HANDBOOK OF INTUITION RESEARCH AS PRACTICE

HANDBOOKS OF BUSINESS AND MANAGEMENT RESEARCH AS PRACTICE

The Elgar Handbooks of Business and Management Research as Practice series aims to take steps to bridge the gap between theoretical research on a given subject and its relevance to practitioners and corporate trainers. They will be rigorous and research-led but will be accessible to and informed by practice. These handbooks are both stimulating to researchers and pertinent to practice-based teachers and higher level students.

Handbook of Intuition Research as Practice

Edited by

Marta Sinclair

Senior Lecturer, Griffith University, Australia

HANDBOOKS OF BUSINESS AND MANAGEMENT RESEARCH AS PRACTICE

Edward Elgar
PUBLISHING

Cheltenham, UK • Northampton, MA, USA

Published by
Edward Elgar Publishing Limited
The Lypiatts
15 Lansdown Road
Cheltenham
Glos GL50 2JA
UK

Edward Elgar Publishing, Inc.
William Pratt House
9 Dewey Court
Northampton
Massachusetts 01060
USA

Paperback edition 2022

A catalogue record for this book
is available from the British Library

Library of Congress Control Number: 2020938628

This book is available electronically in the **Elgar**online
Business subject collection
http://dx.doi.org/10.4337/9781788979757

MIX
Paper from
responsible sources
FSC® C013604

ISBN 978 1 78897 974 0 (cased)
ISBN 978 1 78897 975 7 (eBook)
ISBN 978 1 80392 152 5 (paperback)

Printed and bound by CPI Group (UK) Ltd, Croydon, CR0 4YY

Contents

Contributors

Alessandro Antonietti is Full Professor of Cognitive Psychology at the Catholic University of the Sacred Heart in Milan, Italy. He received a Master's degree in Philosophy, a Specialisation Degree in Psychology and a Ph.D. in Cognitive Psychology and Psycholinguistics. He is editor and member of the board of various international journals. Professor Antonietti carried out experimental studies about learning, creativity, problem solving, decision making, and mental imagery. He is interested in the applications of cognitive issues in the field of instruction and rehabilitation. He devised tests to assess thinking skills and programs to train cognitive abilities.

Bjørn Tallak Bakken is Associate Professor of Crisis Management at the Inland Norway University of Applied Sciences (INN), where he is head of the BA Program in Crisis Management. He holds Master's and Bachelor's degrees from the Norwegian School of Economics and Business Administration (NHH) in Bergen, and a Ph.D. in Business and Economics from the BI Norwegian Business School in Oslo, Norway. His doctoral work is on the psychology of decision making in crisis management. He has published his research in international scientific books and journals, such as the *Journal of Behavioral Decision Making* and *Journal of Contingencies and Crisis Management.*

Alina Bas is an Executive Coach based in New York, USA. She coaches mindful leaders on expanding influence, developing self-awareness, and increasing well-being. Ms. Bas has extensive corporate experience in Organizational Effectiveness and Leadership Development, and has presented in front of audiences at Google, Facebook, The Garrison Institute, MIT, and Academy of Management; she has worked with clients from Oracle, the United Nations, Credit Suisse, Citibank, Google, and Facebook. She holds a Master's degree in Industrial/Organizational Psychology from New York University, USA, and is currently pursuing a Ph.D. at the University of Strathclyde Business School, UK. She is an Amazon #1 best-selling author of *Skeptic's Guide to Intuition* (2013, The Difference Press).

Delfina Biščak earned a Bachelor's degree in the field of International Relations and a Master's degree in Management of Organizations, Human Resources and Knowledge at the Faculty of Social Sciences in Ljubljana, Slovenia. She graduated with a cum laude Master's thesis, titled *Presence of Intuition in the Process of Strategic Decision Making*, which represents the core of her chapter, as well as her first scientific publication within the research field of intuition. She is interested in exploring ways of recognizing, activating and practicing intuition within organizations and raising awareness on the mentioned subject within social sciences study programs.

Raymond Trevor Bradley (Ph.D., Columbia University, New York, USA) has been pioneering the multi-disciplinary application of physics, information science, neuropsychology, psychophysiology, and sociology in research on social systems for 40 years. His work has included studies on charismatic and entrepreneurial systems, experts and novices, holographic social organization, nonlocal intuition, emotional development/management and task performance, tacit collective identity of secret groups, and an award-winning quantum holographic theory of nonlocal interaction. He has published several books and research monographs, including *Charisma and Social Structure* (1999, iUniverse) and *The Coherent Heart* (co-authored, 2006, Institute of HeartMath), numerous articles and book chapters, and has recently completed a new book, *The Lens of Love: Quantum Holographic Eye of Universal Consciousness* (under review).

Heather Cairns-Lee is Affiliate Professor of Leadership at IMD in Switzerland. Her work encompasses the design and delivery of executive learning, research into leadership and organizational development, group facilitation and executive coaching. Her Ph.D. thesis on *How Leaders Make Meaning through Metaphor* won the Emerald/EFMD Award for Outstanding Doctoral Research in 2017 and her program designs have won awards for innovation and impact. Dr. Cairns-Lee is also a Research Fellow at the University of Surrey in the UK, Advisory Board member for the School of Management Fribourg and President of Business Professional Women of Lake Geneva in Switzerland. Her research focuses on sensemaking through metaphor, leadership development and unconscious processes, including intuition and creativity.

Barbara Colombo is Associate Professor at Champlain College, USA, where she is the Head of the Neuroscience Lab. She received a Master's degree in Human Sciences and a second Master's degree in Applied Psychology. She earned her Ph.D. with a dissertation focused on cognitive psychology applied to multimedia learning. She is an active member of the British Psychological Society, the American Psychological Association, the American Society of Neurorehabilitation and the Society for Neuroscience. Her theoretical and research background is in cognitive (neuro)psychology. Her research focuses on cognitive processes like creativity, mental imagery, decision making, and problem solving.

Viktor Dörfler is Senior Lecturer in Information & Knowledge Management at the University of Strathclyde Business School, UK. His research of the human mind focuses on intuition and creativity. Recently, he conducted in-depth open-ended interviews with 17 Nobel Laureates in order to understand the thinking and learning of those at the highest level of expertise. Dr. Dörfler spearheaded the development of an AI software called Doctus (http://www.doctuskbs.com). He has written two books, ten book chapters, 20+ journal papers, and 100+ conference papers. He also delivered a TEDx talk (https://youtu.be/KAXfo-cZ8oY), British Standards Institution (BSI) AI conference talk (https://youtu.be/RkQd1Gjo8Qo) and other talks around the globe on the subject of Human Mind vs. Artificial Intelligence.

Maxim Egorov is an Executive Coach and Executive Trainer based in Germany. He received his Ph.D. from the TUM School of Management, Technical University of Munich, Germany. Dr. Egorov's research interests comprise individual differences in moral intuition, moral judgment and moral decision making, as well as the areas of business ethics, moral leadership and moral leadership development. His research on the interface of these fields has been published in the *Journal of Business Ethics* as well as the *Encyclopedia of Professional and Business Ethics*.

Ariel Nian Gani is a Doctoral Candidate at Radboud University Nijmegen in the Netherlands. He holds an MSc in Business Administration and an M.Phil. in System Dynamics. His Ph.D. dissertation focuses on the use of intuition in the context of entrepreneurial decision making.

Serena Germagnoli is a Developmental Psychologist specialized in learning processes and learning disabilities, as well as in psycho-educational interventions in school and rehabilitation settings. She received her Master's degree in Developmental Psychology and a 2nd level Master's degree in Cognitive Dysfunctions in Developmental Age. She is currently enrolled in a Cognitive Behavioral Psychotherapy school. She mainly deals with neuro-development disorders and cognitive enhancement. She collaborates with the Service of Learning and Educational Psychology at the Catholic University of the Sacred Heart in Milan, Italy, where she is involved in research projects and training courses with children and teachers.

Jenny Gibb received her Ph.D. from the University of Waikato, New Zealand, where she is currently a Senior Lecturer at Waikato Management School. She is a behavioral strategist who explores new ways of organizing capability in goal setting environments. These forms of organizing begin with understanding the psychological drivers and interdependencies between self and others. She is particularly interested in understanding how drivers such as intuition impact on entrepreneurial behavior. She has had work accepted in journals such as *Personnel Review* and *Strategy Management Journal*.

L. Murray Gillin, AM, is Emeritus Professor at Swinburne University of Technology, Melbourne, Adjunct Professor (AGSE) at Swinburne University of Technology, Adjunct Professor (ECIC) at the University of Adelaide, and Academic Convenor of the Pitcher Partners Institute on Entrepreneurship and Innovation (PPIEI) Graduate Programs in Entrepreneurship in Australia. He is the 'grandfather' of entrepreneurship education in Australia where he received the Inaugural Award in 2001 as the Best Entrepreneurial Educator of the Year and BCERC Lifetime Award. Professor Gillin's career commenced in defence science and technology, later as Defence Research Attaché in the Australian Embassy in Washington, DC, USA. Other appointments included Dean of Engineering, Professor of Innovation and

Entrepreneurship, Pro Vice-Chancellor (Industry/Academic Liaison) and Director at the Australian Graduate School of Entrepreneurship at Swinburne University of Technology.

Michael Goller is a Research Associate at the Institute of Educational Science at Paderborn University, Germany. Between October 2018 and March 2020, he served as full visiting professor at the University of Bamberg, Germany. He studied business and human resource education at the University of Jena, Germany, and University of Kent in Canterbury, UK. For his Ph.D., he went to Paderborn and focused on the relationship of human agency and expertise development in the domain of geriatric care nursing. His current research interests comprise the role of human agency in professional learning and development, expertise development and workplace learning in general including in the particular context of digitalization, as well as the integration of formal and informal learning environments.

Michael Grant earned his Ph.D. at Uppsala University, Sweden, where he currently holds the position as Senior Lecturer at the Department of Business Studies. His research focuses on strategic decision-making processes, such as when acquiring a company, and the role of intuition and expertise in the process of making acquisitions. In addition Dr. Grant has more than 20 years of extensive experience from working internationally with mergers and acquisitions.

Andreas Größler is a Professor of Operations Management at University of Stuttgart, Germany. Before that, he held faculty positions at Radboud University in Nijmegen, the Netherlands, and Mannheim University, Germany, where he also received his Ph.D. in Business Administration. He teaches undergraduate, graduate and doctoral courses in business administration and research methodology. His research interests are in the area of operations strategy, behavioral operations management, and dynamic decision making.

Thorvald Hærem earned his Ph.D. at Copenhagen Business School in Denmark and is currently Full Professor at BI Norwegian Business School. His research interests include organizational and individual routines, behavioral decision making, and information processing in organizations. He has published research in such journals as *Journal of Applied Psychology*, *Journal of Behavioral Decision Making*, *Organization Studies*, *Organization Science*, *Leadership Quarterly*, *MIS Quarterly*, *Annual Review of Organizational Psychology and Organizational Behavior*, and *Academy of Management Review*.

Christian Harteis is Full Professor of Education, Educational Management and Research on Further Education at the University of Paderborn, Germany. His research interests comprise a wide area of professional learning and learning at the workplace, particularly intuition and learning from errors. He conducted several empirical studies on intuition in various professional domains. He earned his Ph.D. from the University of Regensburg, Germany, and acts as Editor-in-Chief of the journal *Vocations and Learning: Studies in Vocational and Professional Education*.

Suzanne Henwood earned her MSc and Ph.D. from South Bank University, UK, and is an mBIT Master Coach and Master Trainer, with a background in academia and health care. She runs two companies (mBraining4Success and The Healthy Workplace) and specializes in leadership, psychological safety and stress. Dr. Henwood worked as an Associate Professor in Health and Social Sciences in New Zealand for ten years and remains research active. She writes regularly for numerous publications (*The Great Health Guide: World Wide Coaching Magazine* and *Rapport*) and has written several books and book chapters, such as *NLP and Coaching for Health Care Professionals* (2007, Wiley) and *Practical Leadership in Nursing and Allied Health* (2013, CRC Press).

Paola Iannello is Researcher of General Psychology and Adjunct Professor of Psychology of Personality and Economic Psychology at the Catholic University of the Sacred Heart in Milan, Italy. She received her Master's degree and Ph.D. in Psychology from the Catholic University of Milan, she won a postdoctoral fellowship at the Center for Empirical Research in Economic and Behavioral Sciences (CEREB) at the University of Erfurt, Germany. Her research background is in cognitive psychology. Her specific research interests mainly include decision-making processes, with a focus on intuition and individual differences in both economic and medical decision making.

Lois Isenman received her Ph.D. in Cell Physiology from the University of California at San Francisco, USA, and worked as a biologist for many years. When she realized that her cognitive style was unusually intuitive, she became interested in understanding what intuition actually is and its role in scientific endeavor. She is now affiliated with the Women's Studies Research Center of Brandeis University, USA. Her work resonates scientific perspectives on intuition with foundational personal experiences of intuition. Her recent book *Understanding Intuition: A Journey on and out of Science* was published by Academic Press (2018), an imprint of Elsevier.

Kazuhito Isomura is Professor of Organizational Behaviour at Chuo University in Tokyo, Japan. He earned a Bachelor's, Master's, and a Ph.D. degree at Kyoto University, Japan. He is a leading researcher on Chester Barnard's management thought in Japan. His areas of research are leadership development, corporate strategy, knowledge management, and management history.

Akihiko Kobayashi is Personnel and Administrative Manager at CTC First Contact Corporation. He earned a Bachelor's degree at Komazawa University and an MBA degree at Chuo Graduate School of Strategic Management, Tokyo, Japan. He has had a long career as a Human Resource Manager and his research focuses on this area.

Galang Lufityanto is Assistant Professor of Psychology and the Head of the Mind, Brain, & Behaviour Laboratory at Universitas Gadjah Mada, Indonesia. He earned his Ph.D. in Cognitive Neuroscience from the University of New South Wales, Australia, and completed his post-doc at New York University, USA. His research interest includes consciousness, decision making, and emotion. His article about intuition has been published in *Psychological Science* and was enlisted as The 10 Best Articles of the Year (2016) in Human Behaviour Research by iMotions.

Nora Meziani is Assistant Professor at HEC Montreal, Canada. She earned her Ph.D. in Organization Studies from La Sorbonne University, France, and ESCP Europe. Her background is in Organizational Behaviour and Philosophy, and her research interests include sensemaking, intuition, embodied cognition, and innovative qualitative research methods. She studies these topics from a CCO perspective (Communication as Constitutive of Organizations – especially the Montreal School of Communication) and specializes in discursive and conversational analysis. Empirically, she is interested in artistic and creative organizations (film crews, haute cuisine, etc.), as well as HRO (firefighters, pilots, etc.).

Fredrik Nilsson is Professor of Business Studies, specializing in Accounting, at Uppsala University, Sweden. Previously he was Professor of Economic Information Systems at Linköping University. His research focuses on how information systems are designed and used to formulate and implement strategies. Professor Nilsson has published his research in scientific articles, monographs and book chapters. He has also co-edited several books, such as *Mergers and Acquisitions: The Critical Role of Stakeholders* (2013, Routledge).

Anna-Carin Nordvall earned her Ph.D. in Psychology at Umea University, Sweden, and became Associate Professor at the same university. She is currently a Senior Lecturer at Uppsala University, Department of Business Studies. Her research focuses on decision making and judgment with a special focus on the cognitive processes in different contexts such as consumer behavior and investor risk perception.

Armin Pircher Verdorfer is an Assistant Professor at the Leadership & Management section of the Amsterdam Business School in the Netherlands. After he received his M.S. in Psychology and a BA in Philosophy, he obtained his Ph.D. degree in Industrial Psychology from the University of Innsbruck in Austria. His current research interests are primarily in the areas of leadership and behavioral ethics. His research has been published in such outlets as the *Journal of Business Ethics*, *Journal of Management*, *Journal of Moral Education*, and *Mindfulness*.

Jean E. Pretz is Professor and Chair of the Psychology Department at Elizabethtown College in Elizabethtown, USA. She received her BA in Psychology and Music from Wittenberg University in Springfield, Ohio, USA, and her M.S., M.Phil., and Ph.D. in Psychology from Yale University, USA. She studies decision making with an aim to understand when intuition is insightful and when it is irrational. Participants in her studies have included engineers, nurses, military leaders, and soccer players. Professor Pretz has published over 20 articles in peer-reviewed scholarly journals including *Journal of Behavioral Decision Making*, *Thinking and Reasoning*, and *Journal of Advanced Nursing*.

Amanda L. Price is an instructional designer with the Center for Teaching Excellence at the Pennsylvania State University in Harrisburg, PA, USA. She earned her B.S. in Psychology from the University of Mary Washington, and her M.S. and Ph.D. in Psychology from the University of New Mexico, USA. Her research focuses on intuition and problem solving, with a particular focus on the impact that stress and aging have on these processes. Her published works include peer-reviewed scholarly articles in *Neuropsychologia, Journal of Advanced Nursing*, and *Memory & Cognition.*

Marta Sinclair received an M.A. in Education from George Washington University, USA, and a Ph.D. in Organizational Behavior from The University of Queensland, Australia. She is Senior Lecturer in Management at Griffith University, Australia. She (co-)authored a number of articles and edited chapters on intuition; acted as Editor of this handbook, the *Handbook of Intuition Research* (2011, Edward Elgar Publishing) and the *Handbook of Research Methods on Intuition* (2014, Edward Elgar Publishing), co-authored a practical guide *Intuition for Every Day: We Know More than We Think* (2012, Windpferd) and published her first novel *Woman's Intuition* (2013, Kindle/iTunes). She has over 20 years of management experience from various industries in Europe and USA, including Silicon Valley.

Grant Soosalu is mBIT Founder/Master Trainer and the original co-developer of mBIT, a highly sought after international leadership consultant, trainer and writer with background and expertise in leadership, coaching, psychology, neuro linguistic programming (NLP), behavioral modeling and applied physics. He has advanced degrees and certifications in Psychology, Positive Psychology, Applied Physics and System Development. He is a qualified Total Quality Management (TQM) Trainer, and has achieved Master Practitioner Certification in the behavioral sciences of NLP and Advanced Behavioral Modeling. Mr. Soosalu has extensive background in business development, senior technical consulting, project management and provides coaching and mentoring to CEOs and senior executives around the world.

Bianca Steffen is a Research Associate and Ph.D. Candidate at Institute of Educational Science at the University of Paderborn in Germany. She studied educational science and media science in her Bachelor's degree as well as educational science and gender studies in her Master's degree (both at the University of Paderborn). Her current research interests comprise workplace learning, expertise development and intuition.

Sandra Streukens obtained her Ph.D. in Marketing from Maastricht University, the Netherlands. Currently she is an Associate Professor at the Department of Marketing and Strategy at Hasselt University. Her main research interests include return on marketing, perceived customer value, service management and PLS-SEM. Her work has been published in various journals such as *Journal of the Academy of Marketing Science, Journal of Service Research, European Management Journal, Industrial Marketing Management* and *Long Range Planning.* Her teaching activities focus on quantitative research methods in business and marketing.

Satu Teerikangas is Professor of Management & Organization, University of Turku, Finland, and Honorary Professor in Management, University College London, UK. Her work on the cultural, human and managerial challenges in mergers & acquisitions (M&A) has been published in leading academic outlets, including *Journal of Management*, *British Journal of Management*, and *Human Resource Management*. She is co-editor of the *Handbook of Mergers and Acquisitions* (2012, Oxford University Press), the first to combine financial, strategic and sociocultural perspectives on the study and practice of M&A. Presently, she is shifting her research to the study of sustainability and world-changing agency, for example in the context of circular economy. Prior to an academic career, Professor Teerikangas worked in the oil and gas industry in the Netherlands and the UK.

Marja Turunen is a Postdoctoral Researcher at the University of Turku and Visiting Researcher at Aalto University, Finland. Marja holds a Ph.D. in Strategy and Organization Behavior from Aalto University, an MBA in Strategy and Leadership, and an M.A. in Psychology. Her Ph.D. discovered the consciousness-based view of organizing. Dr. Turunen's current postdoctoral research revolves around storytelling, innovation, and strategic consciousness-based digitalization. Her research has been published in journals including *Technological Forecasting and Social Change*, *Innovation: Management and Organization*, *Academy of Management Proceedings*, as well as several books. Prior to her academic career, she worked in executive positions in global digital, steel and consulting industries.

Liisa Välikangas is Professor of Leadership at Technical University of Denmark in Copenhagen. She is also affiliated with Hanken School of Economics in Helsinki. Previously she had been affiliated with Aalto University in Finland, Stanford University, USA, London Business School, UK, and Keio University in Japan. She is Senior Editor of *Management and Organization Review*, a journal focused on China and emerging markets, published by Cambridge University Press. Her current research focuses on the business and societal implications of advanced technologies and organisational resilience and renewal. Professor Välikangas has consulted and worked with companies globally and served on the board of the Finnish National Innovation Agency, Tekes.

Allard C. R. van Riel is a Professor of Service Innovation Management at Hasselt University in Belgium. He holds a Ph.D. in Service Innovation Management from Maastricht University and an M.A. in Philosophy from the University of Amsterdam, the Netherlands. His research focuses on the identification of facilitators and barriers to success in the management of the service innovation process, with a special focus on the role of cognitive processes. He published his research in *Journal of Product Innovation Management*, *Industrial Marketing Management*, *Journal of Service Research*, *Journal of Business and Industrial Marketing*, and *Journal of Service Management*, among others.

Mingyang Wang completed her Ph.D. degree at the Waikato Management School, University of Waikato, New Zealand. Her research is in the field of entrepreneurship and cognition. The topic of her thesis was *The Role of Intuition and Analytical Decision-making in Entrepreneurial Opportunity Recognition*. She has conducted several research studies on entrepreneurship, cognition, product innovation, dynamic capabilities, and internationalization process, and published a journal article in the *European Business Review*.

Xin Wang is Associate Professor of Management at Beijing Institute of Technology, China, and Deputy Director of Center for Cultural Heritage and Knowledge Creation. She has completed two years as Visiting Scholar at the Center for Collective Intelligence, Sloan School of Management at MIT, USA. Her research interests are focused currently on eastern cultural features and cognitive models in knowledge creation and innovation, the usability of mindfulness observation and visual analogy, and the evolution of intuition and deliberation for insights. She received her Ph.D. from the Department of Information Management at Peking (Beijing) University.

Krista A. White is an Associate Professor in the Department of Advanced Nursing Practice at Georgetown University in Washington, DC, USA, where she teaches graduate-level research, epidemiology, and biostatistics. She earned her MSN from Villanova University and Ph.D. from the University of Nevada, Las Vegas, USA. Her research focuses on clinical decision making in nursing. She developed and validated a quantitative research instrument entitled the Nursing Anxiety and Self-Confidence with Clinical Decision Making (NASC-CDM©) scale, used worldwide. Professor White has published more than 15 articles in peer-reviewed scholarly journals including *Journal of Nursing Education*, *Journal of Advanced Nursing*, *Nurse Educator*, and *Nurse Education Today*.

Jaana Woiceshyn is Professor of Strategy at the Haskayne School of Business, University of Calgary, Canada. Using primarily qualitative methods, she has studied decision making of effective CEOs, adoption of technological innovations in the oil and gas industry, and implementing innovation and change in the health care sector. Her research has appeared in *Organization Studies*, *Long Range Planning*, *Industrial and Corporate Change*, and *Academy of Management Perspectives*, and elsewhere. Before her academic career, Professor Woiceshyn worked for a family business and a management consulting firm. She holds a Ph.D. in Strategic Management from Wharton School of Business, University of Pennsylvania, USA.

Kristen D. Zulkosky is Professor and Director of the Center for Excellence in Practice at Pennsylvania College of Health Sciences in Lancaster, USA. She earned her MSN from Villanova University and Ph.D. from University of Northern Colorado, USA. Her research focuses on using simulation in nursing education. She was also the Project Coordinator on her college's study team for the NCSBN National Simulation Study. She published several articles pertaining to simulation use in nursing education. Professors Zulkosky, White, Price, and Pretz were the recipients of the *Clinical Simulation in Nursing* 2016 award for Simulation Research

Article of the Year titled *Effect of Simulation Role on Clinical Decision-Making Accuracy*.

Acknowledgments

It has been six years since the previous intuition handbook appeared on the shelves but it was well worth waiting. Intuition is gradually entering the mainstream, as witnessed at our annual symposia at the Academy of Management meetings. This third volume would not have been possible without the unwavering support and contributions of all symposium participants and other members of our growing global community of intuition researchers and practitioners. My thanks go foremost to the contributors to this volume who exhibited utmost professionalism, dedication, and courage to share their cutting-edge work. It has been an honor to be a part of their journey.

As usual, the project was made much easier thanks to the expertise of Francine O'Sullivan, Acquisition Editor, who has witnessed the 'birth' of all three intuition handbooks and became a friend along the way, as well as all her colleagues at Edward Elgar Publishing who provided assistance.

Lastly, my life would not be the same without my husband Carl, my best friend and lifelong companion, who showed me the world and shared my sometimes arduous journey without hesitation. It has become a family tradition to adorn the cover of the handbooks with his artwork. Hopefully the piece we selected for this volume will bring a smile to your face.

Marta Sinclair, Editor
June 2020

An introduction to intuition theory and practice: a summary and a research agenda

Marta Sinclair

Welcome to the third handbook in the intuition series by Edward Elgar Publishing. It took ten years to get to this point – and what a journey it has been. We celebrated a decade of annual intuition symposia at the Academy of Management meeting last year, where new collaborations were struck and innovative approaches to intuition research explored. It confirms that intuition is gradually entering the mainstream, as theorists and practitioners alike call for new ways to conduct business and survive in the twenty-first century. It also shows that the initial research has shifted from our original narrow focus on expert intuition using psychology-based tools to a broader investigation of topics that includes a variety of qualitative methods to offer additional richness and depth. Work in the expert stream continues on a more fine-grained scale but it is complemented by insights from other streams and disciplines, reaching as far as neuroscience, quantum physics or clinical studies. Finally, more empirical work started emerging. This does not mean that all conceptual differences have been reconciled but there is a sufficient consensus to move forward under the original premise of our intuition community to 'agree to respectfully disagree.'

This overall development has been reflected in the progression of topics covered in the handbooks. While the first volume addressed mostly conceptual issues, the second volume reviewed an array of applicable methods underpinned by conceptual considerations. Now, with the third volume, it is time to explore what is happening at the workplace and how we can capture it for practice. This is in response to the growing concern about the existing gap between theory and practice. While new intuition theories are being developed and (sometimes) tested, very few of them are converted into practical training tools. On the other hand, intuition practitioners find it challenging to explain what works for them and their clients by the existing theory. A question arises whether these parallel views can be somehow reconciled for the benefit of all. The current handbook takes the first step in this direction.

It was quite challenging to organize the included chapters into individual parts. Many of them contain several themes that bind the whole book together, making their categorization somewhat arbitrary. At the same time, this is encouraging. The fact that some contributions could be placed under multiple headings resonates with the conclusion that intuition does not function in isolation but tends to be integrated with other processes, prevalent in a multitude of professional settings. Interestingly, most of these have been discussed at the intuition symposia since the last handbook. One common theme is the interaction of intuition and reasoning, although for the latter some researchers use different terms that do not always fully overlap, such as rationality, deliberation or analysis. Sadly, this phenomenon is still mostly investigated in the context of decision making, which seems to be the dominant research focus of this handbook. Not enough attention has been paid to problem solving so far, represented only by a few chapters. Another common theme interwoven throughout the handbook is the presence or absence of affect and/or physical sensations that reinforces previous findings about the cognitive and affective components of intuition but goes further than that. It identifies, and in one instance even measures, the impact of specific affective stimuli; it also suggests an explanation of the relationship between (affect-laden) sensing and (cognitively-oriented) sensemaking as part of intuiting. Overall, more researchers started to make a clearer distinction between intuition as the outcome of the process and intuiting as the process itself. Another emerging theme, albeit still in its infancy in terms of empirical research, is the dynamics of intuition as a group phenomenon. Let's have a closer look at how each part contributes to our current knowledge in the field.

Part I profiles a series of empirical studies focused on decision making. As a corollary, many of them explore the role intuition plays in expertise (or lack of it). These studies encompass a variety of professional settings, ranging from finance to nursing and military crisis management. Most of them focus on decisions of strategic nature in traditional industry or service sectors, one chapter takes a microscopic view to examine intuition prevalence in individual stages of the strategic process. But there are also a few contributions that investigate specific characteristics of such decision-making processes among entrepreneurs. This part represents a wide range of field settings and methods, yet all chapters have something in common. They paint a picture of a sophisticated interplay between intuition and reasoning, confirming that these often function in tandem for an optimum result. Another emerging theme of relevance for practice is that of contextuality. Several chapters illustrate that the deployment and/or effectiveness of intuition depend on the situation or configuration. Among the most frequently mentioned factors are task familiarity and complexity, degree of uncertainty, and level of experience.

Part II investigates the 'neurophysiology' of intuition and how it relates to affective and sensory aspects. Contrary to the previous notion of affect as an umbrella term, it discerns different types of feelings and sensations, and attempts to link them to specific phases or expressions of intuition. It also demonstrates that non-conscious emotional stimuli may influence decision-making behavior and deployment of intuition, especially when cognitive resources are tied up elsewhere. A rather provocative idea is that humans may process intuitive information differently through three nervous centers: brain, heart, and gut, where empirical research suggests that the overall balance across the centers may impact performance. Interestingly, heart appears to be the only receptor with a distinct gender difference. This conclusion is supported by findings that affect-laden factors trigger a stronger intuitive response in women, which also raises caution about the use of theoretically congruent instruments. Regardless of gender, affect is heavily present also in moral intuition with practical implications for leader development. The overall message encapsulated in this part is that various forms of affect and sensations need to be studied in specific contexts and/or configurations; the original 'generic' approach is becoming obsolete.

Part III provides an incomplete but much needed introduction to cultural and collective views on intuition. Non-Western research in the field, at least what is published in English, has been scarce so far. In this handbook it is represented by two chapters that hint at an unexplored richness of perspectives. The Japanese contribution offers a rare glimpse into workplace development of intuition through experience in conjunction with logical and holistic thinking. As one of the co-authors noted, intuition in Japanese workplaces is a given (while logic is not). The Chinese study demonstrates on cases from the aerospace industry how a delicate interplay between intuition and deliberation can lead to a breakthrough when conventional thinking is 'stuck.' What both chapters have in common is their high-level holistic approach to different thinking modes. Contrary to the Western paradigm, they do not see them as mutually exclusive and integrate their fractional contributions with more ease. Interestingly, both chapters draw in their theoretical framework on Western concepts and combine them skillfully with traditional native philosophy; a holistic approach seems to permeate even the methodology.

The collective view on intuition is represented by a single chapter that explores not only whether group intuition can occur but if it is possible non-locally, that is, among people who are not physically in the same location. This kind of research is challenging since it assumes interpersonal interaction at a distance that is difficult to explain by means of psychology. To move the investigation forward, some researchers developed a theoretical framework based on quantum physics but there are very few management scholars active in this space. Drawing on such a framework, this chapter suggests new ways of how to study the group phenomenon that has been explored by a few other researchers in local settings but not thoroughly studied so far. It also offers a new explanation for the role of intention, which has been debated in entrepreneurial intuition.

Part IV explores more closely how intuition is used and/or developed in practical settings. The study of work engagement highlights the importance of off-setting intuitive peak moments with relaxation or 'down time' to prevent employee burnout. A great emotional burden is placed also on first-response workers who seem to strengthen their intuition by means of mental simulation that helps them prepare for tragic emergencies. These are examples of work-related situations that nurture intuition but it can be also developed in the classroom, as attested by a university-level entrepreneurship program designed for a finance company. A question arises whether such training could be delivered effectively on a large scale at a younger age. A study of Italian primary school children couched in problem finding suggests that it is indeed possible. It appears that an effective approach to intuition development encompasses problem definition and other problem-solving activities, in which decision making is embedded. This supports the previously noted conclusion that intuition research needs to be broadened beyond the narrow scope of decision making. What all chapters in this part demonstrate is that the use of intuition can be strengthened by training and/or a nurturing environment. They also suggest that effective training can be designed in a multitude of ways, shaped by the specific context.

Part V introduces several new research perspectives. Two of them draw on a verbal approach to surfacing intuition into consciousness so that it can be talked about and shared (which has implications for researching group intuition). One way to do it is to give the surfaced intuition a persona so that it becomes an independent entity, which is fairly common in artistic circles but less so in management. Another way is to use metaphors (captured in words or images) that are 'floated' into consciousness with the help of a language protocol. Both approaches are useful for verbalizing intuition so it can be included in conversations, and thus taken more seriously. They also provide an internal validation for the intuition recipient that makes him/her more willing to speak about it. Finally, practical methods started emerging that give intuition more legitimacy, especially in work situations.

To underline the handbook's focus on bridging theory and practice, the final chapter attempts to reconcile the opposing views of intuition scholars and practitioners on the role of spontaneity in intuition by attributing the effects to different stages of the process. Moreover, it cautions researchers to examine objectively all phenomena (including various aspects of intuition) before labeling them unscientific. This is seconded by the decision to include in the handbook also studies using methods that have been surpassed by later development because we can learn something of value from their findings.

The outlined content resulted in a truly international handbook, made possible by 43 contributors from 18 countries. Our intuition community continues to grow. Yet, non-Western perspectives are still under-represented and we need to engage with more researchers from other parts of the world. The first step is a further integration and/or reconciliation of Western and Eastern perspectives, based on the currently available research. Another area that requires more attention is creative intuition as boundaries between intuition and creativity remain porous and their interaction has not been fully explored. Similarly, intuition in problem solving has been under-researched, especially in non-creative contexts. It is time to expand the prevalent focus on decision making, which could have implications also for the design of training programs. The initial research into collective and group intuition is promising but more needs to be done in this respect as well, utilizing possibly quantum physics, verbal protocols or other yet-to-be developed methods. And there is more work ahead of us. As researchers started exploring the sensing aspect of intuition, clarity needs to be shed on how it relates to felt sense, interoception and the gamut of terminology used in psychotherapy, movement therapy and other practices under the umbrella of clinical intuition. But until we have at least some of these answers, let's learn from the chapters in this handbook what we know so far.

PART I

INTUITION AS PART OF AN INTEGRATED APPROACH TO DECISION MAKING

1. Intuiting and reasoning: facilitating subconscious and conscious processing for better decisions in organizations

Jaana Woiceshyn

Intuition research has long recognized that decision making involves two types of mental processing: intuiting and reasoning, a view known as the dual processing model. Intuiting, or intuition, is commonly understood as rapid, unconscious mental processing based on associative pattern recognition that results in affective judgments, whereas reasoning is viewed as rational, deliberate and linear (Dane & Pratt, 2007). The dual processing model depicts these two processes as alternatives and being in tension, and decision makers as favoring one or the other (Calabretta et al., 2017; Elbanna & Child, 2007; Hodgkinson & Clarke, 2007). Researchers have observed the need to balance the two processes for effective decision making. They also recognize that we still lack a unifying conceptual framework explaining how the two processes are related and how they can be exploited in organizational decision making (Calabretta et al., 2017; Hodgkinson et al., 2009; Lieberman, 2007; Sinclair, 2011; Sinclair & Bas, 2017).

I concur with these researchers about the need to conceptualize intuition and rational analysis as continually interacting and interdependent processes. This view broadly aligns with what some authors call expert intuition (Dane & Pratt, 2009; Kahneman & Klein, 2009). It is argued that experts in any field have "better" intuitive insights because they have more information, based on repeated experiences, stored in memory. They therefore have more to draw from when encountering new, but similar, decision-making situations, which gives them an advantage over non-experts in making efficacious decisions (Klein, 2003; Simon, 1992).

Despite the insights from the research on expert intuition, I agree that a unifying conceptual framework is still needed to explain *how* the processes of intuiting and reasoning are related. To develop such a framework, it is necessary to examine further the key concepts of "intuiting" and "reasoning" and their relationship. A clear conceptual framework is necessary to facilitate effective decision making and for intuition research to impact the practice of intuition in organizations. Dougherty (2018) presents a similar argument about theories of innovation. In her view, innovation theories have focused on explaining "the what" and "the why" but have failed to explain the "the how" and have therefore been ignored by managers responsible for innovation.

Much of the empirical research on intuition in organizational contexts has focused on the decision makers' experience of intuition as a psychological or bodily phenomenon: a sudden, inexplicable insight or a "gut feel" (Dane & Pratt, 2007; Hayashi, 2001; Sadler-Smith, 2016). Therefore, the phenomenon of intuiting is viewed as an obscure process that cannot be described and explained explicitly, leaving "the how" unanswered. As a result, intuiting cannot be taught for exploiting it in decision making.

Here the processes of intuiting and reasoning are approached differently from the mainstream literature. Instead of the prevalent perspectives of cognitive psychology or neuroscience (cf. Akinci & Sadler-Smith, 2012; Hodgkinson et al., 2009), I adopt the perspective of philosophy (epistemology, in particular), to explain reasoning, intuiting and their relationship conceptually, with the goal of increasing our understanding of these phenomena. This epistemological explanation is then illustrated with a case example of a CEO who efficaciously balanced reasoning and intuiting in his own decision making and helped others in his organization to do the same, with good outcomes in multiple dimensions, such as decentralized (faster and more efficacious) decision making, employee satisfaction (low turnover), and financial performance.

The theory of epistemology[1] I use to explain reasoning, intuiting and their relationship is Rand's Objectivism (Rand, 1990; Binswanger, 2014; Peikoff, 1991; Salmieri, 2016) and her view of psycho-epistemology, "the study of man's cognitive processes from the aspect of the *interaction between the conscious mind and the automatic functions of the subconscious*" [italics added] (Rand, 1971: 18). These offer a unique perspective on mental processing, which, I argue, sheds new light on the phenomena of intuiting, reasoning, and their interplay, and facilitates their exploitation in organizational contexts.

INTUITING, REASONING, AND THEIR RELATIONSHIP

Intuiting is the rapid, automatized recall of mental content from the subconscious "storage house" (Rand, 2001: 57) that facilitates fast, efficacious decision making (Hayashi, 2001; Klein, 2003). But mental content – knowledge – must first be acquired through a conscious process of perception and reasoning; otherwise, there would be only random associations but no actual knowledge of reality to retrieve from the subconscious memory files. We acquire and organize knowledge through reasoning. Therefore, reasoning determines what gets stored in memory and how, and what intuiting retrieves from the subconscious for conscious processing in decision-making situations (cf. Rand, 1999: 55).

Unlike the automatized, subconscious recall of knowledge, or intuiting, the explicit reasoning process requires effortful work and determines the validity of our knowledge (its grounding in reality). In addition, the knowledge we are able to hold in conscious awareness is limited (Binswanger, 2014: 131; Rand, 1990: 63). For these reasons, we need to economize our mental resources, by acquiring and integrating our knowledge logically and filing it in our subconscious database accordingly, through reasoning. Such a logical reasoning process yields valid knowledge and enables automatized retrieval of it from the subconscious – intuiting – for making effective decisions. The identification of the reasoning process is what the Objectivist epistemology adds to the insights on expert intuition, to enhance our understanding of efficacious decision making.

Acquiring and integrating knowledge entails forming concepts, to facilitate thinking and action and to save mental space (Binswanger, 2014: 131; Rand, 1990: 63). We form first-level concepts (e.g., ball, dog, man, rolling, barking, walking) from perceptual observations by differentiating and integrating them (for example, by mentally isolating balls from other objects and grouping them together). We then abstract these first-level concepts into higher-level concepts (e.g., toy, pet, animal, motion, vocalizing) through further differentiation and integration. Concepts hold large amounts of knowledge about their units in a condensed form, made possible by *omitting the particular measurements of the concepts' units* and *retaining only their essential characteristic* that gives rise to all the rest. Rand illustrates this with the concept of man, defined as "a rational animal," as opposed to "an animal possessing a thumb." Rationality (the ability to use reason) – and not the possession of a thumb – is the essential human characteristic that gives rise to all the rest, applies to all humans, and differentiates man from all other animals (Rand, 1990: 63–65). Therefore, it must be the differentia of the concept "man" (while "animal" is the genus).

Eventually, we learn to integrate our knowledge into the most abstract and condensed form: principles. Principles are the broadest generalizations (and depend on valid concepts) that help guide our thinking and action for goal achievement (Binswanger, 2014: 305). For example, a principle of furniture design – the form must follow function – guides us in achieving the goal of functional furniture. A principle of a business strategy – a firm must achieve lower costs than its competitors or differentiate its products – helps achieve the goal of above-average profitability.

Logically formed and organized concepts and principles (the products of reasoning) facilitate efficacious intuiting: automatized recall of vast knowledge needed for effective decision making and action. For example, an entrepreneur who conceptualizes the requirements of a successful venture and forms the associated principles by adhering to facts and using logic is able to efficaciously recall and apply knowledge filed under such concepts and principles. An entrepreneur who fails to reason (to form valid, integrated concepts and principles) will intuit to retrieve jumbled, random associations – as opposed to integrated knowledge of reality – which are not helpful for decision making (cf. Woiceshyn, 2009).

Fortunately, valid reasoning can be learned, as Rand has demonstrated and the example of the CEO John Allison illustrates.

REASONING AND INTUITING: JOHN ALLISON'S DEVELOPMENT AND APPLICATION OF PRINCIPLES

John Allison is the retired CEO and Chairman of BB&T, a Fortune 500 bank, whose assets grew more than 33-fold during his 20-year tenure (1989–2008). He also led BB&T through the 2008 financial crisis as one of the strongest financial institutions in the United States. The bank's Annual Report 2008 acknowledged: "It's hard to overstate [John Allison's] influence on BB&T's success." Analysts' reports frequently referred to Allison's role in his bank's stellar performance, and the external awards he received towards the end of his tenure at BB&T also signaled this.

This example is based on my research interview with John Allison after he had retired and on another extensive interview (Hicks, 2011). Materials written by Allison, including the *BB&T Philosophy* (values and principles), as well as his published talks, provided additional data, as did Allison's live speeches that I had the opportunity to hear on a few occasions.

Reasoning and Intuiting Based On Valid, Consistent Principles – to Achieve Values

Starting early in his career, and perhaps unusually for a banker, John Allison studied philosophy as a hobby, specifically Ayn Rand's works but also Aristotle and other philosophers. He wanted to identify and integrate his core values and to correct any contradictions. The core values and the principles to achieve them identified by Allison were: fact-based decision making and objective reasoning, independent thinking, productivity, honesty, integrity, justice (fairness), and pride (see Allison, 2014). He saw (based on his study of philosophy and on observation of facts) the core values and the principles as hierarchically integrated through a chain of abstractions, grounded in observed facts.

Consistent with Rand's philosophy of Objectivism, Allison's set of values and principles rested on specific facts: the requirements of achieving a long-term purpose (a happy life for individuals, long-term profitability for business firms). He identified the focus on reality by using reason (fact-based, objective decision making – or rationality) as the fundamental requirement of achieving long-term goals in both personal life and in business. He then adopted rationality as his primary principle: "use reason to adhere to facts when making decisions." Allison commented on its importance:

> I think most of the really bad management decisions are acts of evasion. Evasion occurs when somebody is presented with some piece of information that on some level or other they know needs to be examined. However, they don't want to examine it because it threatens something they believe about the world, or something they believe about themselves, and they literally don't hear it. (Hicks, 2011: 7)

Table 1.1 *BB&T philosophy: values and principles*

1	**REALITY (FACT-BASED)** The foundation of quality decision making is a careful understanding of the facts.
2	**REASON (OBJECTIVITY)** There is only one "natural resource" – the human mind … We are looking for people who are committed to constantly improving their ability to reason.
3	**INDEPENDENT THINKING** All employees are challenged to use their individual minds to their optimum to make rational decisions. In this context, each of us is *responsible* for what we do and who we are. In addition, *creativity* is strongly encouraged and only possible with independent thought.
4	**PRODUCTIVITY** We are looking for people who want to create, to produce, and who are thereby committed to *turning their thoughts into actions* that improve economic well-being.
5	**HONESTY** Being honest is simply being consistent with reality. To be dishonest is to be in conflict with reality, which is therefore self-defeating.
6	**INTEGRITY** Principles (values) provide carefully thought-out concepts which will lead to our long-term success and happiness. (Integrity means acting consistently with rational principles.)
7	**JUSTICE (FAIRNESS)** Individuals should be evaluated and rewarded objectively (for better or worse) based on their contributions. Those who contribute the most should receive the most. … We do not discriminate based on non-essentials such as race, sex, nationality, etc. We do discriminate based on competency, performance and character. We consciously reject egalitarianism and collectivism.
8	**PRIDE** Pride is the psychological reward we earn from living by our values. Each of us must perform our work in a manner as to be able to be justly proud of what we have accomplished.
9	**SELF-ESTEEM (SELF-MOTIVATION)** We expect our employees to earn positive self-esteem from doing their work well.
10	**TEAMWORK/MUTUAL SUPPORTIVENESS** While independent thought and strong personal goals are critically important, our work is accomplished within teams. … Our work is so complex that it requires an integrated effort among many people to accomplish important tasks.
Our values are held consciously and are logically consistent to fully execute on any one value, you must act consistently with all 10 values. At BB&T values are practical and important!	

Source: Summarized from Allison, 1994; also discussed in-depth in Allison, 2014.

John Allison's values and principles were also integrated in the sense of being consistent. They were all aligned to achieving a long-term purpose, which requires pursuing and practicing not just one of these values and principles but all of them. Adhering to facts by using reason means thinking independently. Using reason and thinking independently must lead to productivity – creation of material values – because we cannot achieve long-term goals merely by thinking; we must also create material values to survive and thrive. Honesty means rejecting that which is unreal, which is the flip-side of adhering to reality by reason. Integrity means pursuing values and applying principles consistently, which is the only way to reach long-term goals. Justice means applying reason to assessing people, granting each person that which he deserves, trading value for value.

John Allison viewed integration of values and principles – grounded in facts and internal consistency – as the cornerstone of his decision-making process and of the success of his company (Allison, 2014: 28–31; Puris, 1999: 228–229). His values and principles did not contradict facts or each other and could therefore guide decision making and action to achieve a long-term purpose. These values and principles also formed the foundation of BB&T's culture. They are summarized in Table 1.1, based on the *BB&T Philosophy* booklet (Allison, 1994; an elaboration of these values can be found also in Woiceshyn, 2012).

Another key element of Allison's ability to apply principles effectively in his decision making was his development of self-awareness. This helped him ensure that his intuiting – the subconscious recall process – was consistent with his explicit reasoning:

> I pursued self-awareness for years … *helping me look at my subconscious emotional premises … and to align those premises with rationality* [italics added]. The goal was to make my emotions reinforce what my mind would decide, instead of emotions making me make the wrong kind of decisions. (Hicks, 2011: 6–7)

Allison concluded by describing how he and his employees benefited from the alignment of reasoning and intuiting:

> I spent a ton of work, first, getting my personal values clear so that I had an integrated philosophy. I had integrity in systems sense, and my beliefs were consistent. … Secondly, trying to help myself think better, not in a raise-your-IQ sense, but eliminating the blind spots in my thinking process and helping the people who work for me do the same and learn from each other in that process. Those things had very high paybacks. (Hicks, 2011: 6–7)

Using Principles to Facilitate Intuiting for Faster, Efficacious Decisions

How does the thinking process work once valid principles (such as those in the *BB&T Philosophy*) have been identified? As Rand argues in her writings on psycho-epistemology (1971, 1999, 2001) – and as we can observe through introspection – principles, once understood, are stored in an individual's subconscious memory files and recalled when the individual encounters a decision situation: to solve a problem, to hire a competent employee, to improve customer service, for example. Some of my earlier empirical research also provides evidence of this, describing the automatized process of the conscious mind retrieving principles from the subconscious and then applying them explicitly to a concrete decision situation, so as to guide behavior for value achievement (Woiceshyn, 2009, 2011).

We can get a sense of this process of recalling and applying principles by understanding how John Allison and his executive team handled challenging decisions, to achieve long-term profitability. Ultimately, it came to recalling the principles in BB&T's philosophy and applying them to avoid the temptation to evade facts and blindly follow competitors, and to make a rational decision instead. As Allison described: "It was about – going back to our philosophy – it was about making objective decisions based on facts, not what you wish was so."

Allison and his executive team's decision to avoid the subprime mortgages and other risky investments that contributed to the 2008 financial crisis illustrates the process of reasoning (applying principles) and intuiting. In a Letter to the Shareholders, John wrote: "We have avoided many of the problems experienced by our competitors, in large part because of the industry's ill-advised rush into subprime mortgages and more risky investment inconsistent with our philosophy and values" (BB&T, 2007: 6). In an interview he elaborated:

> We knew the market was frothy. We also had always run a sound bank. But primarily it was because of our culture, our value system. Our value system enabled us to avoid a lot of the problems that other banks got into, because they weren't consistent with our long-term beliefs. And because of that, we weren't doing a lot of the things some other people were doing. So, that's really what protected us. (Hicks, 2011: 13)

Another principle that guided Allison and his executive team with this decision, besides *adhering to reality through reason (rationality)* and *independent thinking*, was the *trader principle*, an aspect of *justice*. Reflecting on the commitment to the bank's mission to help clients achieve economic success and financial security, he said:

> We believe in the trader principle: value for value. We have a moral obligation to help you [client] be successful, and I expect to make a profit doing it. I'll tell you that. I'm not going to do it for free, but I'm never going to make a decision that I consciously think is going to be bad for my clients ... even if I can make a profit in the short term, because it will always come back to haunt me. (Hicks, 2011: 14)

John Allison and his executive management team also applied the principle of *integrity*. They stuck to the bank's principles even under pressure from analysts and institutional shareholders to follow the competitors' lead and make investments that were rewarding in the short term but destructive in the long term. The record of BB&T's performance during Allison's tenure as CEO shows the pay-off of identifying valid principles and using them in decision making to achieve long-term goals (values).

From CEO's Reasoning and Intuiting to Company-wide Effective Decision Making

It is one thing for the CEO to integrate his values and principles for effective reasoning and intuiting in his decision making, but how did he help others in his organization to do the same? In other words, how was intuiting exploited across the organization to promote better – long-term performance-enhancing – decisions? BB&T's Executive Management Team employed four primary practices to ensure others were able to reason logically and intuit effectively as well: (1) selection (and de-selection) of people, (2) training, (3) communication, and (4) incentive compensation and evaluation.

Employees were carefully selected based on cultural fit; many were attracted to BB&T because of its values and philosophy. BB&T used psychological profiles based on their strongest performers and structured interviews to select the best candidates who identified with the company's values and adopted them as guides to behavior (Allison, 2009). Those who violated the company's values, including high performers, were terminated. John commented: "I always thought if we tolerated a person violating our values, what's the message it sends? We actually haven't had that many people leave for violations. But I think because we always acted consistently with our values, our employees lived our culture" (Hicks, 2011: 8). Another indicator of employees agreeing with the bank's philosophy was its low employee turnover compared to competitors (BB&T, 2006).

The influence of John Allison on reasoning and intuiting at BB&T started well before his tenure as CEO. Every management-level employee completed a training program originally designed by John in the 1970s. All management trainees read Rand's *Atlas Shrugged* (1957) and were told that the novel's basic philosophical principles are the foundation of BB&T's philosophy. Allison commented that the philosophy was taught to everyone who went through the training program over many years. The philosophy was built into all of the bank's training programs, extending to the staff of the firms BB&T acquired. It was discussed and lived by the management who acted consistently with the principles (Hicks, 2011: 8).

An important part of management training was developing self-awareness. After John Allison had participated in a seminar on self-awareness, BB&T bought the company that had delivered it. This company became the operator of the BB&T Leadership Institute, which offered self-awareness seminars as part of the bank's senior management training. Through these seminars, all senior managers were trained to identify their subconscious emotional beliefs that could interfere with rational decision making. John commented: "The goal was to get the filters down to help people be more rational. This was not anything magical, but it was powerful" (Hicks, 2011: 6–7).

Communicating the company philosophy was also important. One of the most critical internal groups who needed to agree with the philosophy was the Executive Management Team. Its members had all joined BB&T about the same time in the 1970s and had gone through the same management development program. They were charged with driving the bank's strategy since the early 1980s. John commented on his and the team's role:

> I think my role was understanding and communicating the philosophy and putting together a team that believed in the philosophy but had very different sets of ways of thinking. And one of the temptations of CEOs to get a bunch of people to think like you do is, I think, a suicide… So everybody on the Executive Management Team, they were highly confident, they were proven, experienced people who agreed deeply with the philosophy but disagreed in lots of other areas and thought differently. (Woiceshyn, 2014)

To help communicate BB&T's vision, mission, purpose and values to all employees, Allison wrote the *BB&T Philosophy* booklet after the largest merger in the bank's history that doubled the number of employees. All employees were required to read the *BB&T Philosophy*, and John gave presentations to them about it, with concrete illustrations about how it applied to real-world situations.

Finally, BB&T's incentive compensation system supported the application of BB&T's values and principles. Employees were compensated based on their living the values and principles and the high achievement that ensued. They were evaluated every six months based on their adherence to the values and principles (BB&T, 2004).

John Allison assessed his role in helping others in his organization to apply principles in their decision making:

> … the unique thing I think I was able to do was make our philosophy very explicit and kind of work through what it meant … If we are going to make a decision based on facts, what does that mean? Like "rationality," what does that mean? Does that mean we'll always be able to analyze all the facts and do the exact right thing? No. But there's a process we are going to go through … We are not going to make decisions on emotionalism, we're not going to have internal politics … that's not rational. (Woiceshyn, 2014)

The premise of the BB&T philosophy, according to John Allison, was that the company's competitive advantage lies in the minds of the employees. In his view, to deliver value to clients and economic return to shareholders, employees needed to adhere to facts and use reason, think independently, be productive, act with integrity, honesty, justice, and pride. In other words, employees needed to reason and intuit effectively. Therefore, much emphasis at BB&T was put on "human systems": communicating clearly and honestly, explaining the bank's philosophy, training the staff to do their jobs well, decentralizing the structure to give employees autonomy to make decisions when dealing with clients, treating employees fairly, and compensating them justly. These human systems were driven by part of the company mission: "creating a place where our employees can learn, grow and be fulfilled in their work."

This was an environment where all employees were trained to reason based on principles first, and then allowed significant autonomy to make decisions by relying on intuiting – automatized, subconscious recall of the shared rational principles and applying them in concrete decision situations to achieve the bank's values. Arguably, such an interplay of reasoning and intuiting yielded fast, efficacious decisions, which contributed to a high level of both customer and employee satisfaction, and to excellent financial performance for the bank.

DISCUSSION AND CONCLUSION

Most research views intuiting and reasoning as alternative processes (Akinci & Sadler-Smith, 2012) that we volitionally activate, depending on context (e.g., brainstorming for new product ideas versus rational calculations of return on investment).

Rand (1971, 1999, 2001) argued that both are constant components of thinking: reasoning (by the conscious mind) guides intuiting (by the subconscious) that, in turn, provides stored mental content for further reasoning. Each depends on the other. Only if the conscious mind integrates knowledge – concepts and principles – logically, can the subconscious store it accordingly, and therefore also retrieve and apply it easily and rapidly when needed to make decisions. This conceptualization of reasoning and intuiting makes their relationship clear. It also explains explicitly that "patterns" in memory (the term used by researchers of expert intuition (Kahneman & Klein, 2009: 516)) are the person's knowledge, held either as integrated concepts and principles at the one end of the spectrum, or as random associations at the other.

Calabretta et al.'s (2017) seven case studies of tensions between rationality and intuition during innovation processes that involved innovating companies and design consultants (designers) provide further evidence of the interdependent nature of rationality and intuition. For example, when these authors identify one of the steps for managing the tension between rationality and intuition – developing the outcome [innovation] through paradoxical thinking – they describe its constituent practices. One is a rational practice of structuring (and collecting) relevant information, and another is an intuitive practice of making connections. These practices are "deeply intertwined." By structuring information, designers "create a body of knowledge from which patterns, associations, and ultimately innovative solutions can more easily emerge" (Calabretta et al., 2017: 381).

This body of design knowledge that allowed designers to create innovative solutions is akin to the body of banking knowledge combined with the BB&T's philosophy (values and principles) that allowed the bank's employees to find solutions for their clients' needs efficaciously, regardless of the particular concretes of any given decision situation.

To exploit intuiting effectively, organizations must first help their members reason logically to acquire and apply knowledge, based on a rational epistemology, such as that proposed by Rand. Only by applying the principle of rationality – adhering to reality by the means of reason (observation and logic) – can an organization's members acquire and hold valid substantive knowledge (concepts and principles) of their work. By the same method, organizations' leaders can form guiding principles for the organization, which everyone can learn to apply, with the help of particular organizational practices.

Only when organizations' shared values and principles are based on valid reasoning, can they guide all members to intuit effectively and make independent decisions. Such an outcome was achieved by BB&T under John Allison's leadership through the practices described above (selection, training, communication, evaluation and incentive compensation), allowing the bank to trust employees to make fast, autonomous decisions, consistent with the company's values and principles. This contributed to strong performance, as measured by employee and customer satisfaction and long-term growth and profitability. As shown by recent research (Calabretta et al., 2017), similar continual interplay of reasoning and intuiting occurs in other organizations as well, with positive performance outcomes (innovation).

The epistemological and psycho-epistemological arguments of Rand and the case evidence in support of continual interplay of reasoning and intuiting outlined here suggest that facilitating integrated reasoning and intuiting by all organizational members can yield factually grounded, efficacious decisions and significant organizational benefits and is therefore worth exploring.

NOTE

1. Rand defines epistemology as "a science devoted to the discovery of the proper methods of acquiring and validating knowledge" (Rand, 1990: 36).

REFERENCES

Akinci, C. & Sadler-Smith, E. 2012. Intuition in management research: A historical review. *International Journal of Management Reviews*, 14: 104–122.

Allison, J.A. 1994. *BB&T Philosophy*. Winston-Salem, NC: BB&T.

Allison, J.A. 2009. Principled leadership. Audio-recorded presentation. Accessed on February 19, 2020 at https://estore.aynrand.org/p/165/principled-leadership-mp3-download.

Allison, J.A. 2014. *The Leadership Crisis and the Free Market Cure*. New York: McGraw-Hill.

BB&T 2004. *Annual Review: Building from Within*. Winston-Salem, NC: BB&T.

BB&T 2006. *Annual Review: There is Opportunity Here*. Winston-Salem, NC: BB&T.

BB&T 2007. *Annual Review: Best Bank in Town Since 1872*. Winston-Salem, NC: BB&T.

BB&T 2008. *Annual Review: Best Bank in Town Since 1872*. Winston-Salem, NC: BB&T.

Binswanger, H. 2014. *How We Know: Epistemology On an Objectivist Foundation*. New York: TOF Publications.

Calabretta, G., Gemser, G. & Wijnberg, N.M. 2017. The interplay between intuition and rationality in strategic decision making: A paradox perspective. *Organization Studies*, 38 (3–4): 365–401.

Dane, E. & Pratt, M.G. 2007. Exploring intuition and its role in managerial decision making. *Academy of Management Review*, 32 (1): 33–54.

Dane, E. & Pratt, M.G. 2009. Conceptualizing and measuring intuition: A review of recent trends. In G.P. Hodgkinson & J.K. Ford (Eds.), *International Review of Industrial and Organizational Psychology*, Vol. 24: 1–40. Chichester, UK: Wiley & Sons.

Dougherty, D. 2018. Managers fail to innovate and academics fail to explain how. *Management and Organization Review*, 14 (1): 229–239, doi: 10.1017/mor.2018.4.

Elbanna, S. & Child, J. 2007. Influences on strategic decision effectiveness: Development and test of an integrative model. *Strategic Management Journal*, 28: 431–453.

Hayashi, A.M. 2001. When to trust your gut. *Harvard Business Review*, 72 (2): 59–65.

Hicks, S. 2011. Interview with John Allison. Kaizen Newsletter, Issue 17, Center for Ethics & Entrepreneurship. Accessed on March 17, 2014 at http://www.ethicsandentrepreneurship.org/20110719/interview-with-john-allison/.

Hodgkinson, G.P. & Clarke, I. 2007. Conceptual note: Exploring the cognitive significance of organizational strategizing: A dual-process framework and research agenda. *Human Relations*, 60: 243–255.

Hodgkinson, G.P., Sadler-Smith, E., Burke, L.A., Claxton, G. & Sparrow, P.R. 2009. Intuition in organization: Implications for strategic management. *Long Range Planning*, 42: 277–297.

Kahneman, D. & Klein, G. 2009. Conditions for intuitive expertise: A failure to disagree. *American Psychologist*, 64 (6): 515–526.

Klein, G. 2003. *The Power of Intuition*. New York: Doubleday.

Lieberman, M.D. 2007. Social cognitive neuroscience: A review of core processes. *Annual Review of Psychology*, 58: 259–289.

Peikoff, L. 1991. *Objectivism: The Philosophy of Ayn Rand*. New York: Penguin.

Puris, M. 1999. *Comeback: How Seven Straight-Shooting CEOs Turned Around Troubled Companies*. New York: Times Books.

Rand, A. 1957. *Atlas Shrugged*. New York: Random House.

Rand, A. 1971. *The Romantic Manifesto*. New York: Penguin.

Rand, A. 1990. *Introduction to Objectivist Epistemology*. Expanded 2nd edition. New York: Penguin.

Rand, A. 1999. *Return of the Primitive: The Anti-industrial Revolution*. New York: Penguin.

Rand, A. 2001. *The Art of Non-fiction*. Ed. R. Mayhew. New York: Penguin.

Sadler-Smith, E. 2016. What happens when you intuit?: Understanding human resource practitioners' subjective experience of intuiting through a novel linguistic method. *Human Relations*, 69 (5): 1069–1093.

Salmieri, G. 2016. The objectivist epistemology. In A. Gotthelf & G. Salmieri (Eds.), *A Companion to Ayn Rand*: 272–318. Blackwell Companions to Philosophy. Chichester, UK: John Wiley & Sons.

Simon, H.A. 1992. What is an explanation of behavior? *Psychological Science*, 3: 150–161.

Sinclair, M. 2011. An integrated framework of intuition. In M. Sinclair (Ed.), *Handbook of Intuition Research*: 4–15. Cheltenham, UK and Northampton, MA, USA: Edward Elgar Publishing.

Sinclair, M. & Bas, A. 2017. *Intuition integration strategy for analytical thinkers*. Paper presented at the symposium Intuition in Organization at the Academy of Management conference. Atlanta, August 5–9.

Woiceshyn, J. 2009. Lessons from 'good minds': How CEOs use intuition, analysis and guiding principles to make strategic decisions. *Long Range Planning*, 42: 298–319.

Woiceshyn, J. 2011. A model for ethical decision making in business: Reasoning, intuition, and rational moral principles. *Journal of Business Ethics*, 104 (3): 311–332.

Woiceshyn, J. 2012. *How to be Profitable and Moral: A Rational Egoist Approach to Business*. Lanham, MD: Hamilton Books.

Woiceshyn, J. 2014. Personal interview with John Allison.

2. Adaptive decision making processes in crisis management[1, 2]

Bjørn Tallak Bakken and Thorvald Hærem

Decision making in real life, such as in managerial and strategic decision making (Ahmed et al., 2014), regularly departs from perfect rationality with its "ideal" of optimization. Instead, the principle of "satisficing" inherent in Simon's (1991) model of bounded rationality recognizes that decision makers' ability to make fully informed decisions is usually hampered by lack of time and information. Instead of spending unlimited time and resources on mapping and comparing every conceivable option based on its associated outcome(s) (i.e., perfect rationality), a manageable number is examined (i.e., bounded rationality). The Recognition-Primed Decision (RPD) model (Klein, 1998, 2003) is an example of a process to use when time is severely limited and little extra information is needed – in addition to personal (expert) knowledge – sparking an intuitive decision process. At the other end of the scale, a "sensemaking" type of process (Barton et al., 2015; Boin et al., 2005; Weick, 1995) triggers extensive searches for extra information, in particular alternative explanations and anomalies that may falsify existing beliefs. Thus, valuable time is spent both in gathering (from a variety of sources), and critically evaluating contextual information before a decision is made in an analytic process.

Unlike "regular" managerial or strategic decision making, crisis management can be seen as a series of decision points that involves both meta-decisions (decisions about what kind of process to use – intuitive or analytic; see e.g., Brehmer, 2002), as well as decisions about the actual decision problem or task. Feasible courses of action (fundamentally shaped and restrained by time and information available) are seldom foreseeable, but instead determined "on the run" as a function of past choices and a host of other factors. This not only makes crisis management decision making an extraordinary complex task, but also paves the way for complex cognitive processing paths – in the form of concurrent, interacting use of intuition and analysis (e.g., Bakken & Hærem, 2011; Hodgkinson & Sadler-Smith, 2018; Sadler-Smith & Hodgkinson, 2016).

There is currently no integrated perspective or framework that attempts to explain the fast-paced, highly uncertain or ambiguous decision making that is typical for crisis management (Boin et al., 2005; Flin, 1996). We propose that a successful crisis management decision maker should be able to flex spontaneously and rapidly between intuitive recognition (à la the RPD model) and analytic "sensemaking," in response to the unpredictable twists and turns of the crisis situation (see Hodgkinson & Healey, 2008). In this chapter, we pose the following research question: *What is the relationship between cognitive style, task familiarity, and the actual usage of intuitive and analytic decision making, when making decisions in a crisis management situation?*

Our study aims at contributing to decision making research and practice. Studies of simultaneous effects of cognitive styles on actual processing are under-represented and fragmented in existing empirical research. As such, the current research is a direct response to "… calls to examine the role individual differences in information processing might play in shaping cognitive functioning in various organizational domains …" (Hodgkinson & Healey, 2008: 402; see also Hodgkinson & Sadler-Smith, 2018). In addition, our research may have implications for practice with respect to recruitment, development, and training of employees and managers in crisis management. A crisis may be understood as "a situation of unanticipated threat to important values and restricted decision time" (Holsti, 1972: 9). Responding to large accidents (such as nuclear power plant failures) and natural disasters (such as tsunamis and earthquakes), as well as opposing security threats, terrorist attacks and military strikes, are all common examples of crisis management. Not surprisingly, effective decision making skills are seen as the cornerstone for successful crisis management (Hidayat et al., 2009).

THEORY

Within a dual-process perspective on cognition, most researchers now agree that intuition and analysis can be conceptualized as parallel and interactive modes of information processing that are served by separate cognitive systems: System 1 and System 2 (Stanovich & West, 2000; see also Epstein, 1990; Hodgkinson & Clarke, 2007; Kahneman, 2002). System 1 processing is context dependent, associative, heuristic, tacit, intuitive, implicit, automatic, and parallel. It is also often accompanied by affect (Dane & Pratt, 2007; Hodgkinson et al., 2009; Pretz & Totz, 2007; Sadler-Smith, 2010; Sinclair & Ashkanasy, 2005). While being fast in usage, robust to stressors, and requiring small cognitive resources, it is slow to learn and unlearn (Hogarth, 2001; Kahneman, 2002; Schneider & Chein, 2003; Schneider & Shiffrin, 1977). System 2 processing is context independent, rule-based, analytic, explicit, serial, slow, but flexible. In contrast to System 1 processing, it is relatively affect-free (Dane & Pratt, 2007; Hodgkinson et al., 2009; Pretz & Totz, 2007).

In a review of dual-process theories, Evans (2008) argues that two patterns emerge. Some dual-process theories are concerned with parallel competing processes of intuitive or analytic nature, while others describe intuition as preconscious processing that contextualizes and shapes subsequent deliberate analytic processing. Klein (1998, 2003) has made an important contribution to research in the field by applying dual-process theory to crisis management. His model of Recognition-Primed Decision (RPD) describes decision making in critical, time-pressured situations as a continuous, revolving process of initial recognition (intuitive sub-process) followed by mental simulation (analytic sub-process). Tests of Klein's (1998, 2003) RPD model indicate that experienced decision makers successfully use a blend of intuitive and analytic processing in such "naturalistic" settings (Kaempf et al., 1996; Ross et al., 2004). These findings are in line with arguments raised by Barnard (1938) who noted that executives to a large extent rely on intuitive responses in complex situations that require fast decision making, while analysis is required when explaining the reasons behind a decision made (see Akinci & Sadler-Smith, 2019; also Sadler-Smith & Hodgkinson, 2016).

Pretz (2011) proposes a more nuanced model, where intuition is supposedly more effective in both low and high complexity tasks, while analysis is appropriate only for tasks of intermediate complexity. However, the type of effective intuition she suggests, differs between low and high complexity tasks where "inferential" intuition works best in low and "holistic" intuition in high complexity tasks. Note that in this case degree of complexity is a perceptual concept – relative to the degree of expertise of the decision maker (Pretz, 2011). "Holistic intuition is likely to be the most appropriate strategy when problems are perceived as highly complex, whether due to lack of experience or simply the large number of variables involved" (Pretz, 2011: 24). Conversely, inferential intuition has its advantages when a decision problem is perceived as relatively simple. This could be because the decision maker has sufficient expertise to solve the problem intuitively, or because the decision problem is simple in itself (few variables with few interconnections). When an expert can depend on his/her intuitive (inferential) judgments, it is because of extensive practical experience with similar tasks (Pretz, 2011).

Among later conceptual advances on intuitive and analytic integration is Sadler-Smith and Hodgkinson's (2016; see also Hodgkinson & Sadler-Smith, 2018) analytic-intervention model (AIM), which proposes that the interplay of intuitive and analytic processing, and their relative influence, depends on the perceived ambiguity/uncertainty of the situation. In their model, the degree of usage of analysis ("analytic intervention") increases with increasing task uncertainty, while usage of intuition decreases with increasing task uncertainty. They argue that the qualitative nature of intuition and analysis changes as task uncertainty increases. Usage of intuition goes through three modes or stages (although depicted as a continuum), as uncertainty increases: Pattern-seeing, pattern-matching, and pattern-sensing. Analytic intervention has corresponding modes or stages: surface, shallow, and deep analytic intervention (Sadler-Smith & Hodgkinson, 2016). In our work, we argue that task (un)-familiarity can be regarded as a proxy for task (un)-certainty, since a familiar task should represent a greater degree of certainty to the decision maker than an unfamiliar task.

A person's intuitive cognitive style refers to that person's preference for automatic, rapid and effortless information processing, whereas an analytic cognitive style refers to preferences for conscious, slow and deliberative information processing (Evans, 2008; Kozhevnikov, 2007; Pacini & Epstein, 1999; Pretz, 2008). A person's cognitive style is predicted to affect both how information is processed as well as the outcome of decision making tasks (Epstein, 1990; Hodgkinson & Clarke, 2007; Pretz et al., 2010; Sinclair & Ashkanasy, 2005; Sternberg & Grigorenko, 1997). It follows from the Cognitive-Experiential Self-Theory of Personality (CEST; Epstein, 1990;

see also Hodgkinson & Sadler-Smith, 2018), and most models of decision making that build on CEST (e.g., Hodgkinson & Clarke, 2007; Klein, 1998, 2003; Sinclair & Ashkanasy, 2005; see also Betsch, 2008; Gore & Sadler-Smith, 2011) that intuitive and analytic cognitive style have direct, positive effects on intuitive and analytic processing, respectively. That is, a decision maker who prefers analysis (s/he has an "analytic cognitive style") will tend to actually use analysis when making decisions (at least, to a greater extent than s/he will use intuition). The opposite will also hold, in that an intuitive cognitive style will lead to actual usage of intuitive processing during decision making. The literature is not clear on whether task conditions (such as task complexity or uncertainty) will have an influence on the style–process relationship but one might speculate that this relationship will be stronger under conditions that are "in sync" with a particular style–process combination (see Hodgkinson & Sadler-Smith, 2018).

We proceeded to test empirically the relationships between cognitive style and actual usage of intuitive and analytic processing, depending on task familiarity (interaction effect). Furthermore, we tested for direct effects between task familiarity and actual usage of intuitive and analytic processing.

METHOD

We conducted an experiment with decision making in crisis management, where N=109 Norwegian military soldiers participated (113 were recruited, but 4 did not complete the experiment). Of these, 12.4 percent were female. Average age was 20.9 years. The soldiers were recruited voluntarily during a training program for international operations. Each soldier was randomly assigned to one of three experimental conditions, where the independent variable was operationalized as varying task familiarity: familiar task – partly familiar task – unfamiliar task. All tasks were content validated by experienced military officers, and involved tactical and operational decision making under high time pressure. See Appendix for the task descriptions used.

In order to assess intuitive and analytic processing in the soldiers' decision making, we used the newly developed Cognitive Processing Questionnaire (CPQ), a five-factor self-report instrument to assess decision making processing in strategic tasks that vary in time pressure and familiarity (Bakken et al., under preparation). The five factors of CPQ are as follows: Affective (intuitive) – to what degree you were guided by your feelings, and whether your decisions felt right or wrong; Knowing (intuitive) – to what degree you knew that you had the information you needed to make a correct decision; Urgency (intuitive) – to what degree you tried to be as quick as possible, and avoid unnecessary delays; Rational (analytic) – to what degree you tried to make sure that your solution was logically correct, and as precise and accurate as possible; Control (analytic) – to what degree it was important to look for errors and anomalies, and adjust a course of action if needed. The cognitive style variables were assessed using the 40-item Rational-Experiential Inventory (REI; Pacini &

Epstein, 1999). The REI inventory has two dimensions, intuitive and analytic, with 20 items each.

RESULTS

Table 2.1 shows means, standard deviations, and correlation coefficients for the two cognitive style variables of REI, and the five cognitive processing variables of CPQ.

Table 2.1 *Means, standard deviations and correlations coefficients*

Variables	Mean	SD	1	2	3	4	5	6
1. REI: Analytic cognitive style	3.8	.45						
2. REI: Intuitive cognitive style	3.4	.47	−.15					
3. CPQ: Rational	3.0	.67	.18	−.22*				
4. CPQ: Control	2.8	.67	.24**	.03	.52***			
5. CPQ: Knowing	3.2	.72	.13	.02	.03	−.11		
6. CPQ: Urgency	3.9	.61	−.04	.18	−.37***	−.37***	.08	
7. CPQ: Affective	3.3	.79	−.29**	.49***	−.20*	−.11	−.06	.16

Notes: N = 109. * p < .05; ** p < .01; *** p < .001 (two-tailed).

Table 2.2 *Intuitive and analytic cognitive styles regressed on each of the five CPQ variables. The dataset is split according to task type: familiar – partly familiar – unfamiliar*

Independent		Dependent				
Task familiarity	Style	CPQ Rational	CPQ Control	CPQ Knowing	CPQ Urgency	CPQ Affective
Familiar	Analytic	.09	.16	.11	.06	−.18
(N = 38)	Intuitive	−.31	−.09	−.19	.27	.66***
	R^2	.12	.04	.06	.07	.53
	R^2 adjusted	.07	−.01	.01	.02	.50
Partly familiar	Analytic	.18	.33⁺	.22	−.15	−.23
(N = 33)	Intuitive	−.13	.14	.01	.22	.27
	R^2	.05	.12	.05	.08	.14
	R^2 adjusted	−.01	.06	−.02	.01	.08
Unfamiliar	Analytic	.34*	.54***	.05	−.04	−.22
(N = 38)	Intuitive	−.17	.28*	.25	.12	.33*
	R^2	.15	.35	.07	.02	.16
	R^2 adjusted	.10	.31	.01	−.04	.11

Notes:
Standardized beta coefficients are shown. N = 109.
⁺ p < .1; * p < .05; ** p < .01; *** p < .001 (two-tailed).

Table 2.2 shows intuitive and analytic cognitive styles regressed on actual usage of cognitive processing (Rational, Control, Knowing, Urgency, and Affective), for each of the task types.

As shown in Table 2.2, we found an interaction effect of degree of familiarity and cognitive style on decision making. In the familiar situation, there was a positive relation between intuitive cognitive style and actual use of intuitive processing (CPQ Affective), as well as in the unfamiliar situation. In the partly familiar situation there was no correlation between intuitive cognitive style and intuitive processing. Furthermore, there was a positive relation between analytic cognitive style and actual use of analytic processing (CPQ Rational and CPQ Control) in the unfamiliar situation, and only marginally significant in the partly familiar situation. There was no relation between analytic style and processing in the familiar situation.

We proceeded to plot the levels of the five CPQ dimensions across the three experimental conditions (task types) (see Figure 2.1). T-test was used to assess the statistical significance of differences in average group level of actual usage of the five types of processing between the conditions. We found that actual usage of analytic processing (CPQ Rational and CPQ Control) is higher for tasks of intermediate uncertainty (partly familiar), than for tasks of low and high uncertainty, which is consistent with Pretz' (2011) predictions. We also found that actual usage of intuitive processing (CPQ Urgency) is higher for tasks of low and high uncertainty, than for tasks of intermediate uncertainty. CPQ Affective had no significant changes in level between task type (degree of familiarity). CPQ Knowing had significant changes, but the levels decreased with decreasing familiarity.

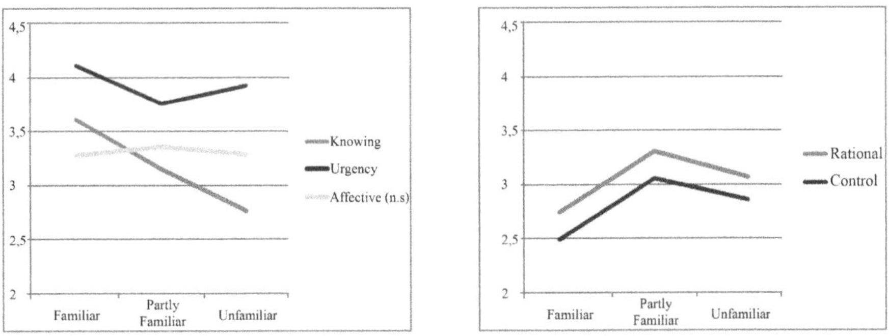

Notes: Left panel shows the three intuitive dimensions, and right panel shows the two analytic dimensions. N.s. = non-significant change between task types.

Figure 2.1 *CPQ levels across experimental condition (task type)*

DISCUSSION

Our results suggest that different sub-processes of intuitive and analytic decision making are instrumental in explaining the mechanisms behind crisis management decision making. These findings support and extend the theories of naturalistic decision making, in particular the roles this literature assigns to both intuitive and analytic decision making (Klein, 1998, 2003; see also Hodgkinson & Clarke, 2007; Hodgkinson & Sadler-Smith, 2018). The literature on naturalistic decision making holds that intuitive processing is important to ensure rapid recognition of solutions and favorable courses of action, and that analytic processing has a role of monitoring the progress and of initiating corrections and adjustments if needed. Several researchers underline the importance of employing "sensemaking" in situations that are new, unexpected, unfamiliar and surprising (see Weick, 1995; Weick et al., 2005); these features are hallmarks of crisis management. The benefits of sensemaking in crises include correction of erroneous beliefs, as well as the discovery of new mechanisms and interpretations. An interesting discovery is the positive association between Knowing and degree of familiarity that appears to be consistent with Pretz's (2011) concept of inferential intuition. This indicates that expert knowledge is the basis of decision making in typical crisis management situations (Klein, 1998, 2003; Pretz, 2011).

In crisis management, restricted time and information are intrinsic parts of the decision problem and efforts to build (shared) situation awareness are considered essential (Valaker et al., 2018), as well as efforts to avoid the judgment biases that are regularly associated with "heuristics" in intuitive judgment and decision making (Kahneman, 2002; see also Hærem et al., 2011). Not only do time and information determine what decisions are feasible, but also the processes through which decisions are reached. Importantly, decisions may affect time and information available for subsequent decisions. A given course of action may free up time; maintain or increase option space; reduce or increase uncertainty.

With this study we have demonstrated the value of exploring the mechanisms linking cognitive style to actual processing, moderated by the degree of familiarity of the task. This area of research currently lacks conclusive studies (see Hodgkinson & Healey, 2008). Furthermore, our conceptualization of cognitive processing is multi-dimensional, meaning that we are likely to capture more of the effects and mechanisms that are at work during decision making in crisis management. In essence, we are about to unravel the "black box" of intuition and analysis. If we interpret our findings in light of Hodgkinson and Clarke's (2007) model of cognitive style and strategy, we may speculate that a decision maker in crisis management should be "cognitively versatile," that is, high on both intuitive and analytic cognitive style, and therefore capable of using intuitive and analytic processing as needed.

What are the practical, day-to-day managerial implications of our findings? In early phases of a crisis, a reactive "first response" strategy may be most effective, when the crisis is still small, and therefore easily handled by resources at hand (that is, the fire engines in the station and firefighters on duty at the outbreak of the incident). For example, when a fire breaks out in a room in a house, and has not yet spread to the entire house, nor to neighboring houses. At this stage, intuitive decision making provides the quickest response, with the recognition of a simple solution (Klein, 1998, 2003) that will be to deploy one or a small number of fire engines and put out the fire directly with water hoses (or nearby fire extinguishers, if available). If, or when, the crisis escalates beyond the point where it can be handled by own resources, the nature of the decision problem changes drastically. For example, when the fire spreads to the entire house, and then from house to house at a rapid pace because of dry weather, flammable materials, and strong winds. In addition, there might be factories or storages nearby with tanks of toxic chemicals that might catch fire and explode – or there might be schools, hospitals and homes for the elderly that need to be evacuated. At this stage, decision making will involve intensive, ad hoc planning for a complex logistics operation, where backup from other fire stations is needed, and also the assistance of other emergency services. Without the proper training and experience, a crisis manager (for example a fire chief) will not be able to perform this analytic task rapidly and correctly enough to handle the crisis (Brehmer, 2002; Bakken & Hærem, 2011).

Limitations

Compared to other research designs, a randomized experiment has the potential to establish inference of causal relationships between independent and dependent variables (Podsakoff & Podsakoff, 2018). In such a design, all variables are held constant (through the randomization process), except for the independent variable; in this case the degree of familiarity of the task. However, the results of an experiment may be difficult to generalize when the experimental setting is abstract or artificial. In our case, all participants were military soldiers who had already accomplished basic military training for international operations. Therefore, the experimental tasks described situations that were natural to the soldiers (Klein, 1998, 2003). In this way, we hope to obtain the best of two design worlds: the generalizability associated with a field experiment and the control of a laboratory experiment (Brehmer & Dörner, 1993).

CONCLUSION

Crisis management is regularly characterized by extreme levels of task complexity, time pressure, uncertainty, and ambiguity. Fortunately, crisis managers are usually well trained in procedures and are often highly experienced (Reason, 1997; Weick & Sutcliffe, 2015). In this study, we have shown that both intuition and analysis are instrumental in crisis management. In a controlled experiment with military personnel as decision makers, exposing them to crisis management situations of varying familiarity, we found that actual usage of intuition and analysis is shaped by both task demands and individual differences (cognitive style). This is in line with the predictions of CEST (Epstein, 1990; Hodgkinson & Sadler-Smith, 2018). As such, the education and training of crisis managers should not emphasize intuitive decision making at the expense of analytic decision making, or vice versa. Instead, our results point in the direction of a balanced model of intuition and analysis (Hodgkinson & Clarke, 2007). Making good decisions in a crisis is not a question of whether to use intuition or analysis, but rather to recognize that the extreme demands of the situation require both to be used. Whether intuition is favorable over analysis at a given stage of a crisis will depend on the perceived familiarity of the situation. Therefore, a successful crisis manager should master both intuitive and analytic decision making, in order to respond appropriately to the situation.

NOTES

1. Thanks to Amund Ole Flesvik for conducting the data collection as part of his master's thesis at the NORD University, Bodø, Norway (Flesvik, 2016). The thesis was written under the supervision of the first author of this chapter. The chapter was written with support from the Interreg project series "CriseIT" (www.criseit.org).
2. An earlier, short version (synopsis) of this chapter was presented at the Intuition in Organizations Symposium at the Academy of Management Annual Meeting, Atlanta, Georgia, August 2017.

REFERENCES

Ahmed, A., Bwisa, H., Otieno, R., & Karanja, K. 2014. Strategic decision making: Process, models, and theories. *Business Management and Strategy*, 5(1): 78–104. http://dx.doi.org/10.5296/bms.v5i1.5267.

Akinci, C., & Sadler-Smith, E. 2019. Collective intuition: Implications for improved decision making and organizational learning. *British Journal of Management*, 30(3): 558–577. doi: 10.1111/1467-8551.12269.

Bakken, B.T., & Hærem, T. 2011. Intuition in crisis management: The secret weapon of successful decision makers. In Sinclair, M. (Ed.), *Handbook of intuition research*: 122–132. Cheltenham, UK and Northampton, MA, USA: Edward Elgar Publishing.

Bakken, B.T., Hærem, T., Hodgkinson, G.P., & Sinclair, M. under preparation. *Development and validation of the Cognitive Processing Questionnaire (CPQ): An instrument for measuring cognitive aspects of decision making.*

Barnard, I.C. 1938. *The functions of the executive.* Cambridge, MA: Harvard University Press.

Barton, M.A., Sutcliffe, K.M., Vogus, T.J., & DeWitt, T. 2015. Performing under uncertainty: Contextualized engagement in wildland firefighting. *Journal of Contingencies and Crisis Management*, 23(2): 74–83.

Betsch, C. 2008. Chronic preferences for intuition and deliberation in decision making: Lessons learned about intuition from an individual differences approach. In Plessner, H., Betsch, C., & Betsch, T. (Eds.), *Intuition in judgment and decision making*: 231–250. New York and London: Lawrence Erlbaum Associates.

Boin, A., 't Hart, P., Stern, E., & Sundelius, B. 2005. *The politics of crisis management. Public leadership under pressure.* Cambridge, UK: Cambridge University Press.

Brehmer, B. 2002. *Learning to control a dynamic system.* Unpublished manuscript, Swedish National Defence College, Stockholm.

Brehmer, B., & Dörner, D. 1993. Experiments with computer-simulated microworlds: Escaping both the narrow straits of the laboratory and the deep blue sea of the field study. *Computers in Human Behavior*, 9: 171–184.
Dane, E., & Pratt, M.G. 2007. Exploring intuition and its role in managerial decision making. *Academy of Management Review*, 32(1): 33–54.
Epstein, S. 1990. Cognitive-experiential self-theory. In Pervin, L.A. (Ed.), *Handbook of personality, theory and research*: 165–192. London: The Guilford Press.
Evans, J.S.B.T. 2008. Dual-processing accounts of reasoning, judgment, and social cognition. *Annual Review of Psychology*, 59: 255–278.
Flesvik, A.O. 2016. *Hvordan påvirkes evnen til å ta gode beslutninger når det oppstår en ikke-gjenkjennbar situasjon?* (How is the decision making ability affected by non-familiar situations?). Master thesis, NORD University, Bodø, Norway.
Flin, R.H. 1996. *Sitting in the hot seat: Leaders and teams for critical incidents*. Chichester: Wiley.
Gore, J., & Sadler-Smith, E. 2011. Unpacking intuition: A process and outcome framework. *Review of General Psychology*, 15(4): 304–316.
Hærem, T., Kuvaas, B., Bakken, B.T., & Karlsen, T. 2011. Do military decision makers behave as predicted by prospect theory? *Journal of Behavioral Decision Making*, 24(5): 482–497.
Hidayat, E.R., Putranto, J.P., & Thjahjono, A.E. 2009. Military decision-making for field commanders. The Indonesian National Army's experience. In Greener, P., & Stouffer, J. (Eds.), *Decision-making: International perspectives*: 37–60. Kingston, Ontario: Canadian Defence Academy Press.
Hodgkinson, G.P., & Clarke, I. 2007. Conceptual note: Exploring the cognitive significance of organizational strategizing: A dual-process framework and research agenda. *Human Relations*, 60: 243–255.
Hodgkinson, G.P., & Healey, M.P. 2008. Cognition in organizations. *Annual Review of Psychology*, 59(1): 387–417.
Hodgkinson, G.P., & Sadler-Smith, E. 2018. The dynamics of intuition and analysis in managerial and organizational decision making. *Academy of Management Perspectives*, 32(4): 473–492.
Hodgkinson, G.P., Sadler-Smith, E., Sinclair, M., & Ashkanasy, N. 2009. More than meets the eye. Intuition and analysis revisited. *Personality and Individual Differences*, 47: 342–346.
Hogarth, R.M. 2001. *Educating intuition*. Chicago and London: The University of Chicago Press.
Holsti, O.R. 1972. *Crises, escalation, war*. London: McGill-Queen's University Press.
Kaempf, G.L., Klein, G., Thordsen, M.L., & Wolf, S. 1996. Decision making in complex naval command-and-control environments. *Human Factors*, 38(2): 220–231.
Kahneman, D. 2002. *Maps of bounded rationality: A perspective on intuitive judgment and choice*. Nobel Prize Lecture. Princeton: Princeton University.
Klein, G. 1998. *Sources of power: How people make decisions*. Cambridge, MA: The MIT Press.
Klein, G. 2003. *Intuition at work*. New York: Doubleday.
Kozhevnikov, M. 2007. Cognitive styles in the context of modern psychology: Toward an integrated framework of cognitive style. *Psychological Bulletin*, 133(3): 464–481.
Pacini, R., & Epstein, S. 1999. The relation of rational and experiential information processing styles to personality, basic beliefs, and the ratio-bias phenomenon. *Journal of Personality and Social Psychology*, 76(6): 972–987.
Podsakoff, P.M., & Podsakoff, N.P. 2018. Experimental designs in management and leadership research: Strengths, limitations, and recommendations for improving publishability. *The Leadership Quarterly*, https://doi.org/10.1016/j.leaqua.2018.11.002.
Pretz, J.E. 2008. Intuition versus analysis: Strategy and experience in complex everyday problem solving. *Memory & Cognition*, 26(3): 554–566.

Pretz, J.E. 2011. Types of intuition: Inferential and holistic. In Sinclair, M. (Ed.), *Handbook of intuition research*: 17–27. Cheltenham, UK and Northampton, MA, USA: Edward Elgar Publishing.

Pretz, J.E., & Totz, K.S. 2007. Measuring individual differences in affective, heuristic, and holistic intuition. *Personality and Individual Differences*, 43: 1247–1257.

Pretz, J.E., Totz, K.S., & Kaufman, S.B. 2010. The effects of mood, cognitive style, and cognitive ability on implicit learning. *Learning and Individual Differences*, 20: 215–219.

Reason, J. 1997. *Managing the risks of organizational accidents*. Aldershot: Ashgate.

Ross, K.G., Klein, G.A., Thunholm, P., Schmitt, J.F., & Baxter, H.C. 2004. The recognition-primed decision model. *Military Review*, July–August: 6–10.

Sadler-Smith, E. 2010. The intuitive style: Relationships with local/global and verbal/visual styles, gender, and superstitious reasoning. *Learning and Individual Differences*, doi: 10.1016/j.lindif.2010.11.013.

Sadler-Smith, E., & Hodgkinson, G.P. 2016. *An Analytic-Intervention Model of managerial intuition*. Paper presented at the Academy of Management Annual Meeting, Anaheim, CA.

Schneider, W., & Chein, J.M. 2003. Controlled & automatic processing: Behavior, theory, and biological mechanisms. *Cognitive Science*, 27: 525–559.

Schneider, W., & Shiffrin, R.M. 1977. Controlled and automatic human information processing: 1. Detection, search, and attention. *Psychological Review*, 84: 1–66.

Simon, H.A. 1991. Bounded rationality and organizational learning. *Organization Science*, 2(1): 125–134.

Sinclair, M., & Ashkanasy, N.M. 2005. Intuition. Myth or a decision-making tool? *Management Learning*, 36(3): 353–370.

Stanovich, K.E., & West, R.E. 2000. Individual differences in reasoning: Implications for the rationality debate? *Behavioral and Brain Sciences*, 23: 645–726.

Sternberg, R.J., & Grigorenko, E.L. 1997. Are cognitive styles still in style? *American Psychologist*, 52(7): 700–712.

Valaker, S., Hærem, T., & Bakken, B.T. 2018. Connecting the dots in counterterrorism: The consequences of communication setting for shared situation awareness and team performance. *Journal of Contingencies and Crisis Management*, 26(4): 425–439.

Weick, K. 1995. *Sensemaking in organisations*. London: Sage.

Weick, K., & Sutcliffe, K.M. 2015. *Managing the unexpected: Sustained performance in a complex world* (3rd ed.). Hoboken, NJ: John Wiley & Sons.

Weick, K.E., Sutcliffe, K.M., & Obstfeld, D. 2005. Organizing and the process of sensemaking. *Organization Science*, 16(4): 409–421.

APPENDIX: TASK DESCRIPTIONS (THREE VARIANTS). TRANSLATED FROM NORWEGIAN BY THE FIRST AUTHOR

Familiar Task

You are in command of an Army reconnaissance unit (squad) in an area with enemy activity. Your unit makes enemy contact ahead. *What do you do?*

You observe that a soldier in your unit falls to the ground and does not get up again. *What do you do?*

You ask for medevac (medical evacuation) and receive orders to move to point Alpha for helicopter transportation, which is four kilometers from your current position. Your unit has marched for one and a half hours when fog sets in. *What do you do?*

Visibility is rapidly down to 50 meters. *What do you do?*

Partly Familiar Task

You are in command of an Army unit that is part of a NATO-led peace enforcement force deployed to a country in the Middle East. Even though the nature of the operation is peace enforcement, the ROEs (Rules of Engagement) clearly specify that intervention and use of force is restricted to operations and self-defense.

It is relatively quiet in the area of operations. There is information that six persons of western background have been taken hostage. According to intelligence, the hostages are held in a house in a village south of the town where you have your base.

You and your unit are on a regular patrolling mission north of town. On your way back to base you and your unit drive through a small village. All of a sudden a person comes running out of a building, heading in your direction. He takes off his jacket and shirt, and appears to have light / white skin. The person waves his hands and shouts. *What do you do?*

It turns out that the person is one of the six hostages referred to in the intelligence report. Immediately after you have started talking to the person, you hear gunshots coming from the same house that the person exited from. It appears that the shots are not directed toward you or your unit. *What do you do?*

Unfamiliar Task

You are in command of an Army unit that is part of a NATO-led peace enforcement force deployed to a country in the Middle East. Even though the nature of the operation is peace enforcement, the ROEs (Rules of Engagement) clearly specify that intervention and use of force is restricted to operations and for self-defense.

Your unit is on a patrolling mission through town. In one of the alleys, one of your soldiers observes that a man is beating a woman with something that looks like an iron bar. The woman collapses after she is hit a few times. As commander of the unit you are informed of this incident over radio. Several people gather around, and shout that you have to interfere. *What do you do?*

After finishing the patrol mission, you and your team are picked up by the unit's two cars. You are in the first car, and you take the main route toward base. Several people are walking on the roadside, but due to the general IED (improvised explosive device) threat toward westerners, you maintain the speed limit of 80 km/h. All of a sudden a child runs out in the road between the two cars. The second car is not able to stop and hits the child, which tumbles across the road. The child does not move. *What do you do?*

[If you choose to stop and get out of the car(s)]

Some local people arrive, pick up the child and run away. A crowd is gathering around the cars. Suddenly you hear gunshots and observe one of your soldiers fall to the ground. *What do you do?*

3. Nursing students' decision making in clinical simulation

Jean E. Pretz, Amanda L. Price, Kristen D. Zulkosky and Krista A. White

Decades of research in social and cognitive psychology have shown that intuition is problematic, leading to predictable biases and errors in judgment (e.g., Kahneman, 2011). Yet others have argued that intuitions can be quite accurate in certain circumstances (e.g., Gigerenzer, 2008). Still others have highlighted the remarkable power of expert intuition (Dane & Pratt, 2007; Klein, 1998). Researchers publishing in the medical and nursing literature have begun to apply some of these concepts to their own research (e.g., Norman & Eva, 2010; Ruth-Sahd, 2003). The field of clinical reasoning and decision making in healthcare settings is fertile ground for the study of intuition, as individuals in these settings often have limited time for decision making and must often rely on incomplete information upon which to base their judgments.

DUAL PROCESS THEORY AND THE LIMITS OF INTUITION

Dual process theories describe two types of cognitive processing, analytical and intuitive (Evans & Stanovich, 2013; Kahneman, 2011). Classic research on cognitive illusions demonstrated numerous ways in which individuals make incorrect judgments under uncertainty, neglect critical information, and make irrational, inconsistent decisions (Tversky & Kahneman, 1974). Dual process theorists characterize cognition in terms of intuitive (Type 1) processing and analytical (Type 2) processing. Some theorists hold a default-interventionist view of the two processes (Evans & Stanovich, 2013). Type 1 thinking is the fast, automatic mode of processing which works well in familiar, predictable situations, but this mode often fails when past experience is lacking or when situations are highly novel. This default mode predominates especially when time is short and cognitive resources are low, leading to predictably vulnerable decision situations. For such decisions, analytical thinking must intervene to overcome the limits of the intuitive processing system (Evans & Stanovich, 2013). Type 2, analytical thinking, requires effort, is limited by the capacity of working memory, and proceeds in a sequential manner, but results in greater accuracy and can be more easily represented explicitly, allowing greater ease of communication. Most dual process theorists emphasize the value of Type 2, analytical processing, over Type 1, intuitive processing (Evans & Stanovich, 2013).

In contrast to this relatively pessimistic view of intuition, other theorists view the two types of processing as more interactive in nature. In his Cognitive-Experiential

Self Theory, Epstein (2011) argued that the two types vary in their level of influence in any one situation. Coget and Keller (2010) propose an integrative model of the "critical decision vortex" in which intuitive processes, analytical processes, and emotion interact to influence decision making in high-stakes situations and unpredictable environments. When providers in the emergency department approach a patient, they first try to apply a rational decision-making process, typically following an algorithm. With a great deal of experience, these processes yield accurate intuitions which increase efficiency and help to detect anomalies in the pattern of symptoms they observe. Emotion can aid decision making by providing empathy for the patient or guiding the provider to respond with a greater sense of urgency. Marcum (2012) has described a similar model in which analytical and intuitive processes can be used to make a medical decision. His model emphasizes the role of metacognition in determining which cognitive process is followed.

STUDIES OF INTUITION IN MEDICAL SETTINGS

The psychology literature on judgment and decision making has been referenced by experts in medical education, articulating the manner in which specific cognitive biases emerge in clinical settings (Croskerry, 2003; Norman & Eva, 2010). Norman and Eva (2010) described clinical examples of availability heuristic, confirmation bias, base rate neglect, and other common cognitive biases, arguing that medical professionals are not immune to these common limitations of human cognition. Croskerry (2003) recommended that medical professionals aim to overcome these biases by relying on analytical thinking. This means slowing down decision making, relying on forward, deductive reasoning from symptoms to diagnosis, and considering alternative diagnoses. He advocated education about cognitive biases and urged medical professionals to integrate metacognition into their clinical reasoning process.

Some models of clinical decision making propose the integration of both intuitive and analytical processes. O'Neill et al. (2005) suggested that intuition may be appropriate and sufficient for familiar situations but that novel situations will require analysis. Marcum (2012) reviewed analytical (hypothetico-deductive) and intuitive (pattern recognition) models of clinical reasoning and proposed his own integrated model that emphasizes the importance of metacognition in determining whether initial intuitive impressions are accurate. If so, then a clinical decision can be made on intuition alone. If metacognitive reflection suggests the pattern is unclear or absent, then analysis should be engaged to form hypotheses about an appropriate diagnosis.

Other researchers have demonstrated the power of analytical, statistical models to outperform human clinical judgment. Dawes et al. (1989) determined that linear models had higher rates of accuracy than expert clinicians. They used weighted linear models based on multiple complex input variables to predict outcomes with remarkable accuracy; however, Hogarth (2001) and others have noted the limitations of these models. Models fail particularly when inputs are difficult to observe or measure precisely and when the cause–effect relationships are highly variable and unpredictable. Whereas many healthcare decisions may be successfully modeled using a statistical algorithm, this approach is likely to fall short in many instances. Many of the highest stakes healthcare decisions must be made very quickly, in the face of incomplete information, and involve numerous interacting variables. These influences limit predictability and render decisions too challenging to be modeled statistically. Professionals operating under these circumstances often have little choice but to rely on an intuitive judgment. Fortunately, some cognitive researchers and practitioners have proposed theories that describe conditions under which intuition is likely to be a successful decision-making strategy.

THE POWER OF INTUITION

In contrast to the prevailing pessimistic view about the value of intuition, some researchers have highlighted the power of intuitive processing in certain circumstances. Gigerenzer (2008) argued that intuitive judgments can be part of an adaptive toolbox, especially when the environmental context is considered. For example, the recognition heuristic suggests that the right answer to a question is usually the alternative that is recognized. When faced with a choice of two possible diagnoses, the one that is recognizable is more likely to be correct. This may be the case because it is a more prevalent diagnosis in the population. This heuristic may not always yield the correct response, but it is a reasonable guess in the face of uncertainty or time restriction. Additional diagnostic tests can be ordered to verify the intuition.

Some research suggests that intuition should not be considered strictly a back-up or second choice strategy but rather, intuition can lead to more accurate judgments than analysis. Wilson and Schooler (1991) described three studies supporting the power of intuition over analysis. For example, in one study, participants in a taste test of strawberry jams either provided a holistic judgment or analytically described reasons for their preferences. Judgments of quality were more closely aligned with expert judgments among those who provided an intuitive, holistic judgment than those who analyzed. Wilson and Schooler argued that analytically articulating reasons for their judgments may have distracted participants from subtle qualities of the jam that were integrated into the holistic judgment but not accounted for in the articulated reasons. Similarly, Pretz (2008) found an advantage of intuition over analysis in a sample of college students. Those students in their first month on campus made better decisions about how to interact with peers and faculty when taking an intuitive as opposed to an analytical approach. Analysis was more successful for students with a few years of experience on campus. Pretz explained that novices were too inexperienced to know what information was relevant in these relatively novel situations, so analysis was more likely to lead to incorrect reasoning. Reliance on holistic intuition was more likely to be accurate in this circumstance where the situation was highly complex.

Research outside the laboratory has revealed the power of expert intuition as well. Klein's (1998) work using the naturalistic decision-making paradigm has shown that experts operating in healthcare settings often develop holistic intuitions that accurately reflect a complex constellation of cues and lead to timely insights into the best options for treatment. Crandall and Getchell-Reiter (1993) documented the sophisticated intuitive expertise of nurses in the neonatal intensive care unit (NICU) using the naturalistic decision-making paradigm. In this paradigm, expert decision making is carefully observed in context, and researchers ask questions to better understand the decision process after the fact. In the NICU study, researchers observed that experienced nurses were able to detect sepsis in infants before the confirmation with diagnostic tests. The nurses' intuitive sense of the infants' behavior gave clues to the dangerous condition, allowing them to treat the infants more successfully than if they had waited for the test to come back positive. Researchers documented the specific cues that were being observed by the intuitive nurses (e.g., unusual lack of irritability in the infant while being handled and tested) and later used that information to instruct novice nurses in the development of their own clinical judgments.

VALIDITY OF INTUITON DEPENDS ON EXPERIENCE AND COMPLEXITY

As a person gains experience in a field, his or her knowledge becomes organized into meaningful schemas (Chase & Simon, 1973). Researchers argue that it takes ten years or 10,000 hours of experience to become an "expert" in a field (Ericsson et al., 2006), though this depends on the domain and the quality of the feedback obtained. With a great deal of experience in a domain, an individual may develop highly elaborated holistic patterns of cues that can be recognized in novel cases. This pattern recognition can occur spontaneously and intuitively (Hammond et al., 1987).

The validity of intuition depends on the experience of the individual making the decision as well as the complexity of the decision itself. Pretz (2011) argued that decision situations that contain a great deal of familiarity will be more likely to be solved via the Type 1 intuitive processing and less likely to require Type 2 analytical processing. Similarly, as an individual gains experience in a field, more complex problems appear less complex as patterns of variables become more easily recognized. The least complex, most familiar problems are more likely to be solved using Type 1 intuitive processing. As problems become more complex, analysis may be required. For individuals with a very high level of expertise, intuitions based on holistic pattern recognition are more likely to be accurate than for those with less expertise. This U-shaped model was also proposed by Baylor (2001) who contrasted immature intuition with mature intuition. The former is characterized by low levels of expertise whereas the latter is characterized by high levels of expertise.

Benner (2001) articulated the development of nursing expertise as the development of intuitive knowledge. In the first few years of education and beginning practice, nurses lack knowledge and therefore intuitive expertise. After gaining a few years of experience, nurses reach competency and approach clinical decision making analytically. At the highest levels of expertise, nurses have excellent intuition because they perceive problems holistically and take into account subtle cues that may not be easily amenable to analysis. According to Benner, intuition should be considered a valuable approach to clinical decision making among the most experienced nurses.

Pretz and Folse (2011) concluded that nurses with a great deal of experience are comfortable relying on their intuition. The study showed that this trust in intuition was clearly linked to nurses' experience because it was not a general personality trait but rather specific to the domain of nursing. Student nurses in the study reported being much less confident in the accuracy of their intuitions, though they nevertheless reported having those intuitions. Ruth-Sahd and Hendy (2005) also found that student nurses are more likely to rely on intuition when they are older, have more clinical experience, and have a great deal of social support. Together, these studies suggest intuitive feelings could be monitored and honed for accuracy during clinical education.

NURSING INTUITON IN SIMULATION STUDY

Nurses are on the front lines of patient care. They are often the first to notice cues to changes in patient status, identifying symptoms that require treatment or further attention by a provider. Nursing education seeks to create situations in which students can practice burgeoning skills related to clinical decision making in a safe and controlled environment that provides as much realism as is practical. Simulation labs are a rich vehicle for education and research in clinical fields. Nurses interact with human patient simulators that have pulses, breath sounds, can speak, and receive nursing treatments including chest compressions and injections. The regular use of simulation experiences in nursing education provides an opportunity for observational and interventional research. Given a controlled simulation scenario, the same complex problem can be presented to multiple participants, and numerous key variables can be manipulated, including time pressure, availability of cues, presence of distractors, expertise of participants, and instructions on how to approach the decision-making process. Participant behavior can be assessed for accuracy, speed, confidence, and various self-reported measures of the experience. In our own work, we showed that simulation can be of value to nursing students, including active participants and observers (Zulkosky et al., 2016).

Past research on the use of intuition in nursing decisions has typically taken a descriptive/phenomenological (Rew & Barrow, 2007) or correlational (e.g., Pretz & Folse, 2011) approach. These approaches are effective in documenting the use of intuition and showing its relationship to relevant variables such as level of experience, but few of the previous studies have shown how use of intuition or analysis relates to accuracy in clinical decision making. One notable exception is a simulation study of emergency room physicians (Harteis, 2011). Harteis and colleagues compared performance of novices, semi-experts, and experts on decision making in two scenarios involving a simulated patient. The researchers manipulated decision-making strategy by applying time pressure to facilitate intuition decision making, and by asking participants to think aloud to facilitate rational decision making. The researchers found that the participant physicians made good decisions in both scenarios. Expertise was positively related to accuracy in decision making for both intuitive and rational approaches. Overall, performance was better using the rational (think-aloud) strategy, but clear conclusions cannot be drawn about the relative value of it as the strategy was confounded with the scenario itself.

Our work examines similar research questions to those posed by Harteis (2011), though we did not manipulate intuitive and rational strategy directly in this design. Using a simulated clinical scenario, we assessed accuracy of decision making along with self-reported measures of decision-making strategy.

Research Design and Hypotheses

In this study, we employed an experimental mixed factorial design (Polit & Beck, 2012). We manipulated roles played by students (e.g., primary nurse vs. observer) and the complexity of the decision (e.g., familiar situation vs. novel situation). Dependent variables were clinical decision accuracy and reliance on intuition or analysis in the decision-making scenario. We expected clinical decision accuracy and reliance on intuition to be greater for the familiar situation than the novel situation, and we expected reliance on intuition to be greater for those in a nurse role as compared to those in an observer role due to the high-stakes nature of the role. We also hypothesized that clinical decision accuracy would be positively related with reliance on intuition for the familiar but not the novel situation, and for participants in a nurse role but not those in a non-nurse role (e.g., family member or observer).

Participants and Procedure

In the reported study, there were 126 undergraduate students enrolled in the fourth semester of an associate degree in nursing program. The participants were primarily women (92.5 percent), Caucasian (86.7 percent), and native English speakers (91.7 percent). Almost half (43 percent) of participants were between 18 and 22 years of age, and another 38 percent were between 23 and 29 years old. Students consented to participate as part of their regular clinical course. The researchers collaborated with course instructors and the simulation lab technician to adapt an existing simulation scenario for the study. A simulation experience in a regular clinical course typically begins with academic discussion about the medical topics and skills that are being developed in the scenario, a pre-briefing experience led by their clinical instructor. After the pre-brief, students receive detailed information about patient history and condition similar to information that would be conveyed during a shift change report in a real clinical situation.

The scenario in the study was run in groups of seven to ten students who were randomly assigned to a role: primary nurse, medication nurse, education nurse, wife of patient, child of patient, or observer. In each group, two to four students were assigned to the role of observer. These students sat outside the simulation room to watch the scenario through a large one-way window into the room, equipped with headphones to hear the conversation in the room. and within view of the monitor displaying vital signs and electrocardiographic rhythm. The nurses and family members entered the room and started to interact with the patient, beginning with assessment of vitals, and then responding to the information obtained through vitals and changes in patient condition. Throughout the simulation, the technician was in the control room acting the voice of the patient, controlling the cardiac monitor, and observing the students in action via a one-way mirror.

The scenario used in this study involved a stable post-operative cardiac patient. Researchers had previously identified two distinct decision points in the scenario when the simulation would pause for data collection. The first decision point happened when the patient complained, "It's getting a little hard to breathe; I cannot get a good breath," reflecting shortness of breath (SOB). The second decision point occurred when the patient reported, "I just do not feel right," and the cardiac monitor reflected increasing heart rate and an erratic cardiac rhythm consistent with atrial fibrillation (AFib). The SOB decision point was selected because it is a relatively familiar situation for student nurses at this level, while the AFib decision point was selected as a relatively novel situation for the participants. Each decision point in the scenario was triggered by the simulation technician according to the planned scenario scripting. Specifically, the pause for the first decision point was prompted by a statement made by the patient, and the pause for the second decision point was prompted whenever students noticed the change on the cardiac monitor.

For each decision point, researchers interrupted the scenario and directed students to work independently for two minutes to write down answers to three brief questions: (a) What are you noticing about the patient right now? (cue acquisition), (b) What do you think is going on right now with the patient? (diagnosis), and (c) What specific action(s) should the nurse take at this time? (action). They were asked to be as complete as possible with their answers in the time allotted. Students also rated the degree to which their responses were based on "gut feeling" on a 1 (not at all) to 10 (completely) scale and "logical analysis" on a 1 (not at all) to 10 (completely) scale. Following the interruption, the scenario resumed and proceeded normally.

Scoring and Analysis

Clinical decision-making accuracy on cue acquisition, diagnosis, and action were scored independently by two doctorally prepared nursing faculty (KDZ and KAW) on a scale of 1 to 4. A score of 1 reflected a completely incorrect response, 2 points were given for correct but vague and missing important information, 3 points were given for responses that included the key correct element but may have been missing other minor information, and 4 points were given for correct responses that were complete. Scores were not normally distributed, so scores of 1 and 2 and scores of 3 and 4 were collapsed and coded as 0 (mostly incorrect) and 1 (correct), respectively. Interrater reliability (intraclass correlation coefficients) ranged from .81 to .98, demonstrating good agreement between the two raters.

Results

As expected, clinical decision accuracy was greater for the more familiar situation (SOB) than the more novel situation (AFib) ($F[2, 238] = 19.59$, $p < .001$), specifically for cue acquisition and action ($p < .01$). Overall, reliance on analysis was higher than reliance on intuition ($F [1, 120] = 41.04$, $p < .0001$) but, contrary to our prediction, there was no interaction with scenario familiarity. We found that self-reported reliance on intuition was similar in both decision points in the simulation scenario. Comparing students in a nurse role (primary nurse, medication nurse, education nurse) to those in a non-nurse role (family member or observer), we discovered that reliance on analysis was similar for all students regardless of role or scenario, but there was an interaction between role and scenario with respect to reliance on intuition. Specifically, we found that primary nurses at the AFib decision point were more likely to report relying on intuition than students in other roles (see Figure 3.1).

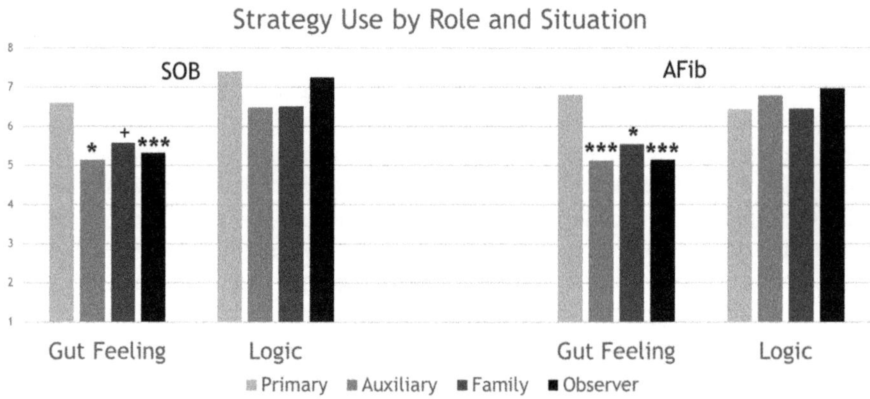

Note: Significance of differences from primary nurse: + $p < .10$; * $p < .05$; ** $p < .01$; *** $p < .001$.

Figure 3.1 *Reliance on intuition and analysis by role and decision point*

When correlating clinical decision accuracy with reliance on intuition or analysis, we found confirmation for our hypotheses. Reliance on intuition was positively associated with overall accuracy in the familiar situation ($r = .214$, $p < .05$), particularly for cue acquisition. Notably, the pattern was reversed for reliance on intuition in the novel situation ($r = -.235$, $p < .01$), though this relationship was found to be driven solely by the observers ($r = -.477$, $p < .01$). Examining the relationship between accuracy and reliance on intuition by participant role revealed that intuition was most strongly associated with accuracy in the familiar situation for the medication and education nurses ($r = .504$, $p < .01$). There was no significant relationship between reliance on intuition and clinical decision accuracy among primary nurses even though they were more likely to rely on intuition in that scenario. Contrary to our prediction, family members were more accurate in the familiar situation when relying on analysis ($r = .423$, $p < .05$) (see Table 3.1).

Table 3.1 *Correlation between clinical decision accuracy and reliance on intuition or analysis by role and decision point*

Simulation Role	Intuition	Analysis	Intuition	Analysis
Primary Nurse	−.335	−.182	−.145	.093
Medication/Education Nurse	.504**	−.161	.067	.102
Family Member	.104	.423*	.083	.181
Observer	.262	.142	−.477**	.062

Note: * $p < .05$; ** $p < .01$.

DISCUSSION AND FUTURE RESEARCH

Simulation is a powerful tool for education and research in healthcare settings. Many aspects of the decision and the decision-making process can be manipulated and/or measured in a safe environment. In our study, we found that nursing students in their fourth semester are more likely to rely on analysis in clinical situations. We also found that they had intuitions during the simulation, confirming the work by Ruth-Sahd and Hendy (2005), but most student nurses were less likely to rely on them, consistent with past work showing a lack of confidence in intuition among novices (Pretz & Folse, 2011). Intuition was reported to be a strategy for more student nurses in the primary nurse role than in other roles, suggesting that intuition is more likely to be used among those in a role with greater responsibility, a high level of perceived pressure, and a strong desire to treat the patient correctly.

Reliance on intuition was associated with greater clinical decision accuracy overall and for medication and education nurses specifically. Notably, observers and family members in the scenario were less accurate when relying on intuition, perhaps because their lower-pressure roles were more amenable to the use of analysis. The value of using an analytic strategy in the simulation is unclear. Students playing the role of a family member were more accurate on the familiar situation when relying on analysis ($r = .423$, $p < .05$), but there was no correlation between analysis and accuracy for those in the observer role ($r = .142$, ns). Analysis was unrelated to accuracy in the novel situation regardless of role.

Our findings also confirm past work emphasizing the importance of the familiarity of the situation. Results showed that the positive relationship between intuition and clinical decision accuracy was found in the familiar situation only. As we discuss in our prior work, for student nurses, encouraging them to attend to their intuition is advisable but only for situations with which they have prior experience (Price et al., 2017).

Conducting research on clinical decision making in a realistic scenario is necessarily challenging. Realistic clinical situations are highly complex and dynamic, even when conducted in a simulated environment. Outcomes of one decision influence the next decision and so on. In our study, we chose to create an open-ended means of assessing student decision processes. This required that responses be coded for accuracy, which is time consuming and requires expert raters. The benefit of this approach is that we could get insight into participants' thoughts at a critical point in the decision process. We were able to obtain their observations about relevant cues, possible diagnoses, and actions that they intended to take. In this study, we relied strictly on two self-report items to determine whether participants were relying on intuition or analysis, which may have produced an incomplete snapshot of their approach. However, this strategy enabled us to get a general sense of their thinking in the critical moment, and our findings show that this rough estimate was significantly related to aspects of decision accuracy, providing some insight into their decision process.

Future work should aim to acquire more complete measures of decision processes. This could be achieved by relying on a think-aloud protocol or a post-hoc narration of their thought processes about decisions made. Ideally observation alone could reveal critical details about participants' decision processes, for example, by coding behavior such as whether participants completed a specific assessment or intervention in response to a prompt from the patient or by examining details recorded on check-sheet protocols. In future studies, researchers could influence participants' decision-making approach by instructing them to rely on intuition or analysis or more overtly manipulating the environment to either require participants to act on their first instinct or hunch (intuition), or to articulate a rationale for every action taken (analysis), similar to the type of manipulation implemented by Harteis (2011). Researchers could also use simulated scenarios to manipulate the presence of distraction or time pressure to influence participants' use of intuition or analysis. The safe environment of a simulation laboratory enables researchers to exert more control over the clinical situation and alleviates concerns about safety among students and instructors. Future work should also aim to examine these decision processes in individuals who are truc experts in the field. Our participants did not have 10 years of experience in the field (Ericsson et al., 2006), so it was not possible to observe the holistic intuition that arises from pattern recognition.

In conclusion, this study shows that the power of intuition may be harnessed even among novice student nurses. When confronted with a high-stakes, time-pressured, familiar scenario even in a simulated clinical situation, student nurses had intuitions about how to respond to their patient. These intuitions were associated with greater clinical accuracy. This does not mean that all intuitions are valid and accurate, but it suggests that these feelings should be acknowledged and could be developed to enhance clinical practice as indicated by some prior research. This is aligned with Benner's (2001) conclusions about the increasing validity of intuition throughout the development of nursing expertise. Similarly, Ruth-Sahd and Hendy (2005) showed that student nurses possess intuitions about their interactions with their patients. These findings support predictions made by Pretz (2011) showing that intuition can be accurate among novices in high-stakes situations with a high level of complexity such as the clinical scenario. This research has demonstrated the value of using simulation for research on intuition in an applied setting. Our study involved very minimal modification of the existing educational learning experience and provided extremely helpful data which can be used to inform nursing education and future research on the validity of intuitive judgment. Researchers have long debated the value of intuition, with some holding more optimistic views than others. Our findings add to a growing body of work demonstrating that intuition is available and accurate even among relative novices in a field in which limitations on time and information prohibit reliance on analytical processing alone.

REFERENCES

Baylor, A.L. 2001. A U-shaped model for the development of intuition by level of expertise. *New Ideas in Psychology*, 19: 237–244.

Benner, P. 2001. *From novice to expert: Excellence and power in clinical nursing practice.* Upper Saddle River, NJ: Prentice Hall.

Chase, W.G., & Simon, H.A. 1973. Perception in chess. *Cognitive Psychology*, 4: 55–81.

Coget, J-F., & Keller, E. 2010. The critical decision vortex: Lessons from the emergency room. *Journal of Management Inquiry*, 19(1): 56–67.

Crandall, B., & Getchell-Reiter, K. 1993. Critical decision method: A technique for eliciting concrete assessment indicators from the intuition of NICU nurses. *Advances in Nursing Science*, 16(1): 42–51.

Croskerry, P. 2003. The importance of cognitive errors in diagnosis and strategies to minimize them. *Academic Medicine*, 78(8): 775–780.

Dane, E., & Pratt, M.G. 2007. Exploring intuition and its role in managerial decision making. *Academy of Management Review*, 32(1): 33–54.

Dawes, R.M., Faust, D., & Meehl, P.E. 1989. Clinical vs. actuarial judgment. *Science*, 243: 1668–1674.

Epstein, S. 2011. The influence of valence and intensity of affect on intuitive processing. In M. Sinclair (Ed.), *Handbook of intuition research*: 37–51. Cheltenham, UK and Northampton, MA, USA: Edward Elgar Publishing.

Ericsson, K.A., Charness, N., Feltovich, P.J., & Hoffman, R.R. (Eds.) 2006. *The Cambridge handbook of expertise and expert performance.* Cambridge: Cambridge University Press.

Evans, J.S.B.T., & Stanovich, K.E. 2013. Dual-process theories of higher cognition: Advancing the debate. *Perspectives on Psychological Science*, 8(3): 223–241. doi: 10.1177/1745691612460685.

Gigerenzer, G. 2008. Why heuristics work. *Perspectives on Psychological Science*, 3: 20–29. doi: 10.1111/j.1745-6916.2008.00058.x.

Hammond, K.R., Hamm, R.M., Grassia, J., & Pearson, T. 1987. Direct comparison of the efficacy of intuitive and analytical cognition in expert judgment. *IEEE Transactions on Systems, Man, and Cybernetics*, 17(5): 753–770.

Harteis, C. 2011. Investigating intuition under the perspective of expertise: Experiences from two experimental studies. In M. Sinclair (Ed.), *Handbook of intuition research*: 116–129. Cheltenham, UK and Northampton, MA, USA: Edward Elgar Publishing.

Hogarth, R.M. 2001. *Educating intuition.* Chicago, IL: University of Chicago Press.

Kahneman, D. 2011. *Thinking fast and slow.* New York: Farrar, Straus, & Giroux.

Klein, G. 1998. *Sources of power.* Cambridge, MA: MIT Press.

Marcum, J.A. 2012. An integrated model of clinical reasoning: Dual-process theory of cognition and metacognition. *Journal of Evaluation in Clinical Practice*, 18: 954–961. doi:10.1111/j.1365-2753.2012.01900.x.

Norman, G.R., & Eva, K.W. 2010. Diagnostic error and clinical reasoning. *Medical Education,* 44: 94–100. doi:10.1111/j.1365-2923.2009.03507.x.

O'Neill, E.S., Dluhy, N.M., & Chin, E. 2005. Modelling novice clinical reasoning for a computerized decision support system. *Journal of Advanced Nursing*, 49(1): 68–77. doi: 10.1111/j.1365-2648.2004.03265.x.

Polit, D.F., & Beck, C.T. 2012. *Nursing research: Generating and assessing evidence for nursing practice* (9th ed.). Philadelphia, PA: Lippincott Williams & Wilkins.

Pretz, J.E. 2008. Intuition versus analysis: Strategy and experience in complex everyday problem solving. *Memory & Cognition*, 36(3): 554–566. doi:10.3758/MC.36.3.554.

Pretz, J.E. 2011. Types of intuition: Inferential and holistic. In M. Sinclair (Ed.), *Handbook of intuition research*: 17–27. Cheltenham, UK and Northampton, MA, USA: Edward Elgar Publishing.

Pretz, J.E., & Folse, V.N. 2011. Nursing experience and preference for intuition in decision making. *Journal of Clinical Nursing*, 20(19–20): 2878–2889. doi:10.1111/j.1365-2702.2011.03705.x.

Price, A., Zulkosky, K., Pretz, J., & White, K. 2017. Accuracy of intuition in clinical decision-making among novice clinicians. *Journal of Advanced Nursing*, 73(5): 1147–1157. doi: 10.1111/jan.13202.

Rew, L., & Barrow, E.M. 2007. State of the science: Intuition in nursing, a generation of studying the phenomenon. *Advances in Nursing Science*, 30: E15–F25.

Ruth-Sahd, L.A., 2003. Intuition: A critical way of knowing in a multicultural nursing curriculum. *Nursing Education Perspectives*, 24(3): 129–134. doi: 10/1043/1536-5026.

Ruth-Sahd, L.A., & Hendy, H.M. 2005. Predictors of novice nurses' use of intuition to guide patient care decisions. *Journal of Nursing Education*, 44(10): 450–458.

Tversky, A., & Kahneman, D. 1974. Judgment under uncertainty: Heuristics and biases. *Science*, 185: 1124–1131.

Wilson, T.D., & Schooler, J.W. 1991. Thinking too much: Introspection can reduce the quality of preferences and decisions. *Journal of Personality and Social Psychology*, 60(2): 181–192. doi:10.1037/0022-3514.60.2.181.

Zulkosky, K.D., White, K.A., Price, A.L., & Pretz, J.E. 2016. Effect of simulation role on clinical decision-making accuracy. *Clinical Simulation in Nursing*, 12(3): 98–106. doi: 10.1016/j.ecns.2016.01.007.

4. The use of intuitive expertise in acquisition-making: an explorative study

Michael Grant, Fredrik Nilsson and Anna-Carin Nordvall

Acquiring a company is one of the most important and complex strategic decisions a business can make. The activities and events leading up to the completion or cancellation of an acquisition, that is, acquisition-making, involve several judgmental tasks of high complexity. Therefore, it is not surprising to find many examples of acquisitions that are failures (e.g., AOL and Time Warner, Daimler Benz and Chrysler), even though there are also examples of successful ones (e.g., Berkshire Hathaway and MidAmerican Energy, InBev and Anheuser Busch) (Pablo, 2016). However, considering the significant impact of acquisition-making on companies involved, it is surprising that our knowledge of how expertise of individuals is used in acquisition-making is so scant.

In this chapter we are especially interested in the use of expertise that is characterized by nonconscious cognitive processes. Following Kahneman and Klein (2009), we call this intuitive expertise. The acquisition-making process is a suitable setting in which to study intuitive expertise as it involves several judgmental tasks of high complexity. It covers the analysis of all aspects of the target company including its employees and its future integration with the acquirer. Moreover, the analysis needs to be carried out in a process characterized by secrecy and with limited access to data and people in the target firm. Consequently, acquisition-making involves judgmental tasks with a high level of uncertainty encompassing a myriad of factors.

The context of this explorative study is serial acquirers. Several studies suggest that serial acquirers typically show positive performance effects. This contrasts the vast majority of performance studies, which use samples of large acquisitions that indicate that acquisitions on average show negative performance effects. Furthermore, serial acquirers organize their acquisition-making in separate, professional organizations managed by people employed for making acquisitions (Chatterjee, 2009; Grant, 2018; Haspeslagh & Jemison, 1991; Trichterborn et al., 2016). The role of these professional acquisition organizations is to collect and analyze information about the target and produce information used by decision-makers, for example, the board of the acquirer. Consequently, the professional acquisition organization plays a vital role, and hence its activities and judgments have a critical impact on decision-making (Grant, 2018).

To the authors' best knowledge, the study by Grant and Nilsson (2019) is the only empirical study of acquisition-making and the use of intuitive expertise. It shows that intuitive expertise plays an important role in the production of strategic and financial rationales (i.e., the key reasons used for making the acquisition). According to Grant and Nilsson (2019) there are reasons to believe that intuitive expertise also plays an important role in other judgmental tasks where high uncertainty prevails, such as negotiations and due diligence. To investigate this, we conducted an explorative study examining in what type of tasks intuitive expertise is used, and how it is used.

INTUITIVE EXPERTISE AND ACQUISITION-MAKING

Acquisition-making usually involves experts with deep and extensive knowledge of many areas. Hence research on intuitive expertise can enhance our knowledge of how acquisitions are made. Below follows a short summary of key references.

Following Kahneman and Klein (2009) the use of intuitive expertise, in contrast to heuristics and biases research (e.g., Kahneman, 2011), usually leads to correct intuitive judgments. In the literature, chess players, expert firemen, military personnel and nurses are early examples of experts using intuitive expertise. Organization and management scholars have studied how intuitive expertise is used in organizations and by management. In spite of this, we have limited knowledge about how intuitive expertise is used in field settings (e.g., Hensman & Sadler-Smith, 2011; Salas et al., 2010; Sinclair, 2011). Field studies with characteristics similar to acquisition-making include how intuitive expertise is used in decision-making by bank loan officers (Lipshitz & Shulimovitz, 2007) and finance executives (Hensman & Sadler-Smith, 2011), by entrepreneurs when deciding what venture to pursue (La Pira & Gillin, 2006), by managers in new service development (van Riel & Lievens, 2004), by CEOs making strategic investment decisions (Woiceshyn, 2009), by investors in early-stage investments (Huang, 2018; Huang & Pearce, 2015), and in the production of strategic and financial rationales (Grant & Nilsson, 2019).

Dual process theories and research on expertise are the theoretical and empirical foundations of research on intuitive expertise. Literature on dual process theories characterizes thinking (i.e., cognition) as two types of processes.[1] The main difference between these two types is working memory, which is necessary in processes of a reflective character (Type 2) but not when intuitive processing is used (Type 1) (Evans, 2008; Evans & Stanovich, 2013; Kahneman, 2011; Stanovich, 1999; Stanovich & West, 2000). The latter is usually characterized as automatic, nonconscious, and associative, and the former as controlled, conscious, and abstract. This type of reflective processing is what scholars and practitioners describe as typical of analytical and rational thinking. However, an intuitive process based on expertise can also be characterized as analytical and rational, even though it is nonconscious.

The effectiveness of Type 1 and Type 2 processes can be explained by how tasks are structured (Dane & Pratt, 2007; Dane et al., 2012; Kahneman & Klein, 2009; Salas et al., 2010; Shapiro & Spence, 1997). If a task can be broken down into sub-processes and solved sequentially, analytical reasoning is appropriate. Tasks that are complex and difficult to break down are best solved by intuitive processes where a holistic approach to problem-solving is necessary (e.g., Dane et al., 2012). These findings are supported by field studies (Grant & Nilsson, 2019; Huang, 2018; Huang & Pearce, 2015). According to literature there is interaction between intuitive and reflective processes (Evans, 2008; Evans & Stanovich, 2013; Kahneman, 2011). For example, experts can quickly find a solution to a complex problem. Subsequently they might consciously reflect upon the answer. In other words, expertise is characterized by the use of both types of processes.

According to Simon (1992: 155), the intuitive process provides the expert with a cue to "information stored in memory." Hence an expert must possess the necessary information and be able to identify and retrieve it. Another way of defining the concept follows Ericsson and Lehmann (1996: 277) that expertise is only present when we are able to observe "consistently superior performance," which implies that expertise is a rare phenomenon in most domains. According to Ericsson and Ward (2007) an absolute minimum of at least ten years of dedicated work is required. However, it is not time per se that is important. Instead the development of expertise requires long experience, an opportunity to get relevant feedback and the possibility of gradually refining skills, that is, deliberate practice (Ericsson, 2006).

AN EXPLORATIVE STUDY

The role of intuitive expertise in acquisition-making is largely unexplored. Therefore, we have chosen to conduct an explorative, interview-based study. We conducted seven exploratory interviews with experts, selected in the following way. First, they were required to have a significant influence on the acquisition-making process. Consequently, we selected acquisition managers and legal managers. The former manage the professional acquisition organization, and together with the legal manager, negotiate the transaction. Moreover, we chose to interview financial and legal advisers as they also influence acquisition-making. Second, we identified and contacted experts in acquisition-making (see Table 4.1) based on one of the researchers' deep knowledge of the Nordic business and M&A community. The expert selection allowed us to follow the acquisition-making process in different stages of decision-making.

Table 4.1 Interviewees

Interviewee	Role in M&A projects	Age	M&A working experience (years)	Experience in the specific firm (years)	Length of interview (minutes)
AM1	Acquisition manager	>50	>15	>20	61
AM2	Acquisition manager	>50	>20	15–20	80
AM3	Acquisition manager	>50	>20	15–20	78
LM1	Legal manager	>50	>20	15–20	55
LM2	Legal manager	40–50	>15	5–10	44
FA	Financial adviser	40–50	>20	>20	51
LA	Legal adviser	>50	>20	>20	64

Five of the interviewees had more than twenty years of experience in acquisition-making, and two had more than fifteen years of experience. In comparison, at least ten years of experience has been found to be required to reach expert performance (Ericsson & Ward, 2007; Simon & Chase, 1973). Ten years should not be seen as fixed but rather used as a point of reference. Arguably, more than fifteen years of experience in acquisition-making should be sufficient to reach expert performance. This claim is also supported by the observation that all of the interviewees worked in highly acquisitive and successful firms. Moreover, the financial adviser has been ranked among the top corporate finance advisers in the Nordic market for several years. Likewise, the legal adviser has for several years been ranked among the top legal M&A advisers in the Swedish market.

All interviewees worked in firms with headquarters in Sweden. With the exception of AM1 and LM1, all of the interviewees were from different companies. AM1 and LM1 worked in a multinational firm in the industrial engineering sector. The firm has presence in more than 180 countries and is among the three leading global companies within its industry. AM2 worked in a leading European ICT firm (information and communication technology). AM3 was employed by a leading European firm in the energy sector. LM2 worked in a multinational firm in the construction and materials sector. The firm has operations in more than 70 countries with worldwide sales. The advisers were members of leading Nordic firms in their respective fields of corporate finance and legal advisory.

Arguably all firms of the interviewees have well-developed processes and structures for making acquisitions and provide ample learning opportunities to their members (e.g., Chatterjee, 2009; Trichterborn et al., 2016). Consequently, these settings provide what Ericsson (2006) calls deliberate practice, an environment for developing expertise through gradually refining performance with opportunities for repetition and feedback.

An interview guide was prepared and included questions such as if the interviewee could recall specific situations when intuition was used, the relation between the use of intuition and analysis, and how open the interviewee was to colleagues about using intuition. The term "gut feeling" was also used when talking about intuition (e.g., to elaborate on how intuitive expertise could be interpreted and understood). In the analysis of our data gut feeling, intuition and intuitive expertise are treated as synonymous (see Huang, 2018; Huang & Pearce, 2015). Even though an interview guide was used, we encouraged the interviewees to speak freely. Interviews lasted 44–80 minutes, with an average of 61 minutes.

Data analysis was an iterative process moving to and from data, findings and literature (Dubois & Gadde, 2014; Langley, 1999). As a first step, all authors listened to the interviews and noted interesting findings. Thereafter, the first author identified themes with supporting quotes from the transcribed interviews. These themes were compared with the initial notes from the authors' reading. The process resulted in a document with themes and ideas, as well as supporting quotes. At a later stage the themes and ideas were revisited and merged into broader themes, from where conclusions were drawn.

RESULTS

The interviews show that judgments based on intuitive expertise are especially salient during due diligence and negotiations. Furthermore, the interviews indicate that judgments related to both the social and the material aspects of various tasks. The social aspects concerned how the expert interpreted what people say, their thoughts and what their aim is. The material aspects related to the physical world such as production facilities, company presentations and financial figures.

Moreover, the study provided us with data on the relation between the use of intuitive expertise and analytical reasoning. For example, during due diligence there was a continuous use of both intuitive expertise and analytical reasoning. Another example is that interviewees, although they relied on intuitive expertise, considered analytical reasoning to be instrumental in transforming intuition into strategic and financial rationales (e.g., business plans and company valuations). In the following three sub-sections, these results are described in more detail. See also Table 4.2 for supporting data. The quotes in Table 4.2, and in the text, are translated from Swedish based on the transcribed interviews. In some cases, quotes are to some extent freely translated.

The Use of Intuitive Expertise in Due Diligence

Due diligence was typically led by the acquisition manager and involved the legal manager, external advisers and internal experts. Usually it included a presentation by the target company's management, site visits and a so-called data room. Interviewees mentioned a range of different tasks where intuitive expertise was used during due diligence. This included the production facilities, a broader assessment of the target company and its management, the business plan of the target, and the identification of potential problem areas. One of the acquisition managers described how he used intuitive expertise to assess the state of the production facilities:

> When you go there, looking at the premises, walking around, you will automatically see at which level of proficiency they are. You do not think about it, it is no analysis. You can see if they are well organized and if the premises are kept clean and in a good condition. All this gives you a first impression. Compare it to a human being … POW! and you have an idea and opinion. The two are very similar. (AM1)

The target's management team in most cases presented their business plan. Assessing the plan and the management's presentation was seen as an essential task in the due diligence. The assessment concerned the quality of the target's management team, whether they believed in the plan and were interested in continuing managing the target also in the future. This was vital because the strategy of the acquirer was often to keep the current management after the acquisition and reduce the risk that they would start a competing business as soon as their non-compete agreement had expired.

Table 4.2 Supporting data

The use of intuitive expertise in due diligence	Data
Intuition was used in a broad assessment of the target. This included production processes, people and the business plan of the target.	… the target company often makes a presentation of some kind. They tell you how they work. Then you get an understanding of their processes, how they monitor their business and how they follow it up. … And you do not have to ask many questions before you see and understand at what level they are in their work. (AM1)
	Then you make an assessment of what kind of people they are, what values they have, how they work, and if they will want to remain. And also if we want them to remain in the business. You get a feeling, and that feeling I also convey when I get home. Often when you meet a company the first time, it can be a few hours, half a day or so. You often sit in a conference room and then you walk around the premises. … Already then there will be an intuitive assessment of the people you meet. (AM1)
	When you meet the management, making a presentation of the company. Very much is based on that. It may be the first time you meet these people. You see the interaction between them. You see who is actually in charge. Does it hold together? Then you can get an intuitive feeling: Do they believe in this? Are they competent? Is this something the owner has orchestrated and asked them to present? Something they really don't believe in? … You can sometimes get a feeling. If they believe in this, or not. (AM3)
Several interviewees described assessment of current management in the target company as critical, as their strategy was to keep the existing management.	Management is perhaps the most important. Do they want to continue, do they want to sell? Will they function in our company? You can do as much due diligence you want, but you have to base it on your own feeling. (LM2)
	The risk that they will start competing activities after the non-compete clause expires. You want a gut feeling about how interested they are in starting competing activities when the clause expires. (LM2)
Intuition was used to identify potential problem areas.	We do a formal legal due diligence where we often bring in a law firm to help us. Then we usually look through the entire material to see if there is something that looks strange. Often it becomes what you call a gut feeling. A feeling that something doesn't hold or is odd. (LM1)
	Then the gut feeling says, wait. Let's not do all the due diligence at once. Let us instead focus on what we feel can be a problem. (LM2)

The use of intuitive expertise in negotiations	Data
Intuition was described as critical for managing the negotiations.	The key in this job is the ability to dance that type of dance. To answer questions that arise, and make the right interpretations and govern [the acquisition process] correctly. And it is completely based on experience. It is like musicality. You are in a situation where parties around you say different things. And then you can play that game in a lot of different ways. It somehow becomes a mixture of game theory but also knowledge of practice. You have an offer. Have they bid this only to be invited to the bidding process? Or is it a real offer? Or should we assume that they are bluffing and will leave? (FA)
	When I negotiate, an important feeling is if your counterpart understands and agrees on our position. … Part of the gut feeling as a negotiator is that you have to give so much concession that your counterpart feels that we have a dialogue. (LA)
A holistic assessment of the situation to get a sense of the competition in an acquisition process.	We recently reached an agreement with a seller. When you looked at their material and how they handled it, you got the feeling that we were alone [the only buyer] … I can't point out exactly what it was. It was an overall assessment which made [me think], there is no serious competition. (LM1)
Negotiations included understanding the seller's side. For example: what are they aiming for, what restrictions do they have, and how will they react.	You try to get an idea of the counterpart's position, and what they are aiming at. It is what you call a collective assessment, in legal language, which is somewhat of a rough estimate. It is a matter of understanding what we can give and what we can get. You try to sense, by judging how they say things and what they emphasize, what they can and cannot let go. (LM1)
	This will be negotiated. There is so much work that can never be described in analytical terms. [For example] When people leave the negotiating table, one has to find out why. It is the underlying process that people cannot see. … These are processes that involve psychology, intuition, feeling, and empathy. (AM2)
Negotiations also encompassed managing or guiding decision-makers in the acquiring firm.	As an experienced adviser, I believe it is part of the gut feeling to be able to guide a client by saying: this you can actually agree with. (LA)
	[Gut feeling is used] when you manage an initial informal price discussion [without involving decision-makers] so that it works, when you need approval from decision-makers and eventually offer a final price in a LOI [Letter of Intent]. (AM1)

Relations between intuitive expertise and analytical reasoning	Data
There was an ongoing interplay or dialogue between intuition and analytical reasoning.	It is basically in some way like an inner dialogue. You get facts and then you believe something … I like to sleep on it. I find that the knowledge that I slowly build up matures, together with new thoughts and new relationships, with the information that grows over time. (AM1)
	The answer is based on a lot of experience, perceptions and learnings, and knowledge of how different parties act in different situations. And how we should play this game and come out on the other side as a winner. It is not a process you can fully describe. It is more about the whole environment, and that this [you feel], this must be right. And then one can question that conclusion from slightly different angles. What if this happens? What if we would not have done this? (FA)
Analytical reasoning was used for testing assessments and judgments based on intuition.	So maybe you test that hypothesis in different ways. … Even with the customer. For example, we have received bids. We go through all the bids, talk to all the bidders so we understand everything. And then we have the picture, this is the situation. We believe this is the best way to move on. Of course, we have that discussion in our team. … And then we take it on to the customer and sit down for a couple of hours and talk about it, at that moment it is tested with senior people with a lot of experience from business decisions. (FA)
	When we build these [acquisition] cases and they are presented in pre-meetings etc. The discussion is often free, what does it feels like? … Is this good and why? If it were your money would you buy it? A very open discussion. To say what you feel. … It [of course] must work technically with all the papers, valuation models, the plan. But then this [open discussion] is another add-on. Does this work, does it feel good? We do this at every acquisition. Not least with this management aspect [the assessment of target management]. (LM2)
Analytical reasoning was used to concretize and create measurable parts.	Can one only be intuitive? No, I don't think so. Because someone needs to judge the intuition so to speak. To assess the intuition, you must create some kind of objective measurable parts. (AM2)
	This is usually the case. If you get a description of the company, you get a page. You look at what business and industry it is in. What growth, invested capital, and profitability it has. Then you can estimate, within 10 percent what this target will cost and what type of buyer there will be. In 90 percent of the cases you do it in 10 minutes. Then, there is still a man-month to produce analysis and material to explain that it is so. … You have already decided based on intuition where this will end, and then the analysis shows that it will be so. So you are comfortable in presenting it because this is how you feel. (FA)

Several interviewees used intuitive expertise in the challenging task of identifying potential problems during the due diligence process. It usually provides limited information and access to the target company, which lends itself to intuition. Furthermore, the process is steered by the seller who tends to set tight deadlines for bids as well as restricting the number of persons involved from the acquirer. The process is also surrounded by secrecy, which adds to the challenge. Intuition was used not only to identify critical areas when information was lacking but also when it was plentiful. An example of the latter was when the legal adviser identified what legal aspects to focus on during due diligence. The legal adviser described that without the required expertise, there was a risk of an overly long and unfocused due diligence report encompassing all legal areas, which provides limited value to the client.

To conclude, the use of intuition seemed vital for due diligence when it came to identifying problem areas and what to focus on. Intuition also enabled a crucial broader assessment of the target company.

The Use of Intuitive Expertise in Negotiations

The acquisition manager, together with the legal manager, was usually leading the internal approval process as well as the negotiation process with the seller. This core team was supported by an external legal adviser. In large acquisitions it was also common that both the acquirer and the seller used financial advisers for support during negotiations. All interviewees described several situations in which intuition was used throughout acquisition-making, from the initiation of the acquisition to the closing or termination of the acquisition. One of the legal managers described how acquisition-making was permeated with intuition, and how there was a continuous and interactive use of intuition and analysis throughout the acquisition:

> You have very limited information. They also give you very little information and still you have to decide a price. You give a price indication to participate in the process and then you receive some more material. And then you give a new price indication, the final negotiations usually follow. Everywhere there is a feeling. You make a judgment, you believe things, and make a conclusion. (LM1)

In line with this account, interviewees described intuition as critical for managing negotiations. It was considered important to understand the seller and especially: What are they actually saying and what does it mean? What are they aiming at? If I do this, how will they react? Why do they react in this way?

The quotes illustrate how the interviewees value the ability to interpret and judge people. An element of this ability and expertise was knowledge about the market and how different firms and individuals have typically acted in previous transactions. For example, how does the seller typically act when they say that they cannot accept this condition of the sale? Is it a test or does it really convey their view?

Negotiations also encompassed how advisers guide a client. One adviser mentioned how long experience and intuition helped when guiding a client to close a deal by recounting similar deals. Another example was during the sensitive phase of informal price discussions. These discussions constitute a difficult challenge to avoid locked positions for future and more formal negotiations. According to the interviews, this requires experience and intuition.

To conclude, the use of intuition seemed vital for negotiations, especially when it came to interpreting and managing people representing the seller. Even though intuitive expertise was important when assessing and managing people, it was also vital in making a holistic assessment of both target and seller.

The Relationship between Intuitive Expertise and Analytical Reasoning

The time-span of acquisition-making, including negotiations and due diligence, is several months. As mentioned earlier, making acquisitions includes many tasks in which intuitive expertise and analytical reasoning are used. Based on the interviews we could discern three patterns regarding the relationship between intuitive expertise and analytical reasoning.

First, there was an ongoing interplay between intuitive expertise and analytical reasoning. All of the interviewees described acquisition-making as being permeated by a myriad of data. This included data received from the seller and the target company, such as management presentations, information memorandum and information provided in the data room, as well as assessments of the management team and other people affected by a possible acquisition. The intuitive expertise was used to identify which aspects of the possible transaction to focus on and, in doing so, to apply more of analytical reasoning to make more informed judgments. The interviewees, exemplified by the quotation below, described it as an interplay or dialogue between intuition and analytical reasoning in which both are needed in making acquisitions.

> The intuitive part sort of massages the data which one has. Somewhere you get a feeling, this feels really good, or [the feeling] that something is wrong. I have to dig deeper into this. Something is not as it should be. (AM1)

Second, several of the interviewees described how judgments based on intuitive expertise were tested analytically. For an adviser, it could be done in discussions with the client. Acquisition and legal managers described that judgments based on intuitive expertise were often challenged and further developed in discussions with other members of the professional acquisition organization, as illustrated in the following quote:

> It is an advantage to be several people. Because people see different things, reflect on these in different ways and so on. When you sit down together and discuss how the counterpart has reacted you get a better picture. (LM1)

Third, analytical reasoning was used to make intuitive judgments tangible and measurable. For example, when producing strategic and financial rationales (e.g., identified synergies and their financial value) a key task was to produce the decision documents presented to decision-makers. These were analytically and logically coherent documents presenting concretized judgments in the form of strategic and financial rationales.

In addition to these three patterns we also discerned, from our interviews, a few examples of situations in which intuitive and analytical judgments conflicted. One example is when the experts at one of the acquiring firms thoroughly discussed their judgments of target management. Even though the target company had many strengths, judgments of target management were more critical. That prompted arguments of whether the acquisition should be aborted or not.

DISCUSSION AND CONCLUSIONS

Our findings of the use of intuitive expertise in acquisition-making add to the few field studies in the area. In the following section these findings are discussed in relation to findings from other field studies. Furthermore, we provide some reflections on the theories we use in our study, that is, dual process theories (Evans, 2008; Evans & Stanovich, 2013; Kahneman, 2011; Stanovich, 1999; Stanovich & West, 2000) and expertise (Ericsson, 2006; Ericsson & Lehmann, 1996). Related to this is the assumption that intuitive expertise is especially effective in tasks of high complexity (Dane & Pratt, 2007; Dane et al., 2012; Kahneman & Klein, 2009; Salas et al., 2010; Shapiro & Spence, 1997). We present our findings in two sections: tasks using intuitive expertise, and the relationship between intuitive and analytical reasoning. For each section the findings are first discussed in relation to those of other field studies, thereafter some reflections related to theory are presented.

Findings on Tasks Using Intuitive Expertise

The study shows that the use of intuitive expertise was critical in acquisition-making. It was used in a wide range of tasks during due diligence and negotiations. These tasks involved judgments of both a social (e.g., people) and/or material (e.g., production facilities) nature. Judgments of a social nature were instrumental in trying to find answers to questions such as: Will target management stay if the company is acquired? Does target management believe in the business plan they present? Intuitive expertise was also important in understanding and interpreting the talk and behavior of people taking part in negotiations.

The findings are in line with previous studies describing the use of intuitive expertise in HR situations (Burke & Miller, 1999), judgments by entrepreneurs of what venture to pursue (La Pira & Gillin, 2006), judgments of loan applicants by bank officers (Lipshitz & Shulimovitz, 2007) and investors' judgments of managers of early stage investments (Huang, 2018; Huang & Pearce, 2015). However, all these studies have focused on judgments of a single individual. We add to this stream of literature by showing that in the process of making acquisitions, judgments arose from judgments of several individuals, such as target management and representatives from the seller. These judgments represented different stakeholders and provided information on different aspects of the target. Together they helped experts in the acquisition organization to form a more coherent opinion of the target company and identify the best way forward (e.g., what to focus on in the due diligence process or how to negotiate).

Furthermore, the results show how intuitive expertise was used in judgments of a material nature, such as assessing production facilities and the quality of the target company's business plan. Some judgments, like those of the production facilities, were to a large extent based on impressionistic information from physical site visits. These findings are similar to the study by Lipshitz and Shulimovitz (2007: 221) on how loan officers used intuitive expertise to assess not only the applicant but also the plant of the applicant, as illustrated by a quote from one of their interviewees: "We visited the plant. It looked well kept, clean and orderly. The secretary had all records at hand, and they were well prepared for our visit."

In addition, we found that judgments, more often than not, included a holistic combination of people, formal documents and other types of information about the seller and the target. For example, evaluating the business plan of the target company was not limited to the plan itself. Other aspects, such as how target management presented the plan and information gathered during the due diligence process, were also assessed. Hence, intuitive expertise was instrumental in making judgments of people, which in turn contributed to a more informed assessment of the plan, an assessment that reached beyond the written text and numbers.

Two studies that have reached similar conclusions are those by Huang (2018) and Huang and Pearce (2015). They show how intuitive expertise is used in the judgment of entrepreneurs and how that assessment affects the analysis of formal documents. Huang and Pearce (2015: 660) describe it as a means to "provide data such as normative value or trustworthiness of the financials or the likelihood of the entrepreneur remaining committed to the business model." Likewise, Lipshitz and Shulimovitz (2007) demonstrate how intuitive expertise was used to assess loan applicants conjointly with the formal application. The linkage between formal plans and people producing these plans is also prominent in the study by Grant and Nilsson (2019). They indicate that intuitive expertise plays an important role in the production of strategic and financial rationales.

In our study we assume that the interviewees are experts in their field and possess domain-relevant schemas (Dane & Pratt, 2007; Kahneman & Klein, 2009). Furthermore, theory and research on intuitive expertise propose and illustrate how it is used in tasks with high complexity, leading to appropriate judgments (e.g., Dane & Pratt, 2007; Dane et al., 2012; Kahneman & Klein, 2009). Our findings are in line with this. We suggest that the characteristics of the acquisition process contribute to high environmental uncertainty and hence task complexity (Dane & Pratt, 2007). These characteristics include: a process steered by the seller and surrounded by secrecy, limited information and access to the target company, and tight deadlines. Additionally, we argue that the tasks identified, that is, due diligence, negotiations, and production of strategic and financial rationales evince high complexity in themselves.

Moreover, our findings show that viewing M&A as a specific domain, or task like Shapiro and Spence (1997) suggest, is too broad a view if we want to understand what type of expertise is required to solve different complex tasks in M&A. Rather, our findings suggest, in line with Kahneman and Klein (2009: 522), that expertise is fractionated, that is, that professional experts can exhibit "genuine expertise in some of their activities but not in others." For example, our findings suggest that a legal professional or an accounting professional without the required expertise in due diligence would not be able to properly identify and assess problem areas in due diligence, related to the legal or accounting area. Taken together, this suggests that we should study the nature of the tasks in order to understand the specific expertise that is required.

Findings on the Relationship between Intuitive and Analytical Reasoning

We have identified three patterns regarding the relationship between intuitive expertise and analytical reasoning. First, our findings show that judgments in acquisition-making are formed in a process using both intuitive expertise and analytical reasoning. This is perhaps not surprising, as due diligence and negotiations include collecting and analyzing a myriad of data as well as judging people in the target company and the seller. Studies of early-stage investments (Huang, 2018; Huang & Pearce, 2015), strategic decision-making (Woiceshyn, 2009), and decision-making by bank executives (Hensman & Sadler-Smith, 2011) corroborate these conclusions by showing a similar pattern of continuous and interrelated use of intuitive expertise and analytical reasoning.

Second, our findings indicate that analytical reasoning was used to test judgments based on intuitive expertise. Several interviewees described it as a deliberate strategy. For example, one of the legal managers described how intuitive judgments of the seller's talk and behavior in negotiations were discussed with other people taking part in the negotiations. The overall objective of these discussions was to further develop and refine judgments of what was said through analytical reasoning. In line with our findings, Woiceshyn (2009) illustrates how effective CEOs used frank and open discussion with others in order to test their intuitively arrived judgments. Similarly, Hensman and Sadler-Smith (2011) describe how bank executives used an analytical and deliberate approach (i.e., rational analysis) to test intuitive hypotheses.

Third, our findings suggest that analytical reasoning was used to concretize and make intuitive judgments measurable in financial terms. As one of the acquisition managers expressed it: "The intuitive drives the business process and the role of the analytical reasoning is to concretize and value it." This is similar to what Hensman and Sadler-Smith (2011: 58) found in their study of bank executives, illustrated in the following quote from one of their interviewees: "You do need to provide somebody with some kind of understanding as to why you've come to this conclusion." The study by Grant and Nilsson (2019) also supports this finding. They describe how strategic and financial rationales were produced to a large extent based on intuitive expertise and later concretized in the presentation of the rationales in decision documents. In line with their conclusions, our study concludes that a key task in all professional acquisition organizations is to produce decision documents that can be presented and understood by decision-makers.

Adding to these three patterns, albeit only with a few examples from the interviews, we found situations in which intuitive and analytical judgments were in conflict. In these situations it seemed that the intuitive judgments prevailed over the analytical judgments. Some earlier studies found a similar pattern of intuitive expertise trumping analytical reasoning when the two are in conflict (Huang & Pearce, 2015; Lipshitz & Shulimovitz, 2007).

Dual process theories provide the behavioral microfoundations for how ideas come to mind based on intuitive and analytical processes and their interactions (Evans, 2008; Evans & Stanovich, 2013; Kahneman, 2011; Stanovich, 1999; Stanovich & West, 2000). Consequently, the concept of decision-making and its outcome concerns these microprocesses. In our study we explored a time perspective of several months and view decision-making as an evolving process in which judgments take place gradually and stepwise (e.g., Mintzberg et al., 1976). This has implications for the outcome of decision-making. For example, even if microprocesses of intuition lead to faulty judgments (e.g., Hodgkinson & Sadler-Smith, 2018; Kahneman, 2011), a longer time perspective allows for a prolonged interaction between intuitive judgments and analytical reasoning. For example, our findings show that there was a deliberate use of analytical reasoning to test intuitive judgments. The finding where analytical reasoning was applied to concretize and make intuitive judgments measurable could also be seen as enabling tests of intuitive judgments. This also provides outsiders the possibility to evaluate such judgments (Kahneman, 2011; Lovallo & Kahneman, 2003).

CONCLUDING COMMENTS AND FUTURE RESEARCH

This is an explorative study with a limited number of interviewees. Consequently, our findings and conclusions should be interpreted with caution. Still, we argue that they provide valuable new knowledge for research on the use of intuitive expertise as well as for acquisition research. First, we identify in what types of acquisition-making tasks intuitive expertise is used and how it is used. This adds to our knowledge about acquisition-making and the role of experts in professional acquisition organizations. Second, our findings of the relationship between intuitive and analytical reasoning corroborate and amplify previous conclusions.

The study is based on retrospective interviews, using these to infer the use of judgments based on intuitive expertise. This method, obviously, imposes limitations on our findings. We therefore suggest that future research should use additional methods to examine our findings and suggestions (for an overview, see for example Sinclair, 2014).

Since the study is explorative, there are several interesting areas for future research. One such area is to further investigate how incongruence between intuitive and analytical judgments affects decision-making. Another area is to examine how the information evaluation occurs in cases of incongruence between intuitive and analytical reasoning. A third area is to explore if and how judgments made by intuitive expertise and judgments made by rational machine decision modeling (e.g., artificial intelligence) differ. By following that line of research, it would be possible to deepen our understanding of potential positive or negative effects of using intuitive expertise. A fourth area is to study how judgments are made collectively. As Akinci and Sadler-Smith (2019) have pointed out, intuitive expertise can also be shared and interpreted by a group. Hence, studying acquisition-making, involving several experts, could add to our knowledge of how judgments are formed.

NOTE

1. Based on Evans and Stanovich (2013) we refer to these as types and not systems. The reason is that the use of the terms System 1 and System 2 (Kahneman, 2011; Stanovich, 1999) could be misinterpreted to mean a two-minds hypothesis.

REFERENCES

Akinci, C., & Sadler-Smith, E. 2019. Collective intuition: Implications for improved decision making and organizational learning. *British Journal of Management*, 30(3): 558–577.

Burke, L.A., & Miller, M.K. 1999. Taking the mystery out of intuitive decision making. *The Academy of Management Executive*, 13(4): 91–99.

Chatterjee, S. 2009. The keys to successful acquisition programmes. *Long Range Planning*, 42(2): 137–163.

Dane, E., & Pratt, M.G. 2007. Exploring intuition and its role in managerial decision making. *Academy of Management Review*, 32(1): 33–54.

Dane, E., Rockmann, K.W., & Pratt, M.G. 2012. When should I trust my gut? Linking domain expertise to intuitive decision–making effectiveness. *Organizational Behavior and Human Decision Processes*, 119(2): 187–194.

Dubois, A., & Gadde, L.E. 2014. 'Systematic combining': A decade later. *Journal of Business Research*, 67(6): 1277–1284.

Ericsson, K.A. 2006. An introduction to the *Cambridge handbook of expertise and expert performance*: Its development, organization, and content. In K.A. Ericsson, N. Charness, P.J. Feltovich, & R.R. Hoffman (Eds.), *The Cambridge Handbook of Expertise and Expert Performance*: 3–19. New York: Cambridge University Press.

Ericsson, K.A., & Lehmann, A.C. 1996. Expert and exceptional performance: Evidence of maximal adaptation to task constraints. *Annual Review of Psychology*, 47(1): 273–305.

Ericsson, K.A., & Ward, P. 2007. Capturing the naturally occurring superior performance of experts in the laboratory: Toward a science of expert and exceptional performance. *Current Directions in Psychological Science*, 16(6): 346–350.

Evans, J.S.B.T. 2008. Dual-processing accounts of reasoning, judgment, and social cognition. *Annual Review of Psychology*, 59: 255–278.

Evans, J.S.B.T., & Stanovich, K.E. 2013. Dual-process theories of higher cognition: Advancing the debate. *Perspectives on Psychological Science*, 8(3): 223–241.

Grant, M. 2018. The role of the professional acquisition organization in acquisition decision-making. In M. Grant, *Making Acquisitions*. Doctoral thesis. Uppsala University. Paper 2 of the Doctoral thesis.

Grant, M., & Nilsson, F. 2019. The production of strategic and financial rationales in capital investments: Judgments based on intuitive expertise. *British Accounting Review*. https://doi.org/10.1016/j.bar.2019.100861.

Haspeslagh, P.C., & Jemison, D.B. 1991. *Managing Acquisitions: Creating Value Through Corporate Renewal*. New York: Free Press.

Hensman, A., & Sadler-Smith, E. 2011. Intuitive decision making in banking and finance. *European Management Journal*, 29(1): 51–66.

Hodgkinson, G.P., & Sadler-Smith, E. 2018. The dynamics of intuition and analysis in managerial and organizational decision making. *Academy of Management Perspectives*, 32(4): 473–492.

Huang, L. 2018. The role of investor gut feel in managing complexity and extreme risk. *Academy of Management Journal*, 61(5): 1821–1847.

Huang, L., & Pearce, J.L. 2015. Managing the unknowable: The effectiveness of early-stage investor gut feel in entrepreneurial investment decisions. *Administrative Science Quarterly*, 60(4): 634–670.

Kahneman, D. 2011. *Thinking, Fast and Slow*. New York: Farrar, Straus and Giroux.

Kahneman, D., & Klein, G. 2009. Conditions for intuitive expertise: A failure to disagree. *American Psychologist*, 64(6): 515–526.

La Pira, F., & Gillin, M. 2006. Non-local intuition and the performance of serial entrepreneurs. *International Journal of Entrepreneurship and Small Business*, 3(1): 17–35.

Langley, A. 1999. Strategies for theorizing from process data. *Academy of Management Review*, 24(4): 691–710.

Lipshitz, R., & Shulimovitz, N. 2007. Intuition and emotion in bank loan officers' credit decisions. *Journal of Cognitive Engineering and Decision Making*, 1(2): 212–233.

Lovallo, D., & Kahneman, D. 2003. Delusions of success. *Harvard Business Review*, 81(7): 56–63.

Mintzberg, H., Raisinghani, D., & Théorêt, A. 1976. The structure of 'unstructured' decision processes. *Administrative Science Quarterly*, 21(2): 246–275.

Pablo, A.L. 2016. Deconstructing M&A research – paradigm progress. In A. Risberg, D.R. King, & O. Meglio (Eds.), *The Routledge Companion to Mergers and Acquisitions*: 383–390. New York: Routledge.

Salas, E., Rosen, M.A., & DiazGranados, D. 2010. Expertise-based intuition and decision making in organizations. *Journal of Management*, 36(4): 941–973.

Shapiro, S., & Spence, M.T. 1997. Managerial intuition: A conceptual and operational framework. *Business Horizons*, 40(1): 63–68.

Simon, H.A. 1992. What is an "explanation" of behavior? *Psychological Science*, 3(3): 150–161.

Simon, H.A., & Chase, W.G. 1973. Skill in chess: Experiments with chess-playing tasks and computer simulation of skilled performance throw light on some human perceptual and memory processes. *American Scientist*, 61(4): 394–403.

Sinclair, M. (Ed.). 2011. *Handbook of Intuition Research*. Cheltenham, UK and Northampton, MA, USA: Edward Elgar Publishing.

Sinclair, M. (Ed.). 2014. *Handbook of Research Methods on Intuition*. Cheltenham, UK and Northampton, MA, USA: Edward Elgar Publishing.

Stanovich, K.E. 1999. *Who is Rational? Studies of Individual Differences in Reasoning*. New York: Psychology Press.

Stanovich, K.E., & West, R.F. 2000. Individual differences in reasoning: Implications for the rationality debate? *Behavioral and Brain Sciences*, 23(5): 645–726.
Trichterborn, A., Zu Knyphausen-Aufseß, D., & Schweizer, L. 2016. How to improve acquisition performance: The role of a dedicated M&A function, M&A learning process, and M&A capability. *Strategic Management Journal*, 37(4): 763–773.
van Riel, A.C.R., & Lievens, A. 2004. New service development in high tech sectors: A decision-making perspective. *International Journal of Service Industry Management*, 15(1): 72–101.
Woiceshyn, J. 2009. Lessons from 'good minds': How CEOs use intuition, analysis and guiding principles to make strategic decisions. *Long Range Planning*, 42(3): 298–319.

5. Uncovering opportunity: expert vs. novice entrepreneurs' use of intuitive and analytical decision-making

Mingyang Wang and Jenny Gibb

Entrepreneurs, as economic actors, seek to exploit opportunities in pursuing wealth creation (Alvarez et al., 2013). As such, entrepreneurship surrounds the seeking out, and acting upon, opportunity (Baron, 2008). Decision-making in entrepreneurship takes place across three stages: opportunity recognition, opportunity evaluation and opportunity exploitation, where in each stage intuitive and analytical processing typically occurs. Intuition is highly relevant in the opportunity recognition phase of business ventures (Sadler-Smith, 2015). The entrepreneurial opportunity recognition stage provides a theoretical foundation to investigate how entrepreneurs "identify a good idea and transform it into an innovative product, which adds value and generates revenue" (Lumpkin & Lichtenstein, 2005: 457).

Nevertheless, we are yet to understand how entrepreneurs' use of intuition interacts with their rational analysis in recognizing opportunity, in situations such as product innovation. In particular, how might different groups of entrepreneurs, such as expert versus novice entrepreneurs, engage in these two decision-making styles? Prior studies suggest expertise plays a vital role in intuitive processing (Baldacchino, 2013; Baron & Ensley, 2006; Gustafsson, 2006). Yet, we do not know whether, and to what extent, expertise is an antecedent to intuitive versus rational processing (Baldacchino et al., 2015). In this study, we examine: *How do expert entrepreneurs' intuitive and analytical decision-making processes differ from those of novice entrepreneurs in recognizing entrepreneurial opportunity?*

Using a multi-case study approach with eight New Zealand software companies, we develop a grounded model of visioning for software product innovation that compares expert and novice founders' use of intuition and analysis in decision-making. We uncover a temporal aspect of visioning that is underpinned by imagination and resilience across these two founder groups. We contribute to Baylor's (2001) U-shaped model of intuition development and explain how entrepreneurial expertise impacts on intuitive and analytical processing towards a firm's growth. Our study also contributes to existing literature on dual processing by examining how different types of entrepreneurs used different combinations of intuition and rational analysis in decision-making processes (Evans, 2007; Hodgkinson & Sadler-Smith, 2018; Sadler-Smith & Hodgkinson, 2016). Further, we extend understanding on entrepreneurial opportunity recognition (Alvarez et al., 2013; Sadler-Smith, 2015) by investigating how these founder groups used intuition and rational analysis to recognize long-term and short-term growth opportunities.

The next section discusses the relevant theoretical concepts, followed by an explanation of the research method used. Then we examine the findings and provide a discussion based on the development of our model, followed by theoretical implications.

THEORY BACKGROUND

Entrepreneurial activities are a function of decision-making and action-taking in recognizing opportunities not previously noticed, especially in uncertain environments (Alvarez et al., 2013). This process often leads to new products and services (Venkataraman & Sarasvathy, 2001) that require entrepreneurial cognition in judging and assessing situations, resource orchestration, and growth (Wright & Stigliani, 2013). Sadler-Smith (2015) suggests entrepreneurs require a sufficient amount of prior knowledge that helps them combine existing ideas in novel and creative ways in discovering new opportunity. He also believes intuition is more relevant in decision-making at opportunity recognition, rather than at the evaluation or exploitation stages. This is due to the greater reliance at this point on non-predictive logic, active scanning, divergent thinking, connecting dots, as well as the use of affect as information.

Entrepreneurial Intuition

Entrepreneurial intuition is defined as "the affectively charged recognition and evaluation of a business venturing opportunity arising as a result of involuntary, rapid, non-conscious, associative processing" (Sadler-Smith, 2015: 213). As such, intuition is a powerful and valuable cognitive and affective asset used in entrepreneurship (Baldacchino et al., 2015; Baron, 2008), especially in times of insufficient information (Blume & Covin, 2011). Intuition is often involved in entrepreneurial process-related matters where effective entrepreneurs need to be able not only to perceive those opportunities which are likely to have potential commercial value but also discriminate between those opportunities that are deemed to have potential value and are not worth pursuing. Sadler-Smith (2015) suggests intuition supports both the spontaneous recognition of important environmental cues that can be recombined in creative ways, and the evaluation of recognized opportunity through, for example, hunches and gut feelings.

Sinclair (2010) provides a conceptual framework that includes three intuitive processes: intuitive expertise, intuitive creation, and intuitive foresight. These three types of intuition can be further refined by the time period involved and by the breadth of information processed. Intuitive expertise draws on stored domain-specific knowledge and is based on the phenomenon described as "deep smarts" (Sadler-Smith & Burke-Smalley, 2015). The distinguishing points between intuitive expertise and entrepreneurial intuition are that intuitive expertise is mostly non-verbal, internal, deliberate thinking is not required, and past pattern recognition is valued. In contrast, entrepreneurial intuition tends to operate pre-verbally where no language exists to describe the process, and enables decision-makers to connect patterns in a new way (Sinclair & Ashkanasy, 2005). Therefore, entrepreneurial intuition is more relevant to the other two processes: intuitive creation and intuitive foresight. Intuitive creation involves a wide range of experience from often unrelated fields or everyday life to create something new. The processing of information appears to be holistic but can be slower than intuitive expertise with accumulated information. This form of intuition is often used when there are many alternatives and possibilities, rather than actual facts that can be proven (Goldberg, 1989). Intuitive foresight can be likened to a future-oriented intuitive expertise where attempts are made to match the foreseen patterns of those from the past, or to intuitive creation if these include broad experiences that can be combined in novel ways.

It is well established that individuals engage in two parallel cognitive systems. The intuitive system is associated with affect, and operates at an automatic, preconscious level (Epstein et al., 1996) that is often called "Type 1" and "System 1" or "X system (reflexive)" (Lieberman, 2007; Sadler-Smith, 2008). The rational system, also called "Type 2", involves processing that is reflective, comparatively slow, detail-focused, and cognitively demanding (Epstein at al., 1996; Evans, 2003, 2010; Lieberman, 2007). The use of intuitive and analytical thinking has appeared in numerous dual process models (Chaiken & Trope, 1999; De Neys & Glumicic, 2008; Evans, 2007; Stanovich & West, 2000). More recently, Sadler-Smith and Hodgkinson (2016) developed an analytical intervention model to explain the intuition–rational analysis relationship with intuitive processing occurring in surface, shallow and deep analytic-intervention. Hodgkinson and Sadler-Smith (2018) categorize all dual process theories into two categories: default-interventionist and parallel-competitive. However, we are yet to understand how different types of decision-makers, such as experts versus novices, might engage in processes that use different combinations of intuition and analysis during entrepreneurial opportunity recognition.

Expertise and the Development of Intuition

Explanations of expertise usually surround the development of individuals' knowledge structures as they move from novice to experts. This approach is largely based on the role of memory in exceptional performances of perception and recognition (Chase & Simon, 1973a, 1973b). These studies suggested that decision-making behaviour has not always completely followed a rational path (Simon, 1955), where experts recognize complex patterns they can use to instantly respond in ways that novices cannot do. The idea of intuition as recognition was based on the premise knowledge had been learnt over time and could be, in part, used to recall beyond immediate consciousness (de Groot, 1986; Harteis & Billett, 2013). From such foundations Dreyfus and Dreyfus (2005) developed a five-stage expertise model. Stage 1, novice, involves using simple rules to determine the task environment and the actions required. Stage 2, advanced beginner, sees the individual beginning to understand the context and to recognize new aspects of the environment. Stage 3, competence, links individuals' greater exposure to experiences with more complex procedures. Stage 4, proficiency, develops once experience is assimilated and intuitive reactions can replace analytical reasoning. Stage 5, expertise, sees the individual as engaging in skilful activity having learnt a repertoire of ways to distinguish between more and less rewarding situations.

In Baylor's (2001) U-shaped model of intuition development, she suggests that there are two different types of intuition based on expertise: immature intuition and mature intuition, each differentiated by the level of subject expertise of the individual. Becoming an expert in a subject requires metacognitive control over one's thought processes at different stages where individuals have acquired a high level of domain-specific knowledge through experience (Dane, 2010). An individual with a less-developed knowledge structure, who acts as a novice, will access immature intuition (Baylor, 2001). Further study by Baldacchino (2013) indicates intuition and cognitive versatility mediate the relationship between experience and opportunity identification. She found that experienced entrepreneurs are more proficient than novices at identifying opportunities. This suggests scholars need to consider cognitive versatility, rather than simply study intuition or analysis in isolation, and to think about how this can be shaped to benefit opportunity identification. Experience and expertise play a vital role in intuitive processing, but the issue of whether and to what extent experience and expertise are antecedents of intuitive processing is unclear (Baldacchino et al., 2015). There is no explanation about how the level of experience or expertise impacts on the way of using both intuition and analysis in entrepreneurial opportunity recognition. As a result, the relationships between three intuitive processes (intuitive expertise, intuitive creation, and intuitive foresight) (Sinclair, 2010) during entrepreneurial opportunity recognition and the level of experience or expertise remain also unclear. We are yet to understand how expert entrepreneurs' intuitive processes in product innovation differ from those of novice entrepreneurs.

METHOD

Data Collection

We used a multi-case study approach in the context of the New Zealand software industry. This industry was selected as an ideal setting to investigate intuitive and analytical decision-making styles given its fast-changing, innovative nature. Using this approach enabled us to obtain in-depth knowledge and to draw comparisons across the cases to ensure replication logic (Eisenhardt, 1991; Yin, 2014). We adopted Lumpkin and Lichtenstein's (2005) definition of entrepreneurial opportunity recognition as the software entrepreneur's ability to identify an innovative idea and transform it into a software product that generates revenue. This study used purposive sampling with the selection of eight fast-growing *Born Global*[1] software companies. Table 5.1 provides further information on these companies, all of which were established in New Zealand, most within the last eight years. We used Dane's (2010) categorization of experts in this study. Experts were defined as those individuals who had ten or more years of CEO experience in the software industry, while novices had less than ten years of CEO experience. The companies were located across different industry sectors (e.g., accounting and payroll, medical and healthcare management), employing between 45 and 2,300 staff.

Semi-structured interviews were conducted between 2011 and 2015. Each interview took approximately one hour. All items on the interview schedule investigated how expert and novice entrepreneurs used intuition and data analytical processes in their decision-making during software product innovation. We also used a variety of data collection techniques to increase content validity, such as direct observation, and secondary data sources, such as documentation, company websites, newspapers and reports.

Data Analysis

We began by developing detailed descriptions to generate initial insight using Yin's (2014) replication approach. We then wrote detailed descriptions for each company. Then we examined the interview transcripts to identify the key issues facing each company. This process led to our identifying the use of intuition and rational analysis in an entrepreneurial opportunity recognition context where we began with 96 categories, coded into first-order categories that collapsed into the second-order themes. Then we aggregated the second-order themes into the theoretical dimensions. In order to do this, we also used Fernandez's (2004) grounded theory method where the categories identified became the basis for new understanding in the theory. Sinclair's (2010) three intuition types formed the foundation for preferred use of intuition. In the process, we uncovered the imagination and resilience constructs where the combined use of intuitive and analytical processing took place towards visioning.

In order to examine how expert versus novice founders engaged in intuitive and analytical decision-making in recognizing opportunity we used the context of four software product innovation areas: new software product, new partnership, new market entry and product feature modification. The eight software company founders were divided into four expert founders in companies: B, C, D and H, and four novice founders in companies: A, E, F and G.

FINDINGS

We examined how expert versus novice founders use intuitive and analytical decision-making in recognizing opportunity across the four software product innovation areas as outlined earlier. We uncovered important differences in the way these two founder types identified opportunity. Expert founders were likely to use their more comprehensive entrepreneurial knowledge structure to sense hidden opportunities. For example, the Company B founder is a famous New Zealand technology

Table 5.1 *Summary of the software companies*

Name of company	Ownership	Location	Type of software	No. of employees	Year of origin	First year export	First export destination	The level of competition	The main competitors overseas	Main markets	The percentage of sales from overseas
A	Private	North Island	Retail web-based point-of-sale	305	2010	2010	US, Australia, Saudi Arabia, South America, Africa	High	US	US, Canada, Australia, UK, Europe	85%
B	Public	North Island	Accounting and payroll	2300	2006	2008	UK	High	US, UK	US, UK	60%
C	Public	North Island	Clinical information	1176	1993	Late 90s	US	Medium	US	US	95%
D	Public	North Island	Crime fighting and security	260	2012	2012	UK, Australia	Low	UK, US	UK, US, Canada, Australia, United Arabic Emirates	80%
E	Public	North Island	Mobile workforce management	45	2009	2010	Australia	High	Canada	Australia, US, UK	80%

Name of company	Ownership	Location	Type of software	No. of employees	Year of origin	First year export	First export destination	The level of competition	The main competitors overseas	Main markets	The percentage of sales from overseas
F	Private	North Island	Online inventory management	74	2010	2010	Australia, UK, Dubai, South Africa	High	Singapore, US, China	Australia	75%
G	Private	South Island	Appointment scheduling	57	2012	2012	Australia	High	Australia, US, UK	Australia, UK, US	80%
H	Private	South Island	Data acquisition systems and education	179	1988	1988	Australia	High	US, Europe, NZ	Australia, Brazil, UK, US, France, Germany, Chile, China, Japan, India, the Middle East	90%

entrepreneur who used his rational understanding and interpretation of prior software product developments to the market to be creatively intuitive in seeking out opportunity for the development of a new product and the transformation of the new software into a business platform. In contrast, novices were found to have a less mature knowledge structure for interpreting past happenings or for considering how things should be done. These founders were more likely to see opportunity for one-off products. For example, Company F, which was new to the software industry, had an idea for a new product, but was less confident in its long-term value to the market.

Visioning

Visioning in this study includes an individual's ability to use their imagination towards product innovation and to use resilience in developing their leadership skills as their company grows. After analysing how all the founders used intuition and analysis to recognize entrepreneurial opportunity we uncovered that both experts and novices used visioning. Within this overarching construct, we found that each group used imagination and resilience differently in perceiving opportunity for new and incremental software product innovation and to forecast technology and market trends; as well as in how they developed their leadership. A key finding was how these two groups used their intuitive and rational process to nurture imagination and resilience towards developing long-term visioning among experts vs. short-term visioning among novices.

Imagination

In this study, we define imagination as the founder's ability to perceive potential opportunity in initiating product innovation, forecasting technology and market trends. "Imagination is a way of seeing and feeling things as they compose an integral whole. It is the large and generous blending of interests at the point where the mind comes in contact with the world. When old and familiar things are made new in experience, there is imagination" (Dewey, 2005: 278). We uncovered how expert founders combined their rational use of prior experience and multi-skill set developed from seeking out prior opportunities to develop a knowledge structure they could use in an intuitive and creative manner to examine and forecast for the future. In contrast, the knowledge structure of novice founders typically led to a more confined and heavier reliance on their interpretation of prior experiences resulting in a more contained use of intuition to do things right when judging future product development opportunities.

Perceiving opportunities

Expert founders perceived more complex opportunities with much of their intuitive processing, together with the rational use of iterative learning and observations of technology and market trends. The founder of Company D reported:

> The three trends we saw cross over are security, big data, and advanced analytics to solve crime problems. No other software companies really dedicate themselves 100 percent to solving these problems. Almost all the decision-making was based on intuition. We ended up with hundreds of presentations, talking to and learning from a lot of people. If I look back at the first presentation or schedule we tried to put together, it was nothing like what we ended up with.

In contrast, novice founders typically perceived and developed a single software product. The idea for the software product usually came from customer feedback or from observing another business. Also, it was found that the knowledge of novice founders often led to a less comprehensive means of processing, with regard to strategic foresight, for their respective companies. The interpretations they made from their knowledge structure and the subsequent intuitive judgements on customer needs saw these founders focus on opportunities for single software product types. In addition, they more readily sought the help of others in growing their business. These founders were more likely to seek partnerships with a well-known or more established software company. For example, the founder of Company A mentioned:

> Building a partnership with PayPal was seen as an opportunity to be a thought leader and also to establish us as a major pioneer in our market. It seems to send a strong message to all our competitors. We saw this partnership as an opportunity for us to build market profile and credibility, to create relationships, and to deliver cool technology to customers. If we did not do the partner project, it would be a mistake because the main benefits we got are all intangible. That leads onto financial rewards, but maybe two or three years down the track.

Initiating software innovation

Expert founders were more likely to use their initiative in seeking out software innovation opportunities in order to imagine and develop original products that used their intuitive creation. These findings support Dane's (2010) conclusions that experts tend to solve problems in a forward-oriented direction, whereas novices tend to work backwards. Intuitive creation often occurs when individuals draw on a wide range of experience in unrelated fields or from everyday life to create something new (Sinclair, 2010). This is exemplified in our study where, for example, the founder of Company B wanted to build a platform between business and government so he initiated work on web services:

> As the internet developed ten years ago, most government departments built their website. More business needs to know to go to each one, there is an easy way to fix this, so we have been working hard since we started about web services into government. We already have the data sitting there, it means now the government departments can just open up their servers, and if we have the data, we can push it straight in, so you get all the compliance work just as a by-product of having good data .... In the long-term, the New Zealand business number is going to be for all our business entities. It would give us an electronic key for every business. This is a great example of where we can lead the world because we are all working with each other.

Novice founders, when compared to expert founders, were more likely to use intuitive expertise to add new features to existing software products. This supports Sinclair's (2010) work where intuitive expertise draws on domain-specific knowledge in the form of expertise accumulated in the past. In our study, these innovative ideas came from customer feedback, other companies' strategies, and partnerships. For example, the founder of Company E explained a new software feature:

> "Job Share" is not a particularly cool feature, but it is commonly requested and can be used by our client base and simply provide job information to our clients' clients. It shared job information with their customers.

Forecasting technology and market trends

In our study, expert founders used intuitive foresight to seek out opportunities in the business environment, markets and industries, using a long-term vision. This intuitive process was evident in their ability to predict what their respective company's future growth stages were going to be. The founder of Company B expressed confidence in his long-term strategic plan and in his ability to predict technology and market trends:

> We spent seven or eight years building online accounting software and focused on doing credit notes and purchase orders. Over the next several years we are going to transform from accounting software to a business platform.

These findings support Sinclair's (2010) comparison of intuitive foresight to a future-oriented intuitive expertise if it matches the foreseen patterns with those from the past, or to intuitive creation if it includes broad experience and combines all in novel ways. In contrast, novice founders were more likely to engage in developing a shorter-term vision that often included following rather than taking market lead. The founder of Company G commented:

> I am comfortable with the idea we only can look at a few months ahead without any real certainty. That is how I deal with these types of situations, just focus on what is going on in the next few months.

Resilience

We adopted Lengnick-Hall et al.'s (2011) definition of organizational resilience capacity to explain the resilience in our study – an entrepreneur's ability to effectively absorb technology and market trends, develop situation-specific responses to, and ultimately engage in, transformative activities to build new products and markets.

Consistent leadership/ownership

Expert founders' resilience in seeking and being prepared to adjust their focus on product innovation opportunity was often linked to the knowledge structures they had built with regard to their learning and leadership skills development that usually accompanied their company's growth. With a greater number of years in which to build expertise across multiple operational and strategic areas, expert founders were able to more readily absorb technology and market trends, develop intuitive responses, and engage in innovative activities to build new products and markets. For example, twenty years ago, the founder of Company C perceived a huge potential opportunity in health software. He learnt and ascertained what the market needed, repositioned the company's software to focus on the health sector, and then gradually built a full range of products for hospitals and the regional health sector. The founder of Company C attributed success to the consistent private ownership/leadership and the unique, comprehensive range of products:

> I think the difference at Company C is that we had consistent ownership and board. Many of our competitors are bought by investors who are looking for exits, so the strategy changes every couple of years. We have just been very consistent. When we started, there were a lot of big competitors. They gradually disappeared one by one, and we became a leading vendor of health solutions after 15 years. We moved from one to another niche area and now have an extensive range of software solutions for hospitals and the regional health sector.

Untested perseverance for leadership

Novice founders, when compared to expert founders, were less likely to learn and develop their leadership skills along with their company's growth, due to their less mature skill set. Their limited experience in a leadership position together with their development of prior experience based on a single product area had not provided a comprehensive knowledge structure. Moreover, founders who had employed a CEO also indicated their untested perseverance and resilience in leadership growth. They were less likely to be able to use rational thinking to learn, understand and absorb new technology and market trends, and to develop their intuitive responses to lead their respective companies during periods of rapid growth. Furthermore, it was found that inconsistent leadership hindered novice founders' ability to develop a long-term vision for company growth. For example, the founder of Company F could not give details of what he expected to happen over the next few years. He said:

> When I started this company, I thought it would be amazing if we became an NZ$10 million-dollar company in a few years. With the opportunities, we set up to be a billion-dollar company.

DISCUSSION AND IMPLICATIONS

We developed a grounded theory model of visioning for software product innovation that compares expert and novice founders' use of intuition and analysis for decision-making in entrepreneurial opportunity recognition (see Figure 5.1). Our study uncovered how expert founders engaged in long-term visioning for technology and market trends compared to novice founders who preferred short-term visioning. We show how visioning is linked to a founder's entrepreneurial knowledge structure and intuitive process. Intuitive process in product innovation can be improved when technical expertise is used to understand and communicate strategic visions. Intuitive process requires the ability of individuals to shift between an intuitive and analytical function (Bastick, 1982). Our founders' intuitive processes helped to solve problems creatively and effectively when there was insufficient information, and also to form visions to perceive, initiate and forecast innovation opportunities (Vaughan, 1979).

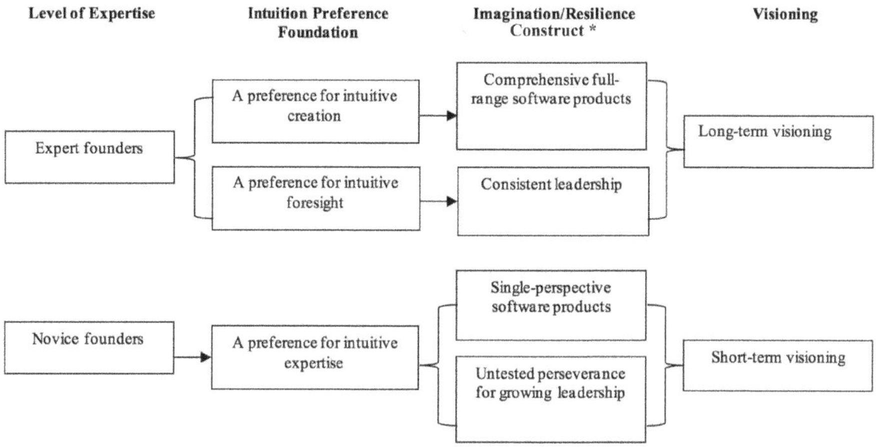

Note: * Constructs combine intuitive and analytical thinking towards visioning, see findings.

Figure 5.1 *Visioning for software product innovation: expert founders vs. novice founders*

We uncovered how founder visioning is underpinned by imagination and resilience. Together these two constructs assisted founders to discover product innovation opportunities and to develop leadership skills as their respective companies grew. Imagination is a mental process that can be used to generate novel images beyond what is already known, where a balance is assumed between conscious and subconscious processing since the individual is never perfectly aware of his or her imagination (Li, 2014). Bringing together images of possibilities with perceptions of reality, Croce (1922/1965: 295) described imagination as the "intellectual intuition of art". Coleridge (1967/1975) distinguishes between primary and secondary imagination. Primary imagination, which is reproductive and based on perception is used by most individuals, while secondary imagination is creative and involves intuition. In our study expert founders, when compared with novice founders, more regularly used intuitive creation to identify immediate product innovation and business opportunities, and intuitive foresight to judge the potential of future opportunity. Expert founders were able to develop a wider product range with a longer-term vision, covering the next five to ten years, with the help of secondary imagination, whereas novice founders preferred short-term visioning that saw them typically focus on a single product in the following months that appeared to draw on primary imagination.

Expert founders engaged in a more comprehensive use of imagination than novice founders. This included experts having a vision for developing their company's future. Our findings support Salas et al.'s (2010) research where expert founders used intuitive creation as a collection of complex patterns in their domain to perceive larger and more meaningful patterns in the environment more rapidly. In this context, intuition acts as "sense-making" where effort is exerted to understand events in order to create order and make sense of what has occurred, what is occurring, and what will occur (Salas et al., 2010). We draw on Sinclair's (2010) conceptualization of "intuitive creation" that we identified among expert founders who preferred to use domain-specific expertise in unrelated fields to create new products. In this instance, it was to judge the intersections between several different market trends or unrelated industries rather than simply relying on customers' requests; and to make rational interpretations based on their existing knowledge structures. Furthermore, it is likely experts regularly draw on collective accounts of intuition from others when independently forming judgements (Akinci & Sadler-Smith, 2019). In contrast, novice founders preferred to use "intuitive expertise" as conceptualized by Sinclair (2010) since they had a limited knowledge structure to engage in analytical thinking and were less inclined to use intuitive creation to think "out of the box" (Baylor, 2001; Sinclair, 2010).

Moreover, in our study the entrepreneurs' use of resilience was found to impact on their visioning. Expert founders were better able to adapt and absorb new concepts during the company's growth, which contributed to their company gaining competitive advantage through a long-term vision in areas such as product development rather than seeking out investors to buy their business. Novice founders, in contrast, lacked resilience and relied on a short-term vision to develop a single software product. Also, novice founders were less able to develop their leadership that would nurture their company growth. Resilience as a concept includes an individual's use of intuition and the recognition of consistent analytical evidence (Fletcher & Sarkar, 2013). As such, resilience is a dynamic process that includes positive adaptation in situations of challenge and adversity that can change over time. The process of resilience highlights how an individual can combine his or her use of intuition and analytical reasoning from situation to situation, which usually leads to changed behaviour over time, particularly with increased expertise. Thus, resilience provides an important link between intuitive creation and foresight (Sinclair, 2010) and analytical thinking towards mature intuition (Baylor, 2001). Resilience is suggested by Krueger (2003) to be a cognitive state that has temporality either prior to or immediately after the target behaviour. Further, our study supports Seeger et al.'s (2005) findings that resilience has a practical and prospective orientation to the future rather than a defensive attitude towards the past.

We observed how expert entrepreneurs developed leadership skills as their company grew. This group of entrepreneurs displayed Sinclair's (2010) "intuitive foresight" that mapped onto patterns they foresaw from the past. Their intuition appeared to originate from prior experience-based ability in recognizing patterns, to act as a conduit to direct knowing (Sinclair & Ashkanasy, 2002). These entrepreneurs relied on intuitive decision-making as a basis for recognizing future venture opportunities in alignment with Hogarth (2001). In contrast, novice founders, who typically did not occupy a CEO position, were less likely to develop leadership skills as their company grew. During the product creation processes, novices learnt from both their limited intuitive expertise and rational knowledge structures to expand and adjust how they recognized opportunity. Expert founders used their mature learning and knowledge structures (Baylor, 2001) to effectively absorb and process information that helped them to use discretion in becoming sensitive to some opportunities but not others (Corbett, 2005, 2006; Dimov, 2007).

Implications

Comparing expert and novice entrepreneurs' use of intuitive and analytical decision-making processes in recognizing entrepreneurial opportunity we make two key contributions to the entrepreneurial intuition literature. First, we show how our visioning construct can be used to explain the development of expertise in both expert and novice decision-makers. We show how expert decision-makers used intuitive creation (Sinclair, 2010) to extend the breadth of imagination in new product development and intuitive foresight (Sinclair, 2010) to imagine leaps towards their company's direction. In each instance experts also called upon their well-developed rational knowledge structure to support their long-term visioning. In contrast, novice decision-makers used intuitive expertise (Sinclair, 2010) to focus on single product development that was accompanied by a rather limited rational knowledge structure towards short-term visioning. We thus extend understanding of Baylor's (2001) U-shaped intuitive processing model, to explain how the U-shape develops between the use of immature intuition by novices and mature intuition by experts. We also demonstrate how resilience is used to create an important link between interpreting the past and imagining the future for both expert and novice decision-makers. In doing so, we extend the understanding of the processes operating towards the bottom of Baylor's (2001) U-shape, where analytical processing takes place.

Furthermore, we illustrate how the use of visioning, together with imagination and resilience, can be used to extend the understanding of dual processes inherent in developing entrepreneurial expertise. By explaining how entrepreneurs engage in an intuitive–rational analysis process to recognize opportunity in product innovation, we contribute to dual process theories (e.g., Evans, 2007; Hodgkinson & Sadler-Smith, 2018; Sadler-Smith & Hodgkinson, 2016). Further, by examining these two entrepreneurial groups we were able to show how expert founders used imagination to perceive a large range of complex, more long-term opportunities than did novices. We also offer insight into the future orientation of resilience and judgement on how intuition and knowledge structure can be used for entrepreneurial opportunity exploration and firm growth (Alvarez et al., 2013; Foss et al., 2007).

NOTE

1. Born Global firms are firms that have undergone faster processes of internationalization than would have been expected for firms of similar size, age, and nature (Lopez et al., 2009).

REFERENCES

Akinci, C., & Sadler-Smith, E. 2019. Collective intuition: Implications for improved decision making and organizational learning. *British Journal of Management*, 30(3): 558–577.

Alvarez, S.A., Barney, J.B., & Anderson, P. 2013. Forming and exploiting opportunities: The implications of discovery and creation processes for entrepreneurial and organizational research. *Organization Science*, 24(1): 301–317.

Baldacchino, L. 2013. *Entrepreneurial experience and opportunity identification: The role of intuition and cognitive versatility.* Doctoral dissertation submitted to the University of Warwick, UK.

Baldacchino, L., Ucbasaran, D., Cabantous, L., & Lockett, A. 2015. Entrepreneurship research on intuition: A critical analysis and research agenda. *International Journal of Management Reviews*, 17(2): 212–231.

Baron, R.A. 2008. The role of affect in entrepreneurial process. *Academy of Management Review*, 33(2): 328–340.

Baron, R.A., & Ensley, M.D. 2006. Opportunity recognition as the detection of meaningful patterns: Evidence from comparisons of novice and experienced entrepreneurs. *Management Science*, 52(6): 1331–1344.

Bastick, T. 1982. *Intuition: How we think and act.* New York: Wiley.

Baylor, A.L. 2001. A U-shaped model for the development of intuition by level of expertise. *New Ideas in Psychology*, 19(3): 237–244.

Blume, B.D., & Covin, J.G. 2011. Attributions to intuition in the venture founding process: Do entrepreneurs actually use intuition or just say that they do? *Journal of Business Venturing*, 26(1): 137–151.

Chaiken, S., & Trope, Y. 1999. *Dual-process theories in social psychology*. New York: Guilford Press.

Chase, W.G., & Simon, H.A. 1973a. The mind's eye in chess. In W.G. Chase (Ed.), *Visual information processing*: 215–281. New York: Academic Press.

Chase, W.G., & Simon, H.A. 1973b. Perception in chess. *Cognitive Psychology*, 4: 55–81.

Coleridge, S.T. 1975. *Biographia literaria* (rev. ed.). New York: Dutton. (Original work published 1967.)

Corbett, A.C. 2005. Experiential learning within the process of opportunity identification and exploitation. *Entrepreneurship Theory and Practice*, 29(4): 473–491.

Corbett, A.C. 2006. Learning asymmetries and the discovery of entrepreneurial opportunities. *Journal of Business Venturing*, 22(1): 97–118.

Croce, B. 1965. *Aesthetic* (rev. ed.). (D. Ainslie, Trans.). N.P.: Noonday Press (Division of Farrer, Straus, & Giroux, USA). (Original work published 1922.)

Dane, E. 2010. Reconsidering the trade-off between expertise and flexibility: A cognitive entrenchment perspective. *Academy of Management Review*, 35(4): 579–603.

de Groot, A.D. 1986. Intuition in chess. *International Computer Chess Association Journal*, 9: 67–75.

De Neys, W., & Glumicic, T. 2008. Conflict monitoring in dual process theories of thinking. *Cognition*, 106(3): 1248–1299.

Dewey, J. 2005. *Art as experience.* New York: Berkley Publishing Group.

Dimov, D. 2007. Beyond the single-person, single-insight attribution in understanding entrepreneurial opportunities. *Entrepreneurship Theory and Practice*, 31(5): 713–731.

Dreyfus, H.L., & Dreyfus, S.E. 2005. Peripheral vision expertise in real world contexts. *Organization Studies*, 26(5): 779–792.

Eisenhardt, K.M. 1991. Better stories and better constructs: The case for rigor and comparative logic. *Academy of Management Review*, 16(3): 620–627.

Epstein, S., Pacini, R., Denes-Raj, V., & Heier, H. 1996. Individual differences in intuitive-experiential and analytical-rational thinking styles. *Journal of Personality and Social Psychology*, 71(2): 390–405.

Evans, J.S.B.T. 2003. In two minds: Dual-process accounts of reasoning. *Trends in Cognitive Sciences*, 7(10): 454–459.

Evans, J.S.B.T. 2007. On the resolution of conflict in dual process theories of reasoning. *Thinking & Reasoning*, 13(4): 321–339.

Evans, J.S.B.T. 2010. *In two minds*. Oxford: Oxford University Press.

Fernandez, W. 2004. Using the Glaserian approach in grounded studies of emerging business practices. *Electronic Journal of Business Research Methods*, 2: 83–95.

Fletcher, D., & Sarkar, M. 2013. Psychological resilience: A review and critique of definitions, concepts, and theory. European Psychologist, 18(1): 12–23.

Foss, K., Foss, N.J., & Klein, P.G. 2007. Original and derived judgement: An entrepreneurial theory of economic organization. *Organization Studies*, 28(12): 1893–1912.

Goldberg, P. 1989. The intuitive experience. In W.H. Agor (Ed.), *Intuition in organizations: leading and managing productively*: 121–134. Newbury Park, CA: Sage.

Gustafsson, V. 2006. *Entrepreneurial decision making: Individuals, tasks and cognitions*. Cheltenham, UK and Northampton, MA, USA: Edward Elgar Publishing.

Harteis, C., & Billett, S. 2013. Intuitive expertise: Theories and empirical evidence. *Educational Research Review*, 9: 145–157.

Hodgkinson, G.P., & Sadler-Smith, E. 2018. The dynamics of intuition and analysis in managerial and organizational decision making. *Academy of Management Perspectives*, 32(4): 473–492.

Hogarth, R.M. 2001. *Educating intuition*. Chicago: University of Chicago Press.

Krueger, N.F. 2003. The cognitive psychology of entrepreneurship. In Z.J. Acs & D.B. Audretsch (Eds.), *Handbook of entrepreneurship research*: 105–140. London: Kluwer Law International.

Lengnick-Hall, C.A., Beck, T.E., & Lengnick-Hall, M.L. 2011. Developing a capacity for organizational resilience through strategic human resource management. *Human Resource Management Review*, 21(3): 243–255.

Li, P. 2014. Toward the geocentric framework of intuition: The Yin-Yang balancing between the Eastern and Western perspectives on intuition. In M. Sinclair (Ed.), *Handbook of research methods on intuition*: 28–41. Cheltenham, UK and Northampton, MA, USA: Edward Elgar Publishing.

Lieberman, M.D. 2007. Social cognitive neuroscience: A review of core processes. *Annual Review of Psychology*, 58: 259–289.

Lopez, L.E., Kundu, S.K., & Ciravegna, L. 2009. Born global or born regional? Evidence from an exploratory study in the Costa Rican software industry. *Journal of International Business Studies*, 40(7): 1228–1238.

Lumpkin, G.T., & Lichtenstein, B.B. 2005. The role of organizational learning in the opportunity-recognition process. *Entrepreneurship Theory and Practice*, 29(4): 451–472.

Sadler-Smith, E. 2008. *Inside intuition*. Abingdon: Routledge.

Sadler-Smith, E. 2015. The role of intuition in entrepreneurship and business venturing decision. *European Journal of Work and Organizational Psychology*, 25(2): 212–225.

Sadler-Smith. E., & Burke-Smalley, L.A. 2015. How much do we really understand about how managers make important decisions? *Organizational Dynamics*, 44(1): 9–16.

Sadler-Smith, E., & Hodgkinson, G.P. 2016. *An annalistic-intervention model of managerial intuition*. Paper presented at the annual meeting of Academy of Management, Anaheim.
Salas, E., Rosen, M.A., & DiazGranados, D. 2010. Expertise-based intuition and decision making in organizations. *Journal of Management*, 36(4): 941–973.
Seeger, M.W., Ulmer, R.R., Novak, J.M., & Sellnow, T. 2005. Post-crisis discourse and organizational change, failure and renewal. *Journal of Organizational Change*, 18(1): 78–95.
Simon, H.A. 1955. A behavioural model of rational choice. *Quarterly Journal of Economics*, 69: 99–118.
Sinclair, M. 2010. Misconceptions about intuition. *Psychological Inquiry*, 21(4): 378–386.
Sinclair, M., & Ashkanasy, N.M. 2002. Intuitive decision-making among leaders: More than shooting from the hip. *Mt Eliza Business Review*, 5(2): 32–38.
Sinclair, M., & Ashkanasy, N.M. 2005. Myth or a decision-making tool? *Management Learning*, 36(3): 353–370.
Stanovich, K.E., & West, R.F. 2000. Individual differences in reasoning: Implications for the rationality debate? *Behavioural and Brain Sciences*, 23(5): 645–665.
Vaughan, F.E. 1979. *Awakening intuition*. Garden City, NY: Anchor Press/Doubleday.
Venkataraman, S., & Sarasvathy, S.D. 2001. *Strategy and entrepreneurship research: Outlines of an untold story*. Darden Business School Working Paper No. 0106.
Wright, M., & Stigliani, I. 2013. Entrepreneurship and growth. *International Small Business Journal*, 31(1): 3–22.
Yin, R.K. 2014. *Case study research: Design and methods* (5th ed.). Thousand Oaks, CA: Sage.

6. Investigating entrepreneurial use of intuition and rationality in decision-making: a QCA approach

Ariel Nian Gani, Allard C. R. van Riel, Sandra Streukens and Andreas Größler

Entrepreneurs approach decision-making tasks in line with their abilities to deal with a combination of (high levels of) environmental volatility (i.e., high levels of environmental uncertainty and dynamics) and time pressure (Shepherd et al., 2015). Extant research suggests that decision-making effectiveness, or the stochastic probability that a decision related to the management of a process positively contributes to its performance (van Riel et al., 2003), is influenced by two distinct cognitive aspects of the decision maker, that is, the use of rationality and/or intuition (Sadler-Smith, 2004). A recent review by Shepherd et al. (2015) shows that entrepreneurship scholars are increasingly interested in examining the combined use of intuition and rationality in entrepreneurial decision-making. On the one hand, intuition could help decision makers cope with ill-structured, ill-informed, and urgent tasks (Sadler-Smith, 2004; Sinclair, 2011). On the other hand, the use of rationality has frequently been argued to benefit managerial decision-making in general. In current entrepreneurship research on the use of intuition and rationality, environmental uncertainty is seen as the task characteristic that primarily affects entrepreneurial decision-making. This research, however, has been unable to establish when and how entrepreneurial decision makers should appropriately *combine* or alternate between intuition and rationality when addressing various tasks.

To address these issues, we propose an innovative empirical approach to investigate the effects of using intuition and rationality in entrepreneurial decision-making. Based on insights from dual-process theory (Epstein et al., 1996; Novak & Hoffman, 2009), we propose that different combinations or *configurations* of intuition and rationality use on the one hand and task characteristics on the other hand can influence the effectiveness or ineffectiveness of entrepreneurial decision-making (cf. Fiss, 2007). (Organizational) configurations have been defined as "multidimensional constellations of conceptually distinct characteristics that commonly occur together" (Meyer et al., 1993: 1175). In the present chapter, a configuration refers to a combination of different levels of dominance of each of the cognitive systems that are used in decision-making and different levels of task characteristics. Thus, we address the following question:

Which configurations of entrepreneurial task characteristics and cognitive information-processing systems' use result in high (low) entrepreneurial decision-making effectiveness?

We address this question using qualitative comparative analysis (QCA). QCA was introduced in sociological research and refers to a set-membership-based analytical technique that is appropriate for complex configuration analyses (Fiss, 2007; Ragin, 2000). In contrast with ubiquitous regression(-like) techniques, QCA focuses on comparing different types of cases (configurations of values on a set of variables) rather than on assessing relationships between variables. This more holistic approach is consistent with previous research that indicated that decision-making effectiveness is the result of an intricate interplay among factors and conditions (Calabretta et al., 2017). By employing this novel approach, we hope to gain a richer insight into what determines decision-making effectiveness under difficult conditions. In addition to introducing the QCA approach into decision-making research, a related aim of the current chapter is to use the QCA results that are described in this study as a launchpad for further research in the domain of entrepreneurial and managerial decision-making under uncertainty.

In the next sections, we discuss the relevant literature, the methods, and several theoretical and practical implications. In the final section of this chapter, we provide an agenda for future research.

COGNITIVE SYSTEMS AND TASK CHARACTERISTICS

In behavioral studies of management and organization, a distinction was made between rational and intuitive cognitive decision-making styles (Barnard, 1938). Further observation of the use of two different cognitive decision-making styles yielded dual-process theory, which suggests the coexistence of two cognitive information-processing systems (see Evans, 2010, for a review). Epstein et al. (1996) specified two ways in which people process information in decision-making: experiential or intuitive and rational. Stanovich and West (2000) then called the two information-processing systems System 1 and System 2, respectively. Kahneman (2011) describes System 1 as a process that operates non-consciously and fast, while System 2 is described as the conscious reasoning system that operates more slowly, and is deliberate and reflective. Dual-process theory suggests that individuals rely on these two distinct but complementary cognitive systems to process information (Evans, 2010).

The intuitive information-processing system relies upon a discrete (instantaneous) cognitive process that uses tacit knowledge to make fast judgments or decisions that appear to be triggered directly by the decision task (van Riel & Horvath, 2014). It subconsciously and instantaneously produces judgments, which distinguishes it from the rational process (Sinclair, 2010). It is considered to be a nonsequential information-processing mode, which is based on affectively charged judgments that result in direct knowing without any use of conscious reasoning (Dane & Pratt, 2007). Dane and Pratt (2007) also argue that intuitive decision-making reflects how tacit knowledge is accessed and used. Overall, these arguments suggest that the use of intuition may indeed be appropriate for decision-making in ill-structured, ill-informed, and pressing task environments or situations (Evans, 2010).

In contrast, the rational information-processing system uses (explicit) information for the purpose of selecting a sensible alternative in the pursuit of one's goals (Epstein et al., 1996). It has been described as an explicit and sequential process using the rules of logic that can be controlled and reproduced by the decision maker. Hough and White (2003) argue that the rational system relies on analysis and systematic scanning. Many scholars (e.g., Epstein et al., 1996; van Riel et al., 2003) argue that the use of the rational system reflects the extent to which a decision-making process involves the collection of relevant information and the reliance upon the analysis of this information in making decisions. These arguments suggest that the use of rationality is appropriate for decision-making in well-informed and well-structured task environments and situations.

Considerable research has established that different cognitive information-processing systems are better suited for different task environments or activities (e.g., Epstein et al., 1996; Hough & White, 2003; Novak & Hoffman, 2009) and that the nature of the task influences the degree to which a rational or intuitive processing system is adopted (e.g., Epstein et al., 1999). Decision task characteristics are defined as the aspects of a decision problem that affect the need for various decision-making resources and approaches (van Riel et al., 2003). In a more recent study, using different types of tasks in decision-making experiments, Novak and Hoffman (2009) also found that cognitive systems' use varied across decision-making tasks. Their study also found that a match between a particular cognitive system that is used in decision-making and the nature of the task led to better task performance. This finding suggests that decision-making effectiveness can be achieved by appropriately employing the cognitive systems that are best suited to deal with the nature (the cognitive requirements) of the decision-making task where the cognitive requirements are determined by the combination of task characteristics. In the context of entrepreneurial decision-making, tasks are often characterized by environmental volatility (environmental uncertainty and dynamics) and significant time pressure (Shepherd et al., 2015).

THE RELATIONSHIP BETWEEN TASK CHARACTERISTICS AND DECISION-MAKING EFFECTIVENESS

Entrepreneurial decision-making is described as an act to manage and transform information, knowledge, and resources into a course of action that results in innovative actions, products, and services that exploit opportunities for economic, societal, and environmental benefit (Mullins & Forlani, 2005). Van Riel et al.'s (2003) definition of decision-making effectiveness considers that "well-made" decisions may sometimes result in unwanted outcomes (and vice versa) because successful outcomes are not only determined by the effectiveness of the decision-making process but also by other factors that cannot be controlled (e.g., environmental dynamics). However, it also suggests that if entrepreneurial decision-making is done according to the most effective decision-making process (e.g., using the appropriate cognitive systems and optimally utilizing all information at hand) under challenging conditions, the chances that the decisions result in positive outcomes will probabilistically increase.

The challenging conditions that entrepreneurial decision makers must deal with are characterized by high levels of environmental volatility and time pressure. Environmental volatility consists of environmental uncertainty and environmental dynamics (Duncan, 1972). Snyder and Glueck (1982) suggested a (negative) causal connection between both constructs. Environmental dynamics refer to the rate of change in relationships between variables (Dess & Beard, 1984). Hough and White (2003), using a simulated decision-making environment, also found that high levels of environmental dynamics diminish strategic decision-making performance because decision makers are unable or slow to respond to rapidly changing situations. Environmental uncertainty refers to situations in which the state of, trends, and responses to the environment are unknown, and decision makers are unable to accurately predict developments due to a lack of high-quality information (Lipshitz & Strauss, 1997). Baum and Wally (2003) found that high levels of uncertainty reduce the speed of strategic decision-making. As a consequence, significant time pressure can decrease decision-making effectiveness (Chu & Spires, 2001) by hampering access to high-quality information and reducing the availability of the necessary time to process it (van Riel et al., 2003).

The discussion above suggests that entrepreneurial task characteristics (i.e., environmental volatility and time pressure) and decision-making effectiveness are negatively related. Increasing degrees of volatility and time pressure may limit the ability of entrepreneurial decision makers to determine the potential effects of their choices or to decide which cognitive information-processing systems (intuition and/or rationality) might be best suited to be used in a decision-making process.

A CONFIGURATION MODEL OF ENTREPRENEURIAL DECISION-MAKING EFFECTIVENESS

After integrating the insights from the literature that is reviewed in the preceding section, we posit that entrepreneurial decision-making effectiveness is a complex, multidimensional phenomenon in which each decision task has many potentially appropriate combinations of the use of cognitive systems that allow decision makers to address the specific requirements of the decision-making task.

As such, the research question guiding the study at hand fits the notion of QCA, which explicitly focuses on the configurations of variables rather than the individual variables (Ordanini et al., 2014). Following this line of reasoning, configuration theory posits that an outcome is rarely the result of a single factor and that factors rarely operate in isolation. Therefore, in line with the literature that was cited in the previous section, the following proposition is put forward:

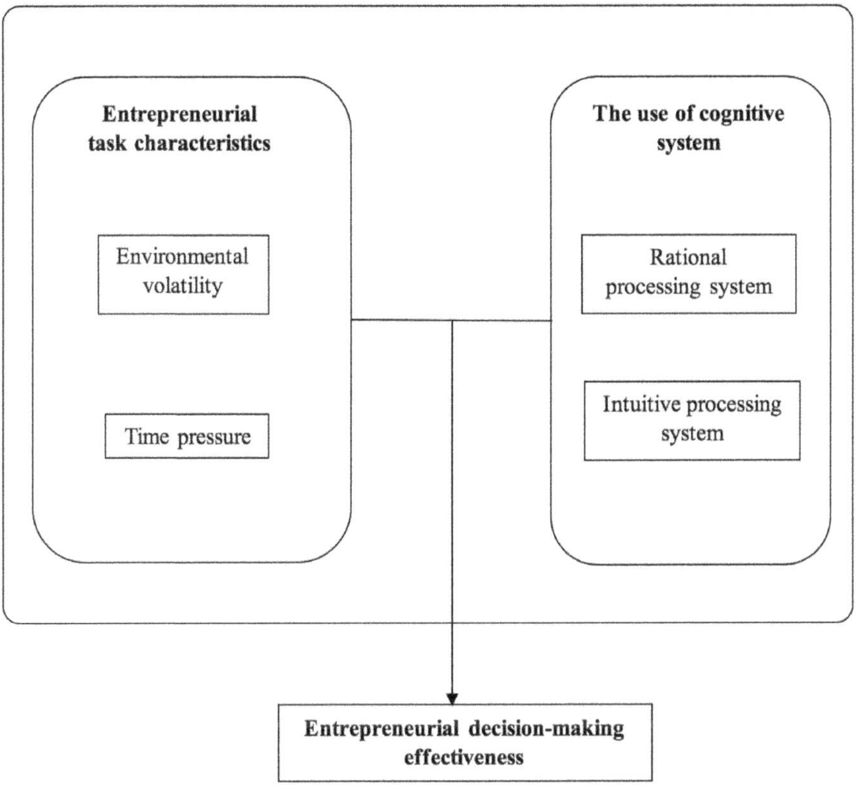

Figure 6.1 *The configurational model of entrepreneurial decision-making effectiveness*

Proposition 1: Effective entrepreneurial decision-making requires the use of both intuition and rationality.

Moreover, configuration theory posits that different configurations can lead to the same outcome ("equifinality"). In the current context and taking Proposition 1 into account, it can therefore be proposed that the combined use of intuition and rationality, as per Proposition 1, leads to decision-making effectiveness under different combinations of task characteristics. More formally, we state the following:

Proposition 2: The combined use of intuition and rationality leads to decision-making effectiveness under different combinations of task characteristics.

Another key feature of configuration theory concerns the property of asymmetry, which implies that configurations leading to the presence of an outcome (i.e., decision-making effectiveness) are not necessarily the same as the solutions leading to the absence of that outcome (i.e., decision-making *in*effectiveness). This leads to the following proposition.

Proposition 3: The absence of rationality and/or intuition leads to decision-making ineffectiveness.

Figure 6.1 provides a graphical overview of the variables and relationships that are used in the current research.

METHOD

The research method that was used was a laboratory experiment employing a computer simulated decision-making task. A dynamic decision-making task was used to stimulate the use of intuition and rationality. The computer simulation game was based on the principles of system dynamics (Sterman, 2000), which is a methodology for studying and managing complex social systems. Dynamic decision-making tasks have been used in previous research related to decision-making (e.g., Bakken & Gilljam, 2003). Research using dynamic decision-making tasks investigates how individuals make decisions when dealing with complex problems. In dynamic decision-making tasks, a series of decisions must be made within a period of time. Then, the state of the system changes based on participants' past decisions. This occurs automatically, and therefore typically creates time pressure.

The CleanStart enterprise simulator served as the dynamic decision-making task in the present research (http://mitsloan.mit.edu/LearningEdge/simulations/cleanstart). This task mimics a "real-world" entrepreneurial environment because it is based on an existing startup company (Sterman, 2014). The objective of the CleanStart simulator is to provide an opportunity for the participants to play the role of the founder and make decisions every quarter as they seek to win customers, improve the product and defeat their competition. There are five decision domains in this task, which are the price of the products, the quantity of employees, the salary and compensation of the employees, the funds that are requested from venture capitalists, and the decision to become a public company or not.

Participants in this research were entrepreneurial decision makers who attended a seminar for personal and professional entrepreneurship development purposes. The seminars (three in total, each lasting four hours) were conducted by the first author in Jakarta, Indonesia. The total number of participants was 116. All participants were Indonesian nationals; they were recruited from small- and medium-sized companies; the average age was 28.11 years; the overall sample included 52 men (44.82 percent) and 64 women (55.17 percent). At the beginning of each experiment, there was a briefing about how to play the game and the user interface of the simulation was explained. The facilitator of the experiment instructed the participants to act as entrepreneurs while playing the decision-making task. During the decision-making experiment, the participants had to make a series of decisions over a 30-minute period. After the time was up, the participants completed a questionnaire based on their experiences while playing the decision-making task.

Validated scales were used to measure the constructs in our model. More specifically, we used the scales of Miller and Friesen (1983) and Omri (2015) to measure perceived environmental volatility, items from Durham et al. (2000) to measure perceived time pressure, and Novak and Hoffman's (2009) situation-specific thinking-style (SSTS) inventory to assess the use of rational and intuitive thinking styles. Finally, a single-item measure was used to gauge the participants' perceived decision-making effectiveness. All constructs were measured using 5- or 7-point Likert-scales with higher scores indicating higher levels of agreement.

DATA ANALYSIS

The psychometric properties of the scales were assessed using the procedures that were outlined in Leroi-Werelds et al. (2014), using SmartPLS3 with J=10,000 bootstrap runs (cf. Streukens & Leroi-Werelds, 2016). Overall, the analysis provided evidence for the existence of each construct's unidimensionality, internal consistency, reliability, item validity, within-method convergent validity, and discriminant validity. Please note that the results of these analyses are available upon request from the authors.

QCA relies on the idea that variables that are drawn from cases (i.e., the variables we measured) can be dichotomized and then turned into a truth table. Consistent with this basic notion of QCA, the original scores pertaining to the constructs' measurements needed to be transformed to reflect the extent to which each respondent could be considered a member of the different configurations. To achieve this aim, the original scale's midpoint was considered as the crossover point (i.e., a membership score of .50), and scores below or above the crossover point are respectively considered as full non-membership (i.e., membership score of 0) or full membership (i.e., membership score of 1) to the set (cf. Ordanini et al., 2014). The truth table, or property space, consisted of all possible combinations of the four predictors (i.e., rationality, intuition, environmental volatility, and time pressure) being either present or not present, thus yielding 16 possible configurations (i.e., 2^4).

Using these membership scores as a starting point, Boolean algebra was used to assign each case to one of the 16 configurations that are relevant to this study (see Ragin, 2008, for the exact computational details). Subsequently, to determine which configurations act as sufficient conditions of effective entrepreneurial decision-making, a cross-case comparison of memberships between the configurations (i.e., causal sets) and the outcome set was required. To find a feasible solution, the criterion for consistency was set to .85 (cf. Leischnig et al., 2016), and a minimum of four best-fit cases was needed for the causal condition (cf. Fiss, 2011).

Table 6.1 *The results of the QCA analysis*

Configurations leading to decision-making effectiveness			
	Raw coverage	Unique coverage	Consistency
INT*RTL*vol*TMPS	0.13	0.13	0.90
	Total coverage = 0.13. Solution consistency = 0.90		
Configurations leading to decision-making *in*effectiveness (i.e., negated outcome)			
	Raw coverage	Unique coverage	Consistency
int*vol	0.19	0.17	0.91
rtl*VOL	0.19	0.06	0.88
rtl*TMPS	0.18	0.04	0.85
			Total coverage = 0.42. Solution consistency = 0.89

In relation to the QCA outcome, the concept of equifinality, which is considered a key advantage of QCA (Fiss, 2011), needs to be mentioned. Equifinality implies the coexistence of alternative solutions or configurations for an outcome of interest. When applied to the situation at hand, QCA is able to unravel the existence of possible alternative configurations of the four variables under study that may lead to decision-making effectiveness.

Finally, in line with the notion of causal asymmetry, the QCA that was described above was performed twice: once for decision-making effectiveness and once for decision-making ineffectiveness. In technical terms, decision-making ineffectiveness is the negated outcome of decision-making effectiveness (see Ragin, 2008, for the computational details). The results of both analyses are presented in Table 6.1.

Overall, the results reveal interesting insights regarding the interplay of rationality and intuition in entrepreneurial decision-making. More specifically, maximizing decision-making effectiveness requires the presence of both rationality and intuition. Moreover, once either rationality or intuition is lacking, ineffective decision-making results. Overall, this provides support for Propositions 1 and 3.

However, task characteristics are relevant and nuance this relationship. Our findings offer a plausible (first) empirical explanation for the argument that the effectiveness of decision-making under difficult conditions (e.g., high time pressure and low volatility) can be achieved by using both intuition and rationality (Groves et al., 2011; van Riel et al., 2003). This result offers partial support for Proposition 2.

DISCUSSION

In this study, we investigated the relationship between the use of rational and intuitive information-processing systems under difficult task conditions and the effectiveness of entrepreneurial decision-making. In accordance with the proposed relationships, we found that achieving decision-making effectiveness requires the use of both rational and intuitive systems. Our results contribute to the extant literature on the role of cognitive information-processing systems in entrepreneurial decision-making by uncovering the complex interaction between intuition and rationality, which leads to high effectiveness. These results contrast the common view that entrepreneurial decision makers generally use the intuitive information-processing system at the expense of the rational system (Groves et al., 2011).

Furthermore, our findings are in line with literature suggesting that the effectiveness of particular cognitive information-processing systems is related to the nature of the task (i.e., the problem) at hand (Akinci & Sadler-Smith, 2012). Mason and Mitroff (1973) distinguished the nature of a task into two categories: "kind" and "wicked" tasks. A "kind" task is characterized by stable cause-and-effect relationships, whereas a "wicked" task is characterized by unstable and unclear cause-and-effect relationships. The characteristics (e.g., high levels of environmental volatility and time pressure) of entrepreneurial decision-making tasks suggest that they can be considered as "wicked" tasks. Therefore, our findings appear to suggest that decision-making effectiveness in "wicked" tasks can be achieved by using a combination of intuition and rationality.

Our findings are relevant for literature suggesting that the freedom to maximize the use of intuition is related to organizational factors, such as accountability and hierarchy (Hensman & Sadler-Smith, 2011). In large and highly diversified organizations, decision makers (e.g., managers and management teams) are held accountable for, and hence have to be able to explain their strategic decisions, and thus they prefer to use a more rational process. Our sample, however, consisted of entrepreneurs of mainly small- and medium-sized companies (which usually have a single business unit). They might be the only decision maker who matters in their company. Smaller companies offer conditions that allow the owner/decision maker to exploit their experience, conduct active experimentation, and practice experiential learning. These conditions allow them to be able to maximize the use of both intuition and rationality in their decision-making process.

It is a common view in the decision-making literature that in the presence of high levels of volatility in decision tasks, the use of an intuitive information-processing system helps to achieve effective decision-making. Our findings, however, appear to show that both cognitive information systems (rational and intuitive) are required to achieve decision-making effectiveness in the entrepreneurial context. This finding seems to suggest that the intuitive system may need some sort of rational support to be effective in entrepreneurial decision-making.

The present study's findings should be considered in the context of several limitations. First, the fact that our analysis only offers partial support for Proposition 2 may be due to an insufficiently precise conceptualization of the entrepreneurial task characteristics. Second, the experiments were conducted in a "semi" fieldwork setting in which many elements could not be controlled by the researchers. This creates potential concern regarding how the participants perceived the task. A better controlled setting, such as a laboratory or a clinical experiment, might increase control over participants' perceptions regarding the decision tasks.

In terms of practical relevance, our findings provide initial empirical evidence that the concrete practice of integrating intuition and rationality leads to higher entrepreneurial decision-making effectiveness. The findings may encourage entrepreneurial decision makers with a preference for a rational approach to integrate intuitive practices into their decision-making processes and vice versa.

Although the results provide initial empirical evidence regarding the intricate interplay between rationality, intuition, and task characteristics, it should be noted that the current configurations only explain 13 percent of the decision-making effectiveness in our sample (i.e., total coverage = .13). Thus, additional research is needed to further understand how and when rationality and intuition contribute to decision-making effectiveness. Therefore, we conclude this chapter with suggestions for further research in this uncharted area.

AGENDA FOR FUTURE RESEARCH

First, more research is needed to study the role of organizational factors influencing the relative use of cognitive systems. This is in line with the observation that the freedom to use intuition is related to organizational factors.

Second, there is a need to further explore the nature of the "wickedness" of entrepreneurial tasks. Throughout the entrepreneurship literature, scholars acknowledge that entrepreneurs perform decision-making tasks under very difficult circumstances. These circumstances are commonly characterized by high levels of uncertainty, high levels of risk, and significant time pressure (Baron, 2008; McMullen & Shepherd, 2006). Our findings provide evidence for the complexity of the interactions between the use of cognitive information-processing systems and environmental characteristics. Such interactions play a role in determining decision-making effectiveness or *in*effectiveness.

Third, the findings in the present chapter point to the fact that some decision-making strategies lead to decision-making effectiveness while others lead to *in*effectiveness. As acknowledged by Dane and Pratt (2007), the use of intuition may come with a dark side as well. Therefore, research is also needed to investigate drivers of decision-making *in*effectiveness under difficult circumstances. Such research will provide insight into the "incomplete" picture of antecedents of decision-making effectiveness and have significant practical implications for entrepreneurial, managerial, and strategic decision-making.

Fourth, the presented study is one of the few empirical studies on entrepreneurial decision-making that focus on the entrepreneurs' actual use of intuitive and/or rational cognitive systems instead of their preference for a particular system. We need more empirical studies that assess the effects of the actual use of intuition and/or rationality on outcome measures related to entrepreneurship (e.g., opportunity identification and exploitation, and growth intentions) to further our knowledge about entrepreneurial decision-making. This is because the use of intuition plays a major role when making decisions about innovation (Hyppänen, 2013). Such research can be approached using the newest theoretical models about the dynamic use of intuition and rationality in decision-making (e.g., the edging and retreating model by Teerikangas & Välikangas, 2014).

Fifth, in this chapter the focus was on decision makers' perceived levels of environmental volatility and time pressure, and their self-reported use of intuition and rationality. Such an approach to investigate one's perceptions regarding particular difficult circumstances does not provide a complete picture of what actually happens inside the brains and bodies of the decision makers. Recent research by Sadler-Smith (2016) regarding what happens when individuals use intuition shows that intuitive judgments involve a process of "bodily awareness." This suggests that (some) intuitive judgments may be somatic. Therefore, we invite scholars who are interested in investigating decision-making under difficult circumstances (e.g., under high levels of environmental volatility and time pressure) to explore the approaches for measuring mechanisms regarding the actual use of intuition in more objective ways, specifically in relation to what happens in the decision makers' bodies and brains (Bakken & Gilljam, 2003). For example, scholars could examine the brains of decision makers who constantly have to deal with difficult circumstances using functional Magnetic Resonance Imaging (fMRI) or Electroencephalography (EEG) to identify the neural signature(s) of intuition use. Scholars may also use electrocardiograms (ECGs) for heart rate variability (beat-to-beat decelerations/accelerations) measurement to examine the relationships between "gut reactions" and intuition.

REFERENCES

Akinci, C., & Sadler-Smith, E. 2012. Intuition in management research: A historical review. *International Journal of Management Reviews*, 14(1): 104–122.

Bakken, B.T., & Gilljam, M. 2003. Dynamic intuition in military command and control: Why it is important, and how it should be developed. *Cognition, Technology & Work*, 5(3): 197–205.

Barnard, C. 1938. *Functions of the executive*. Cambridge, MA: Harvard University Press.

Baron, R.A. 2008. The role of affect in the entrepreneurial process. *Academy of Management Review*, 33(2): 328–340.

Baum, J.R., & Wally, S. 2003. Strategic decision speed and firm performance. *Strategic Management Journal*, 24(11): 1107–1129.

Calabretta, G., Gemser, G., & Wijnberg, N.M. 2017. The interplay between intuition and rationality in strategic decision making: A paradox perspective. *Organization Studies*, 38(3–4): 365–401.

Chu, P.C., & Spires, E.E. 2001. Does time constraint on users negate the efficacy of decision support systems? *Organizational Behavior & Human Decision Processes*, 85(2): 226–249.

Dane, E., & Pratt, M.G. 2007. Exploring intuition and its role in managerial decision making. *Academy of Management Review*, 32(1): 33–54.

Dess, G.G., & Beard, D.W. 1984. Dimensions of organizational task environments. *Administrative Science Quarterly*, 29(1): 52–73.

Duncan, R.B. 1972. Characteristics of organizational environments and perceived environmental uncertainty. *Administrative Science Quarterly*, 17(3): 313–327.

Durham, C.C., Locke, E.A., Poon, J.M.L., & McLeod, P.L. 2000. Effects of group goals and time pressure on group efficacy, information-seeking strategy, and performance. *Human Performance*, 13(2): 115–138.

Epstein, S., Donovan, S., & Denes-Raj, V. 1999. The missing link in the paradox of the Linda conjunction problem: Beyond knowing and thinking of the conjunction rule, the intrinsic appeal of heuristic processing. *Personality and Social Psychology Bulletin*, 25(2): 204–214.

Epstein, S., Pacini, R., Denes-Raj, V., & Heier, H. 1996. Individual differences in intuitive-experiential and analytical-rational thinking styles. *Journal of Personality & Social Psychology*, 71(2): 390–405.

Evans, J.S.B.T. 2010. Intuition and reasoning: A dual-process perspective. *Psychological Inquiry*, 21(4): 313–326.

Fiss, P.C. 2007. A set-theoretic approach to organizational configurations. *Academy of Management Review*, 32(4): 1180–1198.

Fiss, P.C. 2011. Building better causal theories: A fuzzy set approach to typologies in organization research. *Academy of Management Journal*, 54(2): 393–420.

Groves, K., Vance, C., & Choi, D. 2011. Examining entrepreneurial cognition: An occupational analysis of balanced linear and nonlinear thinking and entrepreneurship success. *Journal of Small Business Management*, 49(3): 438–466.

Hensman, A., & Sadler-Smith, E. 2011. Intuitive decision making in banking and finance. *European Management Journal*, 29(1): 51–66.

Hough, J.R., & White, M.A. 2003. Environmental dynamism and strategic decision-making rationality: An examination at the decision level. *Strategic Management Journal*, 24(5): 481–489.

Hyppänen, O. 2013. *Decision makers' use of intuition at the front end of innovation*. Aalto University publication series. Doctoral Dissertations, 1799-4942; 30/2013.

Kahneman, D. 2011. *Thinking, fast and slow*. New York: Doubleday.

Leischnig, A., Henneberg, S.C., & Thornton, S.C. 2016. Net versus combinatory effects of firm and industry antecedents of sales growth. *Journal of Business Research*, 69(9): 3576–3583.

Leroi-Werelds, S., Streukens, S., Brady, M., & Swinnen, G. 2014. Assessing the value of commonly used methods for measuring customer value: A multi-setting empirical study. *Journal of the Academy of Marketing Science*, 42(4): 430–451.

Lipshitz, R., & Strauss, O. 1997. Coping with uncertainty: A naturalistic decision-making analysis. *Organizational Behavior & Human Decision Processes*, 69(2): 149–163.

Mason, R.O., & Mitroff, I.I. 1973. A program for research on management information systems. *Management Science*, 19(5): 475–487.

McMullen, J.S., & Shepherd, D.A. 2006. Entrepreneurial action and the role of uncertainty in the theory of the entrepreneur. *Academy of Management Review*, 31(1): 132–152.

Meyer, A.D., Tsui, A.S., & Hinings, C.R. 1993. Configurational approaches to organizational analysis. *Academy of Management Journal*, 36(6): 1175–1195.

Miller, D., & Friesen, P.H. 1983. Strategy-making and environment: The third link. *Strategic Management Journal*, 4(3): 221–235.

Mullins, J.W., & Forlani, D. 2005. Missing the boat or sinking the boat: A study of new venture decision making. *Journal of Business Venturing*, 20(1): 47–69.

Novak, T.P., & Hoffman, D.L. 2009. The fit of thinking style and situation: New measures of situation-specific experiential and rational cognition. *Journal of Consumer Research*, 36(1): 56–72.

Omri, W. 2015. Innovative behavior and venture performance of SMEs: The moderating effect of environmental dynamism. *European Journal of Innovation Management*, 18(2): 195–217.

Ordanini, A., Parasuraman, A., & Rubera, G. 2014. When the recipe is more important than the ingredients: A qualitative comparative analysis (QCA) of service innovation configurations. *Journal of Service Research*, 17(2): 134–149.

Ragin, C.C. 2000. *Fuzzy-set social science*. Chicago, IL: University of Chicago Press.

Ragin, C.C. 2008. Measurement versus calibration: A set-theoretic approach. In J.M. Box-Steffensmeier, H.E. Brady, & D. Collier (Eds.), *The Oxford handbook of political methodology*: 174–198. Oxford, UK: Oxford University Press.

Sadler-Smith, E. 2004. Cognitive style and the management of small and medium-sized enterprises. *Organization Studies*, 25(2): 155–181.

Sadler-Smith, E. 2016. 'What happens when you intuit?': Understanding human resource practitioners' subjective experience of intuition through a novel linguistic method. *Human Relations*, 69(5): 1069–1093.

Shepherd, D.A., Williams, T.A., & Patzelt, H. 2015. Thinking about entrepreneurial decision making: Review and research agenda. *Journal of Management*, 41(1): 11–46.

Sinclair, M. 2010. Misconceptions about intuition. *Psychological Inquiry*, 21(4): 378–386.

Sinclair, M. 2011. An integrated framework of intuition. In M. Sinclair (Ed.), *Handbook of intuition research*: 3–16. Cheltenham, UK and Northampton, MA, USA: Edward Elgar Publishing.

Snyder, N.H., & Glueck, W.F. 1982. Can environmental volatility be measured objectively? *Academy of Management Journal*, 25(1): 185–192.

Stanovich, K.E., & West, R.F. 2000. Individual differences in reasoning: Implications for the rationality debate? *Behavioral and Brain Sciences*, 23(5): 645–665.

Sterman, J. 2014. Interactive web-based simulations for strategy and sustainability: The MIT Sloan learning edge management flight simulators, Part ii. *System Dynamics Review*, 30(3): 206–231.

Sterman, J.D. 2000. *Business dynamics: Systems thinking and modeling for a complex world.* Boston, MA: Irwin McGraw-Hill.

Streukens, S., & Leroi-Werelds, S. 2016, Bootstrapping and PLS-SEM: A step-by-step guide to get more out of your bootstrap results. *European Management Journal*, 34(6): 618–632.

Teerikangas, S., & Välikangas, L. 2014. Exploring the dynamic of evoking intuition. In M. Sinclair (Ed.), *Handbook of research methods on intuition*: 72–87. Cheltenham, UK and Northampton, MA, USA: Edward Elgar Publishing.

van Riel, A.C.R., & Horvath, C. 2014. Conceptualizing intuition as a mental faculty: Toward a 'critique of intuitive reason' and a process model of intuition. In M. Sinclair (Ed.), *Handbook of research methods on intuition*: 42–56. Cheltenham, UK and Northampton, MA, USA: Edward Elgar Publishing.

van Riel, A.C.R, Ouwersloot, H., & Lemmink, J. 2003. Antecedents of effective decision making: A cognitive approach. Working Paper, *METEOR, Maastricht Research School of Economics of Technology and Organizations*: 1–41.

7. Presence of intuition in the process of strategic decision-making

Delfina Biščak

> But decision making within organizations is only one ripple in a stream of thought flowing back to a time when man, facing uncertainty, sought guidance from the stars. (Buchanan & O'Connell, 2006: 33)

Decision-making is an ancient wisdom and a constant companion of a contemporary human who eventually developed sophisticated problem-solving tools that consequently accelerated decision-making and led to a number of challenges (Buchanan & O'Connell, 2006: 33). Contemporary business environment, however, does not lag behind as it evolves even quicker and therefore demands, as Kovačič et al. (2013) put it, as holistic decision-making as possible. Nowadays, combining intuitive thinking with prevailing logic is not an option, but rather a must. The need for integrated decision-making in the ever-dynamic and complex business environment is therefore increasing along with the need for inclusion of subconscious processes or, better put, "recognition" of what our mind has already included – intuition.

Contemporary studies (e.g., Burke & Miller, 1999; Floyd Fields, 2001; Khatri & Ng, 2000; Martin & Hanlon, 2007; Matzler et al., 2014; Seligman & Kahana, 2009) stress the fact that not a single decision is completely rational nor completely intuitive. And although one might assume this not to be the case in very analytical and rational decision-making environments, such as strategic management, a growing number of studies suggest otherwise. They indicate that rationality and intuition in the decision-making process are interwoven – especially in the field of strategy (Batool et al., 2015; Buchanan & O'Connell, 2006; Calabretta et al., 2017; Hodgkinson & Sadler-Smith, 2018; Ju et al., 2007; Okoli & Watt, 2018; Papulova & Gazova, 2016; Sadler-Smith & Burke, 2009; Shujahat et al., 2017; Sogbossi Bocco & Merunka, 2013; Schreier et al., 2018).

But where exactly and how is this interwovenness reflected when making a strategic decision? In order to define the "space" of strategic decision-making, we first need to examine the contemporary organizational environment. Both in the public and private sector, we quickly discover an increased importance of decision-making, or better said, the need to adopt a "right" decision. This pressure naturally increases as we move up through the organizational ladder because decisions taken at the top have bigger consequences as they affect the entire organization (Buchanan & O'Connell, 2006; Gibson, 2004: 17; Serrat, 2012). This organizational peak usually stands for strategic management, as it is an environment where decisions are not only about long-term planning, but also the long-term coordination of the company (and its objectives) with an unpredictable environment (David, 2001: 5; Mintzberg et al.,

1976). That is why the process of strategic decision-making, which has roots in the classical model of decision-making steeped in the tradition of rationality, is situated in the framework of strategic management.

IMPORTANCE OF INTUITION IN STRATEGIC DECISION-MAKING

Exploration of a possibility to include intuition as part of decision-making in such a rational and demanding environment was inspired not only by the psychological contrast between conscious and subconscious but also by early management studies. For example, Mintzberg and his colleagues (1976) used in-depth studies of 25 complex strategic decision-making processes to distinguish three main phases of strategic decision-making. Similarly, a study when intuition is used in decision-making, conducted by Isenberg (1984), highlights main phases of strategic decision-making. There is a common thread in key studies of organizational and strategic decision-making (Eisenhardt & Zbaracki, 1992; Kahneman, 2003; Mintzberg et al., 1976) suggesting that the strategic decision-making process consists of six (sub) phases: 1. defining a problem, 2. setting goals, 3. gathering information, 4. searching for alternatives, 5. evaluating alternatives, and 6. selecting and adopting a final decision. Hence, the research discussed in this chapter investigated the role of intuition in all of these (sub)phases.

It is questionable whether we can make strategic decisions through all six (sub) phases in perfectly controlled circumstances, with full control over all facts considered. The need to involve the subconscious is therefore worth exploration. Because intuition is a very interdisciplinary subject and its roots run deep in philosophy (Socrates, Plato and Kant; see Akinci & Sadler-Smith, 2012: 105), psychology (Jung and Bruner; see Akinci & Sadler-Smith, 2012: 105) and management (see e.g., Agor, 1984, 1985, 1986a, 1986b; Isenberg, 1984), the definition of intuition for this research is based on the intersection of definitions from the mentioned disciplines. For the purpose of this study, intuition was therefore defined as *a non-rational mental process of subconscious nature, which is characterized by speed and completeness of conclusions while its presence and use depend on the individual (decision-maker).*

IMPORTANCE OF THE ACTUAL STUDY – PURPOSE AND BACKGROUND

Having the above-described contemporary circumstances in mind, as well as the developed definitions, it is possible to perceive the paradox of traditional rational decision-making processes. Despite the entrenched strategic management position that would anticipate the desire to optimize decisions and maximize their potential with the help of rational decision-making processes, strategic management needs to integrate complementary processes, such as intuition.

This paradox inspired the aim of the presented research – to investigate the presence of intuition in the process of strategic decision-making, specifically in all its (sub)phases, and to identify whether its use varies depending on individual intuitive potential. There was a special reason to conduct this research in Slovenia as there is a paucity of such studies in the Slovenian academic (social sciences) context. This research was, to the author's best knowledge, one of the first to measure the presence and inclusion of intuition in the field of strategic management in the country.

The research focused on two aspects. First, it measured the intuitive potential of individual decision-makers and second, it measured the actual use of intuition in the process of strategic decision-making, that is, to what extent intuition was present in different (sub)phases of the strategic decision-making process. The research was guided by the following question: *Through the process of strategic decision-making, is intuition present in all (sub)phases of the process and does its intensity/frequency (number of (sub)phases in which it is detected) differ depending on the intuitive potential of an individual decision-maker?*

Sample

The research sample consisted of 111 Slovenian respondents (out of 250 contacted). As the purpose of the study was not to draw parallels between intuition (its presence and use) and individual work environment, respondents were anonymous. What they all had in common was their professional engagement in the process of strategic decision-making. Out of 111 respondents, 35 percent were male and 65 percent female. The age of the respondents ranged from the 40 to 50 bracket (37 percent), followed by 30 to 40 bracket (30 percent) and 50 to 60 bracket (26 percent). Fifty-six respondents (50 percent) were employed in the public sector and 55 (50 percent) in the private sector. Their participation was solicited by email, contacting major companies that forwarded the online survey to employees whose job description involved strategic management and who were responsible for strategic decisions on a daily basis. The questionnaire introduction explained both intuition and the strategic decision-making process, to ensure respondents could self-select. The companies were selected from databases offered by the Slovenian Management Association, Slovenian Directors' Association, Slovenian Chamber of Commerce and Medical Chamber of Slovenia. These organizations hold information on bigger companies in Slovenia, out of which the ones that had a strategic management layer in their organizational structure were selected.

Individual Intuitive Potential Questionnaire

In line with the two studied aspects described above, the first questionnaire measured the individual intuitive potential. It was assessed with 12 questions provided by Agor's (1985) Intuitive Management Survey (AIM). These 12 questions originate from psychology and have been designed to evaluate individual intuitive abilities (intuitive potential). Agor developed them based on the MBTI psychological instrument (Myers–Briggs Type Indicator, The Myers & Briggs Foundation, 2019). Every question provided two opposite answer options. Every answer had a value of either 0 or 1, with the sum of all answers ranging between 0 (lowest intuitive potential) and 12 (highest intuitive potential).

Use of Intuition Questionnaire

The actual use of intuition in the process of strategic decision-making, was measured with 14 questions drawn from two sources – Agor's AIM and questions developed for this study. The order of questions that form the second part of the questionnaire was designed in a way that they first measure general use of intuition in the decision-making process (in order to detect whether the intuitive potential from the first 12 questions is also practiced in the actual process of strategic decision-making), and second, they measure the use of intuition in each individual (sub)phase of strategic decision-making. The latter is mainly assessed by a question (Q24) listing all six (sub)phases of strategic decision-making for which respondents could choose whether they think they use either reason, intuition or both.

Translating the above methodology into practice, the presence of intuition was demonstrated within individual (sub)phases by analysis of answers to question Q24. The use of intuition according to the level of individual intuitive potential was demonstrated by analysis of results/answers on questions Q24 and Q17 (this question asked respondents whether they used intuition when making important decisions or not) and correlation between both (this way groups of respondents with a certain intuitive potential could be studied according to their opinion about the use of intuition and their actual use of intuition).

Agor's AIM was used as a base for developing the measurement instrument, as the current flood of international literature on intuition in the field of (strategic) management, on the one hand, and a lack of research in the Slovenian social sciences context, on the other hand, showed a clear need to establish the relevance of the research topic with verified measurement criteria. Hence, relying on an instrument developed by a pioneer in the intuition research in social sciences, based on studies of managers (Agor, 1984, 1985, 1986a, 1986b), was a cautious choice. Additionally, the original measure studied the intuitive potential of individual decision-makers and, consequently, the use of intuition in the decision-making process, and was used in other contemporary studies as well (e.g., Floyd Fields, 2001; Oluwabusuyi, 2011). Moreover, Thompson and Borello (1986) analyzed several studies that used the MBTI instrument, which served as a basis for Agor's AIM, and found strong instrument validity and reliability. Agor's AIM is also frequently mentioned as a core known instrument that measures intuitive potential in the field of management (Anshul & Agrasen, 2015: 307).

Last but not least, since Agor's AIM is not limited to study a specific decision-maker or a specific decision area (it was designed on the basis of a wide range of individuals in different sectors, organizations, organizational positions, and circumstances), it is sufficiently general and at the same time sufficiently specific to be useful for measurements within a specific research framework; as it has been the case with this study – in specific (sub)phases of strategic decision-making.

ANALYSIS OF RESULTS

The average intuitive potential of the respondents was 5.8 points, with a standard deviation of 2.84 (see Figure 7.2). But since it was always a whole number, it is more meaningful to note that the majority of the respondents (20.7 percent) had an intuitive potential of 6, while the least frequently recorded score (1.8 percent) was 10. Intuitive potential 0 scored 3.6 percent of respondents, while the maximum intuitive potential of 12 accounted for 2.7 percent of respondents (see Figure 7.1).

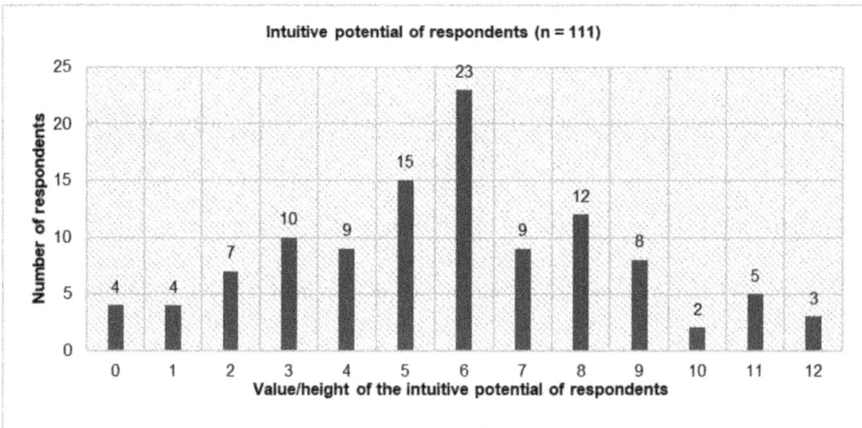

Figure 7.1 *Intuitive potential of the respondents*

As for the use of intuition in the process of strategic decision-making (see Figure 7.3), 87 percent of respondents reported they indeed use intuition in making important decisions; they often identified it in the form of feelings or signals, or simple "knowing" that a particular decision is "right." These feelings/signals were mostly identified as high energy (29 percent), calmness (26 percent), sudden insight (15 percent), excitement (14 percent), with a small number of respondents experiencing heat (5 percent) or no signals at all (3 percent). In their own words, some respondents also described feelings of satisfaction, "feeling that this is it," magnetic attraction or self-affirmation. In terms of circumstances when respondents considered using intuition, 34 percent nominated situations with many possible alternative solutions, followed by situations with little previous practice (25 percent) and under time pressure (22 percent). A few respondents (3 percent) described circumstances when they

Intuitive potential	Q1		Q2		Q3		Q4		Q5		Q6		Q7		Q8		Q9		Q10		Q11		Q12		Intuitive potential height	Number of respondents	Percentage	Cumulative
	1	0	1	0	1	0	1	0	1	0	1	0	1	0	1	0	1	0	1	0	1	0	1	0				
0	0	4	0	4	0	4	0	4	0	4	0	4	0	4	0	4	0	4	0	4	0	4	0	4		4	3,6%	13%
1	0	4	2	2	0	4	0	4	0	4	0	4	0	4	2	2	0	4	0	4	0	4	0	4		4	3,6%	16%
2	0	7	3	4	1	6	1	6	1	6	1	6	0	7	5	2	0	7	0	7	1	6	1	6		7	6,3%	23%
3	0	10	6	4	3	7	2	8	2	8	1	9	4	6	9	1	2	8	0	10	0	10	1	9		10	9,0%	32%
4	5	4	6	3	2	7	3	6	1	8	1	8	2	7	8	1	6	3	0	9	0	9	2	7		9	8,1%	40%
5	7	8	12	3	10	5	9	6	2	13	1	14	6	9	14	1	7	8	0	15	0	15	7	8		15	13,5%	53%
6	9	14	21	2	17	6	12	11	14	9	4	19	10	13	19	4	18	5	3	20	2	21	9	14		23	20,7%	74%
7	6	3	6	3	8	1	6	3	5	4	2	7	6	3	9	0	7	2	1	8	2	7	5	4		9	8,1%	82%
8	11	1	11	1	9	3	10	2	10	2	2	10	11	1	11	1	10	2	1	11	1	11	9	3		12	10,8%	93%
9	6	2	8	0	6	2	8	0	6	2	4	4	6	2	8	0	8	0	5	3	1	7	6	2		8	7,2%	100%
10	2	0	1	1	2	0	2	0	1	1	2	0	1	1	2	0	1	1	2	0	2	0	2	0		2	1,8%	2%
11	5	0	5	0	5	0	5	0	5	0	5	0	5	0	5	0	5	0	5	0	0	5	5	0		5	4,5%	6%
12	3	0	3	0	3	0	3	0	3	0	3	0	3	0	3	0	3	0	3	0	3	0	3	0		3	2,7%	9%
Summary	54	57	84	27	66	45	61	50	50	61	26	85	54	57	95	16	67	44	20	91	12	99	50	61				
Percentage(%)	49	51	76	24	59	41	55	45	45	55	23	77	49	51	86	14	60	40	18	82	11					111	100%	
Number of all responcents	111		111		111		111		111		111		111		111		111		111		111		111					

Valid	Number of individuals	Average	Std. deviation	Minimum	Maximum
111	111	5,8	2,84	0	12

Figure 7.2 Measuring intuitive potential of the respondents – answers on 1st part of questionnaire

examined reasons for and against a certain decision, the suitability of alternatives, or situations when intuition was particularly strong and could not be ignored.

When asked directly, 86 percent of respondents reported using intuition and were able to provide an example of a very important decision when they relied on it. A common thread through provided examples were such circumstances as changing profession, work-related decisions but also private decisions. When asked about the opposite scenario: what kind of signals they experience when they know they are about to make a "wrong" decision, respondents mostly reported mixed or conflicting signals (42 percent) and anxiety (26 percent). An additional 6 percent used such words as depression, restlessness or discomfort. The most common thread when describing circumstances that prevented them from using intuition, 27 percent of respondents identified lack of confidence, followed by overwork (22 percent) and stress (20 percent). Other listed circumstances were fear, uncertainty and lack of belief in intuition. Nevertheless, more than half (64 percent) of respondents were willing to share their use of intuition with others. However, the majority of respondents (78 percent) did not seem to use any particular methods/techniques that would help them with using intuition when making an important decision. Those who did (17 percent), listed techniques such as meditation, solitude or distancing away from the problem. Similarly, the majority of respondents (82 percent) did not use any specific technique to develop their intuitive ability. Those who did, described in their own words examples such as six hats of thinking, meditation or similar.

Intuition is Present Through All (Sub)Phases of the Strategic Decision-Making Process

Use and presence of intuition in the work environment, specifically in strategic decision-making, has been strongly supported by respondents' answers about the (sub)phases in which they use intuition and/or reason. This was measured by a question (Q24) that asked about each of the six (sub)phases and was developed specifically for the purpose of this research (see Figures 7.3 and 7.4).

In the first (sub)phase (defining a problem), reasoning was prevalent (88 percent), as it was in the second (sub)phase (setting goals) (79 percent). A similar pattern was observed in the third (sub)phase (gathering information) where 72 percent of respondents reported reliance on reasoning. However, a shift occurred in the fourth (sub)phase (searching for alternatives) where there was predominance of intuition (66 percent). In the fifth (sub)phase (evaluating alternatives), again reasoning dominates with 59 percent, although the use of intuition is behind just slightly. In the final sixth (sub)phase (selecting and adopting a final decision), the use of reasoning (52 percent) is almost equal to intuition (48 percent). The use of intuition is thus the highest in the fourth (sub)phase and the lowest in the first (sub)phase. Consequently, reliance on reasoning is the highest in the first (sub)phase and the lowest in the fourth (sub)phase.

The data thus shows that intuition was present during the whole process of strategic decision-making. As seen in Figure 7.3, the use of intuition was detected in all six

Intuitive potential	Q13		Q14		Q15		Q16					Q17		Q18							Q19						Q20	
	1	2	1	2	1	2	1	2	3	4	5	1	2	1	2	3	4	5	6	7	1	2	3	4	5	6	1	2
0	3	1	4	0	3	1	0	3	1	0	0	3	1	2	1	1	1	0	0	0	0	1	2	1	2	0	2	2
1	2	2	2	2	4	0	0	2	1	1	0	3	1	0	0	3	1	1	1	0	1	3	4	2	0	0	4	0
2	7	0	4	3	6	1	1	1	3	2	0	6	1	2	1	4	5	1	1	1	1	5	6	2	0	0	5	2
3	10	0	2	8	7	3	0	2	4	3	1	7	3	1	0	6	8	1	1	1	2	6	4	4	0	0	8	2
4	7	2	5	4	6	3	0	1	6	2	0	8	1	1	1	5	4	1	2	1	0	4	7	2	1	0	8	1
5	9	6	6	9	11	4	1	3	7	4	0	12	3	3	3	11	8	3	0	2	7	9	9	8	0	1	12	3
6	22	1	11	12	13	10	3	9	6	3	2	21	2	5	3	8	13	8	1	3	6	8	16	10	0	2	21	2
7	6	3	7	2	5	4	1	3	2	2	1	8	1	3	1	3	4	2	0	1	2	6	6	4	0	1	9	0
8	11	1	8	4	5	7	0	4	5	3	0	12	0	4	0	6	8	3	0	0	8	7	7	9	0	0	11	1
9	5	3	1	7	5	3	0	3	3	2	0	8	0	3	0	3	2	7	0	0	2	4	7	2	0	0	8	0
10	1	1	1	1	1	1	0	1	1	0	0	2	0	2	0	0	1	1	0	2	0	1	2	0	0	1	2	0
11	5	0	2	3	4	1	1	0	1	3	0	4	1	2	1	1	4	1	0	2	2	1	3	4	0	1	5	0
12	2	1	3	0	2	1	0	1	1	1	0	3	0	1	0	1	0	1	1	0	2	1	2	2	0	0	1	2
Summary	90	21	56	55	72	39	7	33	41	26	4	97	14	29	11	52	59	30	7	13	33	56	75	50	3	6	96	15
Percentage(%)	81	19	50	50	65	35	6	30	37	23	4	87	13	14	5	26	29	15	3	6	15	25	34	22	1	3	86	14
Number of all respondents	111		111		111		111					111		111							111						111	

Figure 7.3 *Measuring use of intuition of the respondents – answers on 2nd part of questionnaire*

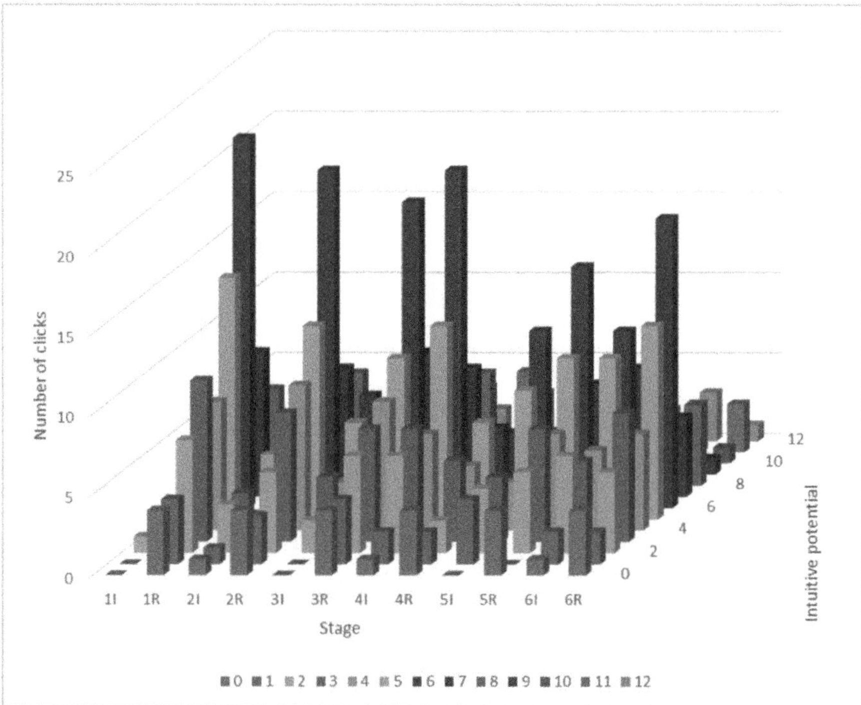

Figure 7.4 *Presence of intuition within different (sub)stages of strategic decision-making based on intuitive potential of respondents*

(sub)phases while its frequency has varied. Similarly, the very presence of intuition (viewed through the lens of the whole sample of 111 respondents) is never recorded as non-existent or as an absolute 0. It is also necessary to emphasize that the use of reasoning is always recorded in each particular phase (along with intuition). Thus, it can be said that intuition is indeed present, in varying strength as opposed to reasoning, in all (sub)phases of the strategic decision-making process.

Intensity of Intuition (Frequency of Use or the Number of Phases in Which it Occurs) in the Process of Strategic Decision-Making Varies Depending on the Intuitive Potential of an Individual Decision-Maker

Analysis of the answers whether respondents consider general use of intuition (Q17) and in which (sub)phases of the process of strategic decision-making they use intuition or reasoning (Q24), whilst taking into consideration their intuitive potential, allowed to study groups of respondents with a certain intuitive potential, their opinion on the use of intuition and their actual use of intuition. In other words, correlation between the mentioned two questions was also measured based on intuitive potential.

These two questions were designed to highlight the contrast between the opinion of the respondents on whether or not (in general terms) they use intuition when making meaningful decisions, and stages where intuition/reasoning is used in the professional decision-making process. Thus, for each individual score of intuitive potential (from 0 to 12), the above answers were analyzed through this lens.

The comparison between respondents' opinion about their use of intuition (Q17) and the level of their intuitive potential (Q1–12) (see Figure 7.5) shows that one's perception of the use of intuition does not depend on the level of intuitive potential. One would expect that the respondent with a lower intuitive potential would believe that he/she does not use intuition when making important decisions. However, as shown in Figure 7.5, the number of respondents who believe that they use intuition while making important decisions is always higher than those who think that they do not; even in cases of respondents with intuitive potential from 0 to 6. The opinion that when making important decisions intuition is used, is thus higher than the opinion that it is not used, in every group of intuitive potential. In addition, the Pearson Correlation Coefficient value of −0.01634 suggests that there is no link between the mentioned variables – results show that there is no connection between the opinion on using intuition when making important decisions and the level of intuitive potential.

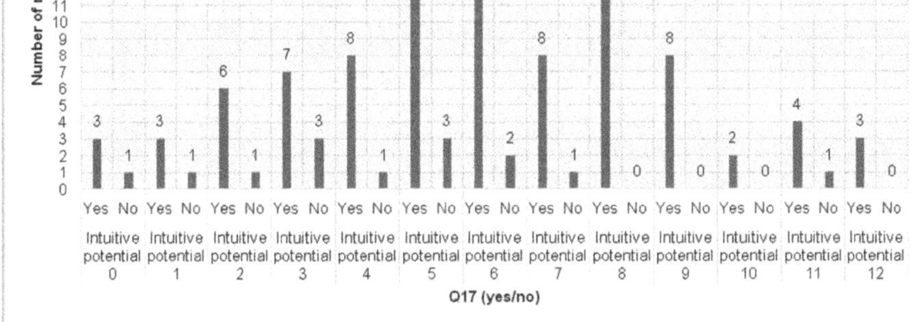

Figure 7.5 *Opinion on using intuition when making the most important decisions, in relation to intuitive potential of respondents (N = 111)*

Regarding the relationship between (sub)phases of the strategic decision-making process where respondents use intuition or reasoning (Q24) and the level of the intuitive potential of respondents, the use of intuition varies depending on the individual (sub)phase of the decision process and the value of the intuitive potential. Intuition is used least in the (sub)phase of problem definition (where the value of the intuitive potential is 0, 1, 3, 10, and 12), in the (sub)phase of collecting information (where the value of the intuitive potential is 0, 1 and 10) and in the (sub)phase of evaluation of alternatives (where the value of the intuitive potential is 0 and 10). Intuition is used most in the (sub)phase of searching alternatives (where the value of the intuitive potential is 6).

The analysis of the relationship between Q17 (whether respondents consider general use of intuition when making important decisions), Q24 (in which (sub) phases of the process of strategic decision-making they use intuition or reasoning) and the intuitive potential of respondents indicates that the level of intuitive potential does not condition one's opinion on the use of intuition when making important decisions (Q17), but it certainly influences the use of intuition in individual (sub) phases of the strategic decision-making process (Q24), as the frequency of intuition use varies. However, the variation does not mean that a higher intuitive potential is a condition for a higher number of phases in which intuition is used (and vice versa). The frequency of using intuition in the case of two higher intuitive potentials (10 and 12) was among the lowest (in the group of respondents with intuitive potential 10, intuition is used in two out of six phases while in the group of respondents with intuitive potential 12, it is used in four out of six stages). Through all phases, intuition is present in groups of respondents with intuitive potentials 2, 4, 5, 6, 7, 8, 9 and 11; for a group of respondents with intuitive potential 1, its frequency is 4; for a group of respondents with intuitive potential 3, its frequency is 5.

Thus, the second part of the research question – whether the presence of intuition (the frequency of use in individual (sub)phases of the strategic decision-making process) varies according to the level of the intuitive potential of respondents, can be confirmed but with a reservation. While differences in the use of intuition among individual intuitive potentials are evident, we cannot summarize them in a single "pattern."

DISCUSSION

The analysis of the online questionnaire results confirmed the presence of intuition in the process of strategic decision-making. Viewed through the lens of the entire sample, intuition is present in all (sub)phases. As previously mentioned, its presence was the highest in the "search for alternatives" and the lowest in the "problem definition" phase.

Translating the above-mentioned findings into the context of studies of intuition in strategic management that have been performed so far, it can be said that they align with the main "inspiration" study – the Isenberg study (1984) that identified five different uses of intuition throughout strategic decision-making: identifying the problem, analyzing problems, developing alternative situations, evaluating alternatives, selecting the best method and implementing the final decision. Conclusions that intuition was present in all (sub)stages of the decision-making process are also consistent with dual process theories and studies (Kahneman, 2003; Sadler-Smith & Shefy, 2004; Sloman, 2002; Stanovich & West, 2000) that take into account both mental processes when it comes to decision-making. In the core of the dual theory, as Stanovich and West (2000: 658) conclude, there are System 1 and System 2 – two types of cognitive systems that influence the decision-making process. System 1 refers to the intuitive decision-maker and takes action quickly and impeccably. Conversely, System 2 requires the use of reason and effort. Time pressure and cognitive burden are understood as its two determinants (Stanovich & West, 2000: 658). The most important conclusion of dual theory is that these systems are not completely independent of each other, as would be expected (Stanovich & West, 2000: 658) The latter means that both reasoning and intuition are present in the decision-making process, which was precisely the case in this study – rationality (reasoning) and intuition were both present in all phases of the strategic decision-making process.

If we turn to the second part of the research question, results that the level of intuitive potential does not condition one's opinion about own use of intuition when making important decisions, are not consistent with Agor's research (1985, 1986b) where managers with a higher intuitive potential used intuition more than those with a lower potential (Agor's study permits the completion of the second part of the questionnaire only for those with an intuitive potential higher than 6). As Agor's research is, to the author's best knowledge, one of the rare examples of measuring intuitive potential in such a way, the above-mentioned results cannot be compared with any other studies.

Nevertheless, the study has provided additional insights into how strategic decision-makers use intuition in combination with reasoning. It is interesting that in the (sub)phase "searching for alternatives," the use of intuition was recorded almost by 100 percent more than the use of reasoning, and that intuition and reasoning in the (sub)phase "selection and adoption of a final decision" were recorded with almost the same number of responses. In addition, it was possible to observe a pattern of increased intuition use from phase to phase (with the exception of the (sub)phase "gathering of information" where reasoning strongly dominated).

LIMITATIONS AND FURTHER RESEARCH

It is necessary to point out some concerns regarding the measurement instruments as well as consequential research results. In terms of wording, the presence of intuition in the first (sub)phase, would perhaps be higher if the phrase "definition of the problem" included the word "perception," expanding the questionnaire item to "perception and consequent definition of the problem." The additional word could possibly allow greater association with intuition, and the respondents might consequently (to a greater extent) be reminded that they also have the option of using intuition.

Moreover, based on the measurements and analyses that relate to the "intensity" of intuition (the frequency of the use or the number of (sub)phases in which it is present) and its variation in relation to the intuitive potential of the respondents, we can observe that intuitive potential of the respondents does not influence the intensity of intuition within individual (under) stages of the strategic decision-making process in a predictable way. Thus, we cannot say that a higher or lower intuitive potential means a higher or lower intuition presence, or that a higher intuitive potential means a higher number of phases in which the respondent stated intuition use or vice versa. Differences in the use of intuition across individual intuitive potentials are evident, but we cannot summarize them in a single pattern. Moreover, Pearson's coefficient showed that there is no link between intuitive potential and one's (positive) opinion about intuition use. Thus, at this point, it is justified to question the measurement instrument of the intuitive potential (the first 12 questions) as well as the size of the research sample.

Starting with the question of adequacy of the used instrument (here it is necessary to point out that it was identical to the original AIM questionnaire, whilst Agor himself created it on the basis of the MBTI), its simplicity can be detrimental. Although summarized by the aforementioned MBTI (The Myers & Briggs Foundation, 2019), intuitive potential may be a too complex variable to be measured with only 12 questions, even if they originate from a world-known set of psychological indicators. In addition, the AIM questionnaire is the product of the 1980s when research on intuition in management has only begun to develop. Since then Sadler-Smith and Burke-Smalley (2015), for instance, have noted quite a number of new measurement trials. Perhaps future research could use Epstein's Rational Experiential Inventory (Epstein et al., 1995) which takes the dual theory (intuition/reasoning) to a new level and examines the dimensions of rational and experiential styles of information processing and consequential decision-making (Sadler-Smith & Burke-Smalley, 2015; The Society for Judgment and Decision Making, 2017). The Rational Experiential Inventory should be able to measure the construct multi-dimensionally and, consequently, provide more complex and possibly reliable results.

Regarding the sample size, the distribution of respondents across individual groups with a certain intuitive potential reduced the sample considerably. The low number of respondents in individual groups may thus also contribute to the unclear link between the level of intuitive potential and the frequency of intuition use. After all, unintentional "rationalization" of intuition may have contributed to the "confusion." By means of the "summary" question (Q24), respondents self-assessed at what stage they use intuition/reasoning. That is to say, the use of the subconscious was consciously assessed, which may have resulted in a pattern of lower frequency of using intuition than it would have otherwise. Moreover, the result was also expressed in connection with the intuitive potential. In future research, it might be helpful to include either an observational method (field study of people who are professionally involved in making strategic decisions in the actual decision-making process) or additional psychometric questions that measure indicators of the use of intuition/reasoning in individual phases.

Nevertheless, the study yielded useful results. The analysis showed that the presence of intuition (frequency of use in individual (sub)phases of the strategic decision process) varies according to the level of intuitive potential. Despite the opposite poles of conscious (reasoning) and subconscious (intuition) information processing, the results hint at the possibility and the ability of their coexistence in the process of strategic decision-making.

REFERENCES

Agor, W.H. 1984. Using intuition to manage organizations in the future. *Business Horizons*, 27(4): 49–54.

Agor, W.H. 1985. *AIM: Agor Intuitive Management survey*. Bryn Mawr, PA: Organization Design and Development.

Agor, W.H. 1986a. The logic of intuition: How top executives make important decisions. *Organizational Dynamics*, 14(3): 5–18.

Agor, W.H. 1986b. *The logic of intuitive decision making: A research based approach for top management*. Westport, CT: Greenwood Press.

Akinci, C., & Sadler-Smith, E. 2012. Intuition in management research: A historical review. *International Journal of Management Reviews*, 14: 104–122.

Anshul, T., & Agrasen, M. 2015. The recruitment of intuitive managers. *European Journal of Business and Management*, 7(4): 305–308.

Batool, N.M., Riaz, M.N., & Riaz, M.A. 2015. Integrated use of rational and intuitive decision making style: Modern trends in organizational decision making. *Pakistan Business Review*, 17(1): 147–161.

Buchanan, L., & O'Connell, A. 2006. A brief history of decision making. *Harvard Business Review*, 84(1): 32–41.

Burke, L.A., & Miller, M.K. 1999. Taking the mystery out of intuitive decision making. *Academy of Management Executive*, 13(4): 91–99.

Calabretta, G., Gemser, G., & Wijnberg, N.M. 2017. The interplay between intuition and rationality in strategic decision making: A paradox perspective. *Organization Studies*, 38(3–4): 365–401.

David, R.F. 2001. *Strategic management: Concepts and cases: A competitive advantage approach*. Upper Saddle River, NJ: Prentice Hall.

Eisenhardt, K., & Zbaracki, M.J. 1992. Strategic decision making. *Strategic Management Journal*, 13: 17–37.

Epstein, N., Pacini, R., Denes-Raj, V., & Heier, H. 1995. *Individual differences in heuristic processing*. Amherst, MA: University of Massachusetts.

Floyd Fields, A. 2001. *A study of intuition in decision-making using organizational engineering methodology*. PhD Dissertation, Nova Southeastern University, Fort Lauderdale, FL.

Gibson, P. 2004. *Administrative office management, Complete course (13th edition)*. Ohio, IL: South-Western Educational Publishing.

Hodgkinson, G.P., & Sadler-Smith, E. 2018. The dynamics of intuition and analysis in managerial and organizational decision making. *Academy of Management Perspectives*, 32(4): 473–492.

Isenberg, D. 1984. How senior managers think. *Harvard Business Review*, November–December: 81–86.

Ju, B., Feng, J., & Miao, C. 2007. Intuitive decision theory analysis and the evaluation model. *Management Science and Engineering*, 1(2): 63–67.

Kahneman, D. 2003. Maps of bounded rationality: Psychology for behavioural economics. *American Economic Review*, 93(5): 1449–1475.

Khatri, N., & Ng, H.A. 2000. The role of intuition in strategic decision making. *Human Relations*, 53: 7–86.

Kovačič, V., Bulc, V., & Battelino, U. 2013. Intuitive decision-making – an indispensable part of integrated decision-making. *HRM*, 11(51): 33–38.
Martin, R., & Hanlon, P. 2007. *An examination of the role of intuition in individual decision making in organisations*. Paper presented at 10th Annual Conference of the Irish Academy of Management, Queens University, Belfast, Ireland, September 5.
Matzler, K., Uzelac, B., & Bauer, F. 2014. The role of intuition and deliberation for exploration and exploitation success. *Creativity and Innovation Management*, 23(3): 252–263.
Mintzberg, H., Rainsinghani, D., & Theoret, A. 1976. The structure of 'unstructured' decision process. *Administrative Science Quarterly*, 21(2): 246–275.
Okoli, J., & Watt, J. 2018. Crisis decision-making: The overlap between intuitive and analytical strategies. *Management Decision*, 56(5): 1122–1134.
Oluwabusuyi, I. 2011. Intuitive managerial decision making in Malaysia and the United States. *Business Intelligence Journal*, 4(2): 312–318.
Papulova, Z., & Gazova, A. 2016. Role of strategic analysis in strategic decision-making. *Procedia Economics and Finance*, 39: 571–579.
Sadler-Smith, E., & Burke, L.A. 2009. Fostering intuition in management education. *Journal of Management Education*, 33(2): 239–262.
Sadler-Smith, E., & Burke-Smalley, L.A. 2015. What do we really understand about how managers make important decisions? *Organizational Dynamics*, 44: 9–16.
Sadler-Smith, E., & Shefy, E. 2004. The intuitive executive: Understanding and applying 'gut feel' in decision-making. *Academy of Management Executive*, 18(4): 76–91.
Schreier, C., Schubert, A., Weber, J., & Farrar, J. 2018. An investigation of the character traits of decision-makers open to intuition as a tool. *Journal on Business Review*, 3(4): 63–69.
Seligman, M.E.P., & Kahana, M. 2009. Unpacking intuition: A conjecture. *Perspectives on Psychological Science*, 4(4): 399–402.
Serrat, O. 2012. *On decision making*. Washington, DC: Asian Development Bank. https://www.researchgate.net/publication/266477995_On_Decision_Making (accessed May 29, 2019).
Shujahat, M., Saddam, H., Javed, S., Malik, M.I., & Thurasamy, R.J.A. 2017. Strategic management model with lens of knowledge management and competitive intelligence: A review approach. *VINE Journal of Information and Knowledge Management Systems*, 47(1): 55–93.
Sloman, S.A. 2002. Two systems of reasoning. In Gilovich, T., Griffin, D., & Kahneman, D. (Eds.), *Heuristics and biases*: 379–396. Cambridge: Cambridge University Press.
Sogbossi Bocco, B., & Merunka, D. 2013. Do leaders of small and medium-sized businesses base decisions on intuition? An empirical investigation among West African managers. *Global Business and Organizational Excellence*, 32(5): 45–52.
Stanovich, K.E., & West, R.F. 2000. Individual differences in reasoning: Implications for the rationality debate? *Behavioural and Brain Sciences*, 23(5): 645–665.
The Myers & Briggs Foundation. 2019. *MBTI basics*. https://www.myersbriggs.org/my-mbti-personality-type/mbti-basics/home.htm?bhcp=1 (accessed July 1, 2019).
The Society for Judgment and Decision Making. 2017. *Rational-Experiential Inventory – 40 item (REI-40 or REI-revised)*. http://tiny.cc/w3c99y (accessed July 1, 2019).
Thompson, B., & Borello, G. 1986. Construct validity of the Myers–Briggs Type Indicator. *Educational and Psychological Measurement*, 46: 745–752.

PART II

DIFFERENT ROLES OF AFFECT IN INTUITING

8. What is feeling, and what is its role in intuition?

Lois Isenman

Feelings bridge the body and the mind. They are so important to intuition because they support an integrated response of the human organism as a whole. In this chapter, I will examine some of the ways feelings bring the mind and body together and also explore the various roles of feeling in intuition. As is my preference, I will integrate scientific perspectives with some intuitions about intuition that have richly informed my understanding of the topic.

There are at least three different kinds of feeling. The most basic is physical feeling, for example, the experience of a tap on the arm. There is also emotional feeling, such as the desire to be near a loved one. In addition, there is cognitive feeling, such as the subtle knowing that a new project, in spite of its apparent promise, will not go well. Although they may seem very different, these three broad categories of feeling are related. Physical feeling is primary because it is directly about the body. Emotional feeling builds on physical feeling (Damasio, 1994; Panksepp, 1998), and cognitive feeling builds on emotional or on physical feeling. Because of their interrelationship, the distinction between the various kinds of feeling is not always clear.

Some may prefer to limit the word *feeling* to conscious experiences. But certain types of feeling tend to occur in the fringe of awareness (James, 1890; Mangan, 2000, Price & Norman, 2008). Indeed, some researchers argue that the divide between what we are aware of and what we are not is an extended continuum, rather than an all or none phenomenon (Cohen et al., 2016; Sandberg & Overgaard, 2015).

Moreover, mental activity is frequently accompanied by feeling even when it does not appear to be. Many experiences have a physical and an emotional, as well as a cognitive, or thought-like, component. We can experience being hungry as contractions in the stomach, as an emotional need, or as a thought. In any instant we might be aware of one component at a conscious level to the exclusion of the others. Yet in the next instant this might change, and some of what was in the background of experience may come to the forefront.

PHYSICAL FEELING

Physical feelings, or bodily sensations, the common denominator of all feeling, are of two different kinds. Some convey information from the outside world and about the body's position in space. The area of the brain that processes this information, the *primary somatosensory cortex*, or the *somatosensory strip*, is located on the outside of the cortex between the parietal and temporal lobes (Penfield & Boldrey, 1937). These bodily feelings are experienced only after they register on the somatosensory strip, which is topographically arranged, or mapped, so that body parts maintain their relationship to each other.

Interoceptive Feeling

The other kind of physical feeling is called *interoceptive* (as opposed to *exteroceptive*) feeling. It reports on the state of the internal organs, or viscera, including stomach distension and heartbeat, aspects of pain and temperature, and a large variety of homeostatic and other mechanisms important to maintaining the body's physiology (Craig, 2002; Tsakiris & De Preester, 2018). This information is sent continuously via the autonomous nervous system and the hormonal system to the cortex, helping to provide a sense of the body as a whole. Interoceptive feelings also report more subjective internal physical experience, such as the experience of sentience, or of being an organism with feelings and subjectivity (Craig, 2010).

The Insula

Both actual and subjective interoceptive feelings activate the *insula* when they arrive in the cortex. A complicated structure with a number of parts and functions, the insula is located deep within the lateral sulcus – the fold that separates the temporal, parietal and frontal lobes. It is important for integrating different aspects of experience (Critchley & Harrison, 2003). It is also a crucial part of *the salience network*, which determines whether attention is directed externally or internally (Menon & Uddin, 2010).

Actual interoceptive feelings first activate the posterior portion of the insula. Like the somatosensory strip, it is topographically organized; it has been called the *primary interoceptive cortex*. Internal bodily feelings then travel to the anterior portion of the insula, where they may be integrated with the more subjective aspects of experience (Craig, 2002).

Until recently, subjective or "imagined" interoceptive feeling, for example, the experienced temperature of an internal probe, as opposed to its actual temperature, were thought to activate only the anterior insula (Barsalou, 2008). But the posterior and the anterior insula are well-interconnected. A current report suggests that intensely imagined emotional experience may also activate the posterior insula (Wilson-Mendenhall et al., 2018). Subjective interoceptive feelings have an important place in emotional experience and in intuition.

EMOTIONAL FEELING

Emotions, together with basic drives, make things matter to us (Damasio, 1994). Different emotions mobilize somewhat different patterns of bodily response as well as generalized bodily arousal in response to environmental conditions that threaten or enhance survival or well-being (Panksepp, 1998; Pert, 1999). As such, emotion provides the motivation for all cognitive activity, including intuition.

Primary and Secondary Emotional Responses

Primary emotional responses occur faster than we can become aware of their cause (James, 1884). The primary emotional centers of the brain are hard-wired to activate immediately without the involvement of the cortex in response to certain threats or supports to human survival. These primary cues are encoded in the genome; for example, a fear response to snake-like motion, or a pleasure response to snuggling up to a warm-bodied, responsive other. Some other objects or events can become strongly associated through conditioning to these genetically prepared cues and also evoke a primary emotional response, for instance, winning or losing money, even play money.

Fear is a particularly well-studied emotion (Lang et al., 2000; LeDoux, 1998). The amygdala, which is central to the fear response, is strongly connected to the autonomic nervous system, the hormonal system, and a large variety of other brain systems and centers. Once it is activated by a primary fear-inducing cue, it causes: (1) changes in the internal organs and other aspects of the internal environment (such as increased heart rate, shallow breathing and dry mouth), (2) changes in behavior (such as freezing in order to take in information), and (3) changes in cognition (such as enhanced alertness and attention) (Damasio, 1994). The three reactions are interactive and feed back on each other, sustaining and often amplifying the response.

Many emotional responses are secondary instead of primary. They trigger the emotional apparatus, such as the amygdala, only after the object or situation has been appraised, or evaluated, by the cortex, with its complex learning and memory systems (Damasio, 1994; LeDoux 1998). Secondary cues are associated with emotion based on past experience, for example, the memory of a vacation spot visited frequently as a child bringing a sense of well-being. Emotional appraisals as well as secondary emotional responses often occur below awareness (LeDoux, 1998), leaving us unaware we are reacting emotionally. Moreover, situations that occur habitually can result in the associated bodily experiences without causing generalized bodily arousal, through what has been named the "as-if" pathway (Damasio, 1994).

Anticipatory Emotional Responses and Interoception

The landmark *Iowa Gambling Experiments* by Damasio and his colleagues showed that unconscious secondary emotion can function in an adaptive, anticipatory way to influence decision making (Bechara et al., 1997). These studies helped give unconscious cognition and intuition scientific credibility. They also spurred interest in the insula and interoception.

The researchers asked normal subjects and a group of patients who had lesions in the ventromedial pre-frontal cortex, accompanied by flat affect and a history of poor decision making, to make a large number of repetitive choices. The ventromedial pre-frontal cortex, which includes portions of the orbital frontal cortex, is part of the value encoding system of the brain. It is strongly interconnected with the amygdala.

The experiment was constructed so that certain choices were risky because they sometimes gave large play-money rewards but at other times large penalties, resulting in a net loss over time. Normal subjects came to prefer the less-risky choices even before they had the feeling that certain ones were safer than others, and long before they became conscious of this feeling. The brain-damaged subjects, in contrast, continued to prefer the risky choices throughout the experiments – even those who figured out which ones were safer. Further experiments confirmed that the brain-damaged subjects were emotionally blind to the long-term consequences of their choices and were instead responding primarily to the promise of short-term gains (Bechara et al., 2000).

The researchers used Galvanic Skin Conductance as a measure of bodily arousal. In normal subjects, anticipating risky choices generated bodily changes based on their past losses. These signals were unavailable to awareness at least initially, nonetheless they began to bias successive choices along adaptive lines. The brain-damaged subjects, in contrast, lacked these bodily responses based on past experience when contemplating making a risky choice. Although their primary emotional response was intact, their lesions interfered with the secondary emotional pathway connecting the pre-frontal cortex and the amygdala.

The researchers proposed that when normal subjects are faced with a decision, the ventromedial pre-frontal cortex, in conjunction with the amygdala and many other brain regions, recreates, or *re-represents*, the bodily states associated with similar past experiences and their sense of goodness or badness. Damasio called these body-based signals that direct personal decision making based on past experience *somatic markers* (Damasio, 1994). A number of recent studies have confirmed various aspects of the somatic marker hypothesis (Dunn et al., 2010; Kandasamy et al., 2016; Werner et al., 2013).

Somatic markers are not necessarily conscious. They can influence decision making even before the question of choice comes to awareness. The advantageous choice or action just occurs. For the somatic markers to become conscious, the ventromedial pre-frontal cortex must first recreate, or re-represent, them in the anterior insula. This may occur either with or without generalized bodily arousal. Conditions of uncertainty, as is the case at least for much of the gambling experiment, tend to lead to the bodily loop and bodily arousal, as opposed to the "as-if" loop (Bechara & Damasio, 2005).

Potentially conscious signals are often referred to as gut feelings. The digestive system has been called a second brain (Mayer, 2011), and many of these feelings may arise in the gut. But Damasio's term is broader and includes various different types of interoceptive feelings. Moreover these signals may appear in consciousness as a thought or as a mental image, along with, or instead of, a bodily feeling. Sometimes they merge elements of all three.

Ordinary emotion can trump the guidance of somatic markers, often for the worse (Bagneux et al., 2013; Wölk et al., 2014). However what worked in the past is not always appropriate to the present situation. Indeed, in some situations, including some investment decisions, brain-damaged patients can perform better than normal subjects because they are less hindered by past experience (Shiv et al., 2005, see also Kandasamy et al., 2016).

METACOGNITIVE FEELING

Damasio suggested that the somatic markers associated with adaptive personal decision making may also play a role in less personal decisions.

> [T]hey … act covertly to highlight in the form of an attentional mechanism, certain components over others, and to control in effect, the go, stop and turn signals necessary for some aspect of the decision-making and planning in nonpersonal, nonsocial domains. (Damasio, 1994: 190)

Evolution often repurposes what worked well in one context for use in a new, more recently evolved one. The body-based markers used by the emotional system to bias choices were retooled to guide higher intellectual activity. This reflects a *metacognitive* use of emotion; metacognition refers to the online mechanisms that guide cognition as it occurs (Metcalfe & Shimamaru, 1994). It reports its directives with feelings that convey a sense of harmony or discord, signifying the absence or the presence of a sense of rightness or knowing (Mangan, 2000).

Consider the sentence, "The sneakers had to be thrown out because the sign blew away" (based on sentences in Auble et al., 1979). We feel a sense of wrongness. When supplied the words *wet concrete*, the sense of wrongness turns into a feeling of rightness and a feeling of knowing what the sentence is about. In many cases, these feelings, if they make it to awareness at all, are very subtle. Unless we are sensitized to them, they are often easy to miss.

Metacognitive Feeling and the Constructions of Intuitions

Metacognitive feelings play a critical role in several different aspects of intuition. As Damasio suggests in the passage above, some metacognitive feelings occur below awareness and automatically bias cognition along the lines of their suggestion, like the somatic markers that influenced normal subjects in the gambling experiments before they became aware that some choices were safer than others. Non-conscious metacognitive feelings can also have a role in the construction of intuitions, as one of my first conscious encounters with metacognitive emotion illustrated. It occurred in an unusual experience in which the boundary between my unconscious and conscious mind was unusually porous.

One evening I heard a new and more penetrating insight into a topic that mystified me as much as it interested me (Isenman, 2004; Isenman, 2018: 177). I wondered if the three pieces of information I already had about the subject were consistent with it. Yet I could not bring these three older pieces of information to awareness. Nonetheless my unconscious mind on its own started comparing each of the three old pieces of information with the new one. I could follow the movement of the three pairs as well as the metacognitive feelings of harmony reporting that each checked out fine, even though the three old pieces of information still remained below awareness. Soon afterward, and again unbidden, a much deeper still intuition that integrated all of the old pieces of information with the new one popped into my mind.

After puzzling a while about the unconscious evaluation process revealed by the experience, I concluded it demonstrates that metacognitive feeling can guide the construction of intuitions by evaluating if the potential strands to be included cohere, or overlap, in a meaningful way, and are not logically inconsistent. It also shows that both the evaluation and subsequent synthesis can proceed even when the potential strands are not available to awareness, and even when the motivation for the synthesis is implicit rather than explicit. (Implicit in my inquiry about whether the old and new information fit together was a desire for a more complete understanding of the topic. This probably remained implicit because I assumed that full understanding of this obscure topic would always elude me.)

The metacognitive feelings I experienced correspond to the feeling of fitting or of relevance. More often, however, what appears in awareness or its fringe is the inverse, the feeling that the information is *not* relevant or does *not* fit together. The discomfort signals to the conscious mind that there is a significant lack of coherence, or disjunction, between two or more items or ideas that have been brought into proximity. This discomfort encourages the conscious mind to bring attention to ameliorating the situation (Mangan, 2000). The feeling of not fitting often points to especially fertile terrain for the emergence of a future intuition (Isenman, 2018). Yet the positive version of these feelings in most cases need not come to awareness or its fringe.

Feelings of Penetration, Illumination, and of Truth

In contrast, a number of different kinds of *positive* metacognitive evaluative feelings that evaluate the *products* of our own or other's cognition do frequently emerge into the fringe of awareness. These include the feeling of illumination, the feeling of penetration, and the feeling of truth (Isenman, 2018). Like the feeling of fitting, they report on the coherence of information, but in addition they signal the emergence of a coherent *whole*. The three are sometimes used to describe the same phenomenon, yet each holds somewhat different potential connotations. Together with feelings of fitting, I view them as falling on a continuum that signals progressively deeper coherence and wholeness (Isenman, 2018).

The feeling of illumination, like the light bulb above the comic book character's head, reports that a significant field of mental coherence has come into focus. All of a sudden, we feel we comprehend something important that seemed problematic to us or we did not previously understand. This feeling may be temporary, as deeper levels of potential complexity and/or contradiction come into focus.

The feeling of penetration, in contrast to illumination, allows for degrees. It can connote going deeper and piercing more subtle levels. It also can imply that satisfactory progress has occurred, but there is even more complexity there than we can currently appreciate.

I like to reserve the feeling of truth for complete penetration, the feeling that one senses the whole of something, its circumference as well as its depth. It represents a field of coherence that includes what is known about a subject at the unconscious as well as the conscious level (Isenman, 2018; Mangan, 2000). Like a fine bell, whose vibrations can be sensed as pressure waves even after they go out of the range of our ordinary hearing, our metacognition can register and report finer and finer levels of reverberating coherence as it penetrates successively deeper into the unconscious mind.

The strongest feelings of truth tend to have an objective quality. Like sensory information, they can appear as if they are coming from outside of the self, conveying a subtle yet hard to ignore authority (Isenman, 2018). Einstein, for example, before the Special Theory of Relativity gained general acceptance, examined a newly published paper claiming to disprove his theory. Although he found nothing wrong with the paper's calculations, he told his secretary that the paper had to be wrong (Holton, 1973). Because of the objectivity and authority a feeling of truth conveys, it also tends to have a grounding quality, sometimes even if it brings unpleasant knowledge. New knowledge may alter the situation, but nonetheless the depth of the fields of coherence associated with a feeling of truth makes it hard to overturn. It might instead become a special case of an enlarged reality, as Newtonian Physics did with the advent of Einsteinian Physics.

Just as ordinary emotion can overrule somatic markers about personal decision making, it can also overrule metacognitive feeling. The stronger, cruder voice of emotion often trumps the generally softer, more subtle metacognitive voice. Moreover when seeking justification to act on an emotional urge, it is not infrequent to misconstrue an emotional signal as a permissive metacognitive one (Isenman, 2018). Because of a need for closure after many hours of work, for example, we might hail a late hour breakthrough as certain, even as we are aware of many loose ends that will indeed unravel the apparent solution the next day.

Nonetheless, human survival in evolution demands that ordinary emotion and metacognitive emotion work together much of the time. Therefore it is not uncommon to experience metacognitive emotion in a dangerous situation where there is no room for error. Ordinary emotion, if it does not jam us, can make us attentive to a subtle, survival-based metacognitive directive (Isenman, 2018).

PHYSICAL FEELINGS AS COGNITIVE SIGNS IN INTUITION

Physical feelings, especially interoceptive feelings, in addition to their participation in emotional and metacognitive feelings, have another role in intuition. They can function as metaphorical signs, or symbols, that help bring unconscious knowledge to awareness. Another experience that has strongly informed my understanding of intuition helps demonstrate this:

> Early in my investigation of intuition, a colleague surprised me by asking for an impromptu definition of intuition. After a moment of searching, the phrase a blink of the eye unexpectedly came to mind. This didn't seem to answer the question, so I looked again. This time a subliminal physical sense of the experience of intuition as a rapid closing and opening somewhere in my chest accompanied the mental experience of seeing a generic signal go down and then up on a graph. (Isenman, 1997: 398)

The image of the closing and then opening of the eye in an eyeblink, as well as the subtle physical feeling of a rapid closing followed by an opening in the chest, are body-based, or embodied, metaphors for intuition. Intuition often begins when the conscious mind does not know how to proceed – a closing. We might be completely blank, recognize a serious contradiction or disjunction in our thinking, or perhaps be immobilized by the swamp of possibilities. When the way forward appears, often only after a while, there is a sense of release – an opening. The image of a signal going down and then up on a graph or oscilloscope, although not a body-based image, reflects the same down/up pattern – and it also seems to refer to my first intuition as a biologist. The recognition that the three images reflected the same pattern of motion – a closing then an opening, a decrease then an increase, or a down then up – was what allowed me to recognize that the initially silly-sounding "blink of the eye" was a valid definition of intuition.

Embodied Cognition

The blink of the eye experience, among many other things, suggests that body-based experience as well as its correspondence with images about the external world are central to intuition. The view that cognition is *embodied*, now favored by many cognitive scientists (Barsalou, 2008; Varela et al., 1992; Wilson, 2002), provides some insight into why this might be so. It proposes that all cognitive development begins with bodily experience. As infants we experience the world completely from the perspective of our bodies and its genetically determined patterns of action. We gradually expand our perceptual and cognitive sphere to include more of the external world by grounding this knowledge in bodily experience. Lakoff and Johnson proposed in 1980 that body-based metaphors are particularly important to the growth of language and also the extension of cognition into novel realms. Some evidence suggests that at least novel metaphors based on bodily experience can activate the corresponding parts of the brain's motor regions (Hampe, 2017).

Metaphors based on spatial orientation

Because we have bodies, spatial orientation is a core element in our meaning making. This includes, among others, the opposites of *in* and *out*, *front* and *back*, and *up* and *down*. These spatial terms serve as linguistic primitives, or unproblematic concepts that provide some of the building blocks of more complex concepts (Tovey, 1996). Spatial primitives and the metaphors based on them allow us to understand a whole variety of experiences relative to our body's orientation in space.

For example, Lakoff and Johnson (1980) explored ten different kinds of metaphorical meanings for the up–down spatial polarity. Here are a few. *Up is good*, as in, things are looking up, and *bad is down*, as in, things are at an all-time low; *up is conscious*, as in, wake up, whereas *down is unconscious*, as in, he dropped off to sleep; and *up is more*, as in, my income rose last year, and *less is down*, as in, her income is in decline.

Intuition, bodily feeling, and the down–up motif

Like most researchers who stress the importance of bodily experience, Lakoff and Johnson focus on the development and expansion of conceptual activity and language. However the blink of the eye experience suggests that, just as the human mind can project bodily experience into the conceptual realm via metaphor, it can also reverse the process. We can experience unconscious conceptual knowledge via bodily experience (Isenman, 2018). A number of recent reports in the literature provide additional evidence for the ability of metaphor to function bidirectionally – from physically based experience to complex knowledge, as well as from complex knowledge to physically based experience (Guo et al., 2013; Zhong & Leonardelli, 2008).

Even very abstract conceptual knowledge can arrive in consciousness through bodily experience or body-based metaphors. As the answer my unconscious provided to the daunting question "What is intuition?" demonstrates, physical feelings and simple patterns of physical feelings, along with metaphors that employ them, can function as cognitive signs or symbols that help bring very complex unconscious knowledge to awareness. By including both elements of the up–down spatial polarity, as well as reversing the sequence in which we most often think about them, it highlights a dynamic process that is central to breakthrough intuition.

The down–up motif, the core of the intuition, together with the specific images that transmitted the pattern, point to the complex interaction that occurs during the experience of intuition between various aspects of mind that are generally seen as opposed to each other. These include the unconscious/conscious, the body/mind, internal/external experience, and the associative/rational. The first of each of these pairs represents what is generally hidden, closer to the natural world, and often denigrated. This *down*, this apparent disadvantaged state, the down–up motif implies, is important and must be respected for the desired *up* to follow. Indeed, the most profound intuitions often begin with not knowing and letting go of our usual ways of knowing.

The Interaction Between Body-Related and Higher Cognitive Brain Regions in Breakthrough Cognition

The capacity of the mind to come up with this complex answer to the question "What is Intuition?" suggests that higher cognitive centers and the insula work together to identify and represent bodily feelings and patterns of bodily feelings that can communicate hidden knowledge to the conscious mind. It is tempting to claim that the higher cognitive centers identify the dynamic core of the intuition – here the down/up motif – based on abstract implicit knowledge and then re-represent the bodily feelings that correspond to it in the anterior insula. Some abstract tacit knowledge may indeed be easier to express via patterns of bodily feelings than via conventional symbols like words.

However, the brain works as a whole, and this is especially true during novel cognition. The interoceptive-tethered insula likely also has a role in identifying the pattern, as do perhaps a variety of motion-related brain regions. With its stored patterns of muscle tension and its subtle motion in response to experience (Barsalou, 2008), the body likely knows much more about certain things than the conceptual mind. The body is also more finely represented on the right, less verbal side of the brain (Damasio, 1994), the side more frequently associated with processing questions that cannot be answered readily (Goel & Grafman, 2000; Goldberg, 2006) as well with the unconscious mind and with intuition. The emergence of the motif most likely depended on a circular interaction between the more abstract conceptual and more body-related regions of the brain. The view of the brain as a complex dynamic system can best account for this circularity as well as the resultant richness and holism of many intuitions, as I have argued elsewhere (Isenman, 2018).

Whatever the details of the co-operation between the more conceptual and the body-tethered areas of the mind, the intuitive process initially taps into knowledge that is unavailable to awareness. This knowledge tends to be truer to authentic experience than conscious knowledge. The conscious mind has a tendency to revise more direct experience to fit into the grid of our established ways of thinking.

FEELING, BRINGING TOGETHER OPPOSITES, AND WHOLENESS: A PERSONAL CONCLUSION

The emphasis on the role of the body and emotion in cognition is relatively new. Until late in the twentieth century, bodily knowledge and emotional knowledge were considered independent of, and even antithetical to, effective cognitive activity (Damasio, 1994; Lakoff, 1987). The body was seen as irrelevant and emotion a contaminant that would lead thought astray. Many of us who grew up in the last century never considered that feelings could have a role in our decision making and thinking. Moreover we did not know that we pay a cost by not being sensitive to this rich source of knowledge.

I first heard the claim that the body could have a role in making complex decisions when I was in graduate school in California in the mid-1970s. As a scientist in training, I immediately rejected the notion as bizarre, yet some part of me was intrigued. When confronted by a particularly important decision about my future that I could not resolve after great mental effort, I decided to give it a try. I sat there and sat there letting the feeling tones associated with the issue course through my body. The answer appeared suddenly from someplace between my body and mind. Accompanying it was a searing image that merged bodily sensation, emotion, and a specific mental picture: the healing fusion of a zigzag split running up the front of my body. The image highlights the split as a serious wound that requires repair. The rupture seems to refer to a number of overlapping polarities. These include, among others, the body and the mind, the unconscious and conscious mind, and what is commonly attributed to the left and right sides of the brain and the right and left sides of the body.

The exercise of using my body as a source of knowledge provided an important corrective to the view that the conscious mind is the source of all decision making, or at least all trustworthy decision making. When the answer appeared, however, it came from neither the body nor the mind, nor the right nor left side of the body or brain, nor the unconscious nor the conscious mind. Rather it came from someplace between each of the pairs. The jagged wound represents the tendency to hold any one side of these pairs as separate from the other side, and to favor it consciously largely to the exclusion of the other.

Feeling is the psychic solvent that dissolves both sides of what we hold to be immiscible and brings them together into solution. Once they connect, each informs and builds on the other. This dynamic interaction heals the wound of partialness and incompletion. It is especially important to intuition, which, as another characterization holds, can be understood as a sense of the whole (Isenman, 1997, 2018). Feeling is a combined mental and physiological openness. It requires letting go of an exclusive identification with the conscious mind and including the body more in experience. Our intuition works best when we do, and when we are sensitive to even very subtle aspects of what might emerge.

REFERENCES

Auble, P.A., Franks, J.J., & Soraci, S.A. 1979. Effort towards comprehension: Elaboration or "aha?" *Memory & Cognition*, 7: 426–434.

Bagneux, V., Font, H., & Bolton, T. 2013. Incidental emotions associated with uncertainty appraisals impair decisions in the Iowa Gambling Task. *Motivation and Emotion*, 37(4): 818–827.

Barsalou, L.W. 2008. Grounded cognition. *Annual Review of Psychology*, 59: 617–645.

Bechara, A., & Damasio, A.R. 2005. The somatic marker hypothesis. *Games & Economic Behavior*, 52: 336–372.

Bechara, A., Damasio, H., Tranel, D., & Damasio, A.R. 1997. Deciding advantageously before knowing the advantageous strategy. *Science*, 275: 1293–1295.

Bechara, A., Tranel, D., & Damasio, H. 2000. Characterization of the decision-making deficit of patients with ventromedial prefrontal cortex lesions. *Brain*, 123: 2189–2202.

Cohen, M.A., Dennett, D.C., & Kanwisher, N. 2016. What is the bandwidth of perceptual experience? *Trends in Cognitive Sciences*, 20(5): 324–335.

Craig, A.D. 2002. How do you feel? Interoception: The sense of the physiological condition of the body. *Nature Reviews Neuroscience*, 3: 655–666.

Craig, A.D. 2010. The sentient self. *Brain Structure & Function*, 214(5–6): 563–577.

Critchley, H.D., & Harrison, N.A. 2003. Visceral influences on brain and behavior. *Neuron*, 77: 624–638.

Damasio, A. 1994. *Descartes' error: Emotion, reason and the human brain*. New York: G.P. Putnam & Sons.

Dunn, B.D., Galton, H.C., Morgan, R., Evans, D., Oliver, C., Meyer, M., Cusack, R., Lawrence, A.D., & Dalgleish, T. 2010. Listening to your heart: How interoception shapes emotion and decision making. *Physiological Sciences*, 21(12): 1835–1844.

Goel, V., & Grafman, J. 2000. The role of the right pre-frontal cortex in ill-structured problem solving. *Neuropsychology*, 17: 415–435.

Goldberg, E. 2006. *The wisdom paradox: How your mind can grow stronger as your brain grows older*. New York: Avery Press.

Guo, X., Li, F., Yang, Z., & Dienes, Z. 2013. Bidirectional transfer between metaphorical related domains in implicit learning of form-meaning connections. *PLoS ONE*, 8(7): e68100.

Hampe, B. 2017. *Metaphor, embodied cognition and discourse*. Cambridge, UK: Cambridge University Press.

Holton, G. 1973. *Thematic origins of scientific thought: Kepler to Einstein*. Cambridge, MA: Harvard University Press.

Isenman, L.D. 1997. Towards an understanding of intuition and its importance in scientific endeavor. *Perspectives in Biology and Medicine*, 40(3): 395–403.

Isenman, L. 2004. *Feelings of rightness in insight formation and intuition*. Abs 133, Toward a Science of Consciousness VI, Tucson, AZ.

Isenman, L. 2018. *Understanding intuition: A journey in and out of science*. Cambridge, MA: Academic Press.

James, W. 1884. What is an emotion? *Mind*, 9: 188–205.

James, W. 1890. *The principles of psychology, Vol. 1*. New York: Holt.

Kandasamy, N., Garfinkel, S.N., Page, L., Hardy, B., Critchley, H.D., Gurnell, M., & Coates, J.M. 2016. Interoceptive ability predicts survival on a London trading floor. *Scientific Reports*, *6*: 32986.

Lakoff, G. 1987. *Women, fire and dangerous things: What categories reveal about the mind*. Chicago: University of Chicago Press.

Lakoff, G., & Johnson, M. 1980. *Metaphors we live by*. Chicago: University of Chicago Press.

Lang, P., Davis, M., & Ohman, A. 2000. Fear and anxiety: Animal models and human cognitive psychophysiology. *Journal of Affective Disorders*, 61: 137–159.

LeDoux J. 1998. *The emotional brain*. New York: Touchstone.

Mangan, B. 2000. Sensation's ghost: The non-sensory 'fringe' of consciousness. *PSYCHE*, 7: https://www.researchgate.net/publication/247487522_Sensation's_ghost_The_non-sensory_fringe_of_consciousness (accessed February 19, 2020).

Mayer, E.A. 2011. Gut feelings: The emerging biology of gut–brain communication. *Nature Reviews Neuroscience*, 12: 453–466.

Menon, V., & Uddin, L.Q. 2010. Saliency, switching, attention and control: A network model of insula function. *Brain Structure and Function*, 214: 655–667.

Metcalfe, J. & Shimamaru, A.P. 1994. *Metacognition: Knowing about knowing*. Cambridge, MA: MIT Press.

Panksepp, J. 1998. *Affective neuroscience: The foundations of human and animal emotions*. New York: Oxford University Press.
Penfield, W., & Boldrey, E. 1937. Somatic motor and sensory representation in the cerebral cortex of man as studied by electrical stimulation. *Brain*, 60: 389–443.
Pert, C.B. 1999. *Molecules of emotion: The science behind mind-body medicine*. New York: Scribner.
Price, M.C., & Norman, E. 2008. Intuitive decisions on the fringes of consciousness: Are they conscious and does it matter? *Judgment and Decision Making*, 3: 28–41.
Sandberg, K., & Overgaard, M. 2015. Using the perceptual awareness scale (PAS). In M. Overgaard (Ed.) *Behavioural methods in consciousness research*: 181–196. Oxford: Oxford University Press.
Shiv, B., Lowenstein, G., & Bechara, A. 2005. The dark side of emotion. *Cognitive Brain Research*, 32(1): 85–92.
Tovey, M. 1996. Spatial metaphors as linguistic primitives: A comparison of UP–DOWN metaphors in three languages. Totem: The University of Western Ontario Journal of Anthropology, 2(1): Article 16.
Tsakiris, M., & De Preester, H. (Eds.) 2018. *The interoceptive mind: From homeostasis to awareness*. Oxford: Oxford University Press.
Varela, F.J., Thompson, E., & Rosch, E. 1992. *The embodied mind: Cognitive science and human experience*. Cambridge, MA: MIT Press.
Werner, N.S., Schweitzer, N., Meindi, T., Duschek, S., Kambeitz, J., & Schandry, R. 2013. Interoceptive awareness moderates neural activity during decision-making. *Biological Psychology*, 94: 498–506.
Wilson, M. 2002. Six views of embodied cognition. *Psychonomic Bulletin & Review*, 9(4): 625–636.
Wilson-Mendenhall, C.D., Henriques, A., & Barsalou, L.W. 2018. Primary interoceptive cortex activity during simulated experiences of the body. *Journal of Cognitive Neuroscience*, 31(2): 221–235.
Wölk, J., Sütterlin, S., Koch, S., Vögele, C., & Schulz, S.E. 2014. Enhanced cardiac perception predicts impaired performance in the Iowa Gambling Task in patients with panic disorder. *Brain and Behavior*, 4(2): 238–246.
Zhong, C.B., & Leonardelli, G. 2008. Cold and lonely: Does social exclusion literally feel cold? *Psychological Science*, 19: 838–842.

9. Psychophysical measurement of intuition

Galang Lufityanto

Intuition is one of the most intriguing phenomena of the human mind. It has been attracting general populous attention for centuries, from the times of ancient Greece until just recently. The notion of intuition as early documented in Greek literature is illustrated as an inner voice characterized by lack of detailed comprehension that may still become an impetus for certain decisions (Hackforth, 1972). More recent literature, however, defines intuition as a sensation of certainty about something in the absence of logical explanation (Hogarth, 2010) that is further characterized as rapid, emotionally charged, and occurring in the absence of awareness (Gigerenzer, 2007; Gladwell, 2007; Myers, 2004). There has been abundant evidence that relates intuition with emotion, such as it is often described as a sense of alarm when something is going wrong (Stolper et al., 2010), or on the contrary, as a sense of excitement about an advantageous situation (Agor, 1987). There seems to be no indication that intuition is identical with a specific type of emotion however, but all evidence of intuition seems to converge with feeling, emotion, or affect (Myers, 2004).

People have been seduced by the notion of intuition as they believe it can bypass demanding rational thought (Gigerenzer, 2007; Gladwell, 2007; Myers, 2004). A study has demonstrated the fallibility of rational thought in situations where available information is overwhelming (Dijksterhuis & Nordgren, 2006). Although this study is not without controversy (for a review, see Newell & Rakow, 2011), it illuminates the limits of human capacity in information processing.

Using intuition, we do not need to analyse each piece of information, but rather, we can use our general impression to make decisions. This notion is somewhat aligned with the proposition of emotion-based decision making (Mikels et al., 2011) which suggests that emotional encoding can prevent overthinking detailed information. Emotion is attached to the general impression of an object/event which could later be utilized during the judgment process.

Indeed, studies have shown that emotion can act as a mental shortcut (Mikels et al., 2011) or biologically relevant feedback (Bechara et al., 1997) in the context of decision making. Emotion can bypass a lengthy analytical thought to expedite decisions due to association between a certain cognitive process and typical emotional responses (Zajonc, 1980). Furthermore, the human brain architecture enables emotional stimuli to be processed very rapidly (Liddell et al., 2005; Tamietto & de Gelder, 2010; Vuilleumier et al., 2002), much earlier than non-emotional or cognitive information. Emotional images travel from the retina to the limbic system via direct pathways that bypass the primary sensory areas. Consequently, we are able to rapidly respond to potentially threat-related objects, even before recognizing what the objects are (Lang et al., 1990).

Academically, the notion of intuition has also been conceptualized in various paradigms which all indicate the existence of a dual-process of information processing in the human mind (for a review, see Evans, 2008). Based on this paradigm, intuition is categorized as System 1 or the default system of humans, whereas its counterpart, rational thinking is part of System 2. System 2 is characterized as fully-conscious, rational, deliberate, and rule-based, while System 1 is more non-conscious, experiential, automatic, and association-based. Intuition is considered as System 1 due to its application of emotion in a non-deliberative way but otherwise can still affect behaviour. Those two systems are thought to co-exist and work in parallel ways. Further, people are thought to be more inclined towards System 1 or System 2 in regards to information processing (Epstein, 1998).

TESTING THE OBJECTIVE PHENOMENON OF INTUITION

Although the measurement of intuition has already generated large interest, particularly for applied purposes, it tends to measure subjective perception towards intuitive ability and not the intuitive ability per se. There was almost no technique which could measure the acquisition of intuition in individuals beyond their perception. The notion of intuition has mostly been investigated using self-reported questionnaires (e.g., Khatri & Ng, 2000; Sinclair et al., 2010) or interviews (e.g., Klein et al., 1986). These techniques are unfortunately prone to self-report bias and therefore their results often contradict with each other (Shirley & Langan-Fox, 1996; Westcott, 1968).

Nevertheless, there are a few recent studies conducted to test the notion of intuition using more tractable and rigorous methodology, including the study by Lufityanto et al. (2016) which utilizes a technique commonly used in psychophysical measurement and neuroscience. It uses a noisy sensory decision making task that forces participants to make a categorical judgment (left/right) on a set of dots which move stochastically (Newsome, 1997; Shadlen & Kiani, 2013) as illustrated in Figure 9.1. While making categorical decisions, participants were presented with emotional images suppressed using interocular suppression techniques (Stein et al., 2011), therefore they did not have visual awareness of the emotional images. Awareness indeed has been long thought to be the core characteristic of intuition. A process commonly described as intuition involves inexplicable feeling that biases a decision. The inability to explain the logic behind this sensation is one reason that intuitive decisions are considered to be products of non-conscious processing (Myers, 2004).

Interocular suppression techniques, such as continuous flash suppression (CFS), allow suppression of a visual stimulus for several seconds (Tsuchiya & Koch, 2005), enough for the stimulus to be processed by the human brain but bypassing visual consciousness. CFS is achieved by presenting one eye with a static stimulus (i.e., the non-dominant eye) and the other eye with a stimulus changing at a rapid rate therefore allowing this particular stimulus to always dominate visual experience. CFS technique often uses salient objects such as bright coloured patterns (e.g., Sklar et al., 2012), thus prompting conscious perception of stimuli processed by the dominant

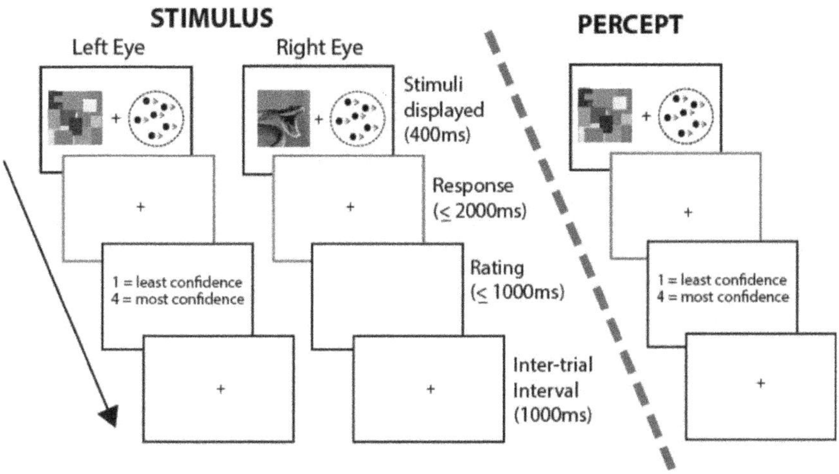

Notes: Participants were presented with stimuli for 400 ms. Following that, a response window appeared for 2,000 ms or otherwise terminated as soon as participants pressed a key responding to the stimuli. During the rating window (1,000 ms) following the response window, participants were asked to indicate their confidence on a 4-point rating scale (1 = least confident, 4 = most confidence). Finally, an inter-trial interval was provided for 1,000 ms.
Source: Lufityanto et al., 2016.

Figure 9.1 *Procedure of the main experiment*

eye, while stimuli presented to the non-dominant eye remain suppressed from visual awareness. Therefore, although people cannot report seeing the images, the early sensory areas in their brain have already captured the visual information.

Further, the CFS technique is an application of binocular rivalry, a natural phenomenon that occurs when two different visual stimuli are presented, one to each eye, therefore causing perceptual competition as only one stimulus is consciously perceived at one time but it will switch to the other stimulus intermittently (Bennur & Gold, 2011; Blake & Logothetis, 2002; Logothetis et al., 1996). Binocular rivalry is often employed in scientific studies aimed to understand the mechanisms underlying human awareness using visual stimuli. Using this technique, awareness can be manipulated from the early stage of sensory processing. The unconscious mind has been extensively studied for a long time, particularly when psychoanalysis became one of the dominant theoretical movements in the psychology discipline (Billig, 2006). However, it is only recently that consciousness has become one of the main topics in experimental psychology, including the study of cognition, perception, and neuroscience. Insights and scientific findings about early sensory processes enable us to test consciousness rigorously.

Studies have indicated that emotional stimuli processed non-consciously can indeed influence complex behaviour. For instance, Almeida and colleagues (2013) found that presenting suppressed emotional images could bias subjective preferences for otherwise neutral stimuli. Participants were presented with images of positive and negative facial expressions suppressed by the CFS technique, following the explicit presentation of neutral Chinese characters. Every character was always paired up with either a positive or negative facial expression, or otherwise with neutral objects in the baseline condition. Subjects rated particular Chinese characters which were associated with a suppressed angry face as the least likeable relative to the baseline condition. This demonstrates that non-conscious induction of emotion can influence complex behaviours.

Likewise, Lufityanto and colleagues (2016) further demonstrated that non-conscious emotional images boosted accuracy in decision making. This boost was accompanied by high confidence among participants in their correct responses. Please note that the study did not find any differential trend between positive and negative emotional images, indicating that intuition does not lean towards a specific emotional valence. This effect was more robust in the difficult task in which adequate information was not available for the decision makers. Using a random dot motion (RDM) task, experimenters can adjust the level of difficulty to mimic natural decision making (Shadlen & Kiani, 2013).

In the RDM tasks, participants are typically presented with coherently and randomly moving dots inside a given aperture. A coherent dot is one that moves coherently in one direction – left or right – over a serial course of time, whereas a random dot does not move continuously in a single direction. Higher coherence in an RDM task means that a greater proportion of the dots in the stimulus is moving together in the same direction (with the remaining dots moving randomly), making the task easier for participants. Conversely, lower coherence makes the task harder and therefore consumes a longer time to respond (Bennur & Gold, 2011).

A study has demonstrated activity in the brain area responsible for accumulating evidence in RDM tasks (Shadlen & Newsome, 2001). Higher coherence of the moving dots, meaning that the stimulus contains a higher proportion of signals in relation to noise – valid information for making decisions. Lufityanto and colleagues (2016) found that the utilization of non-conscious emotional information was more robust in the task involving lower coherence dots, but the effect disappeared as the level of coherence increased. This finding has shown a strict condition where intuition is more powerful, that is, when the information is not enough to be used to make decisions. It dovetails nicely with the previous literature suggesting that intuition is only powerful in the context where valid information does not exist (Hogarth, 2001; Myers, 2004).

Further, using a computational model from physiological data known to be related with non-conscious emotional processing, that is, skin conductance response (Bechara & Damasio, 2005), Lufityanto et al. (2016) demonstrated that emotional information acted as additional information to otherwise lacking categorical relevant information (i.e., coherent moving dots) to make decisions. Moreover, by calculating decision parameters such as reaction times, accuracy, and so on, it was estimated that the value of the non-conscious emotional information was comparable to increasing task-relevant information by ~10 per cent. Nevertheless, this finding suggests that different categorical information, that is, emotional and sensory information, can blend nicely in the decisional process. This insight has therefore provided stronger evidence that intuition exists and can possibly be explained by scientific principles.

SUBJECTIVE FEELING AND PREDISPOSITION OF INTUITION

Perhaps a more interesting finding in Lufityanto et al. (2016) is that people were more confident in their decision in the task where moving dots stimulus was accompanied by suppressed emotional images relative to more neutral images. "Feeling confident" in the context of this study means that participants became more certain of their responses being correct. Please note that participants were not given any feedback therefore they could not rely on external cues other than their own subjective evaluation. It is intriguing that people were persistently confident in their performance even in the absence of explicit feedback. It further prompted some scholars (e.g., Sinclair et al., 2010) to think that there could be a subjective predisposition to intuition; that some people have an innate tendency to act more intuitively than others. Furthermore, this preposition has been more commonly assessed using popular instruments such as the Myers–Briggs Type Indicators (Myers et al., 1998; see Hodgkinson & Sadler-Smith, 2011, for more recent findings), Rational-Experiential Inventory (Pacini & Epstein, 1999), etc. These instruments highlight individual differences in intuition that may be rooted in individual thinking styles.

Further, the Rational-Experiential Inventory (REI) proposes two separate cognitive systems to be used in information processing: (1) rational system, characterized as analytical-based, deliberate, and rather time-consuming, and (2) experiential system which is more emotional-based, intuitive, automatic, and rapid. Participants are asked to rate how accurately each statement describes them using a 5-point Likert response (1 = strongly disagree and 5 = strongly agree). Using a certain formula (Hodgkinson et al., 2009), people can be categorized into rational thinkers and intuitive thinkers.

A later study, using experimental paradigm (Lufityanto & Pearson, 2016), found individual differences in intuitive ability, such as performance in an intuitive decision depending on individual thinking style. This finding is supported by behavioural and physiological data. Some people demonstrated good intuition while others did not. It somehow supports the notion that not everyone is comparably good at intuition (Hogarth, 2001). Using Rational-Experiential Inventory, Lufityanto and Pearson (2016) found that only intuitive thinkers utilized non-conscious emotional information to make decisions, while rational thinkers tended to ignore the emotional information for decisional process. These people acted consistently in two scenarios: (1) where the amount of task-related information was limited and (2) when the people had freedom to collect more information to ponder their decisions (i.e., no time constraint). In their typical experiments, Lufityanto et al. (2016) rapidly presented stimuli for 400 milliseconds to limit flow of information. However, when the time restriction was removed, participants were still biased towards their thinking styles. The latter finding shows that although there is a specific condition where intuition is more preferable (i.e., ambiguous situations), some people will stick with their preferable strategy (i.e., rational vs. intuitive) to make decisions.

Meanwhile, another sample which was categorized as neither intuitive nor rational thinkers showed the ability to switch their strategy, that is, changing from intuitive mode to rational thinking along with the increase of task-related information. When an adequate amount of task-related information was not available, this particular sample resorted to their intuitive strategy. However, as the amount of task-related information increased, they started to ignore the non-conscious emotional information. For that reason, they were named "flexible thinkers". In Lufityanto and Pearson's (2016) data, almost half of the sample were flexible thinkers, leaving a comparable proportion of the sample categorized as intuitive and rational thinkers (~25 per cent each). While the phenomenon of cognitive adaptability has been investigated in numerous studies (Canas et al., 2003; LePine et al., 2000), the phenomenon of flexible thinking which enables individuals to switch cognitive strategy requires further investigation.

One may argue that rational thinkers are merely not sensitive to emotional information. Nevertheless, Lufityanto and Pearson's (2016) data indicated that there was no differential sensitivity between rational and intuitive thinkers in regards to receiving emotional input as indicated from their physiological data, that is, skin conductance response. Both groups experienced an almost comparable increase of arousal level when viewing emotional images. However, their utilization of emotional information in the sensory decision task was different, thus highlighting a preferential strategy which they used for executing the task. While intuitive thinkers relied on non-conscious emotional information, rational thinkers seemed to completely ignore it. It is possible that rational thinkers were simply better at utilizing the task-related information than intuitive thinkers, therefore they did not need additional non-conscious emotional information. Previous work suggests that people with greater cognitive capacity tend to forcefully allocate their executive resources to demanding tasks (De Neys, 2006). However, this assumption requires further investigation.

The separate emotional processing, that is, receiving emotional information and further processing emotional information, is supported by several studies involving physiological measurement and brain imaging techniques. One study suggested that electro-dermal activities had emerged prior to making bad decisions in simulated gambling tasks for normal participants, but this phenomenon was not evident in patients with lesions in the amygdala – an area which is responsible for responding to emotional information (Bechara et al., 1999). However, a follow-up study found poor performance on the same gambling task for those with lesions in the ventromedial prefrontal cortex – a brain area responsible for integrating emotional processing into the decisional process – but having the amygdala intact (Bechara et al., 2000). These two studies demonstrated that the whole emotional processing can be disrupted when brain areas which are particularly responsible for (1) responding to emotional information or/and (2) making use of emotional information for further processes are damaged.

There has been a debate in regards to subjective predisposition of intuition, for example whether some people are better at intuition than others. Nevertheless, a recent study by Lufityanto and Pearson (2016) has at least supported the idea that (1) everyone has a distinct decision making strategy, and (2) the difference is due to the utilization of emotional information (i.e., thinking styles), rather than individual sensitivity to capture the emotional signals. Further investigation is required to illuminate the underlying mechanism, such as whether it is predominantly a product of experience and learning (nurture) or merely biological predisposition (nature).

INTUITION AND COGNITIVE LOAD

People have believed that intuition is more preferable in conditions where our cognitive resources are fully occupied (Hogarth, 2001; Myers, 2004). Consequently, there is a need to confirm that intuition can act as an alternative strategy under this particular condition. The capacity of cognitive resources has been largely investigated in studies of perception, for example selective attention (Lavie et al., 2004) and working memory (for a review, see Baddeley, 2003). For instance, when given two concurrent demanding tasks, performance will most likely be impaired due to multiple allocations of cognitive resources, for example attention (Engle, 2002; Lavie, 2005). Another study demonstrated a worse performance in an arithmetic task when it was given simultaneously with a working memory task (Baddeley et al., 2001).

Even more controversial is the claim that compared to rational thought, non-conscious thought is more central to the decision making process in a scenario where information is overwhelming (Dijksterhuis & Nordgren, 2006). Participants were presented with four hypothetical cars or apartments and then asked to choose the best option. Each option contained multiple information which was intentionally targeted to exhaust participants' cognitive resources. It was found that inaccurate decisions were made by participants who made decisions either (1) straight away or (2) with a short delay between the presentation of information and the decision. However, a group of participants who were given an unrelated anagram task, serving as a distractor prior to choosing cars/apartments (i.e., non-conscious thought group), chose more advantageous options than the comparison groups. Dijksterhuis and Nordgren (2006) interpret this result as evidence that paying attention to all detailed information will otherwise lead to bad decisions. Conversely, diverting attention from the information can increase the probability to make better decisions.

The above-mentioned study is mainly criticized for potentially misleading interpretation of the results. The superiority of non-conscious thought could merely be a result of re-accessing long-term memory process (Newell & Shanks, 2014). In Dijksterhuis' (2004) original experiment, participants were asked to imagine the best cars or apartments according to them, before being presented with information of the cars and apartments. A confirmatory study indeed found a distracting anagram prevented attention to the overwhelming detailed information, it further facilitated for the participants to resort back to their initial subjective impression that had already been preserved in their long-term memory (Lassiter et al., 2009). The superiority of non-conscious thought was no longer evident when participants were not asked to think of the best possible option prior to the presentation of hypothetical cars or apartments. In addition, a comprehensive review of 16 experiments using a similar procedure found no support for the benefit of non-conscious thoughts (Newell & Rakow, 2011). Using Bayesian analysis, the evidence for the benefits of non-conscious thought in decision making was found to be very weak.

Nevertheless, Lufityanto and Pearson (2016) provided much stronger evidence for the superiority on intuition – as one of the outlets of non-conscious thoughts – under conditions where cognitive resources are fully occupied. They investigated whether giving irrelevant additional cognitive burdens, such as those induced by a working memory task, would attenuate accuracy in a concurrent sensory decision task. To test this, they conducted a study in which participants were instructed to retain a digit span from a working memory task, while performing a random dot motion task (RDM) which was presented concurrently with suppressed emotional images as illustrated in Figure 9.2 – following research design of their previous study (Lufityanto et al., 2016) with several modifications.

Further, Lufityanto and Pearson (2016) used the modified version of a digit span working memory task (Anderson et al., 1996) to induce various levels of cognitive load. The procedure of the experiment is illustrated in Figure 9.2. Participants were presented with a series of digits for a brief period of time and instructed to memorize them while performing the RDM task. After completing the task, participants were probed with a similar series of digits where only one number was changed. For instance, participants were presented with digits "7 6 5 4 6 4" in an initial array and were probed with "7 6 6 4 6 4" in a test array (see Figure 9.2). The third digit from the initial array of numbers (i.e., "5") was changed to one value higher ("6") in the later presentation. Participants were later instructed to guess whether the test digit array was higher or lower relative to the initial array by pressing certain keys on computer keyboard.

As for the result, Lufityanto and Pearson (2016) concluded that cognitive load modulates performance in intuitive decisions. They demonstrated that high cognitive loads induced by working memory tasks prompted more intuitive decisions in the RDM task relative to low cognitive loads. Please note that the participants retained eight-digit information in the high cognitive load condition and two-digit information in the low cognitive condition. Based on the preliminary study, it was found that retaining eight-digit information resulted in 75 per cent accuracy among participants. This overall finding supports the belief that intuition is more advantageous under conditions in which our cognitive resources are occupied with something else.

Further it was argued that low cognitive loads did not affect decisions to the same extent as high cognitive loads because participants might still have remaining cognitive resources committed to noisy sensory information in the RDM decision task. The prediction was based on a previous work by Lavie (2005) which showed that low

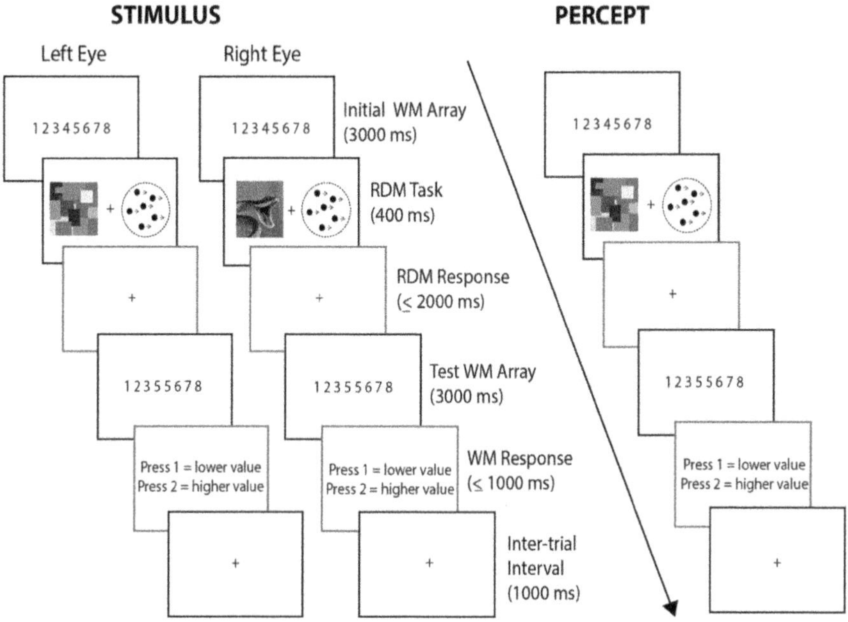

Notes: Participants were presented with an initial digit array that was intermixed between low and high cognitive load trials (i.e., 50 per cent each) for 3,000 ms, following the random dot motion (RDM) stimuli which were concurrently presented with suppressed emotional images for 400 ms. Participants then made decisions about the motion direction on the subsequent response window (up to 2,000 ms), followed by the presentation of a test digit array for 3,000 ms. Finally, the final response window was presented for up to 2,000 ms when participants indicated whether the test digit array was higher than the initial digit array (i.e., pressing key "2"), or lower (pressing key "1").
Source: Lufityanto et al., 2016.

Figure 9.2 *Procedure of the experiment combining a working memory task with a sensory decision task as employed in Lufityanto et al.'s (2016) study*

cognitive loads facilitated unrelated information to be processed simultaneously with target stimuli. In contrast, under high cognitive loads, decisions benefited more from non-conscious emotional information. People might already have occupied their cognitive resources in the high load working memory task, and therefore were less able to execute the RDM task well.

Intuition has been discussed largely in the context of decision making, however scholars have been intrigued by its position relative to other strategies of decision making. A recent study by Lufityanto and Pearson (2016) has shown that intuition is preferable under conditions in which the cognitive resource is restricted. Likewise in a situation where relevant information is not available, overwhelming information can lead to non-effective decisions if we rely only on rational thought. Intuition is therefore preferable under those non-ideal situations.

THE FUTURE CHALLENGE FOR STUDIES OF INTUITION

To sum up, there has been a debate among scholars whether the notion of intuition does exist and can be measured using more objective and tractable methodology (Hogarth, 2010). Using a technique commonly applied in psychophysical studies which enables perceptual consciousness manipulation in a simple decision making paradigm, we can design intuitive decision scenarios in the laboratory setting. The reported findings dovetail nicely with what most people have already believed about intuition characteristics: it is driven by emotion, operated in a non-deliberative and non-conscious fashion, and occurs rapidly (Hogarth, 2001; Myers, 2004).

Although a more objective experimental approach can be applied for studying intuition, the validity of this approach needs to be tested in more complex scenarios or in the natural setting. At least one study found that lateral intraparietal (LIP) activity is related to the process of accumulating evidence in RDM tasks (Shadlen & Newsome, 2001). Higher coherence of moving dots, meaning that the stimulus contains more evidence, gives rise to higher neural firing in the LIP area. Interestingly, the analogous brain area is active during more natural decision making in humans (Daw et al., 2006). Therefore, we can argue that findings using a simple perceptual task could provide insight into the mechanisms underlying more general decision making processes.

All the above-mentioned findings have indicated so far that physiology and psychology are fundamental elements in initiating intuitive decisions. Physiology refers to the individual's ability to capture emotional signals biologically, while psychology refers to what extent individuals utilize the emotional information to perform a task. To understand the phenomenon of intuition we should therefore take into account both physiological and psychological processes of non-conscious emotion – the fuel of intuition – for future research reference.

REFERENCES

Agor, W.H. 1987. The logic of intuition: How top executives make important decisions. *Organizational Dynamics*, 14(3): 5–18.

Almeida, J., Pajtas, P.E., Mahon, B.Z., Nakayama, K., & Caramazza, A. 2013. Affect of the unconscious: Visually suppressed angry faces modulate our decisions. *Cognitive, Affective, & Behavioral Neuroscience*, 13(1): 94–101.

Anderson, J.R., Reder, L.M., & Lebiere, C. 1996. Working memory: Activation limitations on retrieval. *Cognitive Psychology*, 30(3): 221–256.

Baddeley, A. 2003. Working memory: Looking back and looking forward. *Nature Reviews Neuroscience*, 4(10): 829–839.

Baddeley, A., Chincotta, D., & Adlam, A. 2001. Working memory and the control of action: Evidence from task switching. *Journal of Experimental Psychology: General*, 130(4): 641–657.

Bechara, A., & Damasio, A.R. 2005. The somatic marker hypothesis: A neural theory of economic decision. *Games and Economic Behavior*, 52(2): 336–372. doi: 10.1016/j.geb.2004.06.010.

Bechara, A., Damasio, H., Damasio, A.R., & Lee, G.P. 1999. Different contributions of the human amygdala and ventromedial prefrontal cortex to decision making. *Journal of Neuroscience*, 19(13): 5473–5481.

Bechara, A., Damasio, H., Tranel, D., & Damasio, A.R. 1997. Deciding advantageously before knowing the advantageous strategy. *Science*, 275(5304): 1293–1295.

Bechara, A., Tranel, D., & Damasio, H. 2000. Characterization of the decision making impairment of patients with bilateral lesions of the ventromedial prefrontal cortex. *Brain*, 123: 2189–2202.

Bennur, S., & Gold, J.I. 2011. Distinct representations of a perceptual decision and the associated oculomotor plan in the monkey lateral intraparietal area. *The Journal of Neuroscience*, 31(3): 913–921.

Billig, M. 2006. A psychoanalytic discursive psychology: From consciousness to unconsciousness. *Discourse Studies*, 8(1): 17–24.

Blake, R., & Logothetis, N.K. 2002. Visual competition. *Nature Review Neuroscience*, 3(1): 13–21.

Canas, J., Quesada, J., Antolí, A., & Fajardo, I. 2003. Cognitive flexibility and adaptability to environmental changes in dynamic complex problem-solving tasks. *Ergonomics*, 46(5): 482–501.

Daw, N.D., O'Doherty, J.P., Dayan, P., Seymour, B., & Dolan, R.J. 2006. Cortical substrates for exploratory decisions in humans. *Nature*, 441(7095): 876–879.

De Neys, W. 2006. Dual processing in reasoning two systems but one reasoner. *Psychological Science*, 17(5): 428–433.

Dijksterhuis, A. 2004. Think different: The merits of unconscious thought in preference development and decision making. *Journal of Personality and Social Psychology*, 87(5): 586–598.

Dijksterhuis, A., & Nordgren, L.F. 2006. A theory of unconscious thought. *Perspectives on Psychological Science*, 1(2): 95–109.

Engle, R.W. 2002. Working memory capacity as executive attention. *Current Directions in Psychological Science*, 11(1): 19–23.

Epstein, S. 1998. Cognitive-experiential self-theory. In D.F. Barone, M. Hersen, & V.B. Van Hasselt (Eds) *Advanced Personality*: 211–238. New York: Plenum Press.

Evans, J.S.B.T. 2008. Dual-processing accounts of reasoning, judgment, and social cognition. *Annual Review of Psychology*, 59: 255–278.

Gigerenzer, G. 2007. *Gut feelings. Shortcuts to better decision making*. New York: Penguin Books.

Gladwell, M. 2007. *Blink: The power of thinking without thinking*. New York: Hachette Digital.

Hackforth, R. 1972. *Plato: Phaedrus*. Cambridge: Cambridge University Press.

Hodgkinson, G.P., Sadler-Smith, E., Sinclair, M., & Ashkanasy, N.M. 2009. More than meets the eye? Intuition and analysis revisited. *Personality and Individual Differences*, 47(4): 342–346.

Hodgkinson, G.P., & Sadler-Smith, E. 2011. Investigating intuition: Beyond self-report. In M. Sinclair (Ed.) *Handbook of intuition research*: 52–66. Cheltenham, UK and Northampton, MA, USA: Edward Elgar Publishing.

Hogarth, R.M. 2001. *Educating intuition*. Chicago: The University of Chicago Press.

Hogarth, R.M. 2010. Intuition: A challenge for psychological research on decision making. *Psychological Inquiry*, 21: 338–353.

Khatri, N., & Ng, H.A. 2000. The role of intuition in strategic decision making. *Human Relations*, 53(1): 57–86.

Klein, G.A., Calderwood, R., & Clinton-Cirocco, A. 1986. *Rapid decision making on the fire ground*. Paper presented at the Proceedings of the Human Factors and Ergonomics Society annual meeting.

Lang, P.J., Bradley, M.M., & Cuthbert, B.N. 1990. Emotion, attention, and the startle reflex. *Psychological Review*, 97(3): 377–395.
Lassiter, G.D., Lindberg, M.J., González-Vallejo, C., Bellezza, F.S., & Phillips, N.D. 2009. The deliberation-without-attention effect evidence for an artifactual interpretation. *Psychological Science*, 20(6): 671–675.
Lavie, N. 2005. Distracted and confused? Selective attention under load. *Trends in Cognitive Sciences*, 9(2): 75–82.
Lavie, N., Hirst, A., De Fockert, J.W., & Viding, E. 2004. Load theory of selective attention and cognitive control. *Journal of Experimental Psychology: General*, 133(3): 339–354.
LePine, J.A., Colquitt, J.A., & Erez, A. 2000. Adaptability to changing task contexts: Effects of general cognitive ability, conscientiousness, and openness to experience. *Personnel Psychology*, 53(3): 563–593.
Liddell, B.J., Brown, K.J., Kemp, A.H., Barton, M.J., Das, P., Peduto, A., … Williams, L.M. 2005. A direct brainstem–amygdala–cortical alarm system for subliminal signals of fear. *Neuroimage*, 24(1): 235–243.
Logothetis, N.K., Leopold, D.A., & Sheinberg, D.L. 1996. What is rivaling during binocular rivalry? *Nature*, 380(6575): 621–624.
Lufityanto, G., Donkin, C., & Pearson, J. 2016. Measuring intuition nonconscious emotional information boosts decision accuracy and confidence. *Psychological Science*, 27(5): 622–634.
Lufityanto, G., & Pearson, J. 2016. *Decomposing intuition: Information process types modulate non-conscious emotional boast to decision making*. Paper presented at the Australasian Experimental Psychology Conference, Sydney, Australia, April.
Mikels, J.A., Maglio, S.J., Reed, A.E., & Kaplowitz, L.J. 2011. Should I go with my gut? Investigating the benefits of emotion-focused decision making. *Emotion*, 11(4): 743–753. doi: 10.1037/a0023986.
Myers, D.G. 2004. *Intuition. Its powers and perils*. New Haven: Yale University Press.
Myers, I.B., McCaulley, M.H., Quenk, N.L., & Hammer, A.L. 1998. *The MBTI® Manual: A guide to the development and use of the Myers–Briggs Type Indicator*. Palo Alto: Consulting Psychologists Press.
Newell, B.R., & Rakow, T. 2011. Revising beliefs about the merit of unconscious thought: Evidence in favor of the null hypothesis. *Social Cognition*, 29(6): 711–726.
Newell, B.R., & Shanks, D.R. 2014. Unconscious influences on decision making: A critical review. *Behavioral and Brain Sciences*, 37(1): 1–19.
Newsome, W.T. 1997. Deciding about motion: Linking perception to action. *Journal of Comparative Physiology*, 181(1): 5–12.
Pacini, R., & Epstein, S. 1999. The relation of rational and experiential information processing styles to personality, basic beliefs, and the ratio-bias phenomenon. *Journal of Personality and Social Psychology*, 76(6): 972–987.
Shadlen, M.N., & Kiani, R. 2013. Decision making as a window on cognition. *Neuron*, 80(3): 791–806.
Shadlen, M.N., & Newsome, W.T. 2001. Neural basis of a perceptual decision in the parietal cortex (area LIP) of the rhesus monkey. *Journal of Neurophysiology*, 86(4): 1916–1936.
Shirley, D.A., & Langan-Fox, J. 1996. Intuition: A review of the literature. *Psychological Reports*, 79(2): 563–584.
Sinclair, M., Ashkanasy, N.M., & Chattopadhyay, P. 2010. Affective antecedents of intuitive decision making. *Journal of Management & Organization*, 16: 382–398.
Sklar, A.Y., Levy, N., Goldstein, A., Mandel, R., Maril, A., & Hassin, R.R. 2012. Reading and doing arithmetic nonconsciously. *Proceedings of the National Academy of Sciences*, 109(48): 19614–19619. doi: 10.1073/pnas.1211645109.

Stein, T., Hebart, M.N., & Sterzer, P. 2011. Breaking continuous flash suppression: A new measure of unconscious processing during interocular suppression? *Frontiers in Human Neuroscience*, 5: 167.

Stolper, E., van Royen, P., & Dinant, G.J. 2010. The 'sense of alarm' ('gut feeling') in clinical practice. A survey among European general practitioners on recognition and expression. *The European Journal of General Practice*, 16(2): 72–74.

Tamietto, M., & de Gelder, B. 2010. Neural bases of the non-conscious perception of emotional signals. *Nature Neuroscience*, 11: 697–709.

Tsuchiya, N., & Koch, C. 2005. Continuous flash suppression reduces negative afterimages. *Nature Neuroscience*, 8(8): 1096–1101.

Vuilleumier, P., Armony, J., Clarke, K., Husain, M., Driver, J., & Dolan, R. 2002. Neural response to emotional faces with and without awareness: Event-related fMRI in a parietal patient with visual extinction and spatial neglect. *Neuropsychologia*, 40(12): 2156–2166.

Westcott, M.R. 1968. *Toward a contemporary psychology of intuition*. New Jersey: Holt, Rinehart, and Winston.

Zajonc, R.B. 1980. Feeling and thinking: Preferences need no inferences. *American Psychologist*, 35(2): 151–175.

10. Exploring intuition and decision-making across the 'three brains'

Grant Soosalu and Suzanne Henwood

Decision theorists have for some time promoted a twofold approach to decision-making within academic studies. The dual processes are intuitive (System 1) and analytical (System 2), offering two quite different approaches to information processing and ways of thinking. The analytical system has been widely accepted to process information consciously by different functions of the brain. Similarly, the non-conscious intuitive system has largely been seen as one entity, but more recent research suggests that there are at least two quite discrete entities within intuition: located broadly in the heart region and gut region. It is also now clear that we have two separable complex neural adaptive networks in the heart and gut, both of which are shown to play a significant part in decision-making (Armour, 2007; Damasio, 1999; Gershon, 1999).

This chapter will explore other levels of specificity within embodied cognition and intuition utilized in decision-making, with discussion around the separable interoceptive components from the key neural plexuses of the cardiac and enteric regions. Sharing the results of a study to design and validate a tri-brain decision-making tool to establish systemic preference in decision-making, we aim to offer greater theoretical and empirical specificity for the field of decision-making research and propose that researchers begin examining head, heart *and* gut preferences in decision-making mode or style. This differentiated approach will then be applied, through practical case studies, in the disciplines of leadership and teams.

ESTABLISHING THE EXISTENCE OF THE CARDIAC AND ENTERIC NETWORKS

This brief section offers some insight into the key thoughts in the field of cardiac and enteric networks. It is not designed to be a thesis on the two networks, but demonstrates current thinking of the global leaders in each area of practice, to provide an opportunity to further explore this field of knowledge for those who are not yet familiar with it.

What is the Intrinsic Cardiac Network?

Andrew Armour (2007) has shown that the intrinsic neural network in and around the heart is complex, functional and adaptive. We now know that there are numerous heart ganglia, which contain concentrations of neurons and that these communicate with each other to form a complex network that some authors call a second brain. As a result of this research in medicine, the new field of neurocardiology has evolved, working with the heart as a functional 'brain' to express the interplay of the nervous and cardiovascular systems.

While the heart cannot function in the same way as a head brain, Armour (2007) has shown that the heart has the ability to learn independently, store memories and feel and sense information. This information is then sent to the head brain via afferent nerve fibres, which – once they have distributed it to higher brain centres – have an influence on our unique perspective on reality, decision-making, as well as a range of cognitive processing functions and autonomic regulation.

Gomes Silva (2014: 97) quoting current research states that:

> Recent scientific research suggests that consciousness emerges from the brain and body acting together. A growing body of evidence suggests that the heart plays a particular significant role in this process. Far more than a simple pump, the heart, now is recognized by scientists, as a highly complex system with its own functional brain.

It is clear then that the role of the heart in decision-making is worthy of deeper exploration.

What is the Enteric Neural Plexus?

Dr Michael Gershon (1999) in his seminal work describing the enteric neural plexus, which runs from oral cavity to anus, has heralded a rediscovery of work undertaken by Byron Robinson in 1907, who described both an abdominal and pelvic brain. Indeed in both Gershon's and Robinson's work the gut is described as the 'second brain'. However, it could be argued that the gut brain is actually the first of the three brains, as it develops first in both evolutionary and embryological terms prior to heart and head brains in utero.

As with the heart brain, it has been shown that the gut can work independently from the head brain (Gershon, 1999; Goldstein et al., 2013). And, just like with the heart brain, experts demonstrated that the gut brain influences head-based affective information processing, motivation, higher cognitive functioning and intuitive decision-making (Berntson et al., 2003; Holzer, 2017). Again, based on these findings a new field of medicine has evolved: neurogastroenterology, which is now changing the way gut health is treated.

The literature is clear then that both heart and gut play a role in decision-making and should be considered as separate entities in their own right. Hammond (1990) suggests that the proportion of the different components may vary across different contexts, different roles and different types of decision-making, but without conscious awareness of the role of each component, it would be very difficult for individuals to change their decision-making at will to optimize their own performance.

ESTABLISHING THE ROLE OF THREE BRAINS IN DECISION-MAKING

If we accept then that the heart and gut have a role to play in decision-making, it opens up questions around what role specifically. If we look at some examples of this, a pattern starts emerging. In one animal-based study Klarer et al. (2014) investigated the impact of cutting the vagus nerve in rats in relation to anxiety and fear responses and decision-making. Rats who had had the vagus nerve cut were no longer able to respond normally to gut-based fear stimuli, with a significant effect on behaviours and decision-making.

A number of researchers have demonstrated the value of enhancing perception at the heart level, to improve higher level decision-making. For example, Dunn et al. (2010: 1835) suggest that bodily responses are 'pivotal' variables in emoting and intuiting and highlight how cognitive-affective processing follows the heart. And Mayer (2011) suggests that there is an actual neurological basis for someone making a decision on gut feelings and links this to interoceptive memories. Craig (2015) asserts that interoceptive awareness (the ability to sense the internal state of the body) is fundamental to being able to identify the physiological reactions that lead to the integration of somatic sensation, cognitive processing and emotional feeling. There is clearly support for head, heart and gut being seen as interconnected and interdependent and therefore in any model assessing decision-making, we propose that all components need to be taken into account.

It is interesting to note that some authors already promote a tri-brain model of decision-making: head (logic and rational thinking), heart (emotions) and gut (intuition) (e.g., Sadler & Zeidler, 2005) and suggest that each individual has a different 'pattern' or combination of the use of these three systems in practice. Indeed, it is highly likely that the different brains play a role in different aspects of decision-making. This is a key theory underpinning the work in mBraining that measures the role of head, heart and gut in decision-making by means of the newly developed Multiple Brain Preference Questionnaire (MBPQ: Soosalu et al., 2019).

One discipline where the interaction of head, heart and gut is being promoted is leadership. Dotlich et al. (2006) claim that the use of all three neural systems enhances wisdom and effectiveness in decision-making. Similarly, Heifetz and Linsky (2004) demonstrate the importance of the use of heart and gut alongside the head in decision-making with respect to 'adaptive' or wicked problems. It is clear then that some authors believe that "human decisions and actions are much more influenced by intuition and emotional responses than it was previously thought" (Markič, 2009: 54).

While scientific research has established that each human has three brains, it is also known that the ability to perceive the internal functions of the three brains varies considerably from person to person. This is called interoceptive awareness, which is a competency that can be enhanced through directionalized embodied learning. Some interesting work has been done in this area, for example, one study found that people with a higher interoceptive awareness ability reported heightened emotional experiences (Wiens et al., 2000). It is also likely that people with this 'trait' would pay more attention to their heart signals in many areas, including decision-making. Interoceptive awareness is not only relevant to the heart. From a gut brain perspective, Riezzo and colleagues (1996) demonstrated a link between gut interoceptive awareness and stress. A human ability to perceive the function of the multiple brains then may play a pivotal role in decision-making in practice. Fetterman and Robinson (2013) went even further and linked a person's perceived sense of self to either head or heart, and showed a correlation between where a sense of self was located and the preferred information processing and decision-making styles.

Previous Reliance on a Two-Factor Model

Up until now, much of the decision-making literature has combined heart and gut into one domain of 'intuition'. Through the field of mBraining (Soosalu & Oka, 2012), we have been exploring a model with greater specificity, where cardiac and enteric nervous systems are treated as unique and distinguished 'brains', or adaptive neural systems, in their own right.

Drawing on conclusions from previous studies, we might pose a question such as: "How likely would you be to make this decision based on your immediate *feelings* or *gut reaction* to the situation?" (Weber & Lindemann, 2008: 199). Then research would need to separate the heart-based feelings from the gut reactions. In some studies, while each individual question was discrete to heart or gut, the questions were then grouped into an overall subsection called intuition (or affective decision category), and statistically they were not treated separately. This approach was taken, for example, by Betsch (2008: 246), compounding answers to such questions as: "My *feelings* play an important role in my decisions", and "When it comes to trusting people, I can usually rely on my *gut feelings*."

Interestingly, earlier studies by Betsch (2004) had shown that individual preferences for analytical versus intuitive decision-making appeared to be stronger than any shift for contextual orientation. This finding supports the notion that individuals can have a preference for a specific domain they use in decision-making. However, we may do the field of study an injustice by oversimplifying decision-making to two factors.

Sadler-Smith (2016) is one author who has attempted to split 'bodily awareness' into gut intuitions versus emotional feelings. And Böhm and Brun (2008) also reported the need to separate intuition from affect. In mBraining we use head, heart and gut as three discrete components. Indeed, building on their previous work, Soosalu et al. (2019) have been developing a psychometric tool to assess head, heart and gut preferences in decision-making, while wholly acknowledging the interconnected and interrelated nature of the three brains working in one complex system.

The Multiple Brain Preference Questionnaire (MBPQ) showed three reliable factors in line with the prime functions of the three brains as outlined in Soosalu and Oka (2012). Gut feeling around safety (one form of intuition), for example, is very different from heart-based emotions and experiencing, and both components can impact on decision-making in different ways. We propose then a "neurologically informed three-factor model of head, heart and gut" (Soosalu et al., 2019).

Is the Model Affected by Gender?

There is some support that men and women have different preferences in decision-making. Fetterman and Robinson (2013) suggest that more women choose the heart than men and Norris and Epstein (2011) concluded men prefer a more rational approach. Likewise, Sinclair and colleagues (2010) claim that females can access intuition more easily. Conversely, some authors suggest that there is no consistent agreement as to the differences between men and women in decision-making in relation to risk or quality of decisions made (Powell & Ansic, 1997). The use of the two-factor model, which does not focus on heart as discrete from gut in decision-making, may further complicate the critical review of such studies and contribute to the lack of definitive data in this area. We attempted to address this discrepancy when designing the MBPQ. When we collected data on gender with the instrument, we did find that men had lower heart scores than women, but no significant difference was demonstrated in terms of gut scores (Soosalu et al., 2019).

PRACTICAL APPLICATION OF THE THREE-BRAIN MODEL TO LEADERSHIP AND TEAMS

It is claimed in leadership that wise decision-making requires a balance of head, heart and gut (Dotlich et al., 2006), yet only 4 per cent of the sample (n=301) in Soosalu et al.'s study (2019) showed such a balance. The sample, recruited from voluntary participants, was predominantly female (60 males and 241 females, age ranging from 19 to 85 years). Participants were from 20 countries (the majority, 48.5 per cent, from New Zealand) and the sample was therefore not representative of any particular population.

While ethics and morals in decision-making was not the focus of the study, it is interesting to note that Zhong (2011) claims that head-focused decision-making can lead to deception and unethical behaviours, as well as a decrease in altruism. Feinberg and colleagues (2012) also showed an issue with moral judgements when head dominates. In response to that, Egorov et al. (2018) recently highlighted the need for consideration of emotional intuition and Haidt (2001: 814) claims that "moral intuition is a kind of cognition, but it is not a kind of reasoning" and that it is an interpersonal process (thereby also implying the need for heart inclusion). Haidt's work highlights the difference between head-based cognitive reasoning and more intuitive somatic 'knowing'. Mathieson (2007) argues that the complexity of moral decision-making makes it more likely that an integrated approach will be used, rather than any one system being dominant, which implies that there will be a natural tendency to use the multiple components of intelligence in decision-making. For a greater insight into this area, Guzak and Hargrove (2011) offer a good review on the role of intuition in ethical decision-making and allude to the differential of heart and gut intuition. Interestingly though, Soosalu and colleagues (2019) showed that people are not always aware of their own decision-making strategy and may thus not be aware of what aspects of decision-making are in play at any one time.

The three-factor model is still in its infancy in relation to decision-making. In order to explore it in more depth here, the following case studies are offered to highlight some of the coaching and leadership explorations of the three-factor model in practice, illustrating the impact it had on the teams and leaders involved.

The Head, Heart and Gut of Workplace Health and Safety

In 2016, the Northwest Rapid Transit fast-rail project, an $8 billion Australian rail infrastructure project comprising nearly 10,000 workers and involving the construction of 23 km of new rail infrastructure with eight new railway stations, car parking facilities and installation of signalling, mechanical and electrical systems, was rolled out utilizing the mBraining Head, Heart, Gut (HHG) model as the basis for its Workplace Health and Safety (WHS) programme. This included using the MBPQ instrument as part of a series of WHS workshops delivered by TCL Consulting (Morrison et al., 2018) to help leaders at all levels of the project understand their HHG decision-making preferences and to build a team culture that highlighted and accepted the importance of embodied intuitive signals in safety decisions. There is a growing acknowledgement of the importance and need for paying mindful attention to intuitive embodied 'gut feel' signals in health, risk and safety contexts (for example, see Resnik, 2017; Klockner, 2013; Gerber, 2001; Rosanoff, 1999). In evaluating the results of the WHS MBPQ-based programme, the Programme Infrastructure Director, David Jackson, provided the following feedback:

> All my senior and team leaders have completed the Multiple Brain Preference Questionnaire (MBPQ) as part of the Leading Edge No Harm NRTIJV Safety Biotic Leadership program which was rolled across the project in 2016/17. I personally found the survey very useful as it gave me a new perspective on how I and others make decisions with regard to our "head, heart and gut" when leading our teams. It also led to important insights on how others (contractors/stakeholders) make decisions, leading to greater understanding that has helped joint problem-solving and enhanced collaboration. I recommend this survey to any organisation wishing to extend their leadership by looking at themselves and their team members from a different perspective. (Jackson, 2018)

Team Project Leadership and the MBPQ

The MBPQ was also utilized across a series of four major Australian public utility infrastructure projects involving both contractor organizations and the principal utility organization (name withheld for anonymity) contracting them for infrastructure work. The client organization has over $2.7 billion worth of water infrastructure assets in Australia and supplies water to over 300,000 permanent residents over 8,100 square kilometres (Ahiaga-Dagbui et al., 2018). Each project focused on team coaching and facilitation utilizing monthly project leadership programme workshops that examined team intelligence and how it linked to individual neural preferences to access head, heart and gut intelligence. Each team member then explored their personal actions with their like role partners between the organizations and shared any insights back to the group. Common themes presented back were the experience of: tuning into intuitive micro signals, seeking to understand more and the subsequent enhanced communication and team performance. Across the extended time period of the projects, teams reported significantly higher levels of communication, team planning and execution.

At the beginning and end of the project teams scored both themselves and other organization partners across five key project success metrics:

1. Commitment to open communication and respectful relationships.
2. Listening to and considering everyone's perspective and opinion.
3. Timely and well-planned works with adequate controls in place.
4. Positive joint Safety, Quality and Environment (SQE) leadership and reporting.
5. Celebrating key milestones collectively and recognizing positive performance.

Scores of self versus other were averaged and compared from *Before* (at first workshop) to *After* (at final workshop) and produced an overall average across four major projects of a 20 per cent increase in scores across all of the five success metrics. In addition, a survey was undertaken of all project team members by researchers from Deakin University to evaluate the effectiveness of the project facilitation. Results showed that overall the members rated the question item 'Usefulness of understanding brain preference scores', on a scale of 0 to 5, as having a score of 4.2, and 'Effectiveness of workshops for honest communication' as having a score of 4.5 (Ahiaga-Dagbui et al., 2018). As indicative of the success of the facilitation process, the following is an example of a typical feedback from project team members: "The facilitated workshops were a valuable tool that formed a big part of the overall project success. They fostered an open and honest workplace that enabled all facets of the project to be dealt with efficiently" (Ahiaga-Dagbui et al., 2018: 10).

Individual Coaching Using the MBPQ

The MBPQ was also utilized in the same large public utility infrastructure organization in one-on-one leadership coaching. Coaching was performed by John Morrison of Frontline Coach Pty Ltd, an Australian Coaching Services organization trained in the use of the MBPQ. The following two case studies show successful indicative use of the MBPQ in one-on-one leadership coaching.

On the MBPQ, JS, a team leader, had a very high head score with much lower heart and gut scores. His reported challenges in leading his team were that he struggled to engage with his team and as a leader was slow to make decisions, often over-thinking the decisions and struggling to take timely action. Coaching was undertaken to help him explore his preferences, strengths and opportunities for growth. He was tasked with connecting more deeply with heart-based prime functions and competencies and with putting less focus on head-based preferences. Over a period of nine months, undergoing monthly one-on-one coaching sessions, JS significantly increased his team leadership engagement scores and his MBPQ profile on retest showed a lowering of head score and an increase in both heart and gut scores, demonstrating his shift away from an over-thinking cognitive style to a more heart and gut experiential processing preference. This result is in line with the theories outlined in this chapter and the need for a balanced reliance on head, heart and gut in leadership and in decision-making. There were clear objective benefits of ensuring a more integrated approach in practice.

GM, a team leader who had taken over a new team, was finding it difficult to lead and incredibly challenging to construe effective leadership processes and decisions. GM had taken the MBPQ two years earlier in an SQE leadership training with her infrastructure colleagues and recorded a relatively even balance across head, heart and gut scores with heart as the strongest of the three scores. When she retook the MBPQ prior to her first coaching session her brain preference scores had changed with her heart score dropping slightly to be the same as her head score and her gut score dropping lower than the other two scores. In exploring GM's detailed response scores it was uncovered that a number of gut items were scored exceptionally low and she admitted that these gut prime functions had been impacted by her interactions with her new team. As a result she was experiencing her inability to connect with team members at the heart level, which was not the case previously in her career; this in turn impacted her current gut level engagement. GM was coached how to better set boundaries and manage a difficult team more effectively. Over the coaching period her scores on leadership performance increased substantially, and she reported being much more at ease when dealing with her team and setting appropriate boundaries and team behaviours.

When summarizing his experience with the MBPQ in coaching, Morrison (2018) reported that "The MBPQ has provided a profound platform to open up the coaching conversation enabling coachees to gain deeper insights into the way they make decisions and influence others." Overall, we have found that the ability to separate head, heart and gut processes and preferences, in practical application to leadership decision-making and workplace safety decisions, provided participants with valuable insights. Individuals, teams and organizations as a whole appear to appreciate and value the opening up of decision-making processes to a more fine-grained set of head, heart and gut distinctions.

MOVING FORWARD

While there are clearly some areas of further research that would be highly beneficial, the MBPQ instrument appears to be a useful new research and coaching tool and we hope that the sharing of both our theoretical research and the action research translated into practical application of the three-brain model brings fresh directions to ongoing work in the field of intuition in decision-making.

REFERENCES

Ahiaga-Dagbui, D., Tokede, O., Morrison, J., & Juffermans, T. 2018. *Coaching the team towards high-performance – facilitation for infrastructure delivery*. Paper presented at the ICEC-PAQS Conference, 18 November, Sydney, Australia.

Armour, J. 2007. The little brain on the heart. *Cleveland Clinic Journal of Medicine*, 74: S48–S51.

Berntson, G., Sarter, M., & Cacioppo, J. 2003. Ascending visceral regulation of cortical affective information processing. *European Journal of Neuroscience*, 18(8): 2103–2109.

Betsch, C. 2004. Preference for intution and deliberation (PID): An inventory for assessing affect- and cognition-based decision-making. *Zeitschrift für Differentielle und Diagnostische Psychologie*, 25: 179–197.

Betsch, C. 2008. Chronic preferences for intuition and deliberation. In H. Plessner, C. Betsch, & T. Betsch (Eds), *Intuition in judgement and decision making*: 231–248. Mahwah, NJ: Lawrence Erlbaum.

Böhm, G., & Brun, W. 2008. Intuition and affect in risk perception and decision making. *Judgment and Decision Making*, 3(1): 1–4.

Craig, A.D. 2015. *How do you feel? An interoceptive moment with your neurobiological self.* Princeton, NJ: Princeton University Press.

Damasio, A. 1999. *The feeling of what happens: Body and emotion in the making of consciousness*. New York: Harcourt Brace.

Dotlich, D., Cairo, P., & Rhinesmith, S. 2006. *Head, heart & guts – how the world's best companies develop complete leaders*. Hoboken, NJ: Wiley.

Dunn, B., Galton, H., Morgan, R., Evans, D., Oliver, C., Meyer, M., … Dalgleish, T. 2010. Listening to your heart: How interoception shapes emotion experience and intuitive decision making. *Psychological Science*, 21(12): 1835–1844.

Egorov, M., Verdorfer, P.A., & Peus, C. 2018. Taming the emotional dog: Moral intuition and ethically-oriented leader development. *Journal of Business Ethics*, 160(3): 817–834, https://doi.org/10.1007/s10551-018-3876-4.

Feinberg, M., Willer, R., Antonenko, O., & John, O. 2012. Liberating reason from the passions: Overriding intuitinist moral judgements through emotion reappraisal. *Psychological Science*, 23(7): 788–795.

Fetterman, A., & Robinson, M. 2013. Do you use your head or follow your heart? Self location predicts personality, emotion, decision making and performance. *Journal of Personality and Social Pscyhology*, 105(2): 316–334.

Gerber, R. 2001. The concept of common sense in workplace learning and experience. *Education + Training*, 43(2): 72–81, https://doi.org/10.1108/EUM0000000005424.

Gershon, M. 1999. *The second brain – a groundbreaking new understanding of nervous disorders of the stomach and intestine*. New York: Harper Perennial.

Goldstein, A., Hofstra, R., & Burns, A. 2013. Building a brain in the gut: Development of the enteric nervous system. *Clinical Genetics*, 83(4): 307–316.

Gomes Silva, S. 2014. *Engaging touch and movement in somatic experiencing trauma resolution approach*. Retrieved 14 May 2019, from Trauma Healing: https://traumahealing.org/wp-content/uploads/2016/04/engaging-touch-and-movement-in-se-trama-resolution-approach-dissertation-bySoniaGomes-2014.pdf.

Guzak, J.R., & Hargrove, M.B. 2011. The role of intuition in ethical decision making. In M. Sinclair (Ed.), *Handbook of intuition research*: 97–108. Cheltenham, UK and Northampton, MA, USA: Edward Elgar Publishing.
Haidt, J. 2001. The emotional dog and its rational tail: A social intuitionist approach to moral judgment. *Psychological Review*, 108(4): 814–834.
Hammond, K.R. 1990. Intuitive and analytical cognition. Information models. In A.P. Sage (Ed.), *Concise encyclopedia of information processing in systems and organizations*: 301–312. Oxford: Pergamon Press.
Heifetz, R.A., & Linksy, M. 2004. When leadership spells danger. *Educational Leadership*, 61(7): 33–37.
Holzer, P. 2017. Interoception and gut feelings: Unconscious body signals' impact on brain function, behavior and belief processes. In H.-F. Angel, L. Olviedo, R.F. Paloutzian, & A.L.C. Runehov (Eds), *Process of believing: The acquisition, maintenance, and change in creditions*: 435–442. Basel, Switzerland: Springer.
Jackson, D. 2018. *mBIT brain preference survey, senior leader testimonial*. Private email communication, with permission for public dissemination.
Klarer, M., Arnold, M., Gunther, L., Winter, C., Langhans, W., & Meyer, U. 2014. Gut vagal afferents differentially modulate innate anxiety and learned fear. *The Journal of Neuroscience*, 34(21): 7067–7076.
Klockner, H. 2013. *Keeping my mind on the job: The role of mindfulness in workplace safety*. Paper presented at the 1st International Conference on Mindfulness, May, Rome, Italy.
Markič, O. 2009. Rationality and emotions in decision making. *Interdisciplinary Description of Complex Systems*, 7(2): 54–64.
Mathieson, K. 2007. Towards a design science of ethical decision support, *Journal of Business Ethics*, 76: 269–292.
Mayer, E. 2011. Gut feelings: The emerging biology of gut–brain communication. *Nature Reviews Neuroscience*, 12(8): 453–466.
Morrison, J. 2018. *Use of MBPQ in leadership coaching practice*. Private email communication, with permission for public dissemination.
Morrison, J., Fitzgerald, T., & Towan, G. 2018. Safety biotic: Authentic safety leadership. Northwest Rapid Transit. *TCL Consulting Workbook*. Melbourne, Australia.
Norris, P., & Epstein, S. 2011. An experiential thinking style: Its facets and relations with objective and subjective criterion measures. *Journal of Personality*, 79: 1044–1080.
Powell, M., & Ansic, D. 1997. Gender differences in risk behavior in financial decision making. An experimental analysis. *Journal of Economic Psychology*, 18: 605–628.
Resnik, D.B. 2017. The role of intuition in risk/benefit decision-making in human subjects research. *Accountability in Research*, 24(1): 1–29.
Riezzo, G., Porcelli, P., Guerra, V., & Giorgio, I. 1996. Effects of different psychophysiological stressors on the cutaneous electrogastrogram in healthy subjects. *Archives of Physiology and Biochemistry*, 104(3): 282–286.
Robinson, B. 1907. *The abdominal and pelvic brain with autonomic visceral ganglia*. Chicago, IL: Franz Betz Hammond Ind.
Rosanoff, N. 1999. Intuition comes of age: Workplace applications of intuitive skill for occupational and environmental health nurses. *Workplace Health & Safety*, 47(4): 156–162.
Sadler, T., & Zeidler, D. 2005. Patterns of informal reasoning in the context of socioscientific decision-making. *Journal of Research in Science Teaching*, 42(1): 112–138.
Sadler-Smith, E. 2016. What happens when you intuit? Understanding human resource practitioners' subjective experience of intuition through a novel linguistic method. *Human Relations*, 69(5): 1069–1093.
Sinclair, M., Ashkanasy, N., & Chattopadhyay, P. 2010. Affective antecedents of intuitive decision making. *Journal of Management and Organization*, 16: 382–398.

Soosalu, G., Henwood, S., & Deo, A. 2019. Head, heart and gut in decision-making: Development of a Multiple Brain Preference Questionnaire (MBPQ). *Sage Open*, doi: 10.1177/2158244019837439.

Soosalu, G., & Oka, M. 2012. *mBraining: Using your multiple brains to do cool stuff.* Australia: Timebinding Publications.

Weber, E., & Lindemann, P. 2008. From intuition to analysis: Making decisions with your head, your heart, or by the book. In H. Plessner, C. Betsch, & T. Betsch (Eds), *Intuition in judgement and decision making*: 191–207. Mahwah, NJ: Lawrence Erlbaum.

Wiens, S., Mezzacappa, E., & Katkin, E. 2000. Heartbeat detection and the experience of emotions. *Cognition and Emotion*, 14(3): 417–427.

Zhong, C. 2011. The ethical dangers of deliberative decision making. *Administrative Science Quarterly*, 56: 1–25.

11. Are all intuitions the same? Or does it depend on the factor that triggers them?

Marta Sinclair

This chapter discusses the results of a web-based study examining the decision-making processes of strategic decision-makers, and when they subconsciously resort to reasoning or intuition. It is an area that received the attention of management theorists and practitioners because of the impact of strategic decisions on organizational performance (e.g., Khatri & Ng, 2000; Miller & Ireland, 2005; Woiceshyn, 2009). Since this type of decision-making deals frequently with ambiguous problems and uncertain outcomes while facing time pressure, inadequate information, and fast-paced change, which are conditions conducive to intuiting (Sinclair et al., 2002), it has been established that integrating reasoning and intuition could yield superior results (Burke & Miller, 1999; Williams, 2012). Extensive research has been conducted about rational decision-making, however, we need to know more about the intuitive process and what triggers it as opposed to reasoning.

Although recent years have seen more fine-grained research into various facets of intuition, not much is known about factors facilitating or impeding its use. Similarly, theory suggests that intuition is a multifaceted construct (Pretz & Totz, 2007; Sinclair & Ashkanasy, 2005) but the activation of specific components of intuition during decision-making remains to be mapped. In response to these deficiencies, the reported study evaluates the effects of dispositional and contextual factors on the choice of a decision-making process, and the role of affect prior to and during the process.

A number of researchers theorized about possible effects of various factors on the use of intuition versus reasoning. However, there has not been a concerted effort to organize these into a coherent, all-encompassing model until recently (see Sinclair et al., 2002). Moreover, with the exception of cognitive style (Bakken & Hærem, Chapter 2 in this handbook), most assumptions have not been tested empirically. In response to this void, Daniel Kahneman (2003) urged management scholars to explore the antecedent stage of intuitive processing in more depth. In their decision-making model based on dual processing, Sinclair and her colleagues identified three categories of determinants: personal disposition, decision-making context, and affective factors. The presence of affect in the intuition process has been established to a degree (Dane & Pratt, 2007; Sadler-Smith, 2008) but it is yet to be determined whether affect is an integral part of the construct or merely accompanies it (Sinclair, 2010). In an attempt to shed more light on the relationship, this study investigates its two specific aspects: the antecedent role of affect in facilitating the use of intuition or reasoning, and the involvement of affective (vs. cognitive) components of intuitive processing itself. And since levels of affect-related variables have been reported to be higher in women (Booth-Butterfield & Booth-Butterfield, 1990), the study also examines whether there is a gender difference.

DEFINING INTUITION

For the purpose of this research, intuition is defined as 'direct knowing that results from non-conscious, holistic information processing, which draws on cognition and affect' (see Sinclair et al., 2010). This is consistent with the understanding of intuition as a non-conscious, quick pattern recognition and synthesis of past experience and domain-specific expertise (Isenberg, 1984; Simon, 1987). The holistic or non-sequential nature of processing refers to the way information is scanned and retrieved (Raidl & Lubart, 2001). Consequently, as Sinclair and Ashkanasy (2005: 357) suggest, "intuitive processing could be likened to a non-conscious scanning of internal (in memory) and external (in environment) resources in a non-logical, non-temporal manner in order to identify relevant pieces of information that are fitted into the 'solution picture' in a seemingly haphazard way, similar to assembling a jigsaw puzzle." This cognitive perspective has received most attention of intuition researchers so far, focusing on the so-called experience-based type of intuition that draws on tacit knowledge accumulated through experience (e.g., Behling & Eckel, 1991), although the produced information may emerge into consciousness accompanied by affect (e.g., Dane & Pratt, 2007; Sadler-Smith, 2008).

A growing number of conceptualizations started including also affective elements (e.g., Epstein et al., 1996; Petitmengin, 1999; Pretz & Totz, 2007), although their specific function in the intuitive process requires further clarification (Epstein, 2010). In one stream of research, 'affectively charged judgments' (Dane & Pratt, 2007) appear to be retrieved by means of emotionally coded 'somatic markers' (see Damasio, 1994) where the intensity of affect is regulated by the newness of the experienced situation (Bechara, 2004). With repeated activations, the affective link becomes weaker as the feedback is produced cognitively in the working memory (see Sadler-Smith et al., 2008). Both instances represent retrieval of existing schemas of the so-called experience-based or 'expert intuition' (Crossan et al., 1999). A different, more affect-based mechanism seems to be involved in what Crossan and her colleagues labeled 'entrepreneurial intuition.' There, affect-laden attention helps the decision-maker focus on the task while a strong desire (affect-infused intention) triggers intuitive information processing (see Bradley, Chapter 15 in this handbook). Since this mechanism appears to utilize a distinct process, the reported study explores whether the experience-based and affect-based components of intuition may be activated by different factors.

FACTORS INFLUENCING THE CHOICE OF A DECISION-MAKING PROCESS

As suggested by Isenberg (1984) and a number of other researchers (e.g., Burke & Miller, 1999; Williams, 2012), decision-makers tend to switch subconsciously between two modes of information processing. According to the Cognitive-Experiential Self-Theory (CEST: Epstein, 1990), humans process information in parallel: using conscious reasoning and mostly non-conscious experiential processing, which is closely linked to intuition. According to CEST, rational and experiential systems function in a complementary fashion beyond awareness, while each mode supports a different decision-making approach, suitable for a different type of problem solving. Analysis, logic and other types of reasoning are associated with the rational mode that is intentional, mostly verbal, and relatively affect-free. Intuition (as part of the experiential system), on the other hand, is automatic, preconscious, holistic, associationistic, primarily non-verbal, and related to affect (Epstein et al., 1996). It tends to be utilized until a need for conscious processing is activated (Smerek, 2014). Epstein and his colleagues argue that experiential-intuitive mode uses affect as cue for action but their model does not elaborate how it might be linked to intuition. In this respect, the Affect Infusion Model (AIM: Forgas, 1995) offers a plausible explanation. It suggests that the involvement of affect varies according to the type and context of the problem. The model implies that positive mood will facilitate access to intuition while negative mood should block it (and enforce reliance on reasoning). Similarly, intense emotions can act in this dual capacity as a facilitator of intuition (if applied to reinforce the affective charge of the intention) or as an inhibitor (if the decision-maker gets absorbed by the emotion itself) (see Sinclair et al., 2002). Therefore, as Thompson (1967) postulated, decision-makers can benefit from consciously matching their approach with decision-tasks and situation. In order to do so properly, it is necessary to identify first the determinants of each decision-making process. As a starting point, the reported study focused on personal characteristics of the decision-maker in terms of disposition and context.

Personal disposition seems to play a major role in decision-making. Personal differences emerged as important factors from research into experiential information processing conducted by Epstein and his colleagues (1996). Similarly, Cappon (1994) and more recently Betsch (2008) highlighted personality as one of the determinants of an individual's intuitive capacity. Among the personality traits and attitudes that emerged from the literature, five factors seem to affect the choice between rational and intuitive decision-making: (1) cognitive style, (2) attitude to intuition, (3) affective orientation, (4) creativity, and (5) risk tolerance (see Sinclair et al., 2002, for a detailed discussion of each variable).

The role of context in decision-making has been discussed by a number of researchers as well. For example, Raidl and Lubart (2001) concluded that intuitive preference might depend on the specific context. This notion, however, appears to be rather broad. Dane and Pratt (2007) distinguish between factors related to domain knowledge (which seem to be aligned with our understanding of expert intuition) and to the performed task (representing a wider range of contextual factors). Sinclair et al. (2002) proposed a more fine-grained differentiation, grouping variables according to characteristics of the problem, characteristics of the decision, environment of the organization, and personal perceptions of the decision-making situation. The contextual factors at this stage of research are limited to situational personal variables that can be induced by external or internal context. For instance, time pressure may be exerted on decision-makers by the work environment or by their personal problems. In this respect, the literature suggests three types of factors: (1) time pressure, (2) stress, and (3) affective states (represented in the study by mood as the most commonly experienced affect in work settings, see Elsbach & Barr, 1999).

There is also an open question whether the use of intuition may vary for each gender. While some earlier management research supports the commonly held belief that women are more intuitive than men (Agor, 1984), seconded by later physiological findings (Tressoldi et al., 2010), results of other studies have been conflicting. Fisher and Nelson (1996), for example, reported that female executives used a more intuitive approach than their male counterparts, while Taggart and his colleagues (1997) did not find any difference in this respect. Evolutionary theory (see Lieberman, 2000; DePaulo, 1992), however, implies that the decision-making process could be influenced by a different role of affect for males and females. A further investigation is therefore warranted.

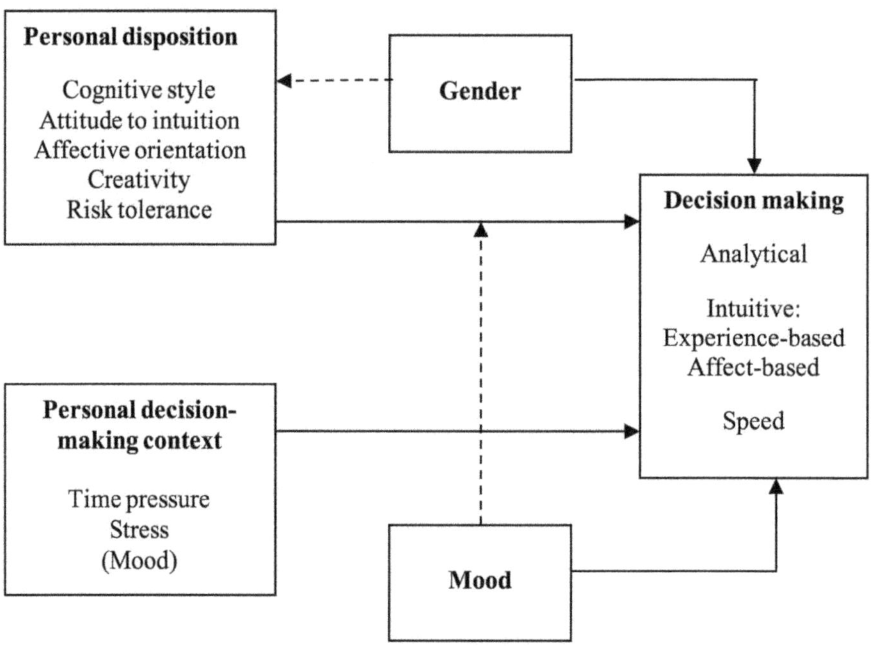

Figure 11.1 *Decision-making model*

The proposed model is depicted in Figure 11.1. It stipulates that whether a decision-maker will employ primarily an intuitive or a rational process is determined by personal disposition, decision-making context, and gender.

METHOD

In order to test the model, a web-based study was designed, targeting managers involved in strategic decision-making. The sample consisted of 217 mid- and top-level managers from Australian and American companies who regularly make strategic decisions with attributes that are conducive to the use of intuition. Specifically, respondents were asked to recall a non-routine decision that they made under time pressure, when they were stressed or upset/happy, did not have enough information, or felt uncertain about the decision success (see Sinclair et al., 2002). The age of participants ranged from 22 to 66 years, with a median of 42. On average, they had 14 years of work experience in the current industry and 11 years of overall management experience. Sixty-six percent were males. Forty-eight percent acted in an executive position, 40 percent as mid-level managers with allocated strategic responsibilities, and those 12 percent who described themselves as first-line decision-makers worked in small flat organizations and were involved in strategic decision-making.

The study consisted of two web-based segments that were available on the research website over a six-month period. In the first segment, participants provided demographic information and were evaluated in terms of their cognitive style, attitude to intuition, affective orientation, creativity, and risk tolerance (for a list of measures, see Table 11.1). In the second segment, participants described a recent decision with the above-specified characteristics. The recollection procedure was modeled on the Critical Incident Technique (Flanagan, 1954; see also Akinci, 2014) that asks respondents to remember a recent incident and answer questions about how they felt, thought, and acted. As part of the process, participants reported how long it took them to make the decision; recalled their mood at the time of the decision; described their decision-making process; and completed decision-making questionnaires.

The decision-making process was assessed threefold by means of questionnaires, content analysis of the described decision, and latency (time taken to make the decision). These three types of measures (see Table 11.1) were applied to ensure robustness of the testing (see Jick, 1979) and, in an exploratory fashion, to evaluate the relationship of individual factors with specific facets of intuition. The intuitive questionnaire had a strong focus on affective aspects of intuition and was contrasted by an analytical/rational questionnaire. The content analysis of decision-makers' descriptions evaluated both affective and experience-based aspects. It was expected to mirror the intuitive questionnaire but, at the same time, detect intuitive use with a stronger involvement of cognitive elements. Since intuition is frequently understood as direct knowing (Behling & Eckel, 1991), which circumvents time-consuming logical processes (Bastick, 1982), it was also hypothesized that intuitive decision-makers will usually decide faster than those using reasoning (Dane & Pratt, 2007; Locke, 2015).

Table 11.1 Dispositional, contextual, and decision-making measures

Factor	Measure	Modifications
Cognitive style	Cognitive Style Index, Allinson & Hayes, 1996	Short version, author
Attitude to intuition	Rational-Experiential Inventory, Experiential Subscale, Pacini & Epstein, 1999	Short version, author
Affective orientation	Affective Orientation Scale, Booth-Butterfield & Booth-Butterfield, 1990	Short version, author
Creativity	Creative Personality Scale, Gough, 1979	none
Risk tolerance	Intolerance of Ambiguity Scale, Budner, 1962	Modified version, author
Time pressure	Time Pressure Scale, author	none
Stress	Stress Scale, author	none
Mood	Positive and Negative Mood Scales, author	none
Intuitive decision-making	General Decision-Making Style Questionnaire, Intuitive Decision-Making Scale, Scott & Bruce, 1995	Modified version, author
Analytical decision-making	General Decision-Making Style Questionnaire, Analytical Decision-Making Scale, Scott & Bruce, 1995	Modified version, author
Intuitive self-description	Content analysis of provided self-descriptions, author	none
Latency	Logarithm of time taken to make the decision, author	none

It was not clear, however, whether this attribute is linked specifically to a particular aspect of intuition.

RESULTS

Descriptive Data

The descriptive statistics are summarized in Table 11.2. As expected, personal disposition variables were moderately correlated with the exception of cognitive style and risk tolerance (.68); both were retained for theoretical reasons. Positive and negative mood correlated only at −.50 ($p < .01$), which supported their treatment as independent factors. The four decision-making measures were also inter-related. There was the anticipated negative correlation between analysis and intuition, measured by intuitive decision-making style and self-description. Latency was correlated positively with analysis. Its relationship with both intuition measures was not significant but in the predicted direction.

Main Effects and Mood Moderations

The relationships were tested in separate hierarchical regressions for each of the four decision-making measures. To maintain a sufficient number of cases per variable

Table 11.2 *Descriptive statistics*

	Variable	*Mean*	SD	1	2	3	4	5	6	7	8	9	10	11	12	13	14	15
	Control																	
1	Hi-tech industry (1=hi-tech; 0=other)	.26	.44	(n/a)														
2	**Gender** (1=male; 2=fem)	1.34	.48	.07	(n/a)													
	Disposition																	
3	Cognitive style	43.97	8.89	.07	.07	(.85)												
4	Attitude to intuition	18.02	3.35	.00	.13^{+}	.44**	(.74)											
5	Affective orientation	27.81	5.16	.02	.29**	.34**	.51**	(.82)										
6	Creativity	6.35	3.55	.01	.01	.41**	.26**	.12^{+}	(n/a)									
7	Risk tolerance	39.92	5.92	.03	–.03	.68**	.39**	.27**	.30**	(.75)								
	Personal context																	
8	Time pressure (1=yes; 2=no)	9.57	2.89	.05	.01	.12^{+}	.08	.06	.04	.06	(.82)							
9	Stress	9.02	2.98	–.00	.14*	–.06	–.04	.18**	–.05	.02	.29**	(.74)						
10	Positive mood	0.51	0.61	–.05	.08	.09	.06	.09	–.09	.01	–.09	–.20**	(n/a)					
11	Negative mood	0.35	0.59	.04	.08	–.01	–.06	.11	.11	.02	.25**	.34**	–.50**	(n/a)				
	Decision-making																	
12	Intuitive DM	20.07	4.41	.12^{+}	.19**	.27**	.31**	.36**	.20**	.17*	.15*	.04	.08	.09	(.71)			
13	Intuitive self-description	3.35	0.98	.08	.25**	.32**	.28**	.29**	.21**	.23**	.03	.11	.01	.05	.42**	(n/a)		
14	Analytical DM	33.05	7.38	–.16*	–.08	–.39**	–.34**	–.28**	–.18**	–.26**	–.12	–.01	–.03	–.02	–.31**	–.30**	(.89)	
15	Latency (latency log)	1.59	1.08	–.02	.02	.01	–.04	–.06	–.10	.03	–.17*	.14*	–.04	–.01	–.08	–.11	.13*	(n/a)

Notes: + $p < .10$; * $p < .05$; ** $p < .01$. $n = 217$.
Scale reliabilities are shown in parentheses on the diagonal.

(see Tabachnick & Fidell, 1996), the full sample was analyzed in separate models for positive and negative mood. All variables included in interactions were centered to deal with possible multicollinearity (Aiken & West, 1991). In Step 1, hi-tech industry dummy was entered as control to account for the assumed difference in decision speed between this and other industry/service sectors, which is a relevant distinction for the studied phenomena. No other control variables were included after a careful evaluation of their relevance and/or significance. Step 2 introduced gender as the most stable factor. Step 3 added all dispositional and contextual variables. In Step 4, positive and negative mood were entered in respective models. Step 5 added positive or negative mood interactions with personal and contextual variables from Step 3. The results of the analyses can be seen in Table 11.3.

In summary, holistic cognitive style had a negative main effect on analytical decision-making and a positive effect on intuitive self-description. A moderation effect was registered on intuitive self-description where strong positive mood neutralized the effect of holistic style. As for attitude to intuition, negative effects of positive attitude were found on analytical style and a marginally positive effect (at $p<.10$) on self-description, although it strengthened to $p<.05$ when negative mood interactions were added. Affective orientation registered a positive effect on intuitive decision-making and a negative effect on latency. Creativity yielded only marginally significant positive effects on intuitive decision-making and negative effects on latency. But there was an interaction between creativity and negative mood on intuitive decision-making and self-description. In both instances, strong negative mood reversed the positive effect of creativity. Risk tolerance had no direct effect but interacted with negative mood on intuitive self-description which facilitated its access to intuition, and with positive mood on intuitive decision-making, which blocked its access. Both results were echoed on the other intuition measure respectively but only with marginal significance. As expected, time pressure predicted latency in the negative direction and stress in the positive direction. All other effects of these two variables were only marginally significant: There was a positive relationship of time pressure with intuitive decision-making and an interaction with negative mood on intuitive decision-making and self-description, in both instances suggesting reduced access to intuition. There was also an interaction of stress with negative mood on intuitive self-description and with positive mood on latency, both in the same direction as time pressure. Surprisingly, neither mood registered any main effect.

Gender Mediation

Whether affective orientation (or any other dispositional variable) would mediate the effect of gender on decision-making style, was tested in a series of hierarchical regressions using the method described by Baron and Kenny (1986), as can be seen in Table 11.4. In Step 1, gender was related only to intuitive decision-making and self-description so the other dependent variables were dropped. Similarly in Step 2, gender was related only to affective orientation so the other dispositional variables were removed. In Step 3, affective orientation predicted both remaining dependent

Table 11.3 Hierarchical regression analysis

Variable	Intuitive DM β/R²		Intuitive Self-Description β/R²		Analytical DM β/R²		Latency β/R²	
	Pos. mood	Neg. mood	Pos. mood	Neg. mood	Pos. mood	Neg. mood	Pos. mood	Neg. mood
Step 1: Control – hi-tech industry	.12+	.12+	.08	.08	–.16*	–.16*	–.02	–.02
ΔR^2	.01+	.01+	.01	.01	.03*	.03*	.00	.00
Step 2: Gender	.20**	.20**	.25**	.25**	–.10	–.10	.02	.02
ΔR^2	.04**	.04**	.06**	.06**	.01	.01	.00	.00
Step 3: Disposition and context								
Cognitive style	.06	.06	.20*	.20*	–.27**	–.27**	.14	.14
Attitude to intuition	.12	.12	.15+	.15+	–.21**	–.21**	.01	.01
Affective orientation	.23**	.23**	.09	.09	–.05	–.05	–.19*	–.19*
Creativity	.12+	.12+	.11	.11	–.07	–.07	–.14+	–.14+
Risk tolerance	–.05	–.05	–.04	–.04	.08	.08	–.00	–.00
Time pressure	.12+	.12+	–.03	–.03	–.09	–.09	–.27**	–.27**
Stress	–.04	–.04	.11	.11	.00	.00	.23**	.23**
ΔR^2	.17**	.17**	.15**	.15**	.24**	.24**	.13**	.13**
Step 4: Mood								
Positive mood	.05	n/a	–.02	n/a	–.01	n/a	–.03	n/a
Negative mood	n/a	.04	n/a	–.00	n/a	.01	n/a	.00
ΔR^2	.00	.00	.00	.00	.00	.00	.00	.00

Variable	Intuitive DM β/R^2		Intuitive Self-Description β/R^2		Analytical DM β/R^2		Latency β/R^2	
	Pos. mood	Neg. mood	Pos. mood	Neg. mood	Pos. mood	Neg. mood	Pos. mood	Neg. mood
Step 5: Mood moderation								
Cognitive style	–.03	.09	–.20*	–.10	–.07	–.11	–.14	.01
Attitude to intuition	–.01	.03	.10	.03	.08	.02	–.09	.15
Affective orientation	.08	–.05	–.05	.05	–.07	–.02	.15+	–.17
Creativity	–.04	–.20**	.11	–.20**	–.01	.14+	.05	–.07
Risk tolerance	–.19*	.18+	–.14+	.28**	.14+	–.10	.11	.03
Time pressure	.02	–.14+	.08	–.13+	.01	.01	–.02	.05
Stress	.02	–.08	.08	–.10+	–.11	.08	–.15+	–.06
ΔR^2	.04	.06*	.07**	.07*	.03	.03	.04	.02

Note: + $p < .10$; * $p < .05$; ** $p < .01$.

Table 11.4 *Gender mediation analysis*

	Criterion variables			
	Intuitive DM	**Intuitive self-description**	**Analytical DM**	**Latency**
Step 1: Correlation between *gender* and *criterion variables*				
Gender	.19**	.25**	–.08	.02
Step 2: Correlation between *gender* and *mediator variables*				
Cognitive style	.07			
Attitude to intuition	.13			
Affective orientation	.29**			
Creativity	.01			
Risk tolerance	.05			
Step 3: Correlation between *mediator variables* and *criterion variables*				
Affective orientation	.36**	.29**	n/a	n/a
Step 4: Correlation between *gender* and *criterion variables* after mediator variables entered				
Affective orientation	.10[a]	.18**	n/a	n/a

Note: * $p < .05$; ** $p < .01$; $n = 217$; [a] full mediation.

variables. In Step 4, which involves adding the significant mediator to each model, gender was no longer a significant predictor of intuitive decision-making when affective orientation was entered, indicating full mediation. It remained significant on intuitive self-description, although at a lesser degree, but a z-test ruled out partial moderation.

DISCUSSION

Results of the study suggest that the choice of intuitive versus analytical/rational decision-making is indeed influenced by personal disposition and context. Some findings corroborate conclusions from previous research (Sinclair et al., 2010). In particular, it was confirmed that intuitive processing is facilitated by holistic cognitive style and heightened emotional awareness, which seems to account in part for a higher reliance on intuition among female decision-makers. Some effects were also enhanced or blocked by strong mood, which appears to have a considerable influence on the choice of a decision-making mode. Even more interestingly, result variations across decision-making measures provided support for the assumption that individual factors *may* interact more with cognitive or affective components of intuition. Although this conclusion is tentative and requires more rigorous testing, it suggests new possibilities for studying intuition in a more fine-grained manner. Therefore, the value of this study lies in opening new areas of inquiry rather than finding definitive answers. In this spirit, some marginally significant results are discussed, not to ascertain their validity but to spur ideas for future research.

Influence of Personal Disposition and Context

As expected, there was a relationship between the preferred cognitive style and the used decision-making mode. Decision-makers who processed information more holistically tended to use a more intuitive approach while analytical thinkers leaned mostly toward logical reasoning. The effect of holistic style on intuition, however, seems to be suppressed by a strong positive mood. It appears that mood at high intensity acts in this instance the same way as a flared-up emotion that made the decision-maker focus on the emotional state, thus blocking access to intuition and reinforcing reliance on reasoning (Sinclair et al., 2002). This is in line with previous research (Sinclair et al., 2010) that found mood effects to be guided more by intensity than valence, especially if decision-makers were not trained how to use the emotional charge to their advantage.

In agreement with theoretical reasoning, the relationship between intuitive decision-making and holistic style could be tied more to experience-based aspects of intuition. This is suggested not only by significant results on intuitive self-description (which assessed both components of intuition but considered experience-based aspects more strongly than the other measure) but also by the lack of results on the affect-based measure. Although these conclusions are tentative, it would be worthwhile to conduct more research in this area, which would be particularly helpful for the study of expert intuition (because of its strong cognitive component). A speculative question arises whether holistic style is impeded by affect because of the style's cognitive nature.

The lack of positive attitude led clearly to more analytical/rational decision-making, which is consistent with the previously outlined reasoning for suppressed intuitions (Dane, 2011). Negative attitude could be one of the factors explaining why dispositional preference for holistic cognitive style does not translate automatically into the use of intuition (see Bakken & Hærem, Chapter 2 in this handbook). On the contrary, marginally significant findings pose a question whether a positive attitude might facilitate access to affect-based components of intuition. It could be that the attitude's affect-laden positive priming (Dane, 2011) might serve as conduit to the corresponding aspects of intuitive processing.

Similarly, awareness of one's emotional states seems to be related to the affect-based aspects of intuition, and also to the speed of reaching decisions. It implies that emotionally aware decision-makers tend to use the affective charge as a conduit to intuition (see Epstein, 1990; Forgas, 1995) and decide faster (see Schoemaker & Russo, 1993). The results also confirmed that female decision-makers used the intuitive approach more than their male counterparts, in part because they were more attuned to their emotions. Consistent with previous research (see Booth-Butterfield & Booth-Butterfield, 1990; Sinclair et al., 2010), females in this study showed a higher emotional awareness than males. Such awareness might act as a conduit to experiential information processing (see Epstein et al., 1996), that in turn would facilitate access to intuition. This conclusion finds support in Soosalu and Henwood's work (see Chapter 10 in this handbook) who found gender differences in heart-based intuition aspects (infused with affect) but not in gut-based aspects (devoid of affect).

Creativity was found to have only a marginal impact on faster decision-making and possibly on the affective component of intuition. Its overall relationship with intuition became more apparent when decision-makers experienced a pronounced mood that acted as a neutralizer. As a result, creativity lost its influence when decision-makers were in a strongly negative mood, which could have evoked the need for a careful deliberation (see Bastick, 1982). It might also be that the negative mood stifled momentary creativity (see Schwartz, 2001) before it could trigger intuitive processing. Another explanation might lie in the consequential relationship between both variables. It is possible that intuition serves as a conduit to creativity, and their interaction thus needs to be studied differently (see Sinclair & Maimone, forthcoming).

Neither risk tolerance exerted much influence on the choice of the decision-making process, unless a strong mood was present. But here the results are more puzzling. While negative mood facilitated access to intuition, positive mood blocked it. As mentioned previously, it could be that high intensity mood acted the same way for both valences (Sinclair et al., 2010) and that each mood interacted with a different aspect of intuition. Since marginal effects were noted respectively also on the other measure, no conclusions can be reached until more research is conducted, preferably using multiple instruments.

Time pressure and stress had obviously a strong impact on decision speed, although in the opposite direction. This raises questions about the overall influence of time pressure (Maule & Svenson, 1993). It seems that it can have a direct effect by helping the decision-maker focus and decide faster, or it can evoke stress that will stall or slow down the decision-making process. In this context, stress could act similarly to an intense blocking emotion (Petitmengin, 1999). Caution should be executed in future studies to differentiate between both constructs.

Marginal findings also raise a question for future research whether time pressure could be linked more to affective components of intuition, which may be accessed without any non-conscious pattern recognition or synthesis, and therefore can occur faster. And should that be the case, would its impact be impeded by negative mood acting as a signpost for deliberation (Cacioppo & Gardner, 1999)? A similar conclusion was reached in a study examining the negative influence of regret on intuition use (Kuhnle & Sinclair, 2011). Since indications about the role of stress were absent, it would be useful to test in the future its newly theorized differential effects, either blocking access to intuition (Petitmengin, 1999) or, under certain conditions, facilitating it (Grant & Langan-Fox, 2014).

Role of Mood and Gender

Surprisingly, positive and negative mood influenced the choice of the decision-making mode only in conjunction with other factors. Moreover, they tended to facilitate or block effects on intuition according to their relationship with the specific factor and the intensity, not their positive or negative valence. This is contrary to previous findings (Elsbach & Barr, 1999). It concurs, however, with the hypothesized conclusion that the effect might depend on how the decision-maker uses the available affective charge (see Palmer, 1998; Sinclair et al., 2002), seconded by findings from experimental research about the role of mood intensity (Sinclair et al., 2010). It seems that decision-makers had difficulties to distinguish between a strong mood and an intense emotion. In the future, it might be necessary to examine their influence separately. Results from this study so far indicate that a strong mood tends to modify the impact of some dispositional factors. It impeded access to intuition for holistic cognitive style and creativity while it enhanced some effects of risk tolerance.

In terms of gender, results conformed to expectations while suggesting a more fine-grained view. Female decision-makers used both components of intuition more but in the case of the affective component it was because of their higher emotional awareness (DePaulo, 1992). It is reasonable to assume that men with similarly developed qualities will be able to use them the same way. For example, empathy experienced by male nurses will probably help them use their intuition more effectively. This is an interesting area for professional development since research suggests that awareness of emotions and conscious mood regulation can be trained (Farrell & Shaw, 1994).

Integrated Decision-Making

Reports provided by decision-makers confirmed findings from previous research about an integrated use of intuition and reasoning (see Burke & Miller, 1999; Williams, 2012). Consistent with a previous experimental study by the author, two-thirds used a combination of intuitive and rational processes. Many decision-makers implied, however, that their primary reliance was on one approach or the other (see Scott & Bruce, 1995). Twenty-four percent stated that they used exclusively reasoning, but only 10 percent acknowledged that they relied solely on intuition. This suggests that the majority of respondents were to some extent 'cognitively versatile,' able to switch between both processing modes as needed (Hodgkinson & Clarke, 2007), a desired quality for strategic decision-making.

The provided descriptions also offered other insights regarding the interface of rational and intuitive modes. Some decision-makers used deliberation to find support or a reason for their initial intuitive assessment, others checked the final outcome of rational analysis against their intuition for confirmation. This finding is aligned with conclusions of other researchers (e.g., Locke, 2015). In many instances, however, this process was iterative in that it was applied as an interim check during the decision-making process, not only in its beginning or final stage. A combined use of intuition and reasoning was reported not only in people-related situations (see Burke & Miller, 1999), which are viewed as the 'soft' side of management, but also when deciding about fact-based issues, such as financial plans or accuracy of technical information. The strategic application of intuition was frequently indicated by such words as 'big picture' or 'holistic approach,' and 'foresight.' These conclusions confirm the usefulness of recognizing which mode the decision-maker uses at the given moment and having the ability to combine both modes skillfully. It also calls for a more fine-grained research into the interaction of both decision-making modes.

LIMITATIONS AND IMPLICATIONS FOR FUTURE RESEARCH

Although some findings are tentative and require replication, they provide a fertile ground for future research that will hopefully bring more clarity about specific phases and aspects of the decision-making process. This is a new line of research that needs to be thoroughly tested, especially the conclusions about experience-based and affective components of intuition, but it is a good start. Result variations across measures suggest that, even though intuition research has progressed considerably, we need to remain vigilant about what we actually measure and whether we can draw general conclusions from it. On the other hand, a comparison of different instruments can provide new insights into particular aspects of intuiting and how to switch to reasoning when needed.

We need also to exercise caution when working with self-report techniques not to overtax recollection abilities of the respondents. More accurate methods in situ started emerging but they are not suitable for large-scale organizational studies. Additional work is to be done also on gender differences and mood effects, with a more controlled arousal level, preferably contrasted with effects of intense emotions. The impact of dispositional factors and their interaction with affect warrants an ongoing attention. As for contextual factors, further categorization is necessary, including factors of non-personal nature, and a careful distinction between possibly differential effects of time pressure and stress.

In terms of practical implications, the qualitative data indicate that, despite advances in dual-process research, there is an ongoing need to explain intuition in specific, practical terms so that its use is properly understood and complemented with reasoning. In this respect, strategic decision-makers would benefit from becoming aware how individual factors impact their choice of a decision-making process so that they can start controlling it more consciously. Overall, the results of this study suggest that there are still many gaps in our understanding how managerial decision-making works. It is evident, however, that personal disposition, affective states, and gender play an important role.

REFERENCES

Agor, W.H. 1984. *Intuitive management: Integrating left and right brain management skills.* New York: Prentice Hall Press.

Aiken, L.S., & West, S.G. 1991. *Multiple regression: Testing and interpreting interactions.* Thousand Oaks: Sage.

Akinci, C. 2014. Capturing intuitions in decision making: A case for the Critical Incident Technique. In M. Sinclair (Ed.), *Handbook of research methods on intuition*: 147–159. Cheltenham, UK and Northampton, MA, USA: Edward Elgar Publishing.

Allinson, C.W., & Hayes, J. 1996. The Cognitive Style Index: A measure of intuition-analysis for organizational research. *Journal of Management Studies*, 33: 119–135.

Baron, R.M., & Kenny, D.A. 1986. The moderator-mediator variable distinction in social psychology research: Conceptual, strategic, and statistical considerations. *Journal of Personality and Social Psychology*, 51: 1173–1182.

Bastick, T. 1982. *Intuition: How we think and act*. New York: John Wiley.

Bechara, A. 2004. The role of emotion in decision-making: Evidence from neurological patients with orbito-frontal damage. *Brain and Cognition*, 55: 30–40.

Behling, O., & Eckel, N.L. 1991. Making sense out of intuition. *Academy of Management Executive*, 5: 46–54.

Betsch, C. 2008. Chronic preferences for intuition and deliberation in decision making: Lessons learned about intuition from an individual differences approach. In H. Plessner, C. Betsch, & T. Betsch (Eds.), *Intuition in judgment in decision making*: 231–248. New York: Taylor & Francis.

Booth-Butterfield, M., & Booth-Butterfield, S. 1990. Conceptualizing affect as information in communication production. *Human Communication Research*, 16: 451–476.

Budner, S. 1962. Intolerance of ambiguity as a personal variable. *Journal of Personality*, 30: 29–50.

Burke, L.A., & Miller, M.K. 1999. Taking the mystery out of intuitive decision making. *Academy of Management Executive*, 13: 91–99.

Cacioppo, J.T., & Gardner, W.L. 1999. Emotion. *Annual Review of Psychology*, 50: 191–214.

Cappon, D. 1994. *Intuition and management: Research and applications*. Westport, CT: Quorum Books.

Crossan, M.M., Lane, H.W., & White, R.E. 1999. An organizational learning framework: From intuition to institution. *Academy of Management Review*, 24: 522–537.

Damasio, A.R. 1994. *Descartes' error: Emotion, reason, and the human brain*. New York: G. P. Putnam's Sons.

Dane, E. 2011. Capturing intuitions 'in flight': Observations from research on attention and mindfulness. In M. Sinclair (Ed.), *Handbook of intuition research*: 217–226. Cheltenham, UK and Northampton, MA, USA: Edward Elgar Publishing.

Dane, E., & Pratt, M.G. 2007. Exploring intuition and its role in managerial decision making. *Academy of Management Review*, 32(1): 33–54.

DePaulo, B. 1992. Nonverbal behavior and self-presentation. *Psychological Bulletin*, 111: 203–243.

Elsbach, K.D., & Barr, P.S. 1999. The effects of mood on individual's use of structured decision protocols. *Organization Science*, 10: 181–198.

Epstein, S. 1990. Cognitive-experiential self-theory. In L. Pervin (Ed.), *Handbook of personality theory and research*: 165–192. New York: Guilford Press.

Epstein, S. 2010. Demystifying intuition: What it is, what it does, and how it does it. *Psychological Inquiry*, 21: 295–312.

Epstein, S., Pacini, R., Denes-Raj, V., & Heier, H. 1996. Individual differences in intuitive-experiential and analytical-rational thinking styles. *Journal of Personality and Social Psychology*, 71: 390–405.

Farrell, J.M., & Shaw, I.A. 1994. Emotional awareness training: A prerequisite to effective cognitive-behavioral treatment of borderline personality disorder. *Cognitive and Behavioral Practice*, 1(1): 71–91.

Fisher, S.R., & Nelson, D.L. 1996. 'Feeling' at the top: An underutilized resource in top management teams. *Journal of Social Behavior and Personality*, 11: 77–90.

Flanagan, J.C. 1954. The Critical Incident Technique (CIT). *Psychological Bulletin*, 51: 327–358.
Forgas, J.P. 1995. Mood and judgment: The Affect Infusion Model (AIM). *Psychological Bulletin*, 117: 39–66.
Gough, H.G. 1979. A creative personality scale for the adjective check list. *Journal of Personality and Social Psychology*, 37: 1398–1405.
Grant, S.L., & Langan-Fox, J. 2014. Stress and the unconscious in intuitive judgement. In M. Sinclair (Ed.), *Handbook of research methods on intuition*: 59–71. Cheltenham, UK and Northampton, MA, USA: Edward Elgar Publishing.
Hodgkinson, G.P., & Clarke, I. 2007. Exploring the cognitive significance of organizational strategizing: A dual-process framework and agenda. *Human Relations*, 60: 243–255.
Isenberg, D.J. 1984. How senior managers think. *Harvard Business Review*, 6: 81–86.
Jick, T.D. 1979. Mixing qualitative and quantitative methods: Triangulation in action. *Administration Science Quarterly*, 24: 602–611.
Kahneman, D. 2003. A perspective on judgment and choice. Mapping bounded rationality. *American Psychologist*, 58(9): 697–720.
Khatri, N., & Ng, H.A. 2000. The role of intuition in strategic decision making. *Human Relations*, 1: 57–86.
Kuhnle, C., & Sinclair, M. 2011. Decision mode as an antecedent of flow, motivational interference, and regret. *Learning and Individual Differences*, 21: 239–243.
Lieberman, M.D. 2000. Intuition: A social cognitive neuroscience approach. *Psychological Bulletin*, 126: 109–137.
Locke, C.C. 2015. When it's safe to rely on intuition (and when it's not). *Harvard Business Review*, April 30. https://hbr.org/2015/04/when-its-safe-to-rely-on-intuition-and-when-its-not (accessed February 15, 2020).
Maule, A.J., & Svenson, O. 1993. Theoretical and empirical approaches to behavioral decision making and their relation to time constraints. In O. Svenson & A.J. Maule (Eds.), *Time pressure and stress in human judgment and decision making*: 3–25. New York: Plenum Press.
Miller, C.C., & Ireland, R.D. 2005. Intuition in strategic decision making: Friend or foe in the fast-paced 21st century? *Academy of Management Executive*, 19: 19–30.
Pacini, R., & Epstein, S. 1999. The relation of rational and experiential information processing styles to personality, basic beliefs, and the ratio-bias phenomenon. *Journal of Personality and Social Psychology*, 76: 972–987.
Palmer, H. 1998. Introduction to inner knowing. In H. Palmer (Ed.), *Inner knowing*: xv–xxi. New York: Jeremy P. Tarcher/Putnam.
Petitmengin, C. 1999. The intuitive experience. *Journal of Consciousness*, 6: 43–77.
Pretz, J.E., & Totz, K.S. 2007. Measuring individual differences in affective, heuristic, and holistic intuition. *Personality and Individual Differences*, 43: 1247–1257.
Raidl, M.-H., & Lubart, T.I. 2001. An empirical study of intuition and creativity. *Imagination, Cognition and Personality*, 20: 217–230.
Sadler-Smith, E. 2008. *Inside intuition*. Abingdon: Routledge.
Sadler-Smith, E., Hodgkinson, G.P., & Sinclair, M. 2008. A matter of feeling? The role of intuition in entrepreneurial decision-making and behavior. In W.J. Zerbe, C.E.J. Härtel, & N.M. Ashkanasy (Eds.), *Research on emotions in organizations, vol. 4*: 35–55. Oxford: Elsevier Publications.
Schoemaker, P.J.H., & Russo, E.J. 1993. A pyramid of decision approaches. *California Management Review*, 36: 9–31.
Schwartz, N. 2001. Feelings as information: Implications for affective influences on information processing. In L.L. Martin & G.L. Clore (Eds.), *Theories of mood and cognition*: 159–176. Mahwah, NJ: Lawrence Erlbaum.
Scott, S.G., & Bruce, R.A. 1995. Decision-making style: The development and assessment of a new measure. *Educational and Psychological Measurement*, 55: 818–831.

Simon, H.A. 1987. Making management decisions: The role of intuition and emotion. *Academy of Management Executive*, 1: 57–64.
Sinclair, M. 2010. Misconceptions about intuition. *Psychological Inquiry*, 21: 378–386.
Sinclair, M., & Ashkanasy, N.M. 2005. Intuition: Myth or a decision-making tool? *Management Learning*, 36(3): 353–370.
Sinclair, M., Ashkanasy, N.M., & Chattopadhyay, P. 2010. Affective antecedents of intuitive decision making. *Journal of Management and Organization*, 16(3): 382–398.
Sinclair, M., Ashkanasy, N.M., Chattopadhyay, P., & Boyle, M.V. 2002. Determinants of intuitive decision-making in management: The moderating role of affect. In N.M. Ashkanasy, W.J. Zerbe, & C.E.J. Härtel (Eds.), *Managing emotions in the workplace*: 143–163. Armonk, NY: ME Sharpe.
Sinclair, M., & Maimone, F. forthcoming. Role of intuition in creativity research – open agenda. In V. Dörfler & M. Stierand (Eds.), *Handbook of creativity research*. Cheltenham, UK and Northampton, MA, USA: Edward Elgar Publishing.
Smerek, R.E. 2014. Why people think deeply: Meta-cognitive cues, task characteristics and thinking dispositions. In M. Sinclair (Ed.), *Handbook of research methods on intuition*: 3–14. Cheltenham, UK and Northampton, MA, USA: Edward Elgar Publishing.
Tabachnick, B.G., & Fidell, L.S. 1996. *Using multivariate statistics, 3rd ed.* New York: Harper Collins.
Taggart, W.M., Valenzi, E., Zalka, L., & Lowe, K.B. 1997. Rational and intuitive styles: Commensurability across respondents' characteristics. *Psychological Reports*, 80: 23–33.
Thompson, J.D. 1967. *Organization in action*. New York: McGraw-Hill.
Tressoldi, P.I., Martinelli, M., Scartezzini, L., & Massaccesi, S. 2010. Further evidence of the possibility of exploiting anticipatory physiological signals to assist implicit intuition of random events. *Journal of Scientific Exploration*, 24(3): 411–424.
Williams, K.C. 2012. Business intuition: The mortar among the bricks of analysis. *Journal of Management Policy and Practice*, 13(5): 48–65.
Woiceshyn, J. 2009. Lessons from 'good minds': How CEOs use intuition, analysis and guiding principles to make strategic decisions. *Long Range Planning*, 42: 298–319.

12. Moral intuition and moral leader development

Maxim Egorov and Armin Pircher Verdorfer

With the proliferation of ethical scandals in business and other societal sectors, leadership researchers have become increasingly interested in the moral dimension of leadership (Brown & Mitchell, 2010; Eisenbeiss, 2012; Lemoine et al., 2018; Peus et al., 2010). Consistent with much prior research in the field of organizational behavior and leadership, we use the terms moral and ethical synonymously in this chapter. Broadly described, moral leadership is how leaders use visible moral traits and actions to lead followers towards a purposeful and ethical direction and, thereby, to shape ethical organizations (Cropanzano & Walumbwa, 2010). Against this backdrop, a perennial question asked by researchers and practitioners is: *How can we effectively develop moral leaders?* To answer this question, it is important to have a thorough understanding of what moral leaders actually do and how underlying moral decision processes occur. While the influence of intuition is well established in the field of organizational decision-making more generally (Akinci & Sadler-Smith, 2011; Hodgkinson & Sadler-Smith, 2018), research on the role of moral intuition for moral leadership is just beginning to emerge (Weaver et al., 2014). Accordingly, current concepts of moral leadership and related notions of moral leader development have a strong focus on rational deliberation, while largely neglecting the potential influence of moral intuition in the leadership process (Egorov et al., 2019b; Weaver et al., 2014).

This chapter explores how moral intuition can enhance our understanding of effective moral leader development. It is suggested that moral intuition complements existing common rational deliberation approaches to moral leader development, and thus offers development opportunities that were formerly unavailable or less adequately considered.

MORAL FORMS OF LEADERSHIP

In the current leadership literature, three approaches to moral leadership have received the most attention (Lemoine et al., 2018). First, Brown et al. (2005: 120) introduced the concept of *ethical leadership*, defined as "the demonstration of normatively appropriate conduct (...) and the promotion of such conduct to followers." In this framework, being an ethical leader rests on a combination of leaders' moral traits, such as integrity, and the use of position power to convey ethical standards to followers. Second, *authentic leadership*, with its foundation in leaders' self-awareness and being true to themselves, also contains a moral component (Gardner et al., 2011). Specifically, authentic leaders are thought to be guided by strong personal moral values, instead of external pressures (Neider & Schriesheim, 2011). Third, *servant leadership* has a moral underpinning in that it frames the leadership process around a genuine other-serving orientation (Eva et al., 2018). Accordingly, servant leaders are generally described as being humble and altruistic with a strong concern for stakeholders' interests and long-term outcomes. While these approaches to moral leadership are, to some degree, rooted in different moral philosophies (e.g., deontology, virtue ethics, and consequentialism; see Lemoine et al., 2018), there are meaningful overlaps too. Most notably, and as mentioned at the outset of this chapter, they all contain the notion of urging followers into a meaningful and ethical direction. Importantly, this requires what researchers in this area have referred to as *ethical competence* (Pohling et al., 2016). In essence, *ethical competence* comprises the ability to identify ethical issues and potential ways to address them as well as to consider the effects on others. Furthermore, it refers to decision-making based on conscious values and normative decision rules and overcoming obstacles and risks for the sake of personal moral principles. That said, it becomes clear that ethical competence, and therefore the above leadership concepts, involve high levels of deliberation and careful thought on the part of leaders. Ethical, authentic, and servant leaders have consistently been described as having strong ethical principles they are aware of and that they consciously use to make moral decisions and to shape their interactions with others.

CURRENT APPROACHES TO MORAL LEADER DEVELOPMENT

In accordance with the discussion above, moral leader development typically seeks to develop leaders' ethical competence with its inherent focus on intentional, deliberative decision-making. An integral part of most interventions in this area are normative knowledge and moral decision-making rules. In their simplest form, such interventions merely convey information about explicit normative expectations regarding ethical and unethical conduct in the workplace (Weber & Wasieleski, 2013). More complex forms seek to teach specific moral leadership styles and their underlying ethical principles and behaviors, mostly in traditional classroom or workshop settings, using lectures, case studies, role-playing, and group discussions (for an overview, see Lohrey, 2016). Other approaches seek to go deeper and to promote deliberative moral reasoning as rooted in Kohlberg's paradigm of cognitive moral development (Kohlberg, 1984). Briefly, moral reasoning at high levels focuses on individual rights and social mutuality as well as universal ethical principles of respect and justice. Lower stages, in contrast, reflect more instrumental thinking (i.e., "what's in it for me") and following commonly accepted social standards and rules to gain approval from others. That said, it is thought that leaders at higher levels are more likely to treat others with dignity and respect, make fair decisions, show concern in the welfare of society and the environment, and replace self-interest with a responsible use of power (Eisenbeiss, 2012). Research in this field has shown that moral reasoning development is promoted by cognitive conflict and socially expanded perspective taking (Snarey & Samuelson, 2008). Accordingly, interventions to enhance moral reasoning usually seek to systematically expose participants to higher stage reasoning. To this end, they typically use expert facilitated discussions of moral dilemmas (Kvalnes & Øverenget, 2012; Lerkiatbundit et al., 2006; Schmidt et al., 2009).

MORAL INTUITION THEORY

Although current approaches to moral leader development focus on rational deliberation and the promotion of conscious moral reasoning, recent advances in the field of moral psychology have challenged this orientation and drawn increasing attention to the unconscious components of moral information processing (Haidt, 2001; Haidt & Joseph, 2004; Reynolds, 2006). A highly influential work in this field is Haidt's (2001) Social Intuitionist Approach, describing the process of moral judgment as an interplay of both *moral reasoning* and *moral intuition*. In this theoretical model, *moral intuition* is defined as "the sudden appearance in consciousness of a moral judgment, including an affective valence (good–bad, like–dislike), without any conscious awareness of having gone through steps of searching, weighing evidence, or inferring a conclusion" (Haidt, 2001: 818). As such, moral intuition comprises two aspects: (1) *moral intuition process* and (2) *moral intuition content* (Weaver et al., 2014).

The *moral intuition process* can be defined as a "rapid (i.e., automatic), nondeliberative (i.e., noninferential), evaluative experience that often is emotionally laden (i.e., accompanied by affective reactions, such as disgust, anger, elevation, etc.)" (Weaver et al., 2014: 101). According to Haidt (2001), this non-deliberative affective response to a moral stimulus is the primary and central component of moral judgment, while the deliberative part of moral reasoning is proposed to occur post-hoc. This means that, in contrast to what rational deliberation approaches assume, the first and immediate reaction of leaders (and followers) to a moral stimulus is affective and precedes conscious reasoning (i.e., deliberately assessing whether something is morally right or wrong) (Haidt, 2001; Egorov & Pircher Verdorfer, 2017; Egorov et al., 2019b; Sadler-Smith, 2012, 2016).

The *content of moral intuition* refers to the foundations of morality, indicating that individuals – leaders and followers – may respond to their environment with different moral intuitions. The most influential approach in this field is the Moral Foundation Theory (MFT; Graham et al., 2013; Haidt & Joseph, 2004). It postulates that "human morality is derived from or constrained by multiple innate mental systems, each shaped by a different evolutionary process" (Graham et al., 2013: 58). In particular, MFT proposes five moral foundations, which are specified as (1) care/harm (i.e., focus on the reduction of suffering, while promoting well-being), (2) fairness/cheating (i.e., focus on a decrease of cheating and an increase of justice, fair und trustful interactions and reciprocity), (3) loyalty/betrayal (i.e., focus on a need of coalition building and punitive actions against outgroups), (4) authority/subversion (i.e., focus on hierarchical relationships), and (5) sanctity/degradation (i.e., focus on purity and cleanliness and an avoidance of contaminants). Thus, the theoretical model indicates that these five moral foundations determine how sensitive leaders and followers respond to different moral stimuli, which values they endorse, and which moral principles they are willing to violate or not (Egorov et al., 2019a, 2019b; Fehr et al., 2015; Weaver et al., 2014).

MORAL INTUITION AND MORAL LEADER DEVELOPMENT

Since moral psychology has been experiencing a "renaissance" (Graham et al., 2011: 368) in recent decades, applied fields such as research on moral leader development have been challenged to integrate these new intuitionist theoretical perspectives on leaders' moral cognition and behavior (Sadler-Smith, 2012; Treviño et al., 2006; Weaver et al., 2014). On this basis, Egorov et al. (2019b) have made suggestions for how moral intuition can be integrated in moral leader development and introduced a conceptual model covering the role of moral intuition processes and moral intuition content in this context (see Figure 12.1).

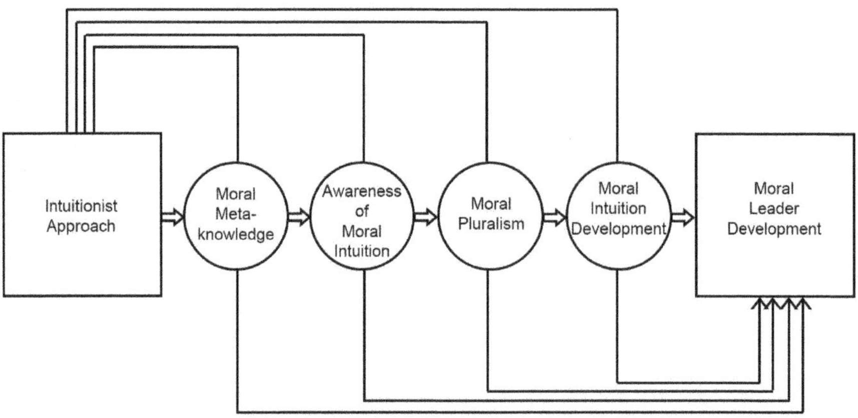

Source: Adapted from Egorov et al., 2019b. Copyright 2018 by Springer Science+Business Media B.V., part of Springer Nature 2018.

Figure 12.1 *A conceptual model of moral leader development*

A key tenet of this model is that the concept of ethical competence, as the basis of moral leadership, must be broadened by including moral intuition. On this basis, four areas are identified, which address the integration of moral intuition in the process of moral leader development: (1) promotion of moral metaknowledge, (2) development of awareness of own moral intuition, (3) consideration of moral pluralism represented in divergent moral intuitions of others, and (4) the purposeful development of moral intuition process and content (see Figure 12.1). While each component can make a contribution on its own, it is assumed that a chronological sequence produces the best result (Egorov et al., 2019b).

Promotion of Leaders' Moral Knowledge about Moral Cognition

Proponents of the intuitionist approach have outlined that the promotion of knowledge about moral cognition and the interaction between moral reasoning and moral intuition represents an important objective of leader development programs (Sadler-Smith, 2012; Weaver et al., 2014). Leaders need to gain a pronounced understanding that beside rational deliberation, also the unconscious process and content of moral intuition determine both their leadership behavior as well as the way it is perceived by their followers. Recent theoretical work by Fehr and colleagues (2015) has supported this assumption in two ways. First, moral intuition can be linked to certain forms of leadership. For instance, aspects of the care/harm or the justice foundations are reflected in theoretical concepts of ethical, authentic, or servant leadership. In turn, issues of loyalty and obedience can be linked to autocratic or paternalistic leadership (Harms et al., 2018). Second, Fehr and colleagues (2015) suggested that moral intuition also plays an important role in the construction of followers' perceptions of leadership. More specifically, followers are thought to perceive those leadership behaviors as moral that correspond with their own moral intuition content or the moral foundations endorsed by the organizational culture (Fehr et al., 2015; Graham et al., 2013). Against this background, leaders who are equipped with a better understanding of the conscious and unconscious components of human morality are likely to develop higher levels of moral complexity, that is, more differentiated and richly connected mental representations of moral issues, and to better regulate their moral decision-making and behavior (Egorov et al., 2019b; Sadler-Smith, 2012).

Development of Leaders' Self-Awareness of Their Own Moral Intuition

While theoretical knowledge about the interplay of moral intuition and moral reasoning allows leaders to better monitor their moral decision-making and behavior (Sadler-Smith, 2012), it is crucial that leaders "understand their own propensities to deliberation or intuition, the factors that influence the activation of each, and the ways" they "can balance each kind of moral judgment in appropriate fashion" (Weaver et al., 2014: 111). In fact, leaders often have limited or biased awareness of how they approach moral issues and the values and principles that underlie their decisions and behaviors (Egorov & Pircher Verdorfer, 2017; Reynolds, 2006;

Sonenshein, 2007; Weaver et al., 2014). Yet, leaders' awareness of specific moral issues and how they respond to them are strongly influenced by both moral intuition processes and moral intuition content. Thus, it is suggested that the inclusion of these features in guided as well as self-reflective practice (Nesbit, 2012) will aid leaders in monitoring, regulating, and integrating their moral decision-making processes.

Integration of Moral Pluralism and Promotion of Leaders' Awareness of Moral Intuitions of Others

As outlined above, MFT suggests that leaders' and followers' understanding of and their sensitivity for what is "normatively appropriate" (Brown et al., 2005: 120) may vary significantly. Furthermore, also the culture in an organization may accentuate a divergent selection of values and principles, which may likewise correspond to divergent moral intuition contents (Cooke & Rousseau, 1988; Fehr et al., 2015). Consequently, besides providing leaders with increased moral knowledge about moral cognition and self-awareness of their own moral intuitions, effective moral leader development also needs to provide them with awareness of moral pluralism and the ability to handle and integrate the moral intuitions of relevant others (Egorov et al., 2019b). This is important for two reasons: First, divergent moral intuitions have been associated with a negative impact on the quality of social interactions on both the individual and the group level (Graham et al., 2013). A lack of sensitivity for divergent moral intuitions of others naturally aggravates this effect because of the "inability to simulate, and therefore appreciate, the visceral responses that motivate another person's moral concerns" (Ditto & Koleva, 2011: 332). Thus, it is crucially important that leaders proactively consider the moral intuitions of their followers. Second, a key assumption in the moral leadership literature is that moral leadership approaches foster followers' moral functioning. However, the pluralistic viewpoint of MFT suggests that leaders may have a rather more differentiated effect on followers, depending on both leaders' and followers' moral intuition and their interplay in the leader–follower dyad. Different types of leadership behaviors may increase and promote divergent types of moral awareness and moral behavior among followers depending on the moral intuitions they trigger. In particular, Fehr and colleagues (2015) argued that leadership behaviors that reflect specific moral foundations and that resonate with the moral intuitions of followers will promote specific value-consistent responses on the side of these followers. For instance, "behavior that is consistent with (a) the care/harm foundation or (b) the fairness/cheating foundation" will motivate followers "to engage in prosocial behavior" (Fehr et al., 2015: 197), while "behavior that is consistent with the authority/subversion moral foundation" is likely to motivate followers to "engage in proleader behavior" (Fehr et al., 2015: 198).

Development of Moral Intuition Process and Content

As a final element of moral leader development that integrates moral intuition, Egorov and colleagues (2019b) discussed whether and how leaders' moral intuitions can be shaped. There is evidence that the plasticity in neural brain structures involved in the development of moral intuitions decreases after late childhood and adolescence (Damasio et al., 1990). At the same time, however, there is no reason to believe that moral socialization stops with adulthood and research has consistently pointed to the positive effects of explicit and implicit learning in this domain (Dane & Pratt, 2007; Lapsley & Narvaez, 2004). That said, leader moral intuition development may be stimulated by "repeated experience, practice, correction of errors, instruction, role modeling, coaching, feedback, and reflection in and on moral actions in a given domain across multiple situations, collectively, and over time" (Sadler-Smith, 2012: 368). For instance, as moral foundations, such as care/harm or fairness/cheating, play a significant role in the conception of prominent moral leadership models, the development of these moral intuition contents could significantly contribute to the development of related leadership styles. Thus, the repeated and consistent exposure to contents related to these foundations in leader development contexts should impact leaders' moral information processing, enhance the formation and accessibility of related knowledge structures represented in leaders' cognitive moral schemas (Lapsley & Narvaez, 2004; Narvaez et al., 2006), and therefore promote the development of related moral intuitions (Egorov et al., 2019b). Yet, Egorov et al. (2019b) also highlighted that the exposure to such contents embedded in leaders' frequent and intense engagement in varying demanding moral environments (Power et al., 1989) and moral interactions (Haidt, 2001; Lapsley & Narvaez, 2004) with peers (Haidt, 2001) would constitute the most promising way of moral intuition development. Real interactions instead of discussing hypothetical dilemmas provide leaders with opportunities to experience moral pluralism as well as competing moral intuitions and, furthermore, to obtain feedback and to reflect on their own cognitive, affective and behavioral moral responses (Haidt, 2001; Sadler-Smith, 2012). Such moral interactions and feedback from peers "may help leaders to challenge their intuitive moral judgments, offer new perspectives and thus stimulate cognitive reappraisal" (Egorov et al., 2019b: 826) as well as a purposeful development of moral intuition process and content.

PRACTICAL IMPLICATIONS

The outlined moral intuition perspective introduces a complementary framework to moral leader development, which offers several implications for practitioners in this field. Most notably, development programs aiming at promoting leaders' moral competence are challenged to purposefully include moral intuition. However, while the idea of integrating moral intuition in moral leader development is novel and promising, it does not call for a completely new set of tools and techniques. Rather, it complements existing approaches by tailoring existing development tools to also address leaders' moral intuitions. Egorov and colleagues (2019b) argue that explicit learning, stimulated in training or coaching contexts, will contribute to the development of leaders' *moral metaknowledge* (see Figure 12.1) – in particular the knowledge about moral reasoning and moral intuition as well as their interplay. Structured reflection, moral intuition-related self-assessments (Graham et al., 2011) as well as engagement with business cases addressing moral intuition process and content (Sadler-Smith, 2012) will foster leaders' *awareness of moral intuition* (see Figure 12.1), as an important part of self-awareness in general. Explicit learning, reflection, ethical discourse with peers (Sekerka et al., 2014) as well as group and moral reframing exercises (Feinberg & Willer, 2013) with peers will foster awareness and integration of *moral pluralism*, while implicit learning, group exercises, and different applications of play (Kark, 2011) will promote leaders' *moral intuition development* as depicted in Figure 12.1.

CONCLUSION

In summary, the growing body of knowledge on moral intuition offers promising paths to the exploration and prediction of ethical and unethical leader behavior. In this chapter, first theoretical and practical implications of this new perspective on moral leader development have been introduced and specified. The purposeful integration of moral intuition into leader development will be highly useful for equipping leaders with the appropriate moral competence and, as many ethical problems in organizations emerge from a failure of leadership (Knights & O'Leary, 2005), help prevent ethical lapses in organizations.

REFERENCES

Akinci, C., & Sadler-Smith, E. 2011. Intuition in management research: A historical review. *International Journal of Management Reviews*, 14(1): 104–122.

Brown, M.E., & Mitchell, M.S. 2010. Ethical and unethical leadership: Exploring new avenues for future research. *Business Ethics Quarterly*, 20(4): 583–616.

Brown, M.E., Treviño, L.K., & Harrison, D.A. 2005. Ethical leadership: A social learning perspective for construct development and testing. *Organizational Behavior and Human Decision Processes*, 97(2): 117–134.

Cooke, R.A., & Rousseau, D.M. 1988. Behavioral norms and expectations: A quantitative approach to the assessment of organizational culture. *Group & Organization Studies*, 13(3): 245–273.

Cropanzano, R., & Walumbwa, F.O. 2010. Moral leadership: A short primer on competing perspectives. In M. Schminke (Ed.), *Managerial ethics: Managing the psychology of morality:* 21–52. New York: Routledge/Taylor & Francis Group.

Damasio, A.R., Tranel, D., & Damasio, H. 1990. Individuals with sociopathic behavior caused by frontal damage fail to respond autonomically to social stimuli. *Behavioural Brain Research*, 41(2): 81–94.

Dane, E., & Pratt, M.G. 2007. Exploring intuition and its role in managerial decision making. *Academy of Management Review*, 32(1): 33–54.

Ditto, P.H., & Koleva, S.P. 2011. Moral empathy gaps and the American culture war. *Emotion Review*, 3(3): 331–332.

Egorov, M., Kalshoven, K., Pircher Verdorfer, A., & Peus, C. 2019a. It's a match: Moralization and the effects of moral foundations congruence on ethical and unethical leadership perception. *Journal of Business Ethics*. doi: 10.1007/s10551-019-04178-9.

Egorov, M., & Pircher Verdorfer, A. 2017. Leadership moral foundations. In D.C. Poff & A.C. Michalos (Eds.), *Encyclopedia of business and professional ethics*: 1–5. Cham: Springer International Publishing.

Egorov, M., Pircher Verdorfer, A., & Peus, C. 2019b. Taming the emotional dog: Moral intuition and ethically-oriented leader development. *Journal of Business Ethics*, 160(3): 817–834. doi:10.1007/s10551-018-3876-4

Eisenbeiss, S.A. 2012. Re-thinking ethical leadership: An interdisciplinary integrative approach. *Leadership Quarterly*, 23(5): 791–808.

Eva, N., Robin, M., Sendjaya, S., van Dierendonck, D., & Liden, R.C. 2018. Servant leadership: A systematic review and call for future research. *The Leadership Quarterly*, 30(1): 111–132.

Fehr, R., Yam, K.C., & Dang, C. 2015. Moralized leadership: The construction and consequences of ethical leader perceptions. *Academy of Management Review*, 40(2): 182–209.

Feinberg, M., & Willer, R. 2013. The moral roots of environmental attitudes. *Psychological Science*, 24(1): 56–62.

Gardner, W.L., Cogliser, C.C., Davis, K.M., & Dickens, M.P. 2011. Authentic leadership: A review of the literature and research agenda. *Leadership Quarterly*, 22(6): 1120–1145.

Graham, J., Haidt, J., Koleva, S., Motyl, M., Iyer, R., Wojcik, S., & Ditto, P.H. 2013. Moral foundations theory: The pragmatic validity of moral pluralism. *Advances in Experimental Social Psychology*, 47: 55–130.

Graham, J., Nosek, B.A., Haidt, J., Iyer, R., Koleva, S., & Ditto, P.H. 2011. Mapping the moral domain. *Journal of Personality and Social Psychology*, 101(2): 366–385.

Haidt, J. 2001. The emotional dog and its rational tail: A social intuitionist approach to moral judgment. *Psychological Review*, 108(4): 814–834.

Haidt, J., & Joseph, C. 2004. Intuitive ethics: How innately prepared intuitions generate culturally variable virtues. *Daedalus*, 133(4): 55–66.

Harms, P.D., Wood, D., Landay, K., Lester, P.B., & Lester, G.V. 2018. Autocratic leaders and authoritarian followers revisited: A review and agenda for the future. *The Leadership Quarterly*, 29(1): 105–122.

Hodgkinson, G., & Sadler-Smith, E. 2018. The dynamics of intuition and analysis in managerial and organizational decision making. *Academy of Management Perspectives*, 32(4): 473–492. doi: 10.5465/amp.2016.0140.

Kark, R. 2011. Games managers play: Play as a form of leadership development. *Academy of Management Learning & Education*, 10(3): 507–527.

Knights, D., & O'Leary, M. 2005. Reflecting on corporate scandals: The failure of ethical leadership. *Business Ethics: A European Review*, 14(4): 359–366.

Kohlberg, L. (Ed.) 1984. *Moral stages and moralization: The cognitive-developmental approach* (Vol. II). San Francisco: Harper & Row.

Kvalnes, Ø., & Øverenget, E. 2012. Ethical navigation in leadership training. *Etikk i praksis: Nordic Journal of Applied Ethics*, 6(1): 58–71.

Lapsley, D.K., & Narvaez, D. 2004. A social-cognitive approach to the moral personality. In D.K. Lapsley & D. Narvaez (Eds.), *Moral development, self and identity*: 189–212. Mahwah, NJ: Erlbaum.

Lemoine, G.J., Hartnell, C.A., & Leroy, H. 2018. Taking stock of moral approaches to leadership: An integrative review of ethical, authentic, and servant leadership. *Academy of Management Annals*, 13(1): 148–187.

Lerkiatbundit, S., Utaipan, P., Laohawiriyanon, C., & Teo, A. 2006. Impact of the Konstanz method of dilemma discussion on moral judgment in allied health students: A randomized controlled study. *Journal of Allied Health*, 35(2): 101–108.

Lohrey, S. 2016. *The effects of servant leadership on follower performance and well-being: Underlying mechanisms, boundary conditions, and the role of training.* Doctoral dissertation, Aston University.

Narvaez, D., Lapsley, D.K., Hagele, S., & Lasky, B. 2006. Moral chronicity and social information processing: Tests of a social cognitive approach to the moral personality. *Journal of Research in Personality*, 40(6): 966–985.

Neider, L.L., & Schriesheim, C.A. 2011. The Authentic Leadership Inventory (ALI): Development and empirical tests. *The Leadership Quarterly*, 22(6): 1146–1164.

Nesbit, P.L. 2012. The role of self-reflection, emotional management of feedback, and self-regulation processes in self-directed leadership development. *Human Resource Development Review*, 11(2): 203–226.

Peus, C., Kerschreiter, R., Frey, D., & Traut-Mattausch, E. 2010. What is the value? Economic effects of ethically-oriented leadership. *Zeitschrift für Psychologie/Journal of Psychology*, 218(4): 198–212.

Pohling, R., Bzdok, D., Eigenstetter, M., Stumpf, S., & Strobel, A. 2016. What is ethical competence? The role of empathy, personal values, and the five-factor model of personality in ethical decision-making. *Journal of Business Ethics*, 137(3): 449–474.

Power, F.C., Higgins, A., & Kohlberg, L. 1989. *Lawrence Kohlberg's approach to moral education.* New York: Columbia University Press.

Reynolds, S.J. 2006. A neurocognitive model of the ethical decision-making process: Implications for study and practice. *Journal of Applied Psychology*, 91(4): 737–748.

Sadler-Smith, E. 2012. Before virtue: Biology, brain, behavior, and the 'moral sense'. *Business Ethics Quarterly*, 22(2): 351–376.

Sadler-Smith, E. 2016. The role of intuition in entrepreneurship and business venturing decisions. *European Journal of Work and Organizational Psychology*, 25(2): 212–225.

Schmidt, C.D., McAdams, C.R., & Foster, V. 2009. Promoting the moral reasoning of undergraduate business students through a deliberate psychological education-based classroom intervention. *Journal of Moral Education*, 38(3): 315–334.

Sekerka, L.E., Godwin, L.N., & Charnigo, R. 2014. Motivating managers to develop their moral curiosity. *Journal of Management Development*, 33(7): 709–722.

Snarey, J., & Samuelson, P. 2008. Moral education in the cognitive developmental tradition: Lawrence Kohlberg's revolutionary ideas. In L. Nucci and D. Narvaez (Eds.), *Handbook on moral and character education*: 53–79. New York: Routledge.

Sonenshein, S. 2007. The role of construction, intuition, and justification in responding to ethical issues at work: The sensemaking-intuition model. *Academy of Management Review*, 32(4): 1022–1040.

Treviño, L.K., Weaver, G.R., & Reynolds, S.J. 2006. Behavioral ethics in organizations: A review. *Journal of Management*, 32(6): 951–990.

Weaver, G.R., Reynolds, S.J., & Brown, M.E. 2014. Moral intuition: Connecting current knowledge to future organizational research and practice. *Journal of Management*, 40(1): 100–129.

Weber, J., & Wasieleski, D.M. 2013. Corporate ethics and compliance programs: A report, analysis and critique. *Journal of Business Ethics*, 112(4): 609–626.

PART III

CULTURAL AND COLLECTIVE VIEWS ON INTUITION

13. Japanese style of 'Genbaism': combining intuitive, logical, and holistic thinking through experience

Kazuhito Isomura and Akihiko Kobayashi

This chapter aims to examine how Japanese organizations understand, use, and develop different thinking methods such as intuitive, logical, and holistic thinking. In general, for Japanese organizations intuition is based on experience at an operational workplace called 'Genba,' the importance of which is emphasized in such representative companies as Toyota, Honda, and Panasonic (Honda Café, 2013; Matsushita, 2007; Nakayama, 1994; Toyota, 2013). In addition, Japanese organizations develop their employees through on-the-job training (OJT) rather than off-the-job training (Off-JT). A management thought called 'Genbaism' is behind this management practice.

Genbaism is well accepted in Japanese companies and is considered the main reason why employees are developed through experience-based learning (Fujimoto, 2013; Kawamata et al., 2005). Genba is regarded as a gold mine where important implicit knowledge is embedded. Employees are expected to get acquainted with it so they can extract behavioral knowledge from what they directly see, hear, and touch as a basis for identifying problems and generating solutions to improve their operations. Intuitive familiarity with Genba thus becomes a basic ability that employees are expected to learn and acquire. It therefore follows that Japanese organizations have a managerial philosophy where experience, knowledge, and thinking are integrated and employees' thinking abilities are developed through experience-based learning. We will illustrate these principles on case studies.

The chapter is designed as follows: first, we review Chester Barnard's views on thinking methods to build an analytical framework; second, we explain the tenets of Genbaism, to clarify how Japanese organizations understand thinking methods; third, we present three cases to illustrate how Japanese organizations use and develop employees' thinking abilities; finally, we summarize the main points and draw conclusions.

ACTION, KNOWLEDGE, AND THINKING

In this section, we discuss Barnard's views on thinking methods because he is one of the first practitioners and theorists who emphasized the importance of intuitive thinking and systematically showed the relationship among action, knowledge, and thinking (Akinci & Sadler-Smith, 2012; Isomura, 2010, 2018; Sadler-Smith, 2019).

Barnard (1937) argued that practitioners face an ever-changing, complex and diverse reality, which is composed of verbalized factors, consciously perceived factors, unconsciously sensed factors, and unknown and unknowable factors. Thus, practitioners daily extract and accumulate different types of knowledge from the reality.

According to Barnard (1936, 1950, 1995), practitioners deal with three different types of knowledge: behavioral knowledge (skill), personal knowledge, and formal knowledge. Behavioral knowledge is important because it is deeply related to intuitive thinking. It is embedded in the body and hard to explain verbally; it includes physical, social, and intellectual skills and is learned by imitation and practice. Barnard (1950) uses three special skills as its examples: the skill of getting along with others, persuasion, and intuitive familiarity. Such intuitive skills are acquired and improved through patient hard work.

Personal knowledge is local, that is, related to a specific time and place; such knowledge does not attract any general interest, and most of it is not recorded officially. It is valuable only for the individual; it is not scientific in character. However, personal knowledge is important because it includes personal ideas, values, and emotions and is essential for dependable behavior. It is the basis of responsible decisions and actions; so, as argued lately, it is significantly related to holistic thinking.

Formal knowledge, on the other hand, is socially recorded and shared; it is generally applicable and attracts general interest. It can be put into books, taught at school, or acquired through deliberate observation and experiment. Such knowledge is a social rather than personal possession. A large amount of formal knowledge has been accumulated in society; thus, it is beyond the capacity of an individual to handle it. Formal knowledge is the basis of logical thinking.

Barnard (1950) argued that action, knowledge, and thinking are in a cyclical process: behavioral knowledge is fundamentally acquired and accumulated through action, changes into forms such as personal and formal knowledge, and returns to action through making a judgment. Barnard suggested that decision-making is the process of thinking, and that action and knowledge are integrated by thinking. Consequently, we propose a model of how action, knowledge, and thinking are interconnected (see Figure 13.1).

According to Barnard (1936), thinking methods should be changed depending on what types of knowledge are mainly dealt with when making a decision. For example, he notes that the method of thinking depends on the nature of knowledge (Barnard, 1945, 1947). If the number of variables is limited and they are accurately measured, logical thinking is appropriate to clarify the relationships among the variables. In contrast, if the number of variables is large and cannot be measured quantitatively, intuitive thinking is more suitable.

Barnard (1936: 302) defines logical thinking as "conscious thinking which could be expressed in words, or other symbols, that is, reasoning." If quantitative data, reliable facts and precise information are available, practitioners can utilize logical

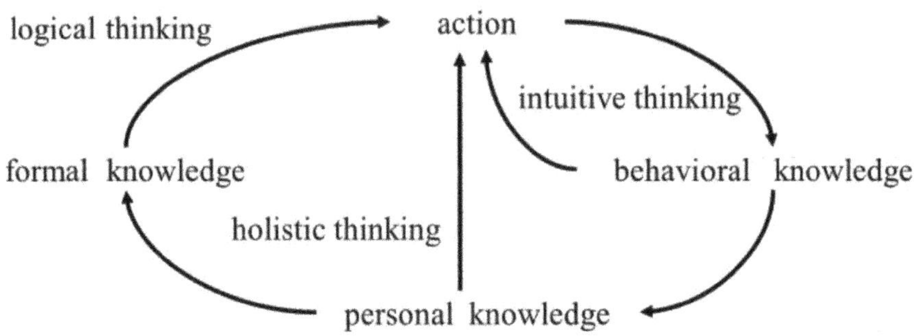

Figure 13.1 A model of integrating action, knowledge, and thinking

thinking. However, if logical thinking is applied in a case where only qualitative and ambiguous information is available, there is a risk that it might be wrong. Logical thinking is useful when precise information, such as formal knowledge and ample time, are available: its purpose is to ascertain or formulate a truth; its focus is on the past and present.

In contrast, Barnard (1936: 302) defines intuitive thoughts as "those not capable of being expressed in words or as reasoning, which is only made known by judgment, decision or action." Intuitive thinking is useful when an immediate decision is required without deep deliberation on the basis of qualitative and ambiguous information, such as behavioral and personal knowledge; its focus is on the present and future.

Barnard also calls intuitive thinking 'strategic reasoning' because it focuses on one 'strategic factor.' "Strategic reasoning involves selecting a single factor and operating on it alone so that the effect may be said to be caused by the change in that factor" (Barnard, 1948: 180). Thus, intuitive thinking identifies and prioritizes a single strategic factor to change.

Intuitive thinking is exploratory and experimental, it is based on a trial-and-error method (Isomura, 2016; Wolf, 1995). Experienced decision makers are familiar with the reality they are facing, so they intuitively choose a strategic factor based on their experience. For them, a strategic factor represents a kind of hypothesis; experienced decision makers verify the results by deciding and taking an action so that they can reduce the uncertainty by experimentation. Then, they re-examine the reality and find a new strategic factor for the next step (Barnard, 1938). Therefore, intuitive thinking is similar to hypothesis-based thinking (Uchida, 2006); it is integrated into action and is mainly used at the operational level.

Barnard (1938) emphasized the importance of the sense of a whole which approximates to holistic thinking; it is based on personal experience and knowledge. Personal knowledge encompasses on-the-spot knowledge accumulated through experience; it is an important source of creativity and responsibility because it includes personal ideas, values, and emotions. The focus of holistic thinking is on the present and future.

Practitioners review their decision processes by utilizing their sense of a whole and modify their judgments when they feel something is wrong. As a result, it is related to risk sensitivity. On the other hand, experienced executives understand the reality as a whole; they often focus on contradictions to find creative problems and solutions (Collins & Porras, 1994; Martin, 2007, 2009); so, it is related to opportunity sensitivity.

Moreover, holistic thinking is indispensable for executives because they must make a judgment based on insufficient evidence and be responsible for the result (Barnard, 1938). Executives learn by repeatedly experiencing such tough judgments, radically changing themselves in the process and developing their personalities. Barnard (1937) argued that personality is a differential capability for social adaptation; it is enhanced or decreased by the social environment's reaction. Difficult moral judgments always test people's personalities. Therefore, executives can be developed through experiencing tough responsible decisions (Isomura, 2010, 2018).

In sum, Barnard suggests that practitioners use and develop three different thinking methods: intuitive thinking, logical thinking, and holistic thinking, which are mainly utilized at the operational, managerial, and executive level respectively. We have adopted Barnard's views as our analytical framework to examine which knowledge and thinking methods Japanese organizations use and develop in their workplace.

WHAT IS 'GENBAISM'?

In this section, we explain the management thought called 'Genbaism,' which is well accepted in Japanese companies. In general, Japanese companies recruit new graduates, employ them for the long term, and develop their skills and knowledge through experience-based learning in their operational workplace. In fact, according to the Ministry of Health, Labor and Welfare (2017), 76 percent of companies recognize the importance of OJT rather than that of Off-JT.

Then, what is Genba? It is literally translated to English as 'a real place' because 'gen' means real or actual while 'ba' means place or space in Japanese. Genba is a place where operations are carried out and value is added (Imai, 2012; Macpherson et al., 2015); it is the shop floor for manufacturers, the store for retailers, and so on. In Japan, Genba is considered a crucial place where something new is always happening. As such, it is perceived as a one-time-only, ever-changing, concrete, and complex phenomenon (Endo, 2014). In line with this understanding, Nonaka and Takeuchi (1995) insist, Genba should be translated as an 'actual place.' Most employees are required to work there and deepen their understanding of it, even if they are candidates for executives.

The nature of Genba can be further clarified by using the concept of 'ba' (Nonaka & Konno, 1998). Ba is considered a shared space for emerging relationships; this space can be physical, virtual, mental, and emotional. Maimone and Sinclair (2014) translate it as 'space of knowledge'; ba is thought of as an organizational space to create emerging change through individual and environmental interactions. Intuition as a form of direct knowing (Sinclair, 2011) plays an important role in noticing new opportunities and a timely response to the emergent change.

According to Toyota (2013), Genba is likened to the real place where actual work is done and value is added. It is one of the most important places in a Toyota factory where time, space, and productivity are crucial and should not be wasted. The philosophy of Genba means that all actions and processes are as transparent as possible; this visibility enables *kaizen*, that is, the philosophy of continuous improvement. The best practice is created by accessing and directly seeing Genba where any problems and solutions are hidden.

Suzuki (2006) defines Genbaism as a management philosophy where all employees from operational level to top management recognize the importance of Genba and regard it as a source of competitive advantage. Genbaism serves as the foundation for quality improvement of products and services. Customer value is created by quality products and services in a factory while customer value is transmitted in a store. In Genba, all necessary information is embedded to solve problems and improve products and services. Therefore, it is also the place where ideas for new products and services are generated.

In Honda, Genbaism is called Sangen Syugi, three reality principles that place emphasis on real place, real thing, and reality. As such, it serves as the base for research and development as well as problem-solving. Honda's philosophy encourages all employees to visit sites of Genba, such as its shop floor and sales office – to see, listen, and touch real things there. Employees are expected to be realistic as they judge on the basis of how they assess Genba (Honda Café, 2013).

Why, then, is Genba important? According to Endo (2014), this is a place where value is created and communicated; organizational knowledge and know-how are accumulated; and employees are developed. Employees must become familiar with Genba first and foremost to extract all necessary knowledge; to deeply understand people and work, including co-workers, clients, business partners, products, services, equipment, business practices, and so on.

Genba is a place where value creation and communication take place. It is a place where operation is carried out, where products and services are created and sold. Therefore, top management is required to visit Genba regularly and pay attention to what happens there in order to improve their value creation and communication. Executives discover in this space potential problems and solutions for their products, services, and operations; moreover, it gives them an opportunity to get creative ideas for the development of their business and the design of competitive strategy.

Genba is a place where organizational knowledge and know-how are accumulated. The Toyota production system is a good example of this (Ohno, 2014) as the company continuously improves operations on the basis of Genbaism. Genba is a workplace where employees think independently without being ordered around by their superiors (Endo, 2014; Kawamata et al., 2005; Nonaka & Takeuchi, 1995; Suzuki, 2006). In fact, in the retail industry, Shimamura and Ryohin Keikaku companies share the same management philosophy with Toyota. They improve their operations by writing comprehensive manuals that are constantly revised in response to employees' propositions. As a result, the manuals are filled with implicit knowledge and know-how created from what employees learn daily in Genba (Isomura & Huang, 2015, 2016).

Moreover, Genba is a place where employees are developed. In Japan, the focus is on their development as knowledge workers. Most employees start their career in Genba and develop their basic skills and knowledge for their future career. This continues when they reach middle management level as they are able to communicate well with employees in Genba which fuels new ideas for designing and developing new products and services (Nonaka & Takeuchi, 1995).

Overall, Genbaism emphasizes the importance of experience at Genba because such experience is imbued with knowledge and thinking. Genbaism allows employees to accumulate behavioral and personal knowledge in Genba and improve their intuitive familiarity through experience. Experience thus becomes the basis for creating and sharing organizational implicit knowledge (Nonaka & Takeuchi, 1995). Not only formal knowledge but also behavioral and personal knowledge are used when employees make their judgments and take their actions. Intuitive thinking plays an important role in finding a problem and building a hypothesis to solve it. Employees first develop a hypothesis on the basis of their experience; then they verify results by taking actions; and finally they modify the hypothesis. This cycle is used to develop their hypothesis-based thinking (Uchida, 2006).

CASE STUDIES OF JAPANESE COMPANIES

In this section, we examine how the management philosophy of Genbaism is introduced to use and develop employees' thinking abilities. First, we briefly explain the overview of Japan's human resource development. Then, we illustrate the application of Genbaism as part of human resources on three cases from retail business, research and development, and trading business respectively.

In Japan, there is a management practice to recruit new graduates regularly every year even though they do not have any work experience. It is said that this management practice enables a low youth unemployment rate. In fact, in 2017 that rate in Japan was 4.7 percent while the average rate of OECD was 11.9 percent in 2017 (OECD, 2017). Then, Japanese organizations develop the new hires for the long term through experience-based learning. This management practice was introduced after World War II and is universally prevalent in Japan (Koda, 2011).

Seven-Eleven Case: Verifying a Hypothesis Created by Intuition through IT System

First, we introduce the case of Seven-Eleven Japan's (SEJ) Operation Field Counsellors (OFCs). SEJ is a franchise chain of convenience stores, most of which are managed by independent owners. OFCs are responsible for supporting multiple stores to increase their sales and profit. SEJ develops all its employees as OFCs at their directly managed store for more than two years (Seven-Eleven Japan, 2018). After that, they are transferred to stores, product development, administration, and other departments. Their experience as OFCs plays a role in having a common language to facilitate all employees' communication.

As a first step, employees learn the basic knowledge and practice how to operate a store as a trainee for five months. Next, they manage a store as an associate store manager or store manager for about two years. During that time, they learn human resource management, the basics of products, management through figures, and so on. Finally, under supervision of an experienced OFC, they work for two months as an assistant field counsellor, setting up a new store and learning how to prepare business documents for analysis.

The core job of OFC is to increase sales and profit by offering appropriate advice to each store's owner. OFCs collect and analyze quantitative data from each store every day. Quantitative data are the result of the past; they do not necessarily tell what will sell well in the future. The situation changes continuously depending on weather, local events or economic conditions. So, first, OFCs are required to build a hypothesis for what to do in each store based on both quantitative and qualitative data. Next, they propose and discuss the hypothesis with owners; then, owners accept and implement it. Finally, OFCs verify the results and improve the hypothesis through information technology such as the point-of-sales (POS) system. As Figure 13.2 shows, the cycle is repeated until a good-selling store is developed that meets customer needs. Thus, hypothesis-based thinking is adopted; thinking and doing are integrated; OFCs develop their basic abilities through this cycle. Such routines take root in daily activities; they are continuously improved. This hypothesis-based thinking corresponds to SEJ's management philosophy: 'responses to changes and back to basics' (Nonaka et al., 2008).

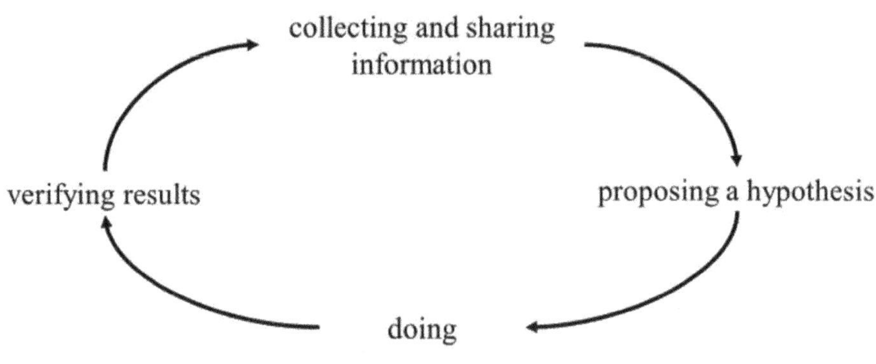

Figure 13.2 Hypothesis-based thinking

Top and middle management are connected through regular meetings held at the headquarters. About 2,700 OFCs assemble every two weeks; they confirm the policy of top management; they share information about customers' trends; and they improve their consulting skills. District and zone meetings are held at the same time. In those meetings, cases are presented to share best practices and discuss intensively how to implement sales initiatives. Therefore, OFCs regularly improve their logical thinking, communication, and decision-making skills through real case discussions.

Here intuitive thinking is mainly used to create a hypothesis by combining behavioral knowledge and quantitative sales data. Behavioral knowledge is verbalized as a hypothesis and OFCs persuade their franchisees to adopt it. The result is verified by the POS system so that OFCs can improve their skills of hypothesis-building and persuasion through this thinking–doing cycle.

Overall, OFCs are developed as knowledge workers to enhance their consulting skills and support their franchisees. Employees' knowledge and skills are used and developed through work experience at Genba; action, knowledge, and thinking are integrated in their daily routines. SEJ's case is exemplary of how intuitive thinking is developed by utilizing the POS system.

Honda Case: Innovative Concept Creation by Group Discussion Using Intuition

Second, we examine the case of Honda's Waigaya. As we explained earlier, Honda has adopted three reality principles as its management philosophy. An intensive meeting method called Waigaya is used as a tool for developing new products. This method is deeply connected with Honda's management philosophy and maintains Honda's corporate culture (Nagasawa & Kino, 2016). The company's fundamental beliefs center on respect for the individual with emphasis on initiative, equality, and trust (Honda, 2020).

Waigaya originates from 'waiwaigayagaya,' that is, jabbering. Homma (2015) defines it as an effective meeting method wherein a group discusses a theme in depth, approaches its essence, and creates an innovation. The aim of Waigaya is to vitalize discussion in order to create a new value and solution; to enable participants to understand each other deeply; and to change the company's atmosphere by increasing the number of collaborators. Therefore, Waigaya is expected to take advantage of a group's collective wisdom by vitalizing communication among all employees.

The aim of Waigaya is to create a concept on the basis of each individual's experience, ideas, and values. A concept should be innovative and change a product's value dramatically. First, participants discuss their own ideas; then, they distill the results of that discussion into a tentative concept; and finally, they create an innovative concept of a new product. In the process, diverse ideas are collected, conflicted, and merged from different people. A concept sheet is made to clarify its corporate policy, a concept, and technical standards to be overcome when realizing the concept. Participants include designers, engineers, production and marketing staff, managers, and so on. They discuss intensively and think deeply in a group; thus, Waigaya is a team-based thinking method (Homma, 2015).

Securing a safe setting for discussion is needed to make Waigaya effective. The atmosphere should be comfortable and relaxed; participants forget each other's workplace, position, age, gender, and so on. That is why Waigaya is often held outside the company. The average number of participants is about ten; a diversity of members is favorable; and guests are sometimes invited to join.

It is important to set a theme to encourage something different. Participants do not rush to achieve results; they enjoy free talking, changing their mindset, and adopting an unconventional approach. To create an innovative concept, they are not afraid of conflicts and contradictions. One session is about three or four hours; such sessions take place intermittently. The whole process takes three to six months, sometimes even a year (Homma, 2015; Kobayashi, 2010).

All participants explore essence through a spiral process. To achieve this, there are mainly three different players: a facilitator, an engineer, and a designer. A designer is an idealist, thoroughly seeking a dream, ready to challenge implicit assumptions and common sense. A designer fully understands the importance of intuitive thinking. In contrast, an engineer is a realist, aiming to produce a realistic product and searching for a creative solution based on formal knowledge and logical thinking. A facilitator balances the two extreme poles and refines their ideas into an innovative concept; they always get back to the reality to verify their hypothesis; and finally, a long-lasting severe tension suddenly leads to a discovery how to solve a problem. Therefore, Waigaya intentionally produces sharp conflicts between an ideal and a reality (Kume, 2006; Shimizu et al., 2018).

Consequently, Waigaya is an intensive discussion method designed to create a new concept through a team-based thinking process. Participants' behavioral knowledge is verbalized and transformed into personal knowledge through a deep group discussion. Honda emphasizes the importance of such knowledge accumulated in Genba because behavioral knowledge is a source of innovation and creation. If personal knowledge is logically analyzed and discussed, it may lose its attractiveness because it is exposed to a criticism from a viewpoint of a scientific procedure. So, Waigaya avoids using formal knowledge or logical thinking intentionally to create an innovative concept. In this process, intuitive thinking is effectively utilized because participants do not need to provide any evidence or any analysis; however, logical thinking is combined to realize an ideal from a viewpoint of technology. A concept must be valuable to inspire resonance among all employees and be shared positively. Such a concept represents a hypothesis that exceeds customers' expectations and does not come from formal knowledge and logical thinking (Homma, 2015).

Sogo Shosa Case: Developing Intuitive Thinking as a Basic Ability at Genba

Third, we examine a case of Sogo Shosha, that is, general trading companies. It establishes a well-designed human development system by combining OJT and Off-JT. Sogo Shosha plays an important role in Japan's economy because it acts as an intermediary for diverse companies and arranges new businesses. It has significantly increased its profit since the 2000s; it also attracts public attention because it develops and provides business leaders for other companies (Sankei Shimbun, 2015).

Sogo Shosha's business model has recently shifted from trading to business investment and management. Its core business used to be trading, brokering a business deal between a buyer and a seller, and getting a commission. The company specialized in importing raw material supplies in upstream business and in exporting clients' products globally in downstream business. However, because information technology has enabled direct transactions since the 1990s, Sogo Shosha faced a serious risk of losing its role as a broker. Therefore, it started investing directly and developing new businesses such as energy, infrastructure, natural resources, IT, retail, and so on. Now, it connects those businesses with traditional trading businesses.

Sogo Shosha's strategy is to dominate each industry's value chain. For example, in importing, it used to buy natural resources from developers and sell them to domestic companies; however, it has started to invest and act as a new developer in an effort to expand its business upstream. On the other hand, in exporting, it has started to support clients' companies to set up factories and sales companies in other countries. Sogo Shosha invests and manages such factories and sales companies by negotiating with diverse stakeholders in foreign countries. In addition, Sogo Shosha used to play a role in financing and distributing as a wholesaler domestically. Now, it is expanding its activities to set up and develop a new business. Thus, Sogo Shosha dominates all processes of the value chain with the aim to increase its profit in the trading business.

Next, we examine what abilities employees are required to possess in those businesses. Sogo Shosha emphasizes the importance of experience at Genba. In fact, according to Iijima (2018), employees have to develop their abilities through their experience. He calls this the power of Genba, intuitive familiarity with Genba. Such abilities include insight to find an opportunity and a risk, ability to respond to changes flexibly, to get things done by approaching difficult tasks aggressively, and communication and negotiation skills to involve and influence stakeholders. On the other hand, Kakiuchi (2018) emphasizes a high sense of ethics, a flexible ability to respond to and handle changes, and ability to get things done to overcome difficulties. Kakiuchi insists that all these abilities are developed through experiencing tough decisions repeatedly; therefore, the company provides its employees with as many opportunities as possible to work as senior or top managers in its global and domestic subsidiaries.

Finally, we examine how Sogo Shosha develops its human resources (Itochu Co., 2018; Mitsubishi Co., 2018). First, new graduates are assigned to work for a division; they learn basic product knowledge and business practice through OJT and build a network of personal connections with clients and business partners. They also learn basic business knowledge and skills such as finance, accounting, credit management, and sales support through Off-JT. Then, they are dispatched to a group company in a foreign country as a trainee. They are expected to improve their language skills and deepen the understanding of cultural differences. They are developed for about eight to ten years to become a trading professional in each division. After that, some of them are dispatched to business schools in a foreign country to improve their formal knowledge and logical thinking.

Next, employees are assigned to work for a group company as a senior or top manager. In this process, they learn change management, insight, execution, commitment, flexibility, how to avoid and handle risk, and hone their decision-making skills, and so on. They also brush up on their communication and negotiation skills and build a network of personal connections. To acquire all these skills and knowledge, they experience tough responsible decisions and negotiations. Thus, once employees accumulate enough experience and knowledge to run a business, they are transferred to a division to start a new business or a subsidiary company.

As a result, Sogo Shosha's employees are developed through accumulating experiences and behavioral knowledge at Genba to improve intuitive thinking. Then, they expand and improve their formal knowledge and skills through Off-JT to enhance logical thinking. Finally, they are required to experience tough and responsible decisions as a senior or top manager to acquire holistic thinking. Employees are systematically developed through repeating the cycle between OJT and Off-JT.

DISCUSSION AND CONCLUSIONS

In summary, first, for Japanese organizations intuition is based on experience at Genba. Intuitive thinking uses behavioral and personal knowledge accumulated at operational workplaces. The philosophy of Genbaism emphasizes the importance of intuitive familiarity with Genba as a basic ability for all employees. This ability is the base of human resource development; it enables all employees to share their deep understanding of people and work. Moreover, employees extract original knowledge from Genba; then, they find and solve problems and produce creative ideas.

Second, Genbaism expects action, knowledge, and intuitive thinking to be integrated when hypothesis-based thinking is used. A hypothesis is created based on experience-based knowledge. The doing–thinking cycle starts from setting a hypothesis, proceeds to taking actions, and ends by verifying and improving it. Therefore, intuitive thinking is not used or developed all by itself. Intuitive thinking can work well with logical thinking once behavioral knowledge is verbalized and abstracted as personal and formal knowledge. Intuitive thinking is mainly used to create a hypothesis that is verified and improved constantly by employees' actions. Such routines take root in their daily activities. Employees are developed by learning and acquiring those routines. Seven-Eleven Japan's case illustrates this principle on the development of employees' intuitive thinking through the POS system.

Third, hypothesis-based thinking is developed through work experience at Genba; however, formal education is also used to develop intuitive skills and to share implicit knowledge. Since intuitive thinking is based on behavioral knowledge created through experience, its process is hard to clarify. However, as Honda's case shows, when behavioral knowledge is transferred to a language form such as personal and formal knowledge, people can share this knowledge and create new knowledge. In fact, intuitive thinking is combined with other thinking methods, such as logical and holistic thinking. As Sogo Shosha's case illustrates, different thinking methods are combined and learned systematically in the process of career development.

Overall, Japanese organizations do not view thinking abilities as separated from action and knowledge. Action, knowledge, and thinking are integrated in daily routines. Thinking abilities are invisible; however, they are visualized as daily routines, especially at the operational level; then, they are constantly verified and improved. Genbaism regards intuitive thinking as a thinking method to create, verify, and improve a hypothesis on the basis of experience. Such hypothesis-based thinking is utilized for the development of intuitive thinking. Thus, Japanese organizations use and develop their employees' thinking abilities through experience-based learning at Genba.

REFERENCES

Akinci, C., & Sadler-Smith, E. 2012. Intuition in management research: A historical review. *International Journal of Management Reviews*, 14: 104–122.

Barnard, C.I. 1936. Mind in everyday affairs. In C. I. Barnard, *The functions of the executive*: 301–322. Cambridge, MA: Harvard University Press.

Barnard, C.I. 1937. Notes on some obscure aspects of human relations. In W.B. Wolf, & H. Iino (Eds.), *Philosophy for managers: Selected papers of Chester I. Barnard*: 63–111. Tokyo: Bunshindo.

Barnard, C.I. 1938. *The functions of the executive*. Cambridge, MA: Harvard University Press.

Barnard, C.I. 1945. Education for executives. In C.I. Barnard, *Organization and management: Selected papers*: 194–206. Cambridge, MA: Harvard University Press.

Barnard, C.I. 1947. Some aspects of organization relevant to industrial research. In W.B. Wolf, & H. Iino (Eds.), *Philosophy for managers: Selected papers of Chester I. Barnard*: 112–121. Tokyo: Bunshindo.

Barnard, C.I. 1948. *Organization and management: Selected papers*. Cambridge, MA: Harvard University Press.

Barnard, C.I. 1950. Skill, knowledge, and judgment. In W.B. Wolf, & H. Iino (Eds.), *Philosophy for managers: Selected papers of Chester I. Barnard*: 129–137. Tokyo: Bunshindo.

Barnard, C.I. 1995. The significance of decisive behaviour in social action: Notes on the nature of decision. *Journal of Management History*, 1(4): 28–87 (original work written in 1940).

Collins, J.C., & Porras, J.I. 1994. *Built to last: Successful habits of visionary companies*. New York: HarperCollins.

Endo, I. 2014. *The theory of Genba: Logic and practice to create remarkable Genba*. Tokyo: Toyo Keizai Inc. (in Japanese).

Fujimoto, T. 2013. *Competitive strategy by Genbaism*. Tokyo: Shinchosya Publishing (in Japanese).

Homma, H. 2015. *Encouragement of Honda's way of Waigaya*. Tokyo: Asahi Shimbun Publication (in Japanese).

Honda, 2020. Honda's philosophy. https://global.honda/about/philosophy.html (accessed February 15, 2020).

Honda Café, 2013. *Honda philosophy*. https://www.honda-cafe.jp/本田宗一郎ミュージアム/honda-philosophy/ (accessed October 23, 2018).

Iijima, A. 2018. Interview with Iijima, Board Chairperson of Mitsui Corporation. *Nikkei Business*, March 19 (in Japanese).

Imai, M. 2012. *Genba kaizen: A commonsense approach to a continuous improvement strategy*. New York: McGraw-Hill Education.
Isomura, K. 2010. Barnard on leadership development: Bridging action and thinking. *Journal of Management History*, 16(2): 216–232.
Isomura, K. 2016. Re-examining Chester Barnard's contributions to knowledge management: Focusing on practical thinking and knowledge. *CGSA Forum*, 14: 1–22.
Isomura, K. 2018. Examining creative leaders' practical-thinking methods on the basis of Chester Barnard's views. *CGSA Forum*, 16: 1–12.
Isomura, K., & Huang, P.-Y. 2015. Shimamura's strategy to avoid competition: Developing a low-cost operating system and evolutionary manuals. *Strategic Direction*, 31(5): 37–39.
Isomura, K., & Huang, P.-Y. 2016. MUJI's way to build a global brand: Integrating value communication into product and store development. *Strategic Direction*, 32(4): 8–11.
Itochu Co. 2018. *Employee relations*. https://www.itochu.co.jp/en/csr/employee/index.html (accessed December 23, 2018).
Kakiuchi, T. 2018. My views on leadership by Kakiuchi, T., President of Mitsubishi Corporation. *Nihon Keizai Shimbun*, January 4 (in Japanese).
Kawamata, H., Soma, T., Kiyoshima, N., Ueki, T., & Nishi, T. 2005. The power of Genba in Japan. *Nikkei Information Strategy*, 14(11): 44–112 (in Japanese).
Kobayashi, S. 2010. *The essence of Honda's innovation*. Tokyo: Nikkei BP (in Japanese).
Koda, H. 2011. The historical development of human resource development management of Japanese companies after the end of World War II: Concepts of ability, skill and competency. *Journal of Creative Management*, 7: 121–133 (in Japanese).
Kume, T. 2006. *How to design inspiration*. Tokyo: Shogakukan (in Japanese).
Macpherson, W.G., Lockhart, J.C., Kavan, H., & Iaquinto, A. 2015. Kaizen: A Japanese philosophy and system for business excellence. *Journal of Business Strategy*, 36(5): 3–9.
Maimone, F., & Sinclair, M. 2014. Dancing in the dark: Creativity, knowledge creation and (emergent) organizational change. *Journal of Organizational Change Management*, 27(2): 344–361.
Martin, R. 2007. How successful leaders think. *Harvard Business Review*, 85(6): 60–67.
Martin, R. 2009. *The opposable mind: Winning through integrative thinking*. Boston, MA: Harvard Business School Press.
Matsushita, K. 2007. *Making managerial decisions*. Kyoto: PHP Research Institute (in Japanese).
Ministry of Health, Labor & Welfare. 2017. *Basic survey of human resource development*. https://www.mhlw.go.jp/file/04-Houdouhappyou-11801500-Shokugyounouryokukaihatsukyoku-Kibansetsubishitsu/0000118619_8.pdf (accessed October 24, 2018).
Mitsubishi Co. 2018. *Training and career development*. https://www.mitsubishicorp.com/jp/ja/about/resource/training.html (accessed December 23, 2018).
Nagasawa, S., & Kino, R. 2016. *Honda's identity and 'Waigaya'*. Tokyo: Doyukan (in Japanese).
Nakayama, M. 1994. *Konosuke Matsushita's intuitive abilities*. Kyoto: PHP Research Institute (in Japanese).
Nonaka. K., & Konno, N. 1998. The concept of 'ba'. *California Management Review*, 40(3): 40–54.
Nonaka, I., & Takeuchi, H. 1995. *The knowledge-creating companies: How Japanese companies create the dynamics of innovation*. New York: Oxford University Press.
Nonaka, I., Toyama, R., & Hirata, T. 2008. *Managing flow: A process theory of the knowledge-based firm*. New York: Palgrave Macmillan.
OECD. 2017. *Youth unemployment rate*. https://data.oecd.org/unemp/youth-unemployment-rate.htm (accessed December 4, 2018).
Ohno, T. 2014. *A basic of Toyota Production System*. Tokyo: JMA Management Center (in Japanese).

Sadler-Smith, E., 2019. Intuition in management. *Oxford Research Encyclopedia for Business and Management.* https://oxfordre.com/business/view/10.1093/acrefore/9780190224851.001.0001/acrefore-9780190224851-e-177?rskey=TolqEE&result=1 (accessed August 23, 2019).

Sankei Shimbun, 2015. *Why are Mitsubishi Corporation's employees invited as a top manager?: The secret of developing managerial leader.* https://www.sankei.com/premium/news/150115/prm1501150002-n1.html (accessed January 7, 2019) (in Japanese).

Seven-Eleven Japan. 2018. *Recruiting information.* http://www.sej.co.jp/recruit/new/recruit/guideline.html (accessed November 10, 2018).

Shimizu, Y., Aoyama, K., Shirasaka, S., Oizumu, K., & Uchida, T. 2018. *The essence of Waigaya.* Tokyo: Nikkan Kogyo Shimbun (in Japanese).

Sinclair, M. 2011. An integrated framework of intuition. In M. Sinclair (Ed.), *Handbook of intuition research*: 3–16. Cheltenham, UK and Northampton, MA, USA: Edward Elgar Publishing.

Suzuki, S. 2006. Japanese corporation and Genbaism. *Journal of Economics, Asia University*, 14(1): 1–15 (in Japanese).

Toyota. 2013. *Genba – Toyota Production System guide.* http://blog.toyota.co.uk/genba-toyota-production-system (accessed October 23, 2018).

Uchida, K. 2006. *The BCG way: The art of hypothesis-driven management.* Tokyo: Toyo Keizai Inc. (in Japanese).

Wolf, W.B. 1995. The Barnard–Simon connection. *Journal of Management History*, 1(4): 88–99.

14. "Wuity" – the proposed third cognitive model for mindful creative problem solving: a case study of two Chinese aerospace projects

Xin Wang

Psychological and cognitive theories as well as management science propose two distinct information processing systems: one is quick, effortless, associative, and intuitive; the other is slow, effortful, analytic, and deliberate. But these systems and their interaction tend to be understood differently in different cultural paradigms. Nisbett and his colleagues find that Westerners tend to engage primarily in context-independent, analytic and conceptual processes, whereas Asians tend to draw first on context-dependent, holistic and intuitive perceptual processes (Nisbett et al., 2001; Peng & Nisbett, 1999). A wealth of psychological and management research has been conducted to resolve the debate whether these two systems run in parallel, as explained by dual-process theories, or if their function can be integrated in an overall framework (Evans & Stanovich, 2013). Current research suggests that the systems may be indeed intertwined. Kruglanski and Gigerenzer (2011) propose that deliberation can become intuitive (*intuitive deliberation*) through practice, they estimate ten thousand hours of training is necessary. On the other hand, intuition can become deliberate (*deliberate intuition*) by training the mind to be attentive. Francisco and Burnett (2008) view deliberate intuition as the intentional engagement of intuitive skills in the service of uncovering hidden relationships and active encouragement in creative problem solving. However, few studies were focused on the transformation, balance and coordination between intuition and analysis. That is where mindfulness could be helpful.

Mindfulness may play a role in reconciling deliberation and intuition and their interaction with the aim to provide a creative solution. It is an important topic in cognitive science, medical science, psychology, and management. Kabat-Zinn (1990) defines mindfulness as a state in which one is highly aware and focused on the reality of the present moment, accepting and acknowledging it, without getting caught up in thoughts that are about the situation or in emotional reactions to the situation. Ellen Langer (1989) believes mindfulness is a simple act of noticing new things, which makes people sensitive to context and perspective. After forty years of study, mindfulness has been widely recognized as a state of mind having a wide conscious attention, which creates both structural and functional brain changes with an altered trait such as neuroplasticity from long-term practice (Dane, 2011a; Goleman & Davidson, 2017). Weick and Sutcliffe (2001, 2011, 2015) in their three management books adopt the term "mindfulness" as a higher-order category for five specific behaviors that are found in high reliability organizations. They illustrate the presence of these behaviors in exemplary stories from nuclear power plants, firefighting crews, hospitals, banks and more. Rather than focus on how to avoid failure or quickly recover from a failure, their emphasis is on the processes of creativity and innovation when creating mindfully something new. Dane (2011b) proposes that mindfulness may enhance the degree to which individuals attend to their intuitions as they arise through an increasing attunement to the outcomes of nonconsciously driven processes. However, more research is needed to connect mindfulness with intuition, deliberation or dual-process theory.

To address the above-mentioned gap, the following research question is investigated: *After getting stuck, how do people achieve creative solutions for scientific problems in a mindful fashion with the integrated power of intuition and deliberation?* The chapter introduces a new integrative cognitive model, based on the Chinese traditional philosophical notion of "Wuity" that allows for a meaningful interaction of both information processing systems. Wuity is defined as a higher cognition with the flexible and imaginative ability to gain intuitive understanding of underlying phenomena, and thus provide an inspirational connection to deliberative thinking for insightful problem solving. Wuity is also a process of mindful observation and visual analogy, embedded in the context of Chinese philosophy (Wang & Gloor, 2018; Wang & Li, 2017, 2018). Therefore, the chapter draws on research from cognitive science, management science and Chinese traditional philosophy to explore the role of higher-level cognition that oscillates between and links intuition and deliberation. Furthermore, it provides evidence how Wuity synthesizes deliberative intuition and visual analogy reasoning to achieve creativity, especially in team processes of innovation.

WUITY AS A HIGHER COGNITION

Wuity emphasizes the need to reach beneath the surface of a problem, to delve deep into its essence, and discover the delicate and hidden relationships that exist at a fundamental level through mindful observation and visual analogy (Hofstadter & Sander, 2013). The concept was first proposed by the Daoist philosopher Zhuangzi 2,000 years ago (Zhuangzi, 2009: 21, *Tianzifang*, line 33), rooted in Chinese indigenous traditions, such as Daoism, Zen Buddhism, and Confucianism. However, Wuity has transcended its religious meaning and has been applied to Chinese cultural practices, such as painting, calligraphy, and poetry, as well as in science disciplines, for example, in Chinese medicine, ancient mathematics, engineering and agriculture. Gradually, it has evolved into a common cognitive model. Yang Yi (2008) sees Wuity as an advantage of the Chinese traditional way of thinking. He states that the Asian concept of Wuity and the Western concept of rationality are two important achievements in the history of human thought, and proposes that they complement each other.

Mindful Observation

Wuity pays more attention to observation than other mindfulness behaviors, which can be traced to the Daoist tradition described in Book of Changes (Yi Jing Editing Group, 1989). On the contrary, the Western view on mindfulness supports a broader range of behaviors, like mindful eating, mindful walking, and mindful listening. Dekeyser and colleagues (2008) point out four aspects: mindful observation, non-aversion, non-judgment, and letting go. Likewise, according to Epstein (2003), a mindful practice includes four core features: attentive observation, critical curiosity, "beginner's mind," and presence. However, all these descriptions of mindfulness emphasize the importance of observing, noticing, or attending to a variety of stimuli, including internal phenomena, such as bodily sensations, cognitions, and emotions, and external phenomena, such as sounds and smells (Dimidjian & Linehan, 2003; Kabat-Zinn, 1990; Segal et al., 2002). Mindful observation means observing and seeing with awareness, which is the careful attending to internal and external phenomena (e.g., thoughts, emotions, sounds, smells, or proprioceptive sensations) (Dimidjian & Linehan, 2003; Linehan, 1993). As Schwartz et al. (2005: 1312) state: "Perhaps the essential characteristic of mindful observation is that you are just watching, observing all facts, both inner and outer, very calmly, clearly and closely." This implies a detachment from things being observed. Learning, therefore, is not solely a matter of what one knows but also who the learners become (Borgo, 2007; Pavlovich & Krahnke, 2012).

Scientific observation usually refers to the observation from binary opposing views, or outward observation, in which subjective observers are separated from the object observed. The effects of observation depend on certain tools, such as eyes, telescopes or microscopes, to observe the external world. Observers must maintain an objective attitude to avoid any personal subjective assumptions affecting results (Daston & Lunbeck, 2011). The limitation of this approach is that it cannot be applied to observing a person's mind and sub-consciousness. On the contrary, mindful observation is from the non-binary opposing or inter-subjective view, also known as inward observation in Daoism or Vipassana (Insight Meditation) in the Buddhist tradition (Kohn, 2008), emphasizing that the observer and the observed are whole or unified. There is no need to distinguish between subjects and objects, observers must carefully perceive and scan what is observed or see intuitively to keep a seamless observation and achieve a deep understanding of relationships of the overall structure and its detailed parts (John-Steiner, 1997). Mindful observation is not opposed to scientific observation, rather it is a kind of scientific thinking, the purpose of which is to find undiscovered parts that have never been attended to.

Visual Analogy and Thinking Model

Contrary to rationality, Wuity makes use of imagery, metaphors and analogy rather than concepts, logics and analysis, but it is also based on reason. Hofstadter and Sander (2013) give a wonderful and insightful account of the role of analogy in cognition, in which analogy is compared to the fuel and fire of thinking and helps to dig through the surface to reach the essence. The Wuity cognitive model is a reflection of the classic Chinese style of visual analogy, named: "Qu Xiang Bi Lei." "Qu" means mindful observing and seeing. "Xiang" means vivid imageries, which may refer to a picture, a phenomenon, mental images, a representation or a symbol of law. Each "Xiang" is concrete and metaphorical, just like "Dao," which provides a practical way of vivid imageries while it hints at a deep meaning of universal law, leading to infinite wisdom. Visual mental images have been described as "seeing with the mind's eye" (Pylyshyn, 2003). The third component, "Bi Lei" refers to the process of analogy, using the nature of one category to describe the nature of another. It aims at revealing the deep connection between them, rather than remaining on the surface. The emphasis is on the common nature of one category instead of special properties of one item. Amit and her colleagues (2017) proposed that humans rely on at least two modes of thought: verbal (or concept) and visual (or imagery). Verbal thinking can be evoked relatively independently of visual imagery. Conversely, individuals can engage in visual imagery even when thinking verbally. Nevertheless, visual thinking is primary since verbal abilities came later during human development.

Creative Insight Harmonizes Two Opposites

Gaining a clear and deep insight is the most productive result of Wuity thinking. Once a good analogy between different domains is found, confusion and contradiction caused by superficial observation will be swept away, and one will enter a transparent state with a clear mind and insights into essence with an enlightened mind. Josipovic (2013, 2014) concluded that when people are in this mindful nondual awareness state, they don't have a strong subject–object dichotomy. The study of insights started in the 1970s as a branch of cognitive psychology. Researchers pointed out that people tend to encounter an obstacle, commonly known as "getting stuck" on their way to an insight (Luo & Niki, 2003). At the same time, insight is considered to be gained through a cognitive restructuring process, which is the only way to the right answer (Epstein, 1984). Taylor and Egeto-Szabo (2017) suggest that, in transformational experiences, a new, stable and permanent "self-system" is established, whereas in temporary awakening experiences the normal "self-system" remains intact, even if temporarily disabled. Two types of transformational experiences are identified: a "secondary shift," in which a person's values and perspective are transformed, and a "primary shift," in which a person's whole "self-system" is replaced, leading to a sense of new identity.

Wuity reconciles the above tension as its style of thought aims to gain intuitive understanding, insights and enlightening through mindful observation and visual analogy. It is a collective thinking model in the classical Chinese culture, but it is also an inherent higher cognitive skill in modern society, achieved by training the mind through mindfulness. Wang and her co-authors introduced Wuity to management innovation. Wang and Gloor (2018) use the case of Elon Musk to demonstrate that Wuity represents creative thinking of innovators both in the East and West, which integrates intuitive and deliberate judgments. Wang and Riopelle (2019) illustrate how to build a shared future through co-Wuity partnership and collaborative innovation networks in a historical case study of moving assembly lines and mass production.

CASE STUDY METHOD

Since the aim of this chapter is to build a new theoretical framework and its interactive process, it adopted the case study method (Eisenhardt, 1989), which provides a rare opportunity to illustrate and expand the relationship among different constructs (Eisenhardt, 1989; Siggelkow, 2007). The chapter presents two cases of Wuity-based innovation in the Chinese aerospace community. The author and her colleagues interviewed renowned professionals (chief scientists, outstanding professionals, talents in scientific and technological innovation) in the field of satellite measurement and control. The interviewees are experts who have been working in this field for years and have made great contributions in knowledge creation (Hooker et al., 2014). The two case studies are: (1) a project on orbit and manifold theory of irregular asteroids near the balancing point (see Jiang et al., 2014) and (2) a project on rescuing an uncontrolled satellite in space, which saved more than 1 billion RMB for China (unpublished data).

Case 1: Project on Orbit and Manifold Theory of Irregular Asteroids Near the Balancing Point

The next six points are excerpts from an interview with respondent G21, which was originally conducted in Chinese and translated into English here.

Respondent G21 began by pointing out that they regarded the motion of an asteroid near thc balancing point to be six-dimensional at the beginning:

1. Then I put a ball in a small bowl to analogize the motion of asteroid near the balancing point. It is easier to understand something abstract when I use imagery analogy. In this way, one six-dimensional space can be divided into six one-dimensional spaces, or three two-dimensional spaces, or one two-dimensional space plus one four-dimensional space. Adopting imagery analogy, I could understand and imagine something abstract by comparing it to something tangible. One-dimensional and two-dimensional spaces are relatively easy to understand through the use of imagery analogy. As for four-dimensional space which could not be further divided, the motion within was not periodic. How could I use the imagery analogy then? I got stuck in thinking.
2. After that, I abandoned all my accumulated knowledge completely.
3. I regard myself to be as ignorant as a baby facing the world of unknown. One day, I thought of the saddle when riding a horse.
4. When one rides in the saddle, he can locate the highest point in this direction of two legs and the lowest point along the horse's mane. Then, I put something on the saddle. If I put a small ball on the smooth surface of the saddle, it will

keep moving periodically without tangential movement or tangential force and will fall with tangential movement or tangential force. The saddle is symmetric, I wonder whether the eigenvalues of four dimensions are symmetrical?

5. I had learned the saddle surface in analytic geometry. Thus, the four-dimensional movement could be analogized. So, the motion near the asteroid equilibrium point is analogous to the projection motion of the four-dimensional subspace relative to the origin.
6. Then, the corresponding eigenvalue equation was figured out. Suddenly, I was shocked. Making a breakthrough, I found the laws of physics were perfectly shown in front of me. There was more shock than happiness in my mind. I felt purified. It was magical. Then I told another member, he danced with delight. He understood when I said it and felt enlightened.

Case 2: Project on Rescuing an Uncontrolled Satellite in Space

Again, the next six points are excerpts from an interview with respondent G22, which was originally conducted in Chinese and translated into English here.

Respondent G22 pointed out they needed to determine the attitude of an uncontrolled detection satellite in order to rescue it:

1. The early ideas went astray. Since the axis of satellite usually pointed to its center, I could determine its attitude by the attitude of its axis. Under normal circumstances, the spinning of axis in space is constant. In this way, the attitude of its axis could be determined and calculated by using formula. However, I felt the axis of that satellite drew a circle, which turned into a round. What's wrong with it? The current thinking model must be wrong and would not do.
2. In this case, I had to think in another way. In those days, I thought about it all day long and it brought me much pressure.
3. I feel that the satellite turned over and one wing was not stretched. It was spinning in the air.
4. It was similar to a person who stretched out one arm and failed to stretch the other one. He was not in a balancing state. The axis which used to point to the center is slanting. How could I calculate its direction and spin angular velocity? If I could not calculate its angle, I could not determine the satellite's attitude, let alone controlling it.
5. At that time my mentor was smoking over there, when it struck me that it may be related to eigenvalue. That day I said I would like to have a smoke. Actually, I have little interest in smoking. I just go there to relax, talking with my mentor and other team members. My mentor was a little addicted to smoking. I learned eigenvalue in college and did not think of this after that. However, it came to me naturally at that moment. When my mentor asked me how it came to my mind, I could not answer. We didn't talk too much in daily life, but I can generate good ideas when being with him.
6. Respondent G1 pointed out that they talked about it later. The thinking model was then settled. Finally, we grasped the law of satellite's motion. At last, we figured out the track of the uncontrolled satellite and rescued it successfully.

CASE ANALYSIS

Next, I will examine the unique impact of Wuity-based thinking on knowledge creation on the basis of the above two cases, using a newly developed framework of knowledge taxonomy: the above-described Qu Xiang Bi Lei cognitive model and Wuity's six-step interactive process (for details, see Wang & Gloor, 2018; Wang & Li, 2017).

Knowledge Taxonomy

The chapter adopts a new knowledge taxonomy proposed by philosopher Jürgen Habermas (1992) who categorizes knowledge into two types: *thematic knowledge* and *unthematic knowledge*. Thematic knowledge is deliberate and discipline-based, unthematic knowledge is intuitive and experience-based. The thematic knowledge is from the scientific world, as the theme and core of social interaction, the effectiveness of thematic knowledge depends on whether the proposition is true, logical, and accurate. Unthematic knowledge comes from our life world and is helpful to interpret obscure thematic knowledge and make it convincing. It relies on one's horizon, connection roles in different fields and accumulation of background information (Lafont & Medina, 1999). Based on Habermas' description, in this chapter unthematic knowledge is defined as knowledge not directly related to tasks and purpose to be achieved, but closely related to life experience, which helps to reach an understanding. Conversely, thematic knowledge is defined as knowledge in a certain field which is directly related to tasks and purpose to be achieved. This distinction was applied to statements from the above interviews, as categorized in Table 14.1.

In Case 1, the motion of asteroids near the balancing point in the four-dimensional space is explained in the form of unthematic knowledge – the motion of a small ball

Table 14.1 Examples of thematic and unthematic knowledge

Case 1	Unthematic Knowledge	When one rides in the saddle, he can locate the highest point in this direction of two legs and the lowest point along the horse's mane. Then, I put something on the saddle. If I put a small ball on the smooth surface of the saddle, it will keep moving periodically without tangential movement or tangential force and will fall with tangential movement or tangential force. The saddle is symmetric.
	Thematic Knowledge	I had learned the saddle surface in analytic geometry. Thus, the four-dimensional movement could be analogized and the corresponding eigenvalue equation was figured out.
Case 2	Unthematic Knowledge	The satellite turned over and one wing was not stretched. It was spinning in the air. It was similar to a person who stretched out one arm and failed to stretch the other. He was not in a balancing state. When a person can't keep his balance while walking, he is likely to fall.
	Thematic Knowledge	The axis which used to point to the center is slanting. How could I calculate its direction and spin angular velocity? If I could not calculate its angle, I could not determine the satellite's attitude, let alone controlling it.

on the saddle surface. It provides a direct explanation and helps generate new thematic knowledge. In Case 2, the detection satellite is spinning in space for one of its wings is not stretched. This thematic knowledge is analogized to a spinning person with one arm not stretched – unthematic knowledge in the life world. As demonstrated, unthematic knowledge explains and helps generate new thematic knowledge, at least to some extent.

It can be seen that the effect of unthematic knowledge on thematic knowledge is twofold. First, it provides an explanation and enables understanding of thematic knowledge. Second, it promotes and generates new thematic knowledge. Therefore, unthematic knowledge from the life world, though not directly related to new thematic knowledge in the scientific micro-world, provides an explanation and enhances understanding of thematic knowledge and helps to form consensus between the two. This is consistent with Habermas' understanding of their relationship. Besides, Wuity-based knowledge creation emphasizes the importance of returning to the starting point. It mainly uses unthematic knowledge in the life world for it is direct and novel, and provides effective support in obtaining the insights of the abstract and strange thematic knowledge. What is to be noted is that these two roles depend on the interaction and combination of thematic and unthematic knowledge. In other words, unthematic knowledge alone will not exert any influence on new thematic knowledge. Likewise, without unthematic knowledge, a new thematic knowledge will not come into being. To summarize, Wuity provides an oscillation process for unthematic (intuitive) knowledge, linking it to and interacting with thematic (deliberate) knowledge, producing mindful creative problem solving as a result.

The Qu Xiang Bi Lei Cognitive Model

"Qu Xiang Bi Lei" has become a cognitive model often used in the Chinese cultural context to solve scientific problems in teams. In the process of team interaction, members link problems in the scientific micro-world with their feelings and experiences in the life world and nature consciously or unconsciously. At the same time, they use metaphor to associate one item in the life world with another in the scientific micro-world to achieve understanding of their relevant property, and thus create new thematic knowledge. The core mechanism of Wuity-based thinking is the adoption of the "Qu Xiang Bi Lei" model. As shown in Table 14.2, unthematic knowledge is closely connected with visual thinking (cognitive model characterized by visual thinking), while thematic knowledge is closely connected with verbal thinking (cognitive model characterized by verbal thinking).

In Case 1, a team member adopts an imagery analogy. By analogizing the motion of asteroids near the balancing point in one-dimensional, two-dimensional and four-dimensional spaces to the motion of the small ball in the bowl and the motion of the ball on the saddle, he obtains the thematic knowledge – eigenvalue equation of the saddle surface and the law of asteroid's motion in the six-dimensional space. He adopts the analogous method of dividing a complex entity into simple parts and converging them back by dividing the motion in a six-dimensional space into those

Table 14.2 Qu Xiang Bi Lei cognitive model

	Qu Xiang Bi Lei
Case 1	The motion of asteroids near the balancing point in the one-dimensional or two-dimensional space (*Thematic Knowledge: Concept 1*)is analogized to the motion of the small ball in the bowl (*Unthematic Knowledge: Imagery 1*). One member puts forward the initial but fuzzy idea of "saddle." The motion of asteroids near the balancing point in the four-dimensional space (*Thematic Knowledge*: *Concept 2*) is analogized to the motion of the ball on the saddle (*Unthematic Knowledge*: *Imagery 2*). The individual finds interlinked connections and common features between the two domains (tangential force influences the motion of asteroids). The individual obtains insights and figures out corresponding eigenvalue equation based on saddle surface (*Thematic Knowledge*: *Concept 2*) (*integrate the concept in thematic knowledge and imagery in unthematic knowledge*).
Case 2	The individual will detect the angle of the satellite (*Thematic Knowledge: Concept 1*) is analogized to a circle on the edge of the axis (*Unthematic Knowledge: Imagery 1*). The individual puts forward the original but fuzzy idea of "satellite in the air spin". The wing not stretched in the probe satellite (*Thematic Knowledge: Concept 2*) is analogized to a person's arm not stretched (*Unthematic Knowledge*: *Imagery 2*). Uncontrolled satellite (*Thematic Knowledge*: *Concept 3*) is analogized to the turning over of a person (*Unthematic Knowledge*: *Imagery 3*). Eigenvalue (*Thematic Knowledge*: *Concept 4*) is analogized to the unique habit of each individual (*Unthematic Knowledge*: *Imagery 4*). The individual finds interlinked connections and common features between the two domains (changes in the spinning angle lead the satellite into an unbalanced state). The individual obtains insight and calculates eigenvalue of the key variable (*Thematic Knowledge*: *Concept 5*) (*integrate the concept in thematic knowledge and imagery in unthematic knowledge*).

in one-dimensional, two-dimensional and four-dimensional spaces and converging them back.

In Case 2, visual analogy is adopted several times. A cross-domain mapping is gradually established by analogizing the component of the satellite (wing), the angle of the satellite (spinning) and uncontrolled satellite (the whole part) to parts of a person's body (arm), posture (slanting) and the whole body motion (turning over). In this way, team members can connect and correspond the context of the satellite with the context of a person.

In this case the team adopts a dynamic and interactive model by integrating Wuity-based thinking and rational thinking. First, the cognitive model characterized by Wuity-based thinking emphasizes the use of imagery analogy. Through the association of one item with the other, a bridge between the thematic and unthematic knowledge, and between life world and the scientific micro-world, is established. Wuity-based thinking explores the interlinked connections and common features between two different domains for an insight. After being tested, innovative solutions are generated. Once the appropriate metaphor is found, one will enter a "transparent" state with an enlightened mind.

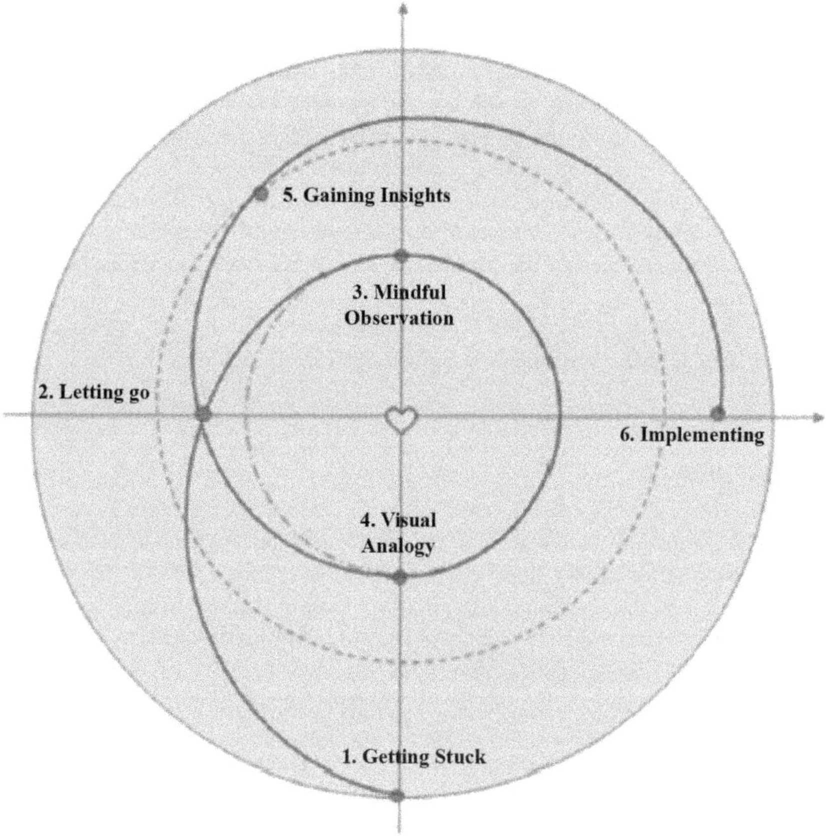

Source: Wang and Gloor, 2018: 172–173.

Figure 14.1 *Wuity's six process steps*

Wuity's Six-Step Interactive Process

Wuity-based innovation goes through six steps, as depicted in Figure 14.1 (see Wang & Gloor, 2018, for more detailed explanation).

1. Getting Stuck – team members get stuck in their thinking when they adopt regular deliberative methods to solve tough problems. No conventional method yields satisfactory results, no matter how hard they try.

2. Letting Go – they make effort to shake away the boundary of the conventional theory by keeping themselves relaxed or reverting to a "beginner's mind."
3. Mindful Observation – they turn to the unthematic knowledge (intuition) and suddenly a fuzzy original idea comes to them.
4. Visual Analogy – benefiting from the heuristic imagery analogy inspired by team interaction and the open interactive relationship between the unthematic knowledge (intuition) in the life world and the thematic knowledge in the scientific world, team-level Wuity-based innovation establishes a cross-domain mapping and helps figure out the interlinked connections and common features.
5. Gaining Insights – they integrate the thematic knowledge (deliberation) and the unthematic knowledge (intuition) to obtain deep intuitive insights (Wuity cognition) into the essence of the problem, which turns separated information into a wholeness.
6. Implementing – team members obtain innovative solutions with new thematic knowledge (deliberation) based on rigorous proof validation.

CONCLUSIONS

Logical deliberation is a cognitive model of deducing a concept from another concept by using the either/or binary logic (Evans, 2008; Wertheimer, 1945). In contrast, when people use visual thinking and verbal thinking at the same time it makes the transformation from an image to a concept possible. During this process, it is crucial to explore the interlinked connections and common features of things between different domains. Visual analogy in the Wuity-based innovation is not applied accidentally, but rather represents a way of thinking deeply rooted in the Eastern culture.

In addition to intuitive/perceptual thinking versus deliberate/rational thinking, this chapter introduces Wuity-based thinking as a cognitive model that integrates both (Li & Cao, 2014). With the help of intuitive imagination, Wuity-based thinking enables one to explore and reach a creative solution by working out interlinked connections and common features between different domains in the face of complex problems. It is possible because Wuity-based thinking does not focus on the existing relationships, but rather on potential ones. It establishes a connection between or among different disciplines or fields which have not been previously linked or connected.

Instead of being rooted in the either/or binary logic, Wuity-based thinking explores the interlinked connections and common features across different domains for an insight. Building on indigenous research on Chinese management and literature in the field of knowledge creation and organizational learning, this chapter proposes a new framework of Wuity-based innovation, informed by findings from the Chinese aerospace industry that interprets the process of Wuity-based knowledge creation by means of Habermas' knowledge taxonomy, "Qu Xiang Bi Lei" cognitive model, and Wuity six-step interactive process. The analysis shows that Wuity-based innovation enables a method of solving problems by returning to the starting point, which not only utilizes thematic knowledge (from the scientific micro-world) to the greatest extent, but also emphasizes exploring novel perspectives by drawing a "scaffolding" inspiration from the unthematic knowledge (from the life world). By following the cognitive model of mindful observation and imagery analogy, team members establish an open cross-domain mapping between a thematic knowledge domain and an unthematic knowledge domain to figure out the interlinked connections between the two for a deep insight.

There are two major accounts of how deliberative and intuitive processes operate: parallel-competitive and default-interventionist theories (Evans & Stanovich, 2013; Healey et al., 2015), much attention has been paid to both Type 1 and Type 2 information processing, but far less to the switch between them (Laureiro-Martínez & Brusoni, 2018). From the viewpoint of this chapter, these processes are complementary: when Type 2 is stuck, Type 1 kicks into action to inspire a vivid interlinked connection and then both of them play a role in gaining an insight, finally Type 2 generates a rational proof. This way, mindfulness and Wuity help reconcile deliberation and intuition to the present moment adaptively and dynamically, and thus dissolve the Western paradox between them by drawing on an overarching framework where Western and Eastern thinking work in unison.

REFERENCES

Amit, E., Hoeflin, C., Hamzah, N., & Fedorenko, E. 2017. An asymmetrical relationship between verbal and visual thinking: Converging evidence from behavior and fMRI. *NeuroImage*, 152: 619–627.

Borgo, D. 2007. Free jazz in the classroom: An ecological approach to music education. *Jazz Perspectives*, 1(1): 61–88.

Dane, E. 2011a. Paying attention to mindfulness and its effects on task performance in the workplace. *Journal of Management*, 37(4): 997–1018.

Dane, E. 2011b. Capturing intuitions 'in flight': Observations from research on attention and mindfulness. In Sinclair, M. (Ed.), *Handbook of intuition research*: 217–226. Cheltenham, UK and Northampton, MA, USA: Edward Elgar Publishing.

Daston, L., & Lunbeck, E. (Eds.) 2011. *Histories of scientific observation*. Chicago, IL: University of Chicago Press.

Dekeyser, M., Raes, F., Leijssen, M., Leysen, S., & Dewulf, D. 2008. Mindfulness skills and interpersonal behaviour. *Personality and Individual Differences*, 44(5): 1235–1245.

Dimidjian, S., & Linehan, M.M. 2003. Defining an agenda for future research on the clinical application of mindfulness practice. *Clinical Psychology: Science and Practice*, 10(2): 166–171.

Eisenhardt, K.M. 1989. Building theories from case study research. *Academy of Management Review*, 14(4): 532–550.

Epstein, R.A. 1984. In defense of the contract at will. *The University of Chicago Law Review*, 51(4): 947–982.

Epstein, R.M. 2003. Mindful practice in action (I): Technical competence, evidence-based medicine, and relationship-centered care. *Families, Systems, & Health*, 21(1): 1–9.

Evans, J.S.B.T. 2008. Dual-processing accounts of reasoning, judgment, and social cognition. *Annual Review Psychology*, 59: 255–278.

Evans, J.S.B.T., & Stanovich, K.E. 2013. Dual-process theories of higher cognition: Advancing the debate. *Perspectives on Psychological Science*, 8(3): 223–241.
Francisco, J.M., & Burnett, C.A. 2008. Deliberate intuition: Giving intuitive insights their rightful place in the creative problem solving thinking skills model. In Puccio, G., Burnett, C., Cabra, J., Fox, J., Keller-Matthews, S., Murdock, M., & Yudess, J. (Eds.), *Proceedings of the 2nd Creativity and Innovation Management Community Conference*: 236–253, Buffalo, NY.
Goleman, D., & Davidson, R.J. 2017. *Altered traits: Science reveals how meditation changes your mind, brain, and body*. New York: Avery.
Habermas, J. 1992. *Postmetaphysical thinking: Philosophical essays*, trans. William Mark Hohengarten. Cambridge, MA: MIT Press.
Healey, M., Vuori, T.O., & Hodgkinson, G. 2015. When teams agree while disagreeing: Reflexion and reflection in shared cognition. *Academy of Management Review*, 40(3): 399–422.
Hofstadter, D., & Sander, E. 2013. *Surfaces and essences: Analogy as the fuel and fire of thinking*. New York: Basic Books.
Hooker, C., Nakamura, J., & Csikszentmihalyi, M. 2014. The group as mentor. In Csikszentmihalyi, M. (Ed.), *The systems model of creativity: The collected works of Mihaly Csikszentmihalyi*: 207–225. Dordrecht: Springer.
Jiang, Y., Baoyin, H., Li, J., & Li, H. 2014. Orbits and manifolds near the equilibrium points around a rotating asteroid. *Astrophysics and Space Science*, 349(1): 83–106.
John-Steiner, V. 1997. *Notebooks of the mind: Explorations of thinking*. Oxford: Oxford University Press.
Josipovic, Z. 2013. Freedom of the mind. *Frontiers in Psychology*, 4: 538.
Josipovic, Z. 2014. Neural correlates of nondual awareness in meditation. *Annals of the New York Academy of Sciences*, 1307(1): 9–18.
Kabat-Zinn, J. 1990. *Full catastrophe living: Using the wisdom of your body and mind to face stress, pain and illness*. New York: Delacourt.
Kohn, L. 2008. *Meditation works: In the Daoist, Buddhist and Hindu traditions*. St Petersburg: Three Pines Press.
Kruglanski, A.W., & Gigerenzer, G. 2011. Intuitive and deliberate judgments are based on common principles. *Psychological Review*, 118(1): 97–109.
Lafont C, Medina J. 1999. The linguistic turn in hermeneutic philosophy. Cambridge, MA: MIT Press.
Langer, E.J. 1989. *Mindfulness*. Boston, MA: Da Capo Press.
Laureiro-Martínez, D., & Brusoni, S. 2018. Cognitive flexibility and adaptive decision-making: Evidence from a laboratory study of expert decision makers. *Strategic Management Journal*, 39(4): 1031–1058.
Li, P.P., & Cao, Y.F. 2014. Wuity: The highest cognition of entrepreneurship. *China Europe Business Review*, (4): 36–43.
Linehan, M. 1993. *Cognitive-behavioral treatment of borderline personality disorder*. New York: Guilford Press.
Luo, J., & Niki, K. 2003. Function of hippocampus in 'insight' of problem solving. *Hippocampus*, 13: 316–23.
Nisbett, R.E., Peng, K., Choi, I., & Norenzayan, A. 2001. Culture and systems of thought: Holistic versus analytic cognition. *Psychological Review*, 108(2): 291–310.
Pavlovich, K., & Krahnke, K. 2012. Empathy, connectedness and organisation. *Journal of Business Ethics*, 105(1): 131–137.
Peng, K., & Nisbett, R.E. 1999. Culture, dialectics, and reasoning about contradiction. *American Psychologist*, 54(9): 741–754.
Pylyshyn, Z. 2003. Return of the mental image: Are there really pictures in the brain? *Trends in Cognitive Sciences*, 7(3): 113–118.

Schwartz, J.M., Stapp, H.P., & Beauregard, M. 2005. Quantum physics in neuroscience and psychology: A neurophysical model of mind–brain interaction. *Philosophical Transactions of the Royal Society B: Biological Sciences*, 360(1458): 1309–1327.

Segal, Z.V., Teasdale, J.D., Williams, J.M., & Gemar, M.C. 2002. The mindfulness-based cognitive therapy adherence scale: Inter-rater reliability, adherence to protocol and treatment distinctiveness. *Clinical Psychology & Psychotherapy*, 9(2): 131–138.

Siggelkow, N. 2007. Persuasion with case studies. *Academy of Management Journal*, 50(1): 20–24.

Taylor, S., & Egeto-Szabo, K. 2017. Exploring awakening experiences: A study of awakening experiences in terms of other triggers, characteristics, duration and after effects. *Journal of Transpersonal Psychology*, 49(1): 45–65.

Wang, X., & Gloor, P.A. 2018. Wuity as higher cognition combining intuitive and deliberate judgments for creativity: Analyzing Elon Musk's way to innovate. In Grippa, F., Leitão, J., Gluesing, J., Riopelle, K., & Gloor, P.A. (Eds.), *Collaborative innovation networks. Studies on entrepreneurship, structural change and industrial dynamics*: 165–182. Cham: Springer.

Wang, X., & Li, P.P. 2017. Conceptual framework of 'Wu'-based innovation at the team level: A case study on indigenous innovation in the context of aerospace projects. *Foreign Economics and Management*, 39(3): 3–23.

Wang, X., & Li, P.P. 2018. Wu-based thinking integrating the East with the West: The analysis of Elon Musk's four metaphors. *Foreign Economics and Management*, 40(1): 124–140.

Wang, X., & Riopelle, K. 2019. Building a shared present and future: Learnings from Henry Ford and Albert Kahn's co-Wuity collaborative innovation network on the moving assembly line and mass production. In Song, Y., Grippa, F., Gloor, P.A., & Leitão, J. (Eds.), *Collaborative innovation networks. Latest insights from social innovation, education, and emerging technologies research*: 3–40. Cham: Springer.

Weick, K.E., & Sutcliffe, K.M. 2001. *Managing the unexpected: Assuring high performance in an age of complexity*. San Francisco, CA: Jossey-Bass.

Weick, K.E., & Sutcliffe, K.M. 2011. *Managing the unexpected: Resilient performance in an age of uncertainty*. San Francisco, CA: Jossey-Bass.

Weick, K.E., & Sutcliffe, K.M. 2015. *Managing the unexpected: Sustained performance in a complex world*. Hoboken, NJ: John Wiley & Sons.

Wertheimer, E. 1945. Glycogen in adipose tissue. *The Journal of Physiology*, 103(4): 359–366.

Yang, Y. 2008. *The general theory of sentiment and Wuity*. Beijing: People's Publishing House.

Yi Jing Editing Group (Ed.). 1989. *Yi Jing in the vernacular*. Beijing: China Folklore.

Zhuangzi. 2009. *The essential writings: With selections from traditional commentaries*. Indianapolis, IN: Hackett Publishing.

15. Group intuition and intentionality: collective action at-a-distance?[1]

Raymond Trevor Bradley

> Since primeval times, people have spoken of strange and sometimes profoundly meaningful personal experiences. Such experiences have been reported by the majority of the world's population and across all cultures. ... These experiences, called "psychic" or psi, suggest the presence of deep, invisible interconnections among people, and between objects and people. The most curious aspect of psi experiences is that they seem to transcend the usual boundaries of time and space. (Dean Radin, *The conscious universe*, 1997: 13)

> Love is a kind of exalted but unspecialized telepathy; the simplest and most universal expression of that mutual gravitation or kinship of spirits which is the foundation of the telepathic law. (F.W.H. Myers, *Human personality and its survival of bodily death*, 1907: 344)

Phenomena that involve action at-a-distance – the transmission of a force or effect by no known physical means – are paradoxical and perplexing. Because they contradict the laws of physics, they defy reason and commonsense and have confounded even the greatest minds in science. Thus, Newton struggled with the nonlocal nature of gravity and Einstein famously dismissed quantum nonlocality as "spooky action at-a-distance." Nowadays, though, action-at-a-distance is known as *nonlocality*. And, following experiments confirming quantum entanglement in the 1980s (the inherent interconnectedness of subatomic particles, no matter how vast the distance), nonlocality is accepted as a scientific fact. Moreover, because the individual particles in particle pairings appear to act is if they instantly "know" what is happening to each other and display an unconditional, unbreakable union, some physicists characterize this bond as "passion at-a-distance." In short, quantum entanglement is not only seen as fundamental to understanding the physical universe but is also thought integral to the question of *consciousness* – including psychic phenomena (Bradley, 2007; Penrose, 1994; Radin, 2006).

Despite a century of evidence of *psychic* effects (human nonlocal communication of information or intention by no known physical means) studies were ignored or vilified by mainstream science (see Radin, 1997). However, a growing number of experiments are now published in leading journals in psychology and even in physics (e.g., Radin et al., 2013), suggesting that psi research is finally gaining some legitimacy. Similarly, where compelling evidence of nonlocal effects was ignored or derided in social science (e.g., Myers, 2002), studies are now appearing in more mainstream publications, like this one.

Most research focuses on the individual, documenting two broad kinds of nonlocal phenomena: extra sensory perception (ESP), the capacity to receive/perceive information about nonlocal objects or events; and psychokinesis (PK), the capacity to intentionally effect a change in a nonlocal object/event. Less studied is *collective* generation of nonlocal effects – *socio-psychic* phenomena. To stimulate urgently needed research, my fourfold purpose here is to: distill what is known; highlight gaps in research; sketch an approach to the question of explanation; and consider the implications for practice. The chapter concludes with a set of principles which may have utility for practice considerations and value as research hypotheses. I begin with a highly compressed overview of the research addressing three key questions: nonlocal communication within the group; collective intuition of nonlocal events; and collective intentional effects on a nonlocal object.

RESEARCH OVERVIEW

Nonlocal Communication

Studies of dyads reveal an implicit energetic channel of communication implicated in regulating interactional dynamics, development, and behavior. This has been documented in mother–fetus interactions in the womb – including those from external social sources, between mothers and infants/toddlers, and is known to influence neurobiological and psychosocial development (Bradley, 2003; Pribram & Bradley, 1998; Schore, 1994). Other studies, using electrophysiological instruments, document heart-to-heart and heart–brain communication (including entrainment) between non-conversing pairs/couples within conversational distance, but with no physical contact (Bradley, 2012; McCraty et al., 2006). And there is evidence of an unconscious channel of nonverbal communication operative in non-touching conversing dyads (e.g., Gregory & Hoyt, 1982). Of note is discovery of an inaudible low frequency band in vocal interactions (beneath 0.5 kHz, *below* normal human hearing range: 15–20 kHz) which operates as an unconscious regulator of relational dynamics (including social status accommodation) and is related to task performance (Gregory et al., 2009).

In a large-scale longitudinal study of 60 urban communes, conducted at Columbia University forty years ago, I found that information about collective order was implicitly encoded in member responses to a sociometric instrument mapping dyadic relations within the group (Bradley, 1987). Although respondents were not asked about group structure, what emerged, when sociograms were constructed, was a highly detailed, coherent hierarchy of power relations extending many levels which I called *global hierarchical coherence*. This raised a basic question: namely, how is it possible to obtain a view of the social *whole* (the group) solely from measurement of its *parts* (individual perceptions of dyadic relations)?

The answer – a novel hypothesis – was suggested by the paradox implied in the question: namely, that information about collective organization is encoded as a *hologram* and tacitly communicated throughout the group to all members (Bradley, 1987). Holographic organization is a field concept in which information about the object as a *whole* is energetically encoded as an interference pattern and distributed by the movement of energy to all parts and locations. This makes it possible to retrieve an image of the whole from *any* point or location in the field.

Using membership turnover as a measure of disturbance or loss of collective memory, I found that only groups with a globally coherent structure of power were able to perpetuate this order through time, despite high levels of turnover or loss of a leader/s. I also found that global coherence was directly related to group survival, was coincident with a dense network of loving bonds, and that, when linked as a complementary balanced coupling, these patterns of love and power predicted group survival some twenty-four months into the future (Bradley & Pribram, 1998). In short, these findings suggest that information about social order is *not* localized to specific parts or positions but is holographically encoded as an *implicit collective consciousness* and communicated *nonlocally*, via the energized field of attachment bonds – love, throughout the group (see Bradley, 1987: 197–274).

This nonlocal nature of collective mind has been found repeatedly in field studies and controlled experiments using a radically different instrumentation – namely, random number generators (RNGs). (RNGs are hardware circuits that use inherent electronic noise to generate truly random bits. Each RNG is attached to a personal computer which continuously collects 200 random bits per second.) The effects of group and global consciousness is registered by RNGs in various settings – meetings, meditations, sports events, ceremonies, natural disasters, and human-caused tragedies; the RNG/s has *no* physical connection to human participants (e.g., Bancel & Nelson, 2008; Jahn et al., 2000; Mason et al., 2007; Nelson, 2002; Radin, 1997, 2006). Studies have consistently found that collectively focused attention generates a shift in RNG behavior to a nonrandom pattern. In social groups, the effect is strongest in those with high social coherence and engaged in an emotionally intense common focus, such as workshops and therapy groups (e.g., Targ & Katra, 2000), plus there is an amplification effect four-times stronger in closely bonded relationships than for that of an individual (Nelson et al., 1991). Studies have also found synchronized group meditation (in large groups with over 1,500 meditators) produce the greatest nonrandom departures, especially when using a specific/advanced technique, such as Transcendental Meditation or "yogic flying" (e.g., Mason et al., 2007). These effects were corroborated in a subsequent experiment using an objective stimulus (binaural-beat audio tones, known as Hemi-Sycn®) to generate a state of "mental coherence," in 14 replications of a group workshop (Radin & Atwater, 2009).

RNGs have also been used to measure *global consciousness* in the ongoing internet-based Global Consciousness Project (GCP), initiated in 1998 by Roger Nelson. Data generated by RNGs are collected continuously from more than 60 sites throughout the world, and analyzed to determine if there is a correlation between global events of mass attention (such as the 2000 Olympic Games Opening Ceremony, the US 9/11 terrorist attacks, the 2004 Sumatra earthquake and tsunami, Obama's reelection, and so forth) and periods of nonrandom order:

> Our research hypothesis predicts the appearance of increasing coherence and structure, or nonrandom trends, in the globally distributed [RNG] data collected during major events

> in the world. The events … share a common feature, namely, that they powerfully engage human attention all around the world, and draw us in large numbers into a common focus. (Nelson, 2002: 550–551)

Because the statistical effect for a single event is "tiny" and difficult to differentiate from noise, data must be accumulated over many replications in order for a "real" effect to become statistically detectable.

The hypothesis has been repeatedly verified by analyses of the aggregated RNG data from world events (e.g., Bancel & Nelson, 2008). The most recent results available of the "cumulative deviation from chance expectation" for 465 world events (August 1998 through April 2014) "are highly significant. The odds against chance are much greater than a billion to one."[2] In commenting on their analysis, Bancel and Nelson point to a collective effect of "*coherent attention or emotional response*" (Bancel & Nelson, 2008: 319; italics added). Moreover, in a follow-up analysis of data from 247 events, Nelson finds that:

1. Events with high emotional intensity generate strongest effects on RNGs, while those neutral or low do not;
2. The emotional valence of the world event to people is significant: "The largest effect sizes in the database are produced by events characterized by fear (4.5 sigma), or compassion and love (3.6 sigma)";
3. There is a "non-local interconnection of human consciousness at an unconscious level"; and,
4. An "unknown mechanism links consciousness with physical systems, yielding detectable changes in their behavior" (Nelson, 2008: 1).

A comment, per point #2, on the emotional valence of the event. Nelson's finding that the two categories of "fear" and "compassion and love" produced the largest effect sizes, suggests the underlying emotion of access – the energetic channel – to nonlocal effects is "love," in the meaning of Myers' epigram at the head of this chapter. If fear is viewed as a negative emotional response to a perceived threat to something one loves (one's own safety/life or that of others, etc.), then fear lies at the negative end and compassion lies at the positive end of an underlying love dimension – as elaborated in my book, *The lens of love* (Bradley, 2018).

In moving to the topics of intuition and intentionality, I want to take a moment to clarify how I view these concepts, as this will inform the discussion that follows. Very briefly, for the technical details are too complex to recount here, perception requires an outgoing wave field of attentional energy and an incoming wave field of energy emitted from the object. Both outgoing and incoming wave fields contain information about their respective sources encoded as quantum holograms in the movement of energy. It is our emotional connection to an object of interest which activates the biological energy required for the act of attention. Tuning into the resonant frequency of the object, attentional focus creates a two-way communication channel between the percipient and the object. *Passionate attentional focus* (which Radin calls "rapt attention") generates a coherent channel of resonating energy through which incoming information from a nonlocal object – including its future potentials – is perceived by the body's psychophysiological systems as intuition. *Passionate intentional focus* transmits a willful thought/desire (encoded as a quantum hologram) instantly to the nonlocal object, via the channel of resonance, where, through a process of vibratory resonance, it can affect the object's potential organization and behavior (see Bradley, 2007, 2018, for the details).

Collective Intuition

Most research on intuition adopts a *cognitive* approach in which intuition is viewed as the brain's extrapolation from stored memory of prior experience (e.g., Myers, 2002). Thus, in their recent article, Akinci and Sadler-Smith (2018: 1) define collective intuition "as independently formed judgement based on domain-specific knowledge, experience and cognitive ability, shared and interpreted collectively." There is, however, convincing evidence of another informational basis for intuitive perception: the *tacit* information about *remote or future – nonlocal –* events processed by the body's psychophysiological systems and perceived as certainty of knowledge or feeling (positive or negative) about something distant or yet to happen (Bradley, 2007; McCraty et al., 2004a). In drawing on this concept of nonlocal intuition, *collective intuition* is signified by shared implicit awareness of remote or future events jointly perceived by the members of a group. There are two distinct levels: a relational and a collective form.

While there is an extensive body of research on nonlocal intuition, virtually all work has been on the individual (see Radin, 1997, 2006). Despite enumerable anecdotal or subjective accounts, there appears to be a dearth of studies on intuition in relationships, other than research on the implicitly "entwined lives" of identical twins when reared apart (Segal, 1999).[3] However, there is work measuring nonlocal communication in a relational setting. To wit, the numerous so-called "staring" studies, spanning many decades, which have consistently found nonlocal effects on a receiver's awareness (measured electrophysiologically) of being "watched" (on a random schedule) by a sender at a remote location (e.g., Braud, 1981). Sheldrake (2013) has corroborated these effects in social media contexts, showing intuitive anticipation by the intended receiver when the sender is engaged in formulating an internet-mediated communication.

Of relevance, also, are the findings from the *presentiment* experiments of the past few decades, which investigate physiological predictors of future *emotional* stimuli, and, hence, are integral to the processing of socio-affective information in our relations and interactions (Bradley, 2003, 2007). Using rigorous experiment protocols and electrophysiological measures, researchers have consistently found that the human autonomic nervous system (ANS) unconsciously responds to randomly selected future emotional stimuli some *four to seven seconds before* the experimental stimulus is presented (see Bradley, 2007; Radin, 1997). Moreover, evidence shows that the heart is directly involved (McCraty et al., 2004a; Tressoldi et al., 2009), and that the heart receives the pre-stimulus information moments *before* the brain

(McCraty et al., 2004b) – suggesting that the heart receives intuition information first, and *then* alerts the brain, via the afferent pathways, for potential decision/action. There was also a noteworthy finding for gender. In female participants (but not males) the *coherent* heart rhythm pattern, induced by intentional activation of a *positive emotion* throughout the experiment, was associated with pre-stimulus perception of an "emotional" stimulus but not for a "calm" one. (Intriguingly, this is consistent with Nelson's finding (above) that events with high emotional intensity generate the strongest mass consciousness effect on RNGs, while those neutral or low do not.)

This has direct bearing on communication of intuitive information in social situations. For the heart is the most powerful generator of energy in our body and it encodes information on our internal states (including our feelings and emotions, and desires and intentions) in patterns of heart rhythm activity, which are communicated nonlocally to those around us (see McCraty et al., 2006). Intersecting with the incoming radiation of energy emissions from all objects, a two-way multi-frequency channel of communication is created between our body and nonlocal objects. It is through this channel of connection that incoming intuition and outgoing intention (described below) is communicated as quantum holographically encoded information, as detailed elsewhere (see Bradley, 2007, 2018).

As noted for relational intuition, there appears to be scarcity of studies on collective intuition, apart from recent work in organizational/management science which pursues a strictly cognitive approach (e.g., Akinci & Sadler-Smith, 2018). A related area concerns flow and performance, and recently research has begun on group flow (Sawyer, 2007) – the emergence of an implicit collective mind that anticipates, coordinates, and guides collaborative activity for optimal performance. While initial results are promising (e.g., Salanova et al., 2014), little is known of the unconscious nonlocal flow dynamics of collective communication and continuously adaptive action.

Returning to the GCP project, there are intriguing data on implicit mass response to certain world events in the database suggestive of collective intuition at the global level of consciousness. As noted above, signal registration from mass focused attention for any given event on the RNG network is typically very weak and also well below the chance expectation threshold. However, for some events the signal structure exceeds chance, and among these are a handful where RNG output deviates from randomness *minutes and even hours before the event* actually occurred. Three of these are natural disasters. In the online GCP database (Table 2: Results for Individual Events), these are: #34, Turkey earthquake; #67, Central American earthquake; and #189, Sumatra earthquake and tsunami. All showed the RNG signal exceeded chance ~15 minutes prior to the actual event.

But one event, with a large departure from chance ($p < 10^6$), was a human-caused catastrophe: the terrorist attacks on the US the morning of September 11, 2001. Independent analysis by Nelson (2002) and Radin (2002) found notable nonrandom departure beginning some *3–4 hours* ***before*** the first plane crashed into the North Tower of the World Trade Center at 8:45 a.m., suggesting *implicit global foreknowledge* of the impending attacks. (The day of September 11 also generated the largest departure from randomness for the year 2001, which was unexplained by artifacts such as electrical disturbances or high mobile phone use.) Indeed, in commenting on a similar antecedent to the Central American earthquake, Nelson observes:

> As in 1999 [Event #34, Turkey earthquake], there is a surprisingly strong deviation *prior* to the first shock. This could be a chance occurence (sic), but it might be interpreted, if found in other cases, to indicate that there is some influence on the Egg [RNG] network that is *a precurso[r]* (sic) to the actual quake. … a suggestion of something like an "earth consciousness" that feels the pressures and tension that lead to the seismic event. (Event #67, Table 2, GCP database; additions in brackets and italics added)

However, the 9/11 terrorist attack response suggests the mechanism is something more than precursor "pressures and tension" to seismic events. It points to an emotional connection to the nonlocal event: unconscious global fear of the terrorist's imminent malevolent actions (Bradley, 2007, 2018).

Another category of events that produce significant RNG nonrandom deviations are synchronized mass prayer/meditation, which sometimes signal a precursor before the event happens (see GCP database). While such results from the GCP are tantalizing and suggestive, more world events displaying such a precursor RNG signal are required for definitive statistical analysis. However, it does seem likely that socially coherent emotion underlies collective intuition, and that collective intuition itself is an intrinsic faculty of global consciousness.

Collective Intentionality

For my purpose here, collective intentionality means "the power of minds to be jointly directed at objects, matters of fact, states of affairs, or values" (Schweikard & Schmid, 2013: 1). This includes instances of an explicit shared awareness and those in which the "joint"/collective action is unconscious. For instance, in my study of communes, mentioned above, a further discovery was dynamic adjustment, over time, to maintain a balanced complementary coupling between the geometries of loving and power relations in surviving groups – presumably by an unconscious intentional collective process. This implicit collective awareness was not evident in non-surviving groups which, instead, were typified by extreme imbalances in the ratio of these two key relational systems (Bradley, 1987: 167–193). To highlight the nature and range of these nonlocal phenomena, I broaden the concept of collective intentionality to include situations in which the collective is the context within which an intentional act occurs. We begin with these.

As surprising as this may seem, there is a large body of rigorous experimental evidence consistently showing that focused mental intention can exert a measurable nonlocal effect on a physical object/system or a living organism/system (e.g., Jahn & Dunne, 1987; Radin, 2006). As noted above for nonlocal effects on RNGs, these effects are typically tiny and subtle, usually becoming statistically detectable in large databases composed of many replications (see Jahn & Dunne, 1987). For instance, in a pioneering experiment, Radin and colleagues (2013) found experienced meditators could mentally "push" photons (massless subatomic particles) generated by an interferometer in a novel variation of the double-slit physics experiment, whereas non-meditators could not. As for intuition, most research is focused on nonlocal intention in individuals. However, if we include instances where a social bond is involved – whether conscious or unconscious – we find compelling evidence of *intentional* nonlocal effects on another person's bodily function, their ANS. For instance, Braud and Schlitz (1991) showed a remote "sender" was able to generate unconscious fluctuations in emotion (measured by electrodermal activity) in a "receiver" purely by *thinking* to arouse or calm that person. Plus, there is evidence that heart and brain entrainment between non-touching pairs/couples and in groups can be intentionally induced (Bradley, 2012). Also, certain kinds of collective activity in unison, such as poetry recitation, praying – including the Buddhist "om" technique (Cysarz et al., 2004), group singing, mantra, chanting (Vickhoff et al., 2013), and other collective rhythmic activity (which induce cardiorespiratory synchronization), spontaneously facilitate a group-wide state of psychophysiological coherence in which the autonomic nervous systems of *all* individuals become synchronized and phase-shifted to an optimal state of function.

Of relational relevance, also, is the large body of experiments investigating the nonlocal effects of distant healers – including intercessory prayer and other healing modalities – which Radin and colleagues (2015) subjected to a rigorous review. They asked two basic questions. First, the all-important "proof of principle" question: "*Does it work?* ... If person A and person B are *strictly isolated* by shielding, distance, or time, is there empirical evidence that A can affect B in any way?" They note that "hundreds of experiments" have been independently replicated in different laboratories throughout the world, and then conclude from the results of metanalyses that: "Cumulatively ... *Yes, A can affect B at a distance*" (Radin et al., 2015: 67; italics added). The second question concerns efficacy: "*Can A in fact heal B?*" On this they find that "The preponderance of evidence for DHI [distant healing intention] effects in simple living systems and for intercessory prayer is at best suggestive of its effectiveness to alter outcomes," while acknowledging that some studies show compelling positive results – particularly with reiki therapy (Radin et al., 2015: 70). In another study, which suggests that love is implicated, Radin and colleagues found nonlocal activation of the patient's ANS when their distant long-term pair mate (friend pairs, partner pairs, married couples, and mother–child pairs) focused "compassionate intention" on the patient. They concluded that "strong motivation to heal and to be healed, and training on how to cultivate and direct compassionate intention, may further enhance this effect" (Radin et al., 2008: 242).

A further line of research concerns the nonlocal intentional effects of synchronized mass group meditation on social order. Numerous studies have found that focused mass meditation intention has a positive impact at the city, state, national, and international levels, by reducing crime, car accidents, hospital admissions, alcohol consumption, and war casualties (Dillbeck et al., 1981; Hagelin et al., 1999; Orme-Johnson et al., 1988); preventing terrorist activity and international armed conflict (Orme-Johnson et al., 2003); improving stock market performance (Cavanaugh et al., 1989); and improving the quality of life (Orme-Johnson et al., 1988). Of import is the discovery of a *time-lag* effect in which the positive force of an intentional meditation on social order (measured by societal indicators) carries forward over several months before dissipating (Hagelin et al., 1999; Orme-Johnson et al., 1988). This has been found for synchronized group meditation as well (Mason et al., 2007).

A final body of research is that conducted by William Tiller and his associates (2005) over a 35-year period on nonlocal intentionality. They developed an ingenious "low tech" electrical device into which a specific intention could be encoded, used as a "surrogate" in a series of elegant experiments. Following their intention to "imprint" the device in group meditations with a "loving heart," they demonstrated that the "imprinted" device created a field of encoded energy which exerted the intended effects both over time (holding the imprinted intention for as much as a year) and nonlocally on various target systems. These targets ranged from the pH behavior of water and air temperature oscillations, to enzyme activity and fruit fly larvae maturation. The targets were shielded by a Faraday cage, had no direct physical connection to, or were distant (as far as 6,000 miles away!) from the device. Some sense of the enormous implications of this landmark work for science, spirituality, consciousness, and healing is summed up in their equation #6.4 (Tiller et al., 2005: 230):

$$\textbf{Mass} \rightleftarrows \textbf{Energy} \rightleftarrows \textbf{Consciousness} \rightleftarrows \textbf{Love}$$

CONCLUSIONS

So, what can we conclude from the overview of evidence on our four basic questions:

1. Nonlocal communication within collectives?
   Although there is great need for more research – both replications and on new topics – we saw evidence of nonlocal interaction in dyadic relations, in social groups, and in mass social aggregations. Also, there seems to be compelling evidence of an implicit collective consciousness operative in groups and at the global level. Thus, the answer appears affirmative.
2. Collective nonlocal intuition?
   There are large gaps in research at both the relational and group levels – the evidence is indirect, at best; studies are urgently needed. At the global level, the RNG data for certain world events are intriguing and suggestive. However, more cases of events displaying a precursor RNG signal are required for a definitive statistical analysis. Thus, while collective intuition seems likely, at this point the answer is inconclusive.
3. Nonlocal collective intentionality?
   While there are gaps in research, in addition to the nonlocal impact of jointly focused minds on RNGs – physical electronic devices, there is the compelling

evidence of nonlocal intentional effects on bodily function at the relational level. To repeat Radin and his co-authors' (2015: 67) conclusion: "Yes, A can effect B at a distance"; however, evidence that "Can A in fact heal B" is "at best suggestive." Also, we found consistent evidence of positive nonlocal effects of mass meditation on social order. And there is Tiller's ground-breaking research showing how intention can be imprinted into a simple electrical device to exert nonlocal influence over time on matter across all levels of scale. Thus, while there are gaps in knowledge and an urgent need for research, the answer appears affirmative.

4. Collective action at-a-distance?
   Overall, on this most basic question, despite the notable gaps in research – particularly on the question of collective intuition, the evidence is consistent and persuasive, and, in some areas, seems beyond question. Thus, the answer appears affirmative.

SKETCH OF A QUANTUM HOLOGRAPHIC ACCOUNT

Beyond these conclusions is another finding of import, for it points to the likely means by which nonlocal interactions occur and has implications for practice. There is consistent evidence, sometimes explicit, other times more subtle, that *emotions* are involved at both the individual and collective levels. In reflecting upon what accounted for the nonrandom departures in their mind-machine experiments, Jahn and Dunne explain:

> Careful application of scientific knowledge and rigor of method, within a permeating atmosphere of "*love*" in the very general sense ... appears particularly pertinent ... for the realization of the phenomena themselves, for it is precisely through the *bonds of consciousness* established between human operators, or with their technical devices and processes, that the anomalous [nonrandom] data seem to emerge. Thus, the spiritual component participates in a very pragmatic sense: *selfless investment of self can affect physical reality.* (Jahn & Dunne, 1987: 293; square brackets and italics added)

This is the *same* understanding that Tiller's research team arrived at and it is of great import. For it appears that the field of emotional connections – our intrinsic bond of *love* to everyone and everything in the universe – is the channel of nonlocal communication. In the thumbnail sketch that follows, this is described as a quantum holographic process which is fully elaborated elsewhere (Bradley, 2007, 2018; Bradley & Tomasino, 2011).

Briefly, passionate attentional focus directed to the object of interest attunes the bio-emotional energy of the percipient's psychophysiological systems, via energetic resonance, to the quantum level of the object and establishes a two-way communication channel. The incoming wave field of energy radiating from the object to the percipient contains information on the object's future potential, encoded as a quantum hologram. The body's perception of such implicit information is experienced as intuition. Propelled by the heart, the outgoing wave field of bio-emotional energy from the percipient during passionate intentional focus contains a quantum hologram encoding mental intention which is communicated to the nonlocal object. Part of the energy wave field containing the quantum hologram is absorbed by the object, via vibratory resonance, enabling the information it contains to *in*-form – give shape to – the object's future organization and behavior. Thus, summed up in the terms of a reformulation of Tiller's equation:

Love —*attunes*→ **Energy** —*enables*→ **Consciousness** —in-*forms*→ **Mass**

These processes are greatly amplified in groups and mass social aggregations when in a coherent state of socio-bio-emotional resonance. As a receptive field, coherent resonance amplifies both incoming nonlocal information, via passionate attention, and the outgoing wave field of intentional energy directed towards the nonlocal object. This not only enhances the system's reception of intuition information, but also strengthens communication of the quantum hologram encoding the passionately held intention. Conversely, in socially incoherent groups, fraught with internal disorder, the wave field of collective energy is too disorganized for signal integrity, thereby impeding communication of information from and to nonlocal sources.

Table 15.1 Principles of nonlocal interaction

1.	Our mind-body is an *energetic field* –a multi-level organization of physio-psychological function which radiates energy emissions containing implicit information on all our internal states and processes.
2.	Within our body, the heart generates the most powerful energetic field; patterns of heart rhythm activity *encode* our emotions, thoughts, and intentions, which are transmitted nonlocally to everyone and everything around us.
3.	*Positive emotions*, like love, generate coherent wave fields of bio-emotional energy, which have immense nonlocal reach and are the access channel to nonlocal interactions.
4.	Sustained *attentional focus* creates a two-way channel of coherent connection, to the nonlocal object, through which intuitive insight/foresight and intentional thought is instantly communicated.
5.	Collective organization is an *energetic field* – the activation of bio-emotional energy from the members' bonds of love and attachment to the group.
6.	Collective organization is *holographic* –a nonlocal field into which the order of the group is encoded and distributed by the movement of energy through all relations to all members.
7.	Nonlocal effects are *amplified* by attentional energetic resonance generated by a commonly held focus in mass social aggregations and in groups high with socio-emotional coherence.
8.	The power of nonlocal effects is *sustained* by repeated sessions and optimized during prolonged states of collective communion, such as synchronized group meditation.

Source: Adapted from *The lens of love*, Chapter 8, Bradley (© 2018).

By way of summary, Table 15.1 presents a set of principles of nonlocal interaction which may have utility in informing practice considerations and value as research hypotheses.

IMPLICATIONS FOR PRACTICE

If coherent emotion is the access channel to the nonlocal domain, then effective emotion regulation techniques (McCraty et al., 2006), advanced meditation practices – such as yoga, and collective activities in unison (which synchronize cardiorespiratory rhythm) should enhance nonlocal interaction potential. When practiced in synchronized sessions in a group, this potential is greatly boosted by the amplification effects of socio-emotional coherence, such as collective communion, and especially in repeated sessions to mitigate the diminishing power of nonlocal effects over time. As long known by ancient spiritual traditions, effective practice and application requires self-less unconditional love and non-attachment to outcomes. Also, the scope of application appears virtually universal, encompassing relational, group, organizational, collective, and global settings (including online social media), across all functional and substantive domains. Furthermore, Tiller's simple device has enormous potential in health and healing when imprinted with a healing intention. And it seems that RNGs could be employed as an early warning system detecting changes in consciousness, both locally and globally:

> Just as changes in seismic meters are used to detect … impending earthquakes, RNG outputs could warn us of changes in collective consciousness … [including] any anticipatory effects … [and] to evaluate preventive and ameliorative measures that utilize collective consciousness … including group meditations to reduce collective stress … [and] to reduce local and global tragedies. (Mason et al., 2007: 315; additions in square brackets added)

However, while studies have investigated mainly "positive" applications – such as distant healing, improved social order, and so forth, there is potential for a "dark" side wherein collective nonlocal effects can be harnessed for malevolent ends – including malicious intention directed to remotely located machines/information processing devices, like computers and servers. Less menacing is that operator feelings and thoughts (whether conscious or unconscious) may also generate anomalous machine behavior when the two are in resonance (Jahn & Dunne, 1987).

In closing, the discoveries of psi research – which include those on collective nonlocal interaction – are revolutionary in their implications. At the most basic level of science, a revision of the fundamental laws of physics is required to explain how nonlocal interactions defy space–time constraints and the temporality of cause and effect. This will spur development of a new socio-psycho-physics which will radically alter our understanding of human consciousness, perception, and agency. For humanity, this paradigm shift in science will transform our conception of reality itself, profoundly empowering our potential, both as individuals and collectively. We stand at the threshold of a potent new era of possibility:

> Someday, after we have mastered the winds, the waves, the tides and gravity, we shall harness for God the *energies of love*. Then for the second time in the history of the world, man will have discovered fire. (Teilhard de Chardin, 1967: 33–34; italics added)

ACKNOWLEDGMENTS

The work on this chapter was fraught with unexpected life events. I am grateful to the editor, Marta Sinclair, for her understanding and patience, and to my wife, Chaarenne, for her helpful comments on an earlier draft and, especially, her unconditional love, faith, and support.

NOTES

1. Space constraints prevent comprehensive citation of references, which are restricted to primary works and examples/illustrations from notable studies.
2. Nelson's conclusion – see http://noosphere.princeton.edu/results/nw.results.html; accessed April 20, 2019.
3. A Google search of "studies of intuition in couples"/ "relationships" or other derivatives produced "no results."

REFERENCES

Akinci, C., & Sadler-Smith, E. 2018. Collective intuition: Implications for improved decision making and organizational learning. *British Journal of Management*; https://doi.org/10.1111/1467-8551.12269.

Bancel, P., & Nelson, R. 2008. The GCP experiment: Design, analytical methods, results. *Journal of Scientific Exploration*, 22: 309–333.

Bradley, R.T. 1987. *Charisma and social structure: A study of love and power, wholeness and transformation*. New York: Paragon Press.

Bradley, R.T. 2003. Love, power, mind, brain, and agency. In D. Loye (Ed.), *The great adventure: Toward a fully human theory of evolution*: 99–150. New York: SUNY Press.

Bradley, R.T. 2007. Psychophysiology of intuition: A quantum-holographic theory of non-local communication. *World Futures*, 63: 61–97.

Bradley, R.T. 2012. Nonlocality, consciousness, and the eye of love. *Consciousness & Development 2.0*. S. Momo, ed., *Spanda Journal*, III.1/2012: 193–205.

Bradley, R.T. 2018. unpublished book manuscript. *The lens of love: Quantum holographic eye of universal consciousness*.

Bradley, R.T., & Pribram, K.H. 1998. Communication and stability in social collectives. *Journal of Social and Evolutionary Systems*, 21: 29–81.

Bradley, R.T., & Tomasino, D. 2011. A quantum-holographic approach to the psychophysiology of intuitive action. In L.P. Dana (Ed.), *World encyclopedia of entrepreneurship*: 318–347. Cheltenham, UK and Northampton, MA, USA: Edward Elgar Publishing.

Braud, W.G. 1981. Psi performance and autonomic system activity. *Journal of the American Society for Psychical Research*, 75: 1–35.

Braud, W.G., & Schlitz, M.J. 1991. Consciousness interactions with remote biological systems: Anomalous intentionality effects. *Subtle Energies*, 2: 1–46.

Cavanaugh, K.L., Orme-Johnson, D.W., & Gelderloos, P. 1989. The effect of the Taste of Utopia Assembly on the World Index of international stock prices. In R.A. Chalmers, G. Clements, H. Schenkluhn, & M. Weinless (Eds.), *Scientific research on Maharishi's transcendental meditation and TM-Sidhi programme: Collected papers*, vol. 4: 2715–2729. Vlodrop, the Netherlands: Maharishi Vedic University Press.

Cysarz, D., von Bonin, D., Lackner, H., Heusser, P., Moser, M., & Bettermann, H. 2004. Oscillations of heart rate and respiration synchronize during poetry recitation. *American Journal of Physiology and Heart Circulation Physiology*, 287: 579–587.

Dillbeck, M.C., Landrith III, G.S., & Orme-Johnson, D.W. 1981. The Transcendental Meditation program and crime rate change in a sample of forty-eight cities. *Journal of Crime and Justice*, 4: 25–45.

Gregory, S.W., & Hoyt, B.R. 1982. Conversation partner mutual adaptation as demonstrated by Fourier series analysis. *Journal of Psycholinguistic Research*, 11: 35–46.

Gregory, S.W., Kalkhoff, W., Harkness, S.K., & Paul, J.L. 2009. Targeted high and low speech frequency bands to right and left ears respectively improve task performance and perceived sociability in dyadic conversations. *Laterality: Asymmetries of Body, Brain and Cognition*, 14(4): 423–440.

Hagelin, J.S., Rainforth, M.V., Orme-Johnson, D.W., Cavanaugh, K.L., Alexander, C.N., Shatkin, S.F., Davies, J.L., Hughes, A.O., & Ross, E. 1999. Effects of the group practice of the Transcendental Meditation program on preventing violent crime in Washington D.C.: Results of the National Demonstration Project, June–July, 1993. *Social Indicators Research*, 47(2): 153–201.

Jahn, R.G., & Dunne, B.J. 1987. *Margins of reality: The role of consciousness in the physical world*. New York-San Diego, CA: Harcourt Brace Jovanovich.

Jahn, R.G., Bradish, G., Dobyns, Y., Lettieri, A., Nelson, R., Mischo, J., Boller, E., Bosch, H., Vaitl, D., Houtkooper, J., & Walter, B. 2000. Mind/machine interaction consortium: PortREG replication experiments. *Journal of Scientific Exploration*, 14(4): 499–555.

Mason, L.I., Patterson, R.P., & Radin, D.I. 2007. Exploratory study: The random number generator and group meditation. *Journal of Scientific Exploration*, 21(2): 295–317.

McCraty, R., Atkinson, M., & Bradley, R.T. 2004a. Electrophysiological evidence of intuition: Part 1. The surprising role of the heart. *Journal of Alternative and Complementary Medicine*, 10(1): 133–143.

McCraty, R., Atkinson, M., & Bradley, R.T. 2004b. Electrophysiological evidence of intuition: Part 2. A system-wide process? *Journal of Alternative and Complementary Medicine*, 10(2): 325–336.

McCraty, R., Atkinson, M., Tomasino, D., & Bradley, R.T. 2006. *The coherent heart: Heart–brain interactions, psychophysiological coherence, and the emergence of system-wide order*. Boulder Creek, CA: Research Center, Institute of HeartMath.

Myers, D.G. 2002. *Intuition: Its powers and perils*. New Haven, CT: Yale University Press.

Myers, F.W.H. 1907. *Human personality and its survival of bodily death*. London and Bombay: Longmans, Green & Co.

Nelson, R. 2002. Coherent consciousness and reduced randomness: Correlations on September 11, 2001. *Journal of Scientific Exploration*, 16(4): 549–570.

Nelson, R. 2008. The emotional nature of global consciousness. Paper for the Bial Foundation 7th Symposium; http:/noosphere.princeton.edu; accessed February 19, 2020.

Nelson, R.D., Dobyns, Y.H., Dunne, B.J., & Jahn, R.G. 1991. Analysis of variance of REG experiments: Operator intention, secondary parameters, database structure, *Technical Note PEAR 91004*, PEAR, Princeton University.

Orme-Johnson, D.W., Alexander, C.N., Davies, J.L., Chandler, H.W., & Larimore, W.E. 1988. International peace project in the Middle East. *Journal of Conflict Resolution*, 32(4): 777–812.

Orme-Johnson, D.W., Dillbeck, M.C., & Alexander, C.N. 2003. Preventing terrorism and international conflict: Effects of large assemblies of participants in the Transcendental Meditation and TM-Sidhi Programs. In C.N. Alexander, K.G. Walton, D.W. Orme-Johnson, R.S. Goodman, & N.J. Pallone (Eds.), *Transcendental meditation in criminal rehabilitation and crime prevention*: 283–302. Philadelphia, PA: The Haworth Press.

Penrose, R. 1994. *Shadows of the mind: A search for the missing science of consciousness*. New York: Oxford University Press.

Pribram, K.H., & Bradley, R.T. 1998. The brain, the Me and the I. In M. Ferrari, & R. Sternberg (Eds.), *Self-awareness: Its nature and development*, Chapter 10: 273–307. New York: The Guilford Press.

Radin, D.I. 1997. *The conscious universe: The scientific truth of psychic phenomena*. San Francisco, CA: HarperEdge.

Radin, D.I. 2002. Exploring the relationship between random physical events and mass human attention: Asking for whom the bell tolls. *Journal of Scientific Exploration*, 16(4): 533–547.

Radin, D.I. 2006. *Entangled minds: Extrasensory experiences in a quantum reality*. New York: Paraview Pocket Books.

Radin, D.I., & Atwater, F.H. 2009. Exploratory evidence for correlations between entrained coherence and random physical systems. *Journal of Scientific Exploration*, 23(3): 263–272.

Radin, D.I., Michel, L., Johnston, J., & Delorme, A. 2013. Psychophysical interactions with a double-slit interference pattern. *Physics Essays*, 26(4): 553–556.

Radin, D.I., Schlitz, M.J., & Baur, C. 2015. Distant healing intention therapies: An overview of the scientific evidence. *Global Advances in Health Medicine*, 4(Suppl): 67–71.

Radin, D.I., Stone, J., Levine, E., Eskandarnejad, S., Schlitz, M., Kozak, L., Mandel, D., & Hayssen, G. 2008. Compassionate intention as a therapeutic intervention by partners of cancer patients: Effects of distant intention on the patients' autonomic nervous system. *Explore*, 4(4): 235–243.

Salanova, M., Rodríguez-Sánchez, A.M., Schaufeli, W.B., & Cifre, E. 2014. Flowing together: A longitudinal study of collective efficacy and collective flow among workgroups. *Journal of Psychology*, 148(4): 435–455.

Sawyer, K. 2007. *Group genius: The creative power of collaboration*. New York: Basic Books.

Schore, A.N. 1994. *Affect regulation and the origin of the self: The neurobiology of emotional development*. Hillsdale, NJ: Lawrence Erlbaum Associates.

Schweikard, D.P., & Schmid, H.B. 2013. Collective intentionality. *The Stanford encyclopedia of philosophy* (Summer 2013 Edition), Edward N. Zalta (Ed.), https://plato.stanford.edu/archives/sum2013/entries/collective-intentionality; accessed March 23, 2019.

Segal, N.L. 1999. *Entwined lives: Twins and what they tell us about human behavior*. New York: Dutton Books, The Penguin Group.

Sheldrake, R. 2013. *The sense of being stared at: And other unexplained powers of human minds*. Rochester, VT; Toronto, Canada: Park Free Press.

Targ, R., & Katra, J.E. 2000. Remote viewing in a group setting. *Journal of Scientific Exploration*, 14: 107–114.

Teilhard de Chardin, P. 1967. *On love*. New York: Harper & Row.

Tiller, W.A., Dibble, W.E., & Fandel, J.G. 2005. *Some science adventures with real magic*. Walnut Creek, CA: Pavior Publishing.

Tressoldi, P.E., Martinelli, M., Zaccaria, E., & Massaccesi, S. 2009. Implicit intuition: How heart rate can contribute to prediction of future events. *Journal of the Society for Psychical Research*, 73(894): 1–16.

Vickhoff, B., Malmgren, H., Åström, R., Nyberg, G., Ekström, S., Engwall, M., Snygg, J., Nilsson, M., & Jörnsten, R. 2013. Music structure determines heart rate variability of singers. *Frontiers of Psychology*, July 9.| doi: 10.3389/fpsyg.2013.00334.

PART IV

DEVELOPING INTUITION IN PRACTICAL SETTINGS

16. Resourcing intuition in practice

Satu Teerikangas, Marja Turunen and Liisa Välikangas

The study of intuition is gaining momentum in management research. The use of intuitive forms of knowing has been found critical in demanding work contexts (Agor, 1989; Weick, 1993). The bulk of extant research on intuition in organizations, however, contrasts intuition with rational accounts (Akinci & Sadler-Smith, 2012; Baldacchino et al., 2015; Simon, 1987). Investigations conducted in organizational settings have focused on the managerial and entrepreneurial faculties of intuition (Baldacchino et al., 2015; Dane & Pratt, 2007; Isenberg, 1984) rather than intuiting as a resourcing practice, which is the focus of this chapter.

Despite recent research on institutionalizing intuition in organizations (Calabretta et al., 2017; Crossan et al., 1999), there is a lack of empirical research on the practices of intuiting in organizational contexts. Little is known about the factors that enable intuiting in work contexts (Crossan et al., 2011; Isaack, 1978; Sinclair, 2011). Furthermore, prior conceptualizations have favored static forms of intuition, considering it as a noun (Sadler-Smith, 2016) instead of active forms, with a focus on the practice of intuiting. In sum, less is known about the preconditions of intuitive knowing practices at work, and about how intuition could be awakened and harnessed within organizational settings.

To fill this void in literature, in this chapter we examine how intuition can be evoked (Vaughan, 1979) and practiced in organizations and work contexts. Our focus is on strategic intuition. Whilst expert intuition correlates with one's degree of professional exposure and expertise, strategic intuition is at the grasp of all professionals, in the everyday work experience. Strategic intuition refers to fleeting moments, when one captures a meaningful insight (Dane, 2011; Duggan & Mason, 2011). Interestingly, research on the factors predictive of strategic intuition is in need of development (Duggan & Mason, 2011).

This chapter builds on the concept of 'engagement as intuiting in practice' (Teerikangas & Välikangas, 2014). Our previous research findings led us to propose that engaging moments, experienced either via high, intense engagement 'edges' or calmer, reflective moments of 'retreating' (Teerikangas & Välikangas, 2012), offer opportunities to tap into one's intuition. In this chapter, we extend this earlier work to propose individual, interpersonal and organizational-level practices enabling professionals to engage (Kahn, 1990) in being 'their authentic best selves,' or rather, their intuiting best selves in contemporary work contexts. By enabling personal engagement, these practices allow for tapping into one's intuition, that is, *intuiting*

(Sadler-Smith, 2016). Engagement thus becomes a means of tuning into one's intuitive resource.

The experience of intuiting is fleeting and vulnerable (Isenberg, 1984; Duggan, 2013). Moments of intuition can remain unnoticed or blotted out by professionals themselves. Dane (2011) argues that the degree to which intuitions are noticed depends on one's degree of attention. Attention refers to a state of being mindfully in the present moment. The fact that not all instances of intuition are consciously attended to by the individual him/herself makes intuition difficult to capture using conventional methodologies (Sinclair, 2011, 2014). Our research design enabled us to serendipitously capture the practice of intuiting in organizational settings. Our findings are based on a two-year Finnish Technology Agency-funded research project, totaling 55 interviews across four contexts of professionals engaging in demanding work (Teerikangas & Välikangas, 2012). Interesting is that we did not initially seek to study intuition. We sought to explore the dynamics of personal engagement (Kahn, 1990) in contemporary work contexts. Our findings, however, led us to observe that the cycle of engagement, via its edging and retreating moments, offers a means of capturing intuition in flight. In other words, the concepts of intuition and intuiting emerged serendipitously in our research findings (see Teerikangas & Välikangas, 2014). Our research design thus led us to surprise intuition by deliberately not focusing on it.

Our findings are theoretically positioned as follows. On the one hand, we build the concept of 'intuiting in practice' on the understanding of practice in social theory (Bourdieu, 1977; Schatzki et al., 2001). Theories of practice offer a means of appreciating *how* actors engage in a certain activity. It is via regular practice that routines and structures emerge and become prone to re-negotiation (Giddens, 1986). As Giddens (1986) suggests, practices thus matter from a longer-term organizational or societal structuration perspective. In strategic management, the practice turn (Whittington, 2006) posits that strategy is what people *do* in organizations. Likewise, we see that intuition refers to the engaged activity of intuiting, which we term intuiting as a practice.

On the other hand, we build on resourcing theory, which explores how resources are brought into use, be it through organizational processes, individual or collective action (Feldman, 2004; Feldman & Orlikowski, 2011; Howard-Grenville, 2007; Sonenshein, 2013). This leads to viewing resources as "mutable sources of energy" (Feldman, 2004: 295), as they are (re)created through and in action. While the role of individuals in shaping resources has been acknowledged (Quinn & Worline, 2008; Sonenshein, 2013), to the best of our knowledge, this line of work has not yet been extended to explore the resourcing of intuition. In this chapter, we focus on this aspect via engagement.

Our chapter moves next to presenting the findings on two fronts. First, we provide an overview of the activities enabling intuiting in practice via edging and retreating. Thereafter, we identify individual, interpersonal, managerial, and organizational practices enabling personal engagement, that is, intuiting in practice. Whilst our explicit focus is on the means of enabling engagement in contemporary work contexts, our underlying argument is that it is in their engagement that professionals find the means of intuiting in practice. The main contribution of the chapter is in offering an appreciation of the resourcing of intuition in contemporary work contexts. We argue that engagement offers a channel toward intuiting in practice. It is in their engagement that professionals resource their intuition, and in doing so, their personal and the collective human capital in organizations.

METHODS

Our research approach is rooted in grounded theory-building (Glaser & Strauss, 1967) in four research settings ST1–ST4. Study STI was set in the Helsinki area-based research and development unit of a global high-technology engineering organization. The second investigation (ST2) is set amidst information technology (IT) consulting. In the third investigation (ST3), we moved beyond corporations to study employee engagement across professions and work contexts. In ST1–3, we sampled highly engaged professionals for our interviews. In the fourth investigation (ST4), we explored the engagement dynamics of young professionals; one that had graduated within 1–3 years and others pursuing postgraduate degrees. Interviewees (ST4) represented a mix of vocational (i.e., the arts, medicine, law) and professional (i.e., business studies, engineering) backgrounds in Finland and China. In total, this encompassed interviews with 55 professionals: nine research and development engineers (ST1), six consultants engaged in strategic IT design and consulting (ST2), 16 established experts across professions (ST3), and 24 junior professionals (ST4). In ST1 and ST2, an element of ethnographic observation was involved, as we visited company premises regularly and engaged in ongoing discussions and regular workshops with company representatives.

Our analysis followed three broadly definable stages. In the first stage, we coded each interview openly, line-by-line. This open coding led to the identification of a number of first order categories that were mapped onto second order themes, and further to aggregate dimensions (Gioia et al., 2012). We observed that, though termed differently, the main findings were converging across the four investigations. Beyond a contribution to the literature on engagement, we continued our discovery and exploration of parallel literatures. We realized that our findings also mapped onto the intuition literature. Further, there appeared to be a resourcing dimension to the findings. In the third stage, we went back to the original interviews to re-analyze the codes emerging from the data.

INTUITING AS A PRACTICE

We start presenting our findings with an overview of the practices that enabled interviewed professionals to engage in work contexts, that is, intuit in practice. We observed engagement to offer a double-edged sword in that it requires a rhythmic balance between high engagement 'edges' on the one hand, and calmer-engagement 'retreats' on the other hand. It is via an ongoing balance of edging–retreating cycles that engagement can be maintained. Such a dyadic rhythm has been found to characterize the breakthrough work of professionals, be they scientists, authors, or artists (see review in Pang, 2017).

Reaching the Edge

We build upon research on engagement (Kahn, 1990) in evoking an intuiting practice. Engagement is a state of turning into one's best self (Kahn, 1990). According to Kahn (2010: 30, cited in Fletcher, 2017), engagement is "both delicate and fragile, and quite resilient ... it can be broken with a word, said in the wrong way at the wrong time ... (yet) engagement (can) ... blossom like a malnourished child suddenly fed and loved." Consequently, an engagement 'edge' (Goldberg, 1985) in our research is theorized as *a shift into an intuiting mode*, beyond the rational mind into unknown territory where it is possible to "grasp the world as a whole, in flux" (Langer, 2011: 114). The mind identifies new categories (Langer, 2011) and novel combinations of existing ones (Scharmer, 2009). Duggan (2013) calls these sparking moments strategic intuition. Next, we look at activities enabling high engagement edging.

A sense of meaning. A sense of meaning appears to be a prerequisite to high engagement. Consultants in ST2 felt they made a difference to the success of their customer companies. Engineers in ST1 drew their engagement from advancing knowledge, working with the latest technology, and thus shaping the future. Interviewees across the four studies felt that through their work, they are making the world a better place. Beyond societal meaning, professionals in ST2 were proud to work for a top-tier corporation, while engineers in ST1 felt engaged with propagating the firm's technological vision in the world.

Aspirational goals help trigger meaning. The consulting organization highlighted the significance of dreaming big (ST2/2), whereas engineers observed the significance of "seeing the bigger picture" (ST1/Workshop). In contrast, experiences of low engagement were ascribed to activities where the objective was unclear or where there is a cacophony of viewpoints. There is an element of timing, though. Engineers in ST1 experienced difficulties in securing high levels of engagement in projects with a long life cycle. Senior consultants at ST2 did not experience this challenge, given that their projects had a shorter time span.

Meaning is also experienced via achievement, such as success at one's task or victory in competition. Moments of high engagement were thus recalled in ST2, when winning a major project. In contrast, low engagement experiences were recalled in situations in which one had a low sense of achievement. The task might take (too) long, one feels one does not move forward, or there is little visibility to one's achievements (ST4).

A sense of challenge. When describing activities bearing a challenge, interviewees experienced being at stake. In ST1, interviewees mentioned "mission impossible" projects (ST1/7). Equally, work pressures and deadlines created a sense of urgency.

For consultants in ST2, demanding tasks and tight deadlines offered stretch and personal growth. Younger interviewees in ST4 recalled instances of acute danger or sports competitions: "I have to perform, as the success of the game in that moment depends on me" (ST4/16). The activity needs to be balanced in one's comfort zone, though. Some noted that when the task is too difficult or too easy, one slips back into low engagement (ST4). These findings parallel Csikszentmihalyi's (1997) classic work on flow, suggesting that individuals experience moments of 'flow' by engaging themselves toward challenging tasks. However, this experience is distracted if the task represents too high or too low a challenge.

Furthermore, Csikszentmihalyi (1997) observes that individuals can undergo uncomfortable feelings, such as fear, before engaging in an activity. However, as one remembers the pleasant experience of flow, one's readiness to overcome challenges increases. This was echoed in our findings, as interviewees observed that high engagement may involve pain and difficulty. Individuals reported stress, negative feelings, and anxiety in the phase preceding the peak experience (edging). Thus a project manager in ST1 noted how for her, stress works as a precursor to high engagement. A novelist (ST4/11) remarked that he tends to become anxious, nervous and nearly paralyzed prior to starting to write his work up. He observed similar experiences among his artist colleagues. Experienced project managers in ST1 explained how the sign of a promising team is that it is capable of undergoing a crisis together.

A sense of renewal. Interviewees experienced work contexts endowed with a culture of ongoing development and renewal as engaging. Renewal characterized the work culture at ST2's consulting organization. Consulting assignments require innovative approaches. Projects are interdisciplinary and cross-functional, consultants rotate across projects, and new recruits are involved. A senior consultant described the organization as "a world of improvisation" (ST2/3). In engineering teams (ST1), project managers underlined how task variety and staff rotation created a sense of renewal. In such work contexts, individuals observed: "I enjoy my current job, as I keep learning, it challenges me to learn" (ST1/7), or "there is a sense of learning, of moving forward" (ST2/4). In contrast, low engagement experiences were recalled during periods when there was little new to learn, or when one was simply doing the same task over and over again. Shifting contexts also evoked a sense of renewal, be it through travel, music or physical activity (ST4). Moving to a new country was engaging to an engineer in ST1(4). A consultant in ST2(2) recounted that for him, renewal occurred frequently on his way home while driving; he gets an idea and is eager to share it at the office in the morning.

Retreating Activities

The quotes above highlight the intensity of edging, that is, the high engagement experience. While pleasant and addictive, there is a need to balance activities with respect to their intensity. In particular, an occasional decreasing of tempo is important. We term engagement experiences with lower intensity as *retreating*. With the concept of 'retreat' we mean an act of 'a letting go' (Scharmer, 2009) of downloaded presuppositions, which in turn opens new opportunities and spaces for intuiting (Pang, 2017). Extant research shows that our mind processes information when we divert our conscious attention elsewhere (Dijksterhuis & Aarts, 2010, cited in Duggan & Mason, 2011). Downtime parallels creative productivity (Pang, 2017).

Based on our findings, retreating can take two forms. First, informants acknowledged the significance of time off work. This refers to holidays, daily recovery or being in-between jobs. A need for recovery following particularly intense periods of work was emphasized: "We should recognize that individuals need a break in between intensive projects. They cannot give 100% immediately" (ST1/9). An executive highlighted how she needs recovery time, when engaging in new, demanding roles, such as a new job. Second, interviewees reported the need to recover on a daily basis. A professional emphasized "the need to turn off 'the machine' for a few days, so that it does not continuously overheat" (ST3/7). Interviewees also experienced retreating while working on less demanding chores such as time keeping or administration. A professional in ST3 ascribed daily routines in the role as a critical backbone in an engaged life, whereas another professional in ST3 described routines as providing a structure for engagement. Such routine activities offer a balance to highly intense edging experiences.

These findings echo extant research positing that a retreat can be reached in several ways depending on the task and individual or organizational preferences. Examples include deliberate mindful practices in controlling consciousness (Langer, 2011; Turunen, 2014) or shifting deliberately into repetitive or routine work, thus occupying the rational mind and opening a space for intuition to emerge (Langer, 2011). Also, a pause, such as resting (a nap, shower, coffee break), changing the focus of activities, such as a short walk or physical exercise, or aesthetic or ethical exposure (Dörfler & Ackermann, 2012) may elicit a phase of retreating (Pang, 2017).

Given the hectic pace of work, retreating appears idealistic, though. Interviewees felt that the pace of corporate life does not provide sufficient opportunities for recovery. In some cases, retreats from work were often taken autonomously, with or without the employer's support. Engagement in the two studied company contexts was defined in a one-sided manner as edging only. Yet interviewees did not consider constant delivery feasible. An engineer from ST1 noted: "You cannot ask people to deliver forever without a break."

Rhythm of Edges and Retreats

Our findings show that engagement at the level of the individual is bounded. Given the high intensity of edging instances, interviewees observed that they cannot remain at the peak too long. There are physical (e.g., hunger) and cognitive (e.g., information overload) limits to high engagement. Ultimately, continuous high engagement can lead to burnout. This explains that the resourcing of engagement needs to be regulated; there is a need to temporarily retreat from the high intensity of the edging experience, be it in the form of rest or activities of lesser intensity (see Figure 16.1). In parallel, a limit to retreating was observed – extended periods of retreating were experienced as conducive to disengagement. There is thus a need to regulate the edging–retreating cycle. In sum, intuiting in practice bears a rhythmic and bounded nature.

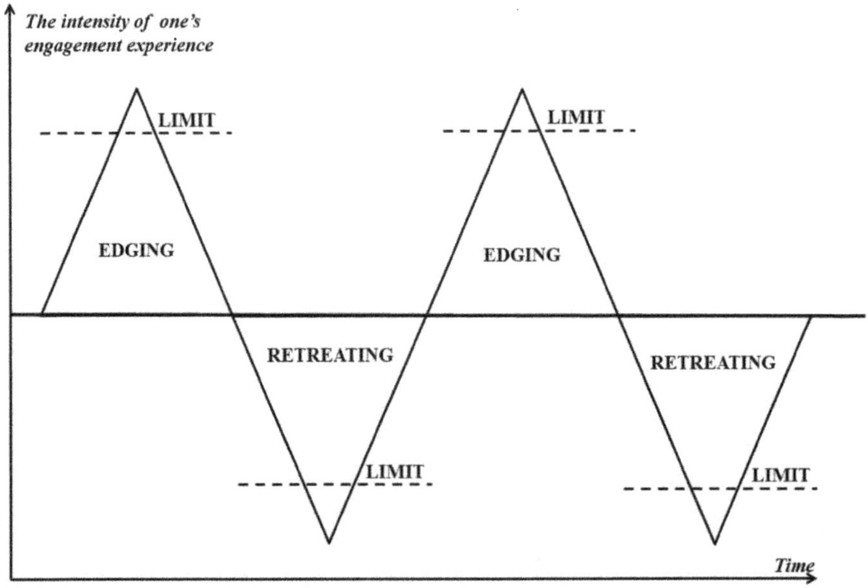

Figure 16.1 Intuition as a practice via engagement edges and retreat

When individuals do not retreat after an intense period of activity, they risk burnout. Interviewees identified limits to edging. "I am not myself anymore" (ST4/3), "I do not have much time for myself" (ST4/24), "there is a limited amount of things that I can be engaged with" (ST4/6), and "there is too much going on" (ST4/11): these are all feelings that signal that a retreat is timely. Interviewees indicated that such limits were reached when they were engaged in many intense activities simultaneously or when entering new environments. Hunger was mentioned as a physical limit to engagement. While edging has its limits, in a similar vein, interviewees saw an excess of less-intense activities as leading to disengagement and apathy. It appears that just as high engagement is addictive, experiences at lower intensity lead to decreased levels of energy, and to disengagement.

Ideally, one is able to balance between high intensity edging and lower intensity retreating experiences. This was recognized with respect to the need to seek "sustainable engagement" (ST1/workshop) instead of peaks only. Engineers in ST1 recognized the need for both; ideally, a healthy work–life balance is achieved. Professionals in ST3 noted the significance of regulating one's activities; otherwise highly engaging work "takes over one's life" (ST3/4). Younger interviewees in ST4 noted that both high and low engagement instances are important. Engagement thus appears to be a balancing act between edges and retreats.

AGENCY AND THE RESOURCING OF INTUITING IN PRACTICE

Taking a closer look at practices supportive of high engagement edges, we found these to be enabled by actions undertaken either by oneself, directly by others, be it colleagues or managers, or indirectly by the work environment. From a resourcing lens (Feldman, 2004), high engagement, or intuiting, is thus resourced via individual, interpersonal, managerial or organizational agency.

The Role of the Self

Is engagement intrinsically or extrinsically driven? Based on our findings, we observe that individuals have a role in engaging themselves. Instead of waiting for engagement to occur, the majority of our interviewees took proactive action to engage themselves. In so doing, they were consciously resourcing their own engagement. The reader is reminded that our interviewees (ST1–ST3) were sampled based on their high engagement.

The role of the self is manifest in actively involving oneself in engaging activities. Engaged interviewees sought meaningful careers and life missions and renewal in their work. Second, by reframing their mindset from negativity to positivity, from crisis to opportunity, from a difficult present to a more pleasant past, they actively tuned their cognitive and emotional capacities. Recalling that a certain emotional and cognitive mindset is characteristic of the edging experience, it appears that individuals, having experienced such instances, are capable of consciously manipulating their cognitive and emotional capacities in this direction. Thus by self-engaging, these individuals are acting upon their own mind, turning it into an engaging resource. Third, interviewees managed their engagement by actively engaging themselves, creating engagement across all their activities, and making conscious choices as to what kinds of activities they focus on. They also set high objectives. Finally, by actively seeking to engage others, regardless of one's own level of engagement, they bear an engaging agency toward others. They consider other individuals as malleable energy resources that can be engaged.

When actively drawing and utilizing the self, it appears that individuals move from occasional experiences of edging to a lifestyle and a quasi permanent state of engagement. This does not mean that these individuals are in an ongoing state of peak engagement, or edging. Rather, mastering their self as an engaging resource provides them the opportunity of actively creating engagement experiences in their lives. They follow the engagement cycles of edging and retreating. Given their addictive nature, these experiences spark further engagement. As a result, these individuals manage, that is, resource, their own engagement.

The Role of Others, Managers and Work Contexts

Paralleling the active role of the self, the individual's organizational surrounding bears an effect on one's capacity to engage. This parallels Maimone and Sinclair's (2014) notion of organizational space (Lefebvre, 1991). This leads to asking whether an organization's space (or spaces) is (are) supportive of employees' engagement. We observed that 'others,' be they colleagues, customers, managers, or work contexts, play a role in enabling engagement.

Beyond engaging themselves, individuals bear an engaging capacity toward one another. Interviewees observed that when one is engaged, this engagement becomes engaging and inspiring toward others, for example, colleagues and customers. This parallels findings on emotional contagion (Barsade, 2002) as well as on how employees' engagement levels are felt by customers (Salanova et al., 2005). What is more, the importance of an emotionally safe work atmosphere was raised as a prerequisite to high engagement (Kahn, 1990). Given the authenticity of the high engagement edge, it requires the sense of safety to take action and to dare to take risks (Teerikangas & Välikangas, 2012). Open, respectful and genuine interactions are examples of an emotionally safe work atmosphere. This highlights that whether personally engaged or not, individuals are involved in engaging others. This brings an element of responsibility to work and non-work interactions. Through a feedback mechanism, the engaging of others is likely to feedback onto the engager (Barsade, 2002), though we as yet have little explicit evidence of this via this research project.

The role of managers is critical. If their managerial paradigm is human-centric, they genuinely appreciate the significance of work engagement. Engagement matters toward work performance; research has established the performance consequences of engagement with regards to individual well-being and performance, team creativity, customer satisfaction, and organizational performance (Britt et al., 2005; Harter et al., 2002; Salanova et al., 2005). What is more, the role of the manager resembles the role of the engaged self. By edging themselves, they become involved in engaging activities, and thus show to their work community that it is safe to seek peak experiences. Further, they provide opportunities for team members to edge, be it via small nudges, or by providing autonomy and responsibility for team members. The role of managers in creating an emotionally safe work atmosphere is critical (Kahn, 1990). Managers also engage others. In a managerial role, the significance of acknowledging success and rewarding good results comes to the fore. All the while, basic hygiene factors need to be in place. This, over time, may lead to positive spirals of engagement (Feldman & Worline, 2012; Fredrickson & Joiner, 2018). This is collective resourcing of intuition at work. Such effects might explain why the studied ST2 consulting organization was considered an island of high engagement amid the larger parent firm, or why the interviewed engineers in ST1 had created flourishing work environments in their respective teams.

Finally, work contexts matter. Workplaces where the external business environment has been interpreted as an opportunity translate this challenge into an engaging activity bearing meaning, challenge and renewal. Human resource practices can be strategically attuned to support the continuous professional development of staff, for example, via rotation and renewal. Recruiting can strategically support engagement. Office and physical work arrangements can be made conducive to engagement. For one, physical proximity matters, even in virtual teams. For another, there is a need for uninterrupted spaces allowing focused work. Third, the role of physical spaces such as offices or meeting rooms was raised.

We hold in our theorizing that intuiting as a practice has a social dimension. Individuals and organizations carry assumptions of intuiting; this in turn affects the use of intuiting (Fletcher, 2017; Hutchins, 1995; Vaughan, 1979). Further, intuiting can be collectively practiced (Akinci & Sadler□Smith, 2018; Scharmer, 2009; Turunen, 2015). Certain contexts (Elbanna, 2015) and contextual cues (Leavitt et al., 2016) in organizations may enhance intuiting. Alternatively, organizational practices may restrict (Prince & Priporas, 2018) or jeopardize the harnessing of intuition or intuition-based outcomes.

It appears that through individual, interpersonal, managerial and workplace activity, it is possible to collectively resource the organization's human capital toward higher degrees of engagement. When this occurs, it is more likely that professionals tune and tap into their intuitive resources and forms of knowing, as they have opportunities and the emotional safety to engage. Interestingly, the active role of the self further amplifies the resourcing of intuition. In such a situation, many or all of the organizational members are engaged and engage one another. This was implicit in the corporate cases of ST1 and ST2.

CONCLUSIONS AND MANAGERIAL IMPLICATIONS

Our findings contribute to the emerging body of literature on intuition at the workplace (Calabretta et al., 2017; Crossan et al., 1999) by identifying practices enabling strategic intuiting at work (Duggan & Mason, 2011). As intuition might best be captured 'in flight,' our findings suggest approaching it via a secondary angle, here via engagement. Given that engagement edges and retreats provide opportunities for tapping into one's intuition, our findings suggest that engagement is a means of tapping into an organization's intuitive sources of knowing. From the perspective of intuiting, our findings are a call for professionals and employers to recognize that personal engagement (Kahn, 1990) matters performance-wise, but further, it bears secondary effects, for example, with respect to intuiting. Intuition seems to easily escape our grasp be it in research or practice. We hope that our findings offer, via the lens of engagement, a tangible lever for contemporary professionals, managers, and human resource practitioners to approach intuition in a way that is understandable, readily available and close to contemporary work practice.

Reading the findings from an intuition perspective, the following implications are observed. If intuition is to be sought, then professionals need to secure a balanced, ongoing rhythm between high engagement edges and calmer-engagement retreats. If employers seek a highly engaged and intuiting workforce, the strategic significance of intense edges and letting go via retreats needs to be acknowledged and provided for. In other words, the key to high engagement and intuiting rests in the duality of the edge–retreat cycle, not in one or the other. This finding echoes studies on breakthrough thinkers' and professionals' work schedules (Pang, 2017), whilst also resonating with classics on work–life balance and the work well-being literature. Taking a critical stance, historically known breakthrough thinkers worked intensively an average of 4–5 hours a day, whilst respecting their need to play, explore and rest (Pang, 2017). This leads us to asking whether contemporary work practices require too much, or whether in so doing, only average instead of exceptional performance is reached.

For another, the role of each professional with respect to mastering the degree and intensity of engagement in one's own activities, career and life comes to the fore. Engaged individuals are involved in engaging activities, they self-engage themselves, whilst engaging others. Via such practices, they come to resource their own intuition. Third, the role of everyone in the organization with respect to securing the intuitive potential of others matters. The question for each professional is – am I an

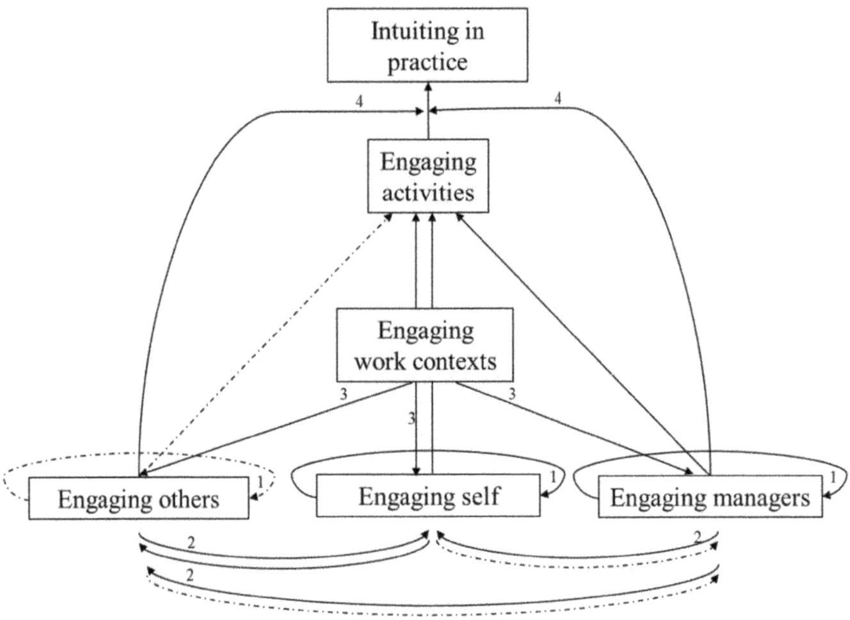

Legend:
Dotted lines refer to implied findings.
1: The role of individuals in reframing and managing their own engagement.
2: The role of engaging interactions toward others.
3: The role of engaging work contexts in recruiting talent.
4: The role of others in creating emotional safety in support of the edging experience.

Figure 16.2 The resourcing of intuiting in practice

engager, do I engage others? Fourth, the role of managers is central with respect to engaging themselves and enabling the engagement of others. Fifth, human resource practices, such as recruitment, that are supportive of engagement matter. Finally, physical spaces create engagement, and thus enable intuiting.

In summary, agency practices, whether at individual, interpersonal, managerial or organizational levels, and physical spaces are involved in continuously resourcing an organization's human capital pool. The question is – are these practices and is this resourcing supportive of intuiting? Our findings are a call to consciously focus on resourcing the engagement of oneself and others. In so doing, the individual's and the collective's intuitive resources are being tapped into. At a time when organizations are facing continuous change, it could be that such practices enable contemporary professionals to surf on the intuitive edge and in so doing, lead from the emerging future (Scharmer, 2009). Figure 16.2 summarizes our arguments on the resourcing of intuiting in practice.

In closing, the chapter calls for employers, practitioners and professionals to take workplace engagement seriously. Not only does engagement bear well-being and performance effects (Britt et al., 2005; Harter et al., 2002; Salanova et al., 2005), it also offers opportunities for individuals to tap into and resource their individual and collective intuitive sources of knowing. Under increasingly complex and demanding work contexts, is intuitive engagement the intelligence of the future?

REFERENCES

Agor, W.H. 1989. *Intuition in organizations, leading and managing productively*. London: Sage.

Akinci, C., & Sadler-Smith, E. 2012. Intuition in management research: A historical review. *International Journal of Management Reviews*, 14(1): 104–122.

Akinci, C., & Sadler-Smith, E. 2018. Collective intuition: Implications for improved decision making and organizational learning. *British Journal of Management*: 1–20, doi: 10.1111/1467-8551.12269.

Baldacchino, L., Ucbasaran, D., Cabantous, L., & Lockett, A. 2015. Entrepreneurship research on intuition: A critical analysis and research agenda. *International Journal of Management Reviews*, 17(2): 212–231.

Barsade, S.G. 2002. The ripple effect: Emotional contagion and its influence on group behavior. *Administrative Science Quarterly*, 47(4): 644–675.

Bourdieu, P. 1977. *Outline of a theory of practice*. Cambridge: Cambridge University Press.

Britt, T.W., Castro, C.A., & Adler, A.B. 2005. Self-engagement, stressors, and health: A longitudinal study. *Personality and Social Psychology Bulletin*, 31(11): 1475–1486.

Calabretta, G., Gemser, G., & Wijnberg, N.M. 2017. The interplay between intuition and rationality in strategic decision making: A paradox perspective. *Organization Studies*, 38(3–4): 365–401.

Crossan, M.M., Lane, H.W., & White, R.E. 1999. An organizational learning framework: From intuition to institution. *Academy of Management Review*, 24(3): 522–537.

Crossan, M.M., Maurer, C.C., & White, R.E. 2011. Reflections on the 2009 AMR decade award: Do we have a theory of organizational learning? *Academy of Management Review*, 36(3): 446–460.

Csikszentmihalyi, M. 1997. *Finding flow: The psychology of engagement with everyday life*. London: Basic Books.

Dane, E. 2011. Capturing intuitions 'in flight': Observations from research on attention and mindfulness. In M. Sinclair (Ed.), *Handbook of intuition research*: 217–226. Cheltenham, UK and Northampton, MA, USA: Edward Elgar Publishing.

Dane, E., & Pratt, M.G. 2007. Exploring intuition and its role in managerial decision making. *Academy of Management Review*, 32(1): 33–54.

Dijksterhuis, A., & Aarts, H. 2010. Goals, attention, and (un)consciousness. *Annual Review of Psychology*, 61: 467–490.

Dörfler, V., & Ackermann, F. 2012. Understanding intuition: The case for two forms of intuition. *Management Learning*, 43(5): 545–564.

Duggan, W. 2013. *Strategic intuition: The creative spark in human achievement*. New York: Columbia University Press.

Duggan, W., & Mason, M. 2011. Strategic intuition. In M. Sinclair (Ed.), *Handbook of intuition research:* 79–87. Cheltenham, UK and Northampton, MA, USA: Edward Elgar Publishing.

Elbanna, S. 2015. Intuition in project management and missing links: Analyzing the predicating effects of environment and the mediating role of reflexivity. *International Journal of Project Management*, 33(6): 1236–1248.

Feldman, M. 2004. Resources in emerging structures and processes of change. *Organization Science*, 15(3): 295–309.

Feldman, M.S., & Orlikowski, W.J. 2011. Theorizing practice and practicing theory. *Organization Science*, 22(5): 1240–1253.

Feldman, M.S., & Worline, M. 2012. Resources, resourcing and applicative cycles in organizations. In K.S. Cameron, & G.S. Spreitzer (Eds.), *The Oxford handbook of positive organizational scholarship*: 629–641. Oxford: Oxford University Press.

Fletcher, L. 2017. The everyday experiences of personal role engagement: What matters most? *Human Resource Development Quarterly*, 28(4): 451–479.

Fredrickson, B.L., & Joiner, T. 2018. Reflections on positive emotions and upward spirals. *Perspectives on Psychological Science*, 13(2): 194–199.

Giddens, A. 1986. *The constitution of society: Outline of a theory of structuration*. Berkeley, CA: University of California Press.

Gioia, D.A., Corley, K.G., & Hamilton, A.L. 2012. Seeking qualitative rigor in inductive research: Notes on the Gioia methodology. *Organizational Research Methods*, 16(1): 15–31.

Glaser, B.J., & Strauss, A.L. 1967. *The discovery of grounded theory*. Chicago, IL: Aldine Publishing Company.

Goldberg, P. 1985. *The intuitive edge*. New York: Tarcher.

Harter, J.K., Schmidt, F.L., & Hayes, T.L. 2002. Business-unit-level relationship between employee satisfaction, employee engagement, and business outcomes: A meta-analysis. *Journal of Applied Psychology*, 87(2): 268–279.

Howard-Grenville, J.A. 2007. Developing issue-selling effectiveness over time: Issue selling as resourcing. *Organization Science*, 18: 560–577.

Hutchins, E. 1995. *Cognition in the wild*. Boston, MA: MIT Press.

Isaack, T.S. 1978. Intuition: An ignored dimension of management. *Academy of Management Review*, 3: 917–922.

Isenberg, D. 1984. How senior managers think? *Harvard Business Review*, 62(6): 81–90.

Kahn, W.A. 1990. Psychological conditions of personal engagement and disengagement at work. *Academy of Management Journal*, 33(4): 692–724.

Kahn, W.A. 2010. The essence of engagement: Lessons from the field. In S.L. Albrecht (Ed.), *Handbook of employee engagement. Perspectives, issues, research, and practice*: 20–30. Cheltenham, UK and Northampton, MA, USA: Edward Elgar Publishing.

Langer, E.J. 2011. *Mindfulness*. 25th Anniversary Edition. Boston, MA: Da Capo Press.

Leavitt, K., Zhu, L., & Aquino, K. 2016. Good without knowing it: Subtle contextual cues can activate moral identity and reshape moral intuition. *Journal of Business Ethics*, 137(4): 785–800.

Lefebvre, H. 1991. *The production of space*. Oxford: Blackwell.

Maimone, F., & Sinclair, M. 2014. Dancing in the dark: Creativity, knowledge creation and (emergent) organizational change. *Journal of Organizational Change Management*, 27(2): 344–361.

Pang, A.S-J. 2017. *Rest: Why you get more done when you work less*. London: Penguin Life, Random House.

Prince, M., & Priporas, C. 2018. Using intuitive awakening for business students to enhance strategic thinking skills. *Australasian Marketing Journal*, 26(2): 157–162.

Quinn, R., & Worline, M. 2008. Enabling courageous collective action: Conversations from United Airlines flight 93. *Organization Science*, 19(4): 497–516.

Sadler-Smith, E. 2016. What happens when you intuit? Understanding human resource practitioners' subjective experience of intuition through a novel linguistic method. *Human Relations*, 69(5): 1069–1093.

Salanova, M., Agut, S., & Peiro, J.M. 2005. Linking organizational resources and work engagement to employee performance and customer loyalty: The mediation of service climate. *Journal of Applied Psychology*, 90(6): 1217–1227.

Scharmer, C.O. 2009. *Theory U*. San Francisco: Berrett-Koehler.

Schatzki, T., Knorr-Cetina, K., & von Savigny, E. 2001. *The practice turn in contemporary theory*. New York: Routledge.

Simon, H.A. 1987. Making management decisions: The role of intuition and emotion. *Academy of Management Perspectives*, 1(1): 57–64.

Sinclair, M. 2011. *Handbook of intuition research*. Cheltenham, UK and Northampton, MA, USA: Edward Elgar Publishing.

Sinclair, M. 2014. *Handbook of research methods on intuition*. Cheltenham, UK and Northampton, MA, USA: Edward Elgar Publishing.

Sonenshein, S. 2013. How organizations foster the creative use of resources. *Academy of Management Journal*, 57(3): 814–848.

Teerikangas, S., & Välikangas, L. 2012. Engaged employees! An actor perspective to innovation. In T. Pitsis, E. Dehlin, & A. Simpson (Eds.), *Handbook on organizational and management innovation*: 54–97. Cheltenham, UK and Northampton, MA, USA: Edward Elgar Publishing.

Teerikangas, S., & Välikangas, L. 2014. Exploring the dynamic of evoking intuition. In M. Sinclair (Ed.), *Handbook of research methods on intuition:* 72–87. Cheltenham, UK and Northampton, MA, USA: Edward Elgar Publishing.

Turunen, M. 2014. Consciousness view of organizations. In D.M. Boje, & T.L. Henderson (Eds.), *Being quantum: Ontological storytelling in the age of antinarrative*: 385–403. Newcastle Upon Tyne, UK: Cambridge Scholars Publishing.

Turunen, M. 2015. *Toward a consciousness-based view of organizing*. Helsinki: Unigrafia.

Vaughan, F.E. 1979. *Awakening intuition*. New York: Anchor.

Weick, K.E. 1993. The collapse of sensemaking in organizations: The Mann Gulch disaster. *Administrative Science Quarterly*, 38(4): 628–652.

Whittington, R. 2006. Completing the practice turn in strategy research. *Organization Studies*, 27(5): 613–634.

17. Facilitating intuitive decision-making and an entrepreneurial mindset in corporate culture – a case study

L. Murray Gillin

Most scholars agree that what differentiates entrepreneurs from other actors in the economy is their behaviour (Bradley et al., 2011). Dane and Pratt (2007: 48) highlight significant aspects of entrepreneurial behaviour as "the interplay between rational and intuitive decision-making". Likewise, in terms of the cognitive basis of making moral judgments and decisions, social psychologist Haidt (2013: 53) identifies the crucial components as "intuition and reasoning". Within this context, Kreuger (2007) emphasizes the significance of entrepreneurial intentions, entrepreneurial attitudes, deep cognitive structures and deep beliefs. All these findings demonstrate the importance of a holistic view of entrepreneurial behaviour, opportunity focus, decision-making and the spiritual/moral understandings that drive the successful entrepreneur's mindset.

Creating new products through opportunity recognition and creative decision-making processes is the 'front-end' of innovation (Hyppänen, 2013). Indeed, co-creation practices (Frow et al., 2016; Sarasvathy & Venkataraman, 2011) emphasize collaboration and interaction among multiple actors through the integration of human, material and financial resources to deliver value propositions perceived by the customer/user as innovation. Such perceptions of added value in the marketplace are seen as elements resulting from intuitive insight and decisive actions, associated with entrepreneurial behaviour and expressed as a corporate-wide culture (Malewska, 2019). The identified creativity and cognitive style are associated with individual differences in perceiving, behaving and solving problems (Ming-Huei et al., 2015), and as such are critical to the majority of high performing global industries and business executives (Henry & de Bruin, 2011). Intuitive decision-making behaviours that contribute to effective entrepreneurship and innovation include insight/perceiving, gut feel, intuition, 'knowing' a decision is right, solving problems, taking decisions and relating to others – and what is referred to as non-local intuition (Armstrong et al., 2012; Bradley et al., 2011; La Pira & Gillin, 2006; Sadler-Smith & Shefy, 2004).

Examples of such decision-making surrounding opportunity recognition, creativity, intuition and divergent thinking (reasoning) have largely been studied from a cognitive perspective using both conscious and unconscious processes, including pattern recognition and memory retrieval (Akinci, 2014; Mitchell et al., 2002, 2005; Shane, 2003). Importantly, Blume and Covin (2011) argue for caution when attributing intuition in decision-making as decisions around venture creation are influenced by a number of factors. However, Cunha (2007) suggests the rational view of decision-making needs to be harmonized with the intuitive and improvisational modes in order to provide a richer and more integrated understanding of entrepreneurial behaviour. Significantly, Dane and Pratt (2007) have concluded that the practice of intuitive decision-making may be more relevant to executive decision-makers dealing with strategy, investment and related management issues. Both Kickul et al. (2010) and Dane and Pratt (2007) also observe that intuition pertains less to learning the process but more to the way how learning and information is accessed and practised. Therefore, the effective use of explicit and implicit learning philosophies to influence intuitive decision-making practice depends on establishing a rigorous and complex cognitive framework. Intuitive perception, in this respect, enables decision-makers to process cues from sensed opportunities and behave entrepreneurially in delivering innovations in the marketplace.

The presented case review how a strategic intervention within a large middle-market financial services partnership in Melbourne, Australia, using an in-house delivered university post-graduate entrepreneurship education program, cultivates an entrepreneurial mindset and an effective innovation culture amongst company staff. The intervention produces a measured change in staff decision-making style from analytical to a more intuitive style. Also assessed is the resulting management style (entrepreneurial mindset) and how it impacts the firm's internal environment, strategic motivation and performance.

ENTREPRENEURIAL COGNITIVE STYLE

Organizational psychologists identify entrepreneurial behaviour, or cultural expression in terms of 'individual cognitive style' (Allinson et al., 2000; Armstrong et al., 2012; Norris & Epstein, 2011), as including the following characteristics: individual differences in perceiving reality, responding to opportunities, solving problems, and taking decisions arising from intuitive thinking or information processing outside of awareness by automatically learning from experience (i.e., experiential processing). Nandram et al. (2018) objectivize these perceptions and subtle cues (both internal and external) in terms of conscious emotions, thoughts, perceptions and information. In considering distinctions between expert and novice entrepreneurs, Wang et al. (2018) identify cognitively based intuition (seeing the bigger picture, sense making) and affectively based intuition (gut feeling) as needed for effective decision-making in innovation. Such cognitive intuition is more strongly exhibited by expert entrepreneurs. Both aspects (cognitive and affect) are not in conflict or exclusive but work simultaneously (Akinci & Sadler-Smith, 2012; Dane & Pratt, 2007; Hodgkinson et al., 2009; Sinclair et al., 2009). Other aspects of entrepreneurial intuition, such as the level of faith in intuition (Hicks et al., 2010) and the quantum approach to 'non-local' intuition (electrophysiology measures), are not the focus of this chapter but were reviewed elsewhere (see Bradley et al., 2011).

In seeking to further understand an entrepreneur's propensity for intuitive decision-making, this discussion is based on both cognitive and affective elements being part of the same experiential system. Sinclair et al. (2009) argue that formal mental simulation contributes creativity to an entrepreneurial business venture. Perhaps this can be called an 'entrepreneurial mindset'. Sinclair (2010) has proposed the term 'intuitive foresight' as a forward-looking intuition. Blume and Covin (2011) identify eight factors associated with the strength of an entrepreneur's attributions to intuition when making a venture founding decision. One of these factors – the strength of the entrepreneur's intuitive cognitive style, is contingent upon the individual's perception that intuition is an acceptable basis for decision-making. In reference to strategic cognition, Narayanan et al. (2011) portray strategy formulation as a complex activity consisting of scanning, sense making and decision-making, with the structure and process of cognition significantly influencing the framing of decisions. In considering our understanding of the role of culture/entrepreneurial behaviour in delivering effective innovations, Chaston and Sadler-Smith (2012) suggest a greater need to focus attention on the unique attributes of creative entrepreneurs and their effects on organizational process and performance. Such a focus may also be studied under the concept of entrepreneurial mindset.

Choice of Cognitive Style Index (CSI)

Given the cognitive underpinnings (discussed above) of the entrepreneurial mindset, entrepreneurial decision-making, entrepreneurial culture and other similar conceptualizations of entrepreneurial cognitions (Akinci & Sadler-Smith, 2013; Allinson et al., 2000; Armstrong et al., 2012; Chaston & Sadler-Smith, 2012; Haynie et al., 2010), it is appropriate to consider the choice of the 'Cognitive Style Index' (CSI) as a tool for this study to measure (or as a proxy for) the propensity of entrepreneurial decision-making behaviour and its relationship with culture.

The self-administered index (CSI: Allinson & Hayes, 1996) is designed to test the participant's propensity for 'intuitive decision-making' compared to 'analytic decision-making' on a continuum from one extreme to the other, with the premise that successful entrepreneurs would be skewed towards the intuitive decision-making end of the continuum (Allinson & Hayes, 2012). Alternatively, Hodgkinson and Sadler-Smith (2003a, 2003b) view the propensity for intuitive and analytic cognition as representing two poles where a person may not be just high on one and low on the other (as suggested by the continuum model), but also high on both or low on both at the same time. This alternative view, or 'dual-process', has been described by Evans (2003: 458) as "two minds in one brain".

Hodgkinson et al. (2009) have reviewed differences in the continuum versus dual-process models to describe decision-making style associated with the dimensions of intuition/experientiality and analysis/rationality and concluded the dual-process model has a more convincing theoretical basis. That said, their findings show that for CSI, the analytical and intuitive factors appear to overlap and interrelate, thus limiting any absolute use of CSI values (derived from Allinson & Hayes' 1996 concept) in cognitive style research.

Over many years, the author has used the CSI measure (Allinson & Hayes, 2012) to initially screen and identify serial entrepreneurs participating in a study of 'heart rate variability', intuition and opportunity decision-making (La Pira & Gillin, 2006). From 2003 to 2019 some 300 serial entrepreneurs, post-graduate students studying entrepreneurship and interested managers seeking to improve the entrepreneurial behaviour/culture inside their organizations have completed a CSI measure. Analysis and interpretation of these results found the CSI score to be a robust and reliable indicator of entrepreneurial intent. Given this finding, and the need to maintain consistency with these previous studies, all measures of decision-making style in this study are based on the standard CSI measure (Allinson & Hayes, 1996).

ENTREPRENEURIAL MINDSET

Entrepreneurial mindset (EM) (Haynie et al., 2010; Ireland et al., 2003; Shepherd et al., 2010) is a way of thinking about opportunities and effective innovation that surface in the firm's external and internal environment. By adopting an entrepreneurial mindset, Ireland et al. (2003) claim managers increase their ability to both recognize opportunities and facilitate necessary resources to 'make-it-happen'. This outcome results in an entrepreneurial culture and effective entrepreneurial leadership impacting the firm's strategic management, innovation and wealth creation. In considering how entrepreneurial either an individual's mindset or an organization's culture is, Shepherd et al. (2010: 60) comment that "interdependencies exist between the manager's mindset and the staff/organisation culture such that entrepreneurial culture and entrepreneurial mindset are inextricably interwoven". Similarly, in considering the concept of cognition and decision-making, Haidt (2013: 52) finds that emotions/gut feel/intuition and reasoning form a continuum of information processing where "contrasting emotion with cognition is therefore pointless".

In seeking to measure entrepreneurial mindset, Davis et al. (2015) developed the Entrepreneurial Mindset Profile (EMP), comprising a large set of individual characteristics including entrepreneurial personality and associated skill sets. A meta-analysis (Stewart & Roth, 2007) of the link between 'achievement motivation' and 'entrepreneurial status' found that entrepreneurs demonstrated reliably higher achievement motivation than managers. In addition, entrepreneurs demonstrated a higher 'risk propensity' than managers. In each case growth-oriented entrepreneurs were characterized by significantly greater levels of EM than managers. It is noted by Davis et al. (2015) that these results are based on an almost total reliance on self-report data.

Using the 'opportunity screening tool' template, developed by Timmons et al. (2011), Hazelton and Gillin (2019) adapted this tool for the self-assessment of EM amongst selected nursing trailblazers in the health industry and also for senior partners associated with the financial services partnership reviewed in the presented case.

Four dimensions: *leadership*, *decision-making*, *behaviour* and *awareness*, were used to describe entrepreneurial performance. Each dimension was scaled, as indicated in Figure 17.1, to measure the propensity for action on a five-point scale.

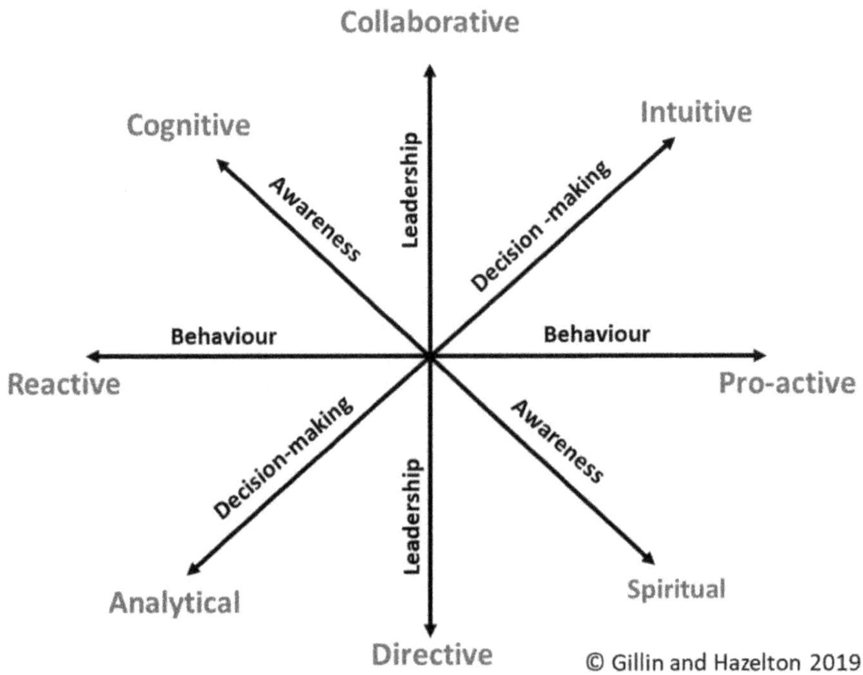

Figure 17.1 *Entrepreneurial dimensions associated with evaluated personal propensities*

The implication for displaying these action styles is to provide holistic understanding of the selected partner's entrepreneurial mindset as achieved after participation in an entrepreneurial learning pedagogy. Such information refers to the partner's personal development, and by extension, corporate entrepreneurial behaviour that contributes to effective innovations that are valued by the partners in the partnership together with clients of the firm.

The use of an EMP, as Davis et al. (2015) conclude, can provide would-be entrepreneurs with a greater insight into how their entrepreneurial motives and skills might affect outcomes; it can be valuable for organizations when constructing entrepreneurial teams; and it can enable university staff to develop teaching programs that help students understand EM as a concept and use it to grasp their own unique entrepreneurial being.

ENTREPRENEURIAL EDUCATION INTERVENTION: A CASE STUDY

The studied financial services firm is a partnership in Melbourne, Australia, providing financial and corporate advisory services to the 'middle-market' and family-based businesses. This 30-year-old firm (600 staff) faces ongoing change and business disruptions, including compliance conformity, technology changes, speed of regulatory change and an aging population. In 2010 the firm recognized the need to seek an appropriate strategy, identify ways to continue to be successful, learn quickly, be ahead of the game and see change coming rather than simply reacting to it.

Following an internal entrepreneurial health audit identifying the firm's need for more effective staff creativity and cross-discipline teamwork (Gillin et al., 2018), the partners chose to invest in an education intervention where the focus would not be on general management skills but on the development of creative skills and practices, nurturing an entrepreneurial culture that identifies opportunities and effectively delivers innovations needed in the marketplace. One partner noted:

> We've always been an entrepreneurial firm with a strong entrepreneurial legacy from the founding partners. The intervention will reinforce that entrepreneurial behaviour; it's the next natural step. (Partner 6)

Based on a specification for post-graduate entrepreneurial education at the Master's level and accredited by AACSB, the supporting brief included the following requirements: provide a nested group of post-graduate award programs at Graduate Certificate, Graduate Diploma and Master's level; deliver quality and integrated learning through a team of experienced professors, inspiring pracademics and dynamic entrepreneurs, using a portfolio of learning practices (Neck et al., 2014); apply the concept of *theory for practice sake rather than theory for theory sake*; integrate curriculum design with academic materials, experiential learning, entrepreneurial theory, practice and experience; teach from in-house and external case studies in the Harvard style; incorporate an applied research project selected from firm/client identified opportunities; use the block teaching mode to meet staff availability; direct students to search for opportunities to evaluate early in the first term; seek application of learning to in-house business practice and/or with family business clients; teach innovation as the 'tool' of the entrepreneur where innovation is defined as "the process that endows a recognized opportunity with the capacity to add value to an already existent invention, product, process or service and at a price a customer will pay" (author definition); and develop an international dimension to entrepreneurship.

The selected provider was the Entrepreneurship, Commercialisation and Innovation Centre (ECIC) at the University of Adelaide (2011–2016). Since 2017 the provider is the Australian Graduate School of Entrepreneurship (AGSE), Swinburne University of Technology. All contracted staff, teaching in the Melbourne office of the partnership, were highly experienced with a proven track record for delivering behavioural change from the applied learning methods. In particular, each staff member was academically qualified at PhD/Master's level, passionate to exchange knowledge and practice, inspirational in presentation, and committed to a holistic mindset in entrepreneurial education. Emphasis was placed on staff developing the human dimensions – intellectual, emotional and spiritual – to further effective decision-making and entrepreneurial behaviour. Learning practices included use of creative tools and mindsets to both identify and evaluate opportunities; workshops with practising serial entrepreneurs; exercises and practice in emotional and spiritual intelligence; student case writing of corporate entrepreneurial outcomes; ethical discussions around entrepreneurial mindset and the dimensions of leadership, decision-making, behaviour and awareness.

On average, the student cohort for each yearly intake (for a seven-year period) was around 20 comprising partners, principals and senior managers of the firm. The groups ranged in age from 32 to 54 years, were predominantly male (overall 20 per cent female) and mainly Caucasian. Some 120 students completed various levels of the program (40 Graduate Certificates, 60 Graduate Diplomas and 20 Master's degrees). All students completed a CSI survey on entry and repeated it after exiting the courses and gaining further experience in the firm. In addition, structured interviews were conducted with a selection of partners to elucidate observed changes in staff behaviour in terms of opportunity identification and post-course behaviours. In 2019 selected partners of the firm, including the four who completed the Master's degree, were surveyed with an instrument to evaluate personal EM propensity.

ENTREPRENEURIAL EDUCATION EFFECTS

Decision-Making Style

In the first two years of the entrepreneurship program (2011 and 2012) when using CSI to measure changes in propensity for intuitive decision-making, only a little change was observed (see mean values in light grey bars, Figure 17.2). Indeed, the scores were close to the world mean for managers (on the analytical side of the mid-point) as determined from international testing (Allinson et al., 2000). However, over subsequent years (2013 to 2017) the decision style score moved below the mid-point, towards a more intuitive style, reaching a mean score close to the world mean for entrepreneurs. This significant shift from 2010 to 2017 represented a change of 17.8 per cent (Gillin et al., 2018). Re-measurement of CSI levels of previously graduated staff in 2018 (see Figure 17.2) suggests they either maintained or marginally improved their propensity for intuitive decision-making after their completion of the program. The outliers for each cohort are also shown.

Entrepreneurial Mindset

Completion of the Entrepreneurial Mindset survey by a cross section of firm partners in 2019 (see Figure 17.3) indicates that those partners who completed the (in-house)

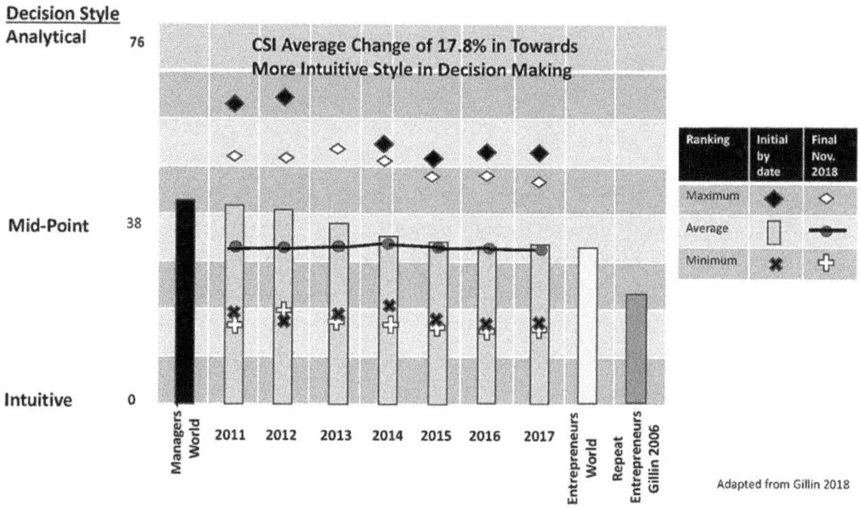

Figure 17.2 *Cognitive Style Index (CSI): Participants in entrepreneurship course – at start of each course 2011–2017 and re-measured in November 2018*

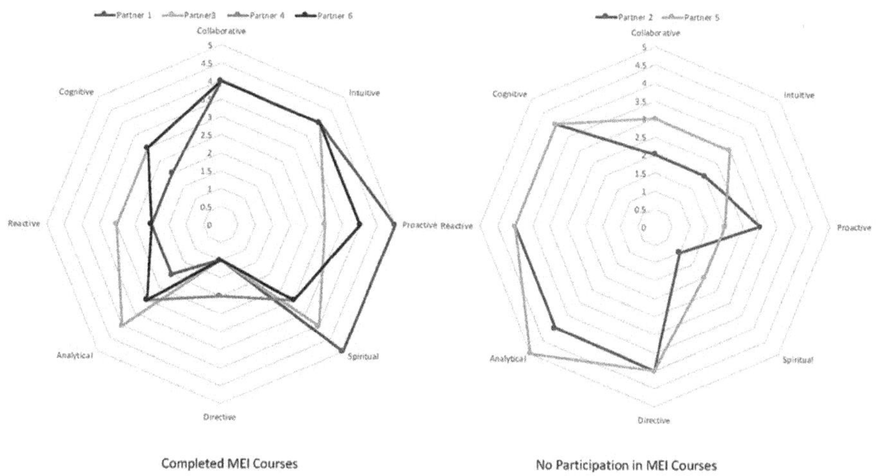

Figure 17.3 *Entrepreneurial mindset propensities for six partners*

Master of Entrepreneurship and Innovation, namely Partners 1, 3, 4 and 6, show a greater propensity for intuitive EM characteristics over the general partnership, represented by Partners 2 and 5.

Partner Interviews

Development of the firm's entrepreneurial culture and EM characteristics following participation in the education intervention are best understood by considering comments extracted from structured interviews with partners who completed 4, 8 or 12 course units. These interviews reveal a significantly positive attitude towards entrepreneurship within the organization, and a broad range of initiatives that support a corporate entrepreneurial strategy. The findings are grouped around the four dimensions of entrepreneurial mindset, as shown in Figure 17.3 with the associated characteristics:

Behaviour – Pro-active/Reactive:

- It is generally accepted by the senior partnership that if you don't continually adapt and change as a professional practice, you risk irrelevancy in the market. Entrepreneurship and a willingness to innovate are seen as essential. (Partner 4)
- We have to be proactive and responsive, anticipating our clients' needs so that we are a step ahead. There is a great level of complexity, complexity around regulation, accounting rules, taxation rules ... You need to be more anticipatory, ahead of the curve, see the problems before the problems occur ... The next evolution is all about preventing the problems, predicting the future, creating the future ... That is the direction we are going as a firm. (Partner 3)

Decision-Making – Intuitive/Analytical:

- We want our staff to continually look outside the firm, understand what the opportunities might be for us to grow and for us to better service our clients. This has always been encouraged by management. If there are good ideas, if they're well thought through, you want partners to have a go. If it works, fantastic, if it doesn't work, fine, we move on. (Managing Partner)
- We're not prepared to put the reputation of the firm at risk, but we are prepared to invest in growing the business through innovation, and if some of those initiatives work, great, if not, we move on. (Managing Partner)
- We don't encourage risk as an end in itself. At the same time, we have supported some 'risky' projects that had a good business plan. (Partner 1)

Leadership – Collaborative/Directive:

- We're aware that not tapping into the innate, innovative abilities of over 600 staff, that we're relying on a small partner group. So, there's a lost opportunity. An innovation committee was formed recently with a view to addressing this point, looking at ways of germinating ideas, capturing ideas, and funding them, across the firm. We need to harness the power of everybody. (Partner 3)

- We have supported projects related to entrepreneurship of the next generation, projects on entrepreneurship incubators. Through the Institute we have captured a lot of intellectual property that we want to develop further. We need to leverage off some of the projects that have been developed by those who have completed the master's course. (Partner 6)

Awareness – Spirituality/Cognitive:

- We're now dealing more with entrepreneurs, and we have the confidence to do it. (Managing Partner)
- It enables us to initiate new conversations with our clients. It's a different conversation, it enables us to inspire our clients and make them more aspirational. It gives you the capacity to empathize with your clients better and engage with them better. (Partner 6)
- The type of work that our people were doing has changed … We were looking for a reskilling of our core capabilities around the provision of valuable business advice, and it was too important to leave it to others, essentially. This in-house program is a key ingredient in the education of an 'aware' business advisor. (Partner 3)

THINKING DISPOSITIONS ON CULTURE CHANGE AND BEHAVIOUR

The claustrophobic impact of a focus on compliance in accounting and financial services can take precedence over the necessary attention and time required to develop staff in the firm's commitment to deliver specialist advising services to their clients and to build a high degree of trust. One solution identified by partners of the studied firm was to consider a strategic initiative to cultivate corporate entrepreneurship, intuitive decision-making style and an entrepreneurial mindset amongst staff across the organization, with a focus on identifying and evaluating opportunities, and also sharing these skills with clients in order to grow both the firm and client businesses. Such strategic approach produces added value in the marketplace (Malewska, 2019) and develops staff with strong cognitive-based intuitive behaviour better suited to manage uncertainty (Wang et al., 2018).

After seven years of in-house entrepreneurship education within the firm, as reported above, it is clear that an effective change, both in firm and personal entrepreneurial behaviour, is the key to innovation, productivity and effective competition. By enhancing intuitive decision-making skills and developing an entrepreneurial mindset, the measured changes amongst course participants confirm that entrepreneurial thinking and associated behaviour as well as practice can be taught (Neck et al., 2014). Indeed, this case confirms that exposure of staff to selected pedagogical principles, appropriate entrepreneurship education programs and inspirational lecturing staff can and does affect changes in participants both personally and corporately in regard to opportunity focus, entrepreneurial mindset and strategic culture (Davis et al., 2015). As Kickul et al. (2010) showed, this impact pertains less to learning the process but rather to the way how learning and information is accessed and practised. In addition, the reported findings confirm the conclusion of Sadler-Smith (2016) that businesses exercising strong intuitive cognition in decision-making are more likely to identify opportunities that can be turned into new business markets (and innovation).

Significantly, results from this longitudinal case study have demonstrated the value of Cognitive Style Index (CSI) for assessing the impact of entrepreneurship learning/training aimed at the development of staff culture and practice that is both passionate and committed to being opportunity focused, creative, team-based, providing outstanding service to clients and delivering effective innovation that grows the business. This finding confirms Blume and Covin's (2011) conclusion that the strength of the entrepreneur's intuitive cognitive style is contingent upon the individual's perception that intuition is an acceptable basis for decision-making. There has been much debate over the theoretical foundations of Allinson et al.'s (2000) CSI instrument and it is accepted that a dual-process-based index would produce more precise measures. However, in this study the CSI is robust enough to provide confidence in assessing staff change/behaviours resulting from entrepreneurship education and training.

Importantly, the administration of the CSI over a seven-year period in each entry cohort provides a valuable insight into the long-term impact of such entrepreneurship learning. Even when tested several years after the initial course experience, the participating staff have retained their propensity towards intuitive decision-making style. This experience can guide academics in developing teaching programs that enable students to understand EM as a concept and their own unique entrepreneurial being (Davis et al., 2015).

It is worth noting that the CSI was administered to participants as they entered a new cohort of the program. They had no formal course work in the degree program before taking the CSI. Yet each successive cohort on entry indicated a higher propensity towards intuitive decision-making than the previous one. This was not understood until analysing the comments made by partners in the structured interviews. It became clear that as each cohort progressed through the program, the participants were sharing their learning, sharing new opportunities, socializing and developing a new culture. The partners claimed that as existing staff observed the change they sought to associate with it and finally apply to do the course. This effective change in corporate culture was captured by the CSI testing. As partners noted:

> What I see now is that the type of conversations that the people who have been through the program have with their clients is very different. They are far more forward looking, they are open to questions, they are more conscious of the client's environment, their competitive situation and the opportunities, and they will engage more holistically with the client. (Partner 3)
>
> A lot of the innovation that is happening internally in the firm comes from projects that were developed during the course. You can see the difference in the people who have done the course. There's no question about it. (Partner 6)

This is in accord with the findings of Ireland et al. (2003) that managers who recognize and drive opportunities in the organization add to the development of an entrepreneurial culture by impacting firm strategic management, innovation and wealth creation.

In addition, results of the EM survey of selected partners confirm Shepherd et al.'s (2010) finding that personal entrepreneurial mindset is inextricably interwoven with an expressed organizational entrepreneurial culture. The four dimensions of EM (Hazelton & Gillin, 2019) and their associated characteristic propensities (see Figure 17.1) provide a good match with the rankings of personal style in the sample of six partners. Importantly, the interwoven nature of corporate culture and personal mindset is further confirmed by those partners with an entrepreneurship Master's degree who showed a strong propensity towards collaborative leadership, intuitive decision-making, pro-active behaviour and spiritual awareness in overall performance when compared to the non-participant partners. In line with Dane and Pratt (2007), these EM partners acknowledge the valuable contribution to entrepreneurial mindset formation that the entrepreneurial education programs have made to the firm and their employees by establishing a rigorous and complex cognitive framework. One partner observed:

> It puts you into the mindset of what an entrepreneur would be thinking. It helps in framing the questions and framing the structure. (Partner 3)

Overall, developing a strong intuitive decision-making mindset within the firm culture feeds into enhanced opportunity recognition and creative skills to deliver opportunities that can be turned into new business markets (and innovation). It also confirms Sadler-Smith's (2016) observation that staff with positive intuitive decision-making style produces much stronger outcomes when compared with individuals possessing a mainly analytical cognitive style. The reported study confirms also the observation of Davis et al. (2015) that entrepreneur-minded decision-makers demonstrate a higher 'risk propensity' than managers.

CONCLUSIONS

This seven-year commitment to entrepreneurship in-house education by participating staff (partners and senior managers) and continued financial investment by the firm have resulted in a significant change in the firm's culture. The development of dynamic staff with an opportunity focus and a positive increase in propensity for intuitive thinking and decision-making, correlate strongly with the increase in innovation culture and improvement in the firm's competitiveness and profitability.

These results have demonstrated the value of the Cognitive Style Index (CSI) for assessing changes in thinking and decision-making styles following participation in a purpose-designed entrepreneurship education program. The establishment and recognition of the importance of intuition and intuitive decision-making style for the development of an entrepreneurial mindset may not create theory of itself but intuition theory will need to be consistent with these observations. It would be instructive if a dual-process-based instrument could be used in conjunction with entrepreneurial learning to further assess validity of the appropriate theory construction.

The case study shows that 'firm-partner management' has a passionate commitment to further developing intuitive thinking and decision-making amongst staff as part of the entrepreneurial mindset within the firm. Significantly, the findings demonstrate the importance of a holistic view of entrepreneurial behaviour, opportunity focus, decision-making and the spiritual/moral understanding that drive a successful entrepreneur mindset. This new way of thinking about opportunities is now an established entrepreneurial strategy that involves the firm's external environment and the commitments, decisions and actions necessary to pursue them, especially under conditions of uncertainty that commonly accompany rapid and significant environmental changes.

REFERENCES

Akinci, C. 2014. Capturing intuitions in decision making: A case for the Critical Incident Technique. In M. Sinclair (Ed.), *Handbook of research methods on intuition*: 147–159. Cheltenham, UK and Northampton, MA, USA: Edward Elgar Publishing.

Akinci, C., & Sadler-Smith, E. 2012. Intuition in management research: A historical review. *International Journal of Management Reviews*, 14(1): 104–122.

Akinci, C., & Sadler-Smith, E. 2013. Assessing individual differences in experiential (intuitive) and rational (analytical) cognitive styles. *International Journal of Selection and Assessment*, 21(2): 211–221.

Allinson, W.C., Chell, E., & Hayes, J. 2000. Intuition and entrepreneurial behavior. *European Journal of Work and Organizational Psychology*, 9(1): 31–43.

Allinson, W.C., & Hayes, J. 1996. The Cognitive Style Index: A measure of intuition-analysis for organizational research. *Journal of Management Studies*, 1: 119–135.

Allinson, W.C., & Hayes, J. 2012. *The Cognitive Style Index: Technical manual and user guide*. London: Pearson Education.

Armstrong, S., Cools, E., & Sadler-Smith, E. 2012. Role of cognitive styles in business and management: Reviewing 40 years of research. *International Journal of Management Reviews*, 14(3): 238–262.

Blume, B.D., & Covin, J.G. 2011. Attributions to intuition in the venture founding process: Do entrepreneurs actually use intuition or just say that they do? *Journal of Business Venturing*, 26(1): 137–151.

Bradley, R.T., Gillin, L.M., McCraty, R., & Atkinson, M. 2011. Non-local intuition in entrepreneurs and non-entrepreneurs: Results of two experiments using electrophysiological measures. *International Journal of Entrepreneurship and Small Business*, 12(3): 343–372.

Chaston, I., & Sadler-Smith, E. 2012. Entrepreneurial cognition, entrepreneurial orientation and firm capability in the creative industries. *British Journal of Management*, 23(3): 415–432.

Cunha, M.P. 2007. Entrepreneurship as decision making: Rational, intuitive and improvisational approaches. *Journal of Enterprising Culture*, 15(1): 1–20.

Dane, E., & Pratt, M.G. 2007. Exploring intuition and its role in managerial decision making. *Academy of Management Review*, 32(1): 30–54.

Davis, M.H., Hall, J.A., & Mayer, P.S. 2015. October 19. Developing a new measure of entrepreneurial mindset: Reality, validity, and implications for practitioners. *Consulting*

Psychology Journal: Practice and Research. Advance online publication. http://dx.doi.org/10.1037/cpb0000045.

Evans, J.S.B.T. 2003. In two minds: Dual-process accounts of reasoning. *Trends in Cognitive Sciences*, 7(10): 454–459.

Frow, P., McColl-Kennedy, J.R., & Payne, A. 2016. Co-creation practices: Their role in shaping a health care ecosystem. *Industrial Marketing Management*, 56: 24–39.

Gillin, L.M., Gagliardi, R., Hougaz, L., Knowles, D., & Langhammer, M. 2018. Teaching companies how to be entrepreneurial: Cultural change at all levels. *Journal of Business Strategy*, https://doi.org/10.1108/JBS-09-2017-0138.

Haidt, J. 2013. *The righteous mind*. New York: Vintage Books.

Haynie, J.M., Shepherd, D., Mosakowski, E., & Earley, P.C. 2010. A situated metacognitive model of the entrepreneurial mindset. *Journal of Business Venturing*, 25: 217–229.

Hazelton, L.M., & Gillin, L.M. 2019. *Nursing ecosystems: Opportunities for trailblazer practice innovations*. National Nursing Forum, 20–23 August, Hobart, Tasmania.

Henry, C., & de Bruin, A. 2011. *Entrepreneurship and the creative economy: Process, practice and policy*. Cheltenham, UK and Northampton, MA, USA: Edward Elgar Publishing.

Hicks, J.A., Cicero, D.C., Trent, J., Burton, C.M., & King, L.A. 2010. Positive affect, intuition, and feelings of meaning. *Journal of Personality & Social Psychology*, 98(6): 967–979.

Hodgkinson, G.P., & Sadler-Smith, E. 2003a. Complex or unitary? A critique and empirical re-assessment of the Allinson–Hayes Cognitive Style Index. *Journal of Occupational and Organizational Psychology*, 76: 243–268.

Hodgkinson, G.P. & Sadler-Smith, E. 2003b (Response). Reflections on reflections on the nature of intuition, analysis and the construct validity of the Cognitive Style Index. *Journal of Occupational and Organizational Psychology*, 76: 279–281.

Hodgkinson, G.P., Sadler-Smith, E., Sinclair, M., & Ashkanasy, N.M. 2009. More than meets the eye? Intuition and analysis revisited. *Personality and Individual Differences*, 47: 342–346.

Hyppänen, O. 2013. *Decision makers' use of intuition at the front end of innovation*. Doctoral dissertation, Aalto University. School of Science. Retrieved 21 February 2020 from https://aaltodoc.aalto.fi/bitstream/handle/123456789/8843/isbn9789526050300.pdf?sequenc=1.

Ireland, R.D., Hitt, M.A., & Simon, D.G. 2003. A model of strategic entrepreneurship: The construct and its dimensions. *Journal of Management*, 29(6): 963–989.

Kickul, J., Gundry, L.K., Barbosa, S.D., & Simms, S. 2010. One style does not fit all: The role of cognitive style in entrepreneurship education. *International Journal of Entrepreneurship and Small Business*, 9(1): 36–57.

Kreuger, N.F. Jr. 2007. What lies beneath? The experiential essence of entrepreneurial thinking. *Entrepreneurship Theory and Practice*, 31(1): 123–138.

La Pira, F., & Gillin, L.M. 2006. Non-local intuition and the performance of serial entrepreneurs. *International Journal of Entrepreneurship and Small Business*, 3(1): 17–35.

Malewska, K. 2019. Intuition and entrepreneurship in management practice. *Journal of Business and Economics*, 9(1): 34–48.

Ming-Huei, C., Yu-Yu, C., & Ya-Hsun, L. 2015. Creativity cognitive style, conflict, and career success for creative entrepreneurs. *Journal of Business Research*, 68: 906–910.

Mitchell, J.R., Friga, P.N., & Mitchell, R.K. 2005. Untangling the intuition mess: Intuition as a construct in entrepreneurship research. *Entrepreneurship Theory & Practice*, 29(6): 653–679.

Mitchell, R.K., Smith, J.B., Morse, E.A., Seawright, K., Peredo, A.M., & McKenzie, B. 2002. Are entrepreneurial cognitions universal? Assessing entrepreneurial cognitions across cultures. *Entrepreneurship Theory and Practice*, 26(4): 9–32.

Nandram, S.S., Mourmont, G., Smith, E.K., Heaton, D.P., & Bindlish, P.K. 2018. Understanding entrepreneurial decision-making by objectivizing subtle cues. *Journal of Management, Spirituality & Religion*, 15(5): 398–423.

Narayanan, V.K., Zame, L.J., & Kemmerer, B. 2011. The cognitive perspective in strategy: An integrative review. *Journal of Management*, 37(1): 305–351.

Neck, H.M., Greene, P.G., & Brush, C.G. 2014. *Teaching entrepreneurship: A practice-based approach*. Cheltenham, UK and Northampton, MA, USA: Edward Elgar Publishing.

Norris, P., & Epstein, S. 2011. An experiential thinking style: Its facets and relations with objective and subjective criterion measures. *Journal of Personality*, 79(5): 1043–1079.

Sadler-Smith, E. 2016. The role of intuition in entrepreneurship and business venturing decisions. *European Journal of Work and Organizational Psychology*, 25(2): 212–225.

Sadler-Smith, E., & Shefy, E. 2004. The intuitive executive: Understanding and applying 'gut feel' in decision-making. *Academy of Management Executive*, 18(4): 76–91.

Sarasvathy, S.D., & Venkataraman, S. 2011. Entrepreneurship as method: Open questions for an entrepreneurial future. *Entrepreneurship Theory and Practice*, 35(1): 113–135.

Shane, S. 2003. *A general theory of entrepreneurship: The individual–opportunity nexus*. Cheltenham, UK and Northampton, MA, USA: Edward Elgar Publishing.

Shepherd, D.A., Patzelt, H., & Haynie, J.M. 2010. Entrepreneurial spirals: Deviation-amplifying loops of an entrepreneurial mindset. *Entrepreneurship Theory and Practice*, 34(1): 59–82.

Sinclair, M. 2010. Misconceptions about intuition. *Psychological Enquiry*, 21: 1–9.

Sinclair, M., Sadler-Smith, E., & Hodgkinson, G.P. 2009. The role of intuition in strategic decision-making. In L. Costanzo and R.B. McKay (Eds), *The handbook of research in strategy and foresight*: 393–417. Cheltenham, UK and Northampton, MA, USA: Edward Elgar Publishing.

Stewart, W.K. Jr., & Roth, P.L. 2007. A meta□analysis of achievement motivation differences between entrepreneurs and managers. *Journal of Small Business Management*, 45(4): 401–421.

Timmons, J.A., Gillin, L.M., Burshstein, S.L., & Spinelli, S. 2011. *New venture creation – Entrepreneurship for the 21st century: A pacific rim perspective*. Sydney, Australia: McGraw-Hill.

Wang, M., Gibb, J., & Sinha, P.N. 2018. Entrepreneurial decision-making styles: Developing a dynamic intuitive-analytic capability, *Academy of Management Proceedings*, 2018(1): 13841.

18. The contribution of mental simulation to the development of intuition

Bianca Steffen, Michael Goller and Christian Harteis

Many professionals are confronted with tasks that require effective performance on the basis of incomplete or contradictory information. Crisis response workers are appropriate examples because they support individuals after the sudden death of a relative but have limited time and opportunities to determine how best to help them. It is the particular characteristic of intuition that decisions are based on recognized situational patterns rather than deliberate consideration; however, the development of intuition is not fully understood. This study explores the contribution of mental simulations to the development of intuition. The term mental simulation describes a set of occurrences rehearsed by an individual (Klein, 2003). These simulations are based on experiential knowledge, and they are used for evaluating possible courses of action. They may result in episodic memory units that establish schemata enabling professionals to take action or to make decisions intuitively.

This chapter is structured as follows: First, the dual-process theory provides a basis for the distinction between conscious and unconscious cognition. Next, the concepts of intuition and mental simulation are elaborated. Crisis response work is described in terms of its tasks, aims, and relevance to the concepts under consideration. The interview study and the qualitative content analysis are then explained. The major part of this contribution, the presentation and discussion of the findings, follows. The conclusion offers suggestions for researchers and practitioners.

DUAL-PROCESS THEORY OF INFORMATION PROCESSING

Fast judgment by professionals is most commonly explained by the dual-process theory (Bruner, 1962; Evans, 2011; Sloman, 2002), which argues that there are two permanently parallel modes of information processing. The different concepts emphasize different distinctions between the two systems, nevertheless their key ideas are similar. Hammond (1993) describes the dual process as a continuum between two poles: *System 1*, the intuitive system, and *System 2*, the rational system. Similarly, Epstein (2010) distinguishes between an experiential system and a rational/analytic system whereas the intuitive system is a subset of the experiential system. In both theories every decision can be placed along this continuum in relation to the strength of the influences of the systems. The main characteristics of both systems are described in Table 18.1.

Table 18.1 Dual-process theory

System 1: Intuitive	System 2: Reflective
Fast processing	Slow processing
High-capacity operation	Low-capacity operation
Independent of working memory and cognitive ability	Heavily dependent on working memory
Independent of individual differences in cognitive ability	Related to individual differences in cognitive ability
Associative access to knowledge base	

Source: Evans, 2011.

INTUITION AS PATTERN RECOGNITION

Expertise is the ability to reliably perform extraordinarily in one's domain (Dreyfus, 2004; Ericsson, 2006; Gruber, 1999). It consists of three elements: a broad knowledge base, a wide set of routines, and intuition as a particular quality of knowledge (Harteis, 2017). Whereas the first two elements have been widely investigated, less is known about the development and application of intuition.

Sinclair (2011) has offered a framework for the most common conceptualizations of intuition. The basic distinction is the placement of intuition in the decision-making process: a quality of knowledge, an ability, or an action. This chapter defines intuition as a quality of knowledge that is needed for recognizing cues and patterns in complex situations. These patterns could be small and opaque hints that distinguish situations. Such recognition allows professionals to access their tacit knowledge bases directly to make quick and successful decisions in uncertain non-routine situations (Chase & Simon, 1973; Dreyfus, 2004; Glöckner & Witteman, 2010). Tacit knowledge is implicit knowledge developed through experience and can hardly be verbalized. Situational awareness is another concept for describing the process through which professionals retrieve knowledge about their circumstances (Busby & Witucki-Brown, 2011); it emphasizes the process of pattern recognition. Intuition itself can be used to make appropriate decisions and, therefore, to act appropriately in insecure and novel situations (Klein, 2008). Professionals know a solution without deliberately thinking about or evaluating the options. They can rely on the input from *System 1* and, thus, act quickly and associatively without requiring conscious control. It follows that intuition is independent of working memory and cognitive ability, which refers to an individual's intellectual and general problem-solving ability.

Intuitive decision-making does not always lead to desired outcomes, even for experts (Kahnemann & Klein, 2009). It must be noted that fast associative decision-making with incomplete information can be based on false heuristics and, consequently, lead to wrong decisions (Kahnemann & Klein, 2009). Baylor (2001) proposes a U-shaped model for the development of expertise in which she claims that novices and experts tend to make more intuitive decisions than intermediates whereas their intuitive decision-making differs in the underlying knowledge structure. However, this chapter focuses on the development of successful intuition of professionals in all stages of competence development.

In conclusion, professionals who have to make decisions in complex non-routine situations on the basis of incomplete information must rely heavily on intuitive pattern recognition. Nevertheless, their development of intuition remains unclear.

MENTAL SIMULATION

The evidence suggests that mental simulation is one of the factors that foster the development of intuition (Klein, 2003; Sonnentag & Kleine, 2000). It can be interpreted as a particular form of deliberate practice (Billett et al., 2018; Ericsson, 2018). Other deliberate practices supporting expertise development include agentic information and feedback seeking and receiving (Goller, 2017). Mental simulation describes the process in which individuals mentally rehearse difficult scenarios to evaluate possible courses of action (Klein, 2008). Within imagined situations, decisions are evaluated to prepare for challenging tasks that might be faced in the future. By training mentally for these situations, individuals establish episodic knowledge that can build schemata. Consequently, when faced with a situation simulated beforehand (or a comparable situation), professionals feel prepared, and they can act immediately because they have a plan of action at hand. The mental effort and the extensive use of working memory locate mental simulation closer to *System 2* operations.

Four major outcomes of mental simulations are assumed. First, professionals are enabled to develop rich schemata and mental models. Mental models are naturally evolving representations of a process, and they are built and modified by interaction with the process (Norman, 1983). Second, professionals are enabled to solve problems and to make appropriate decisions within a limited time span. Kappes and Morewedge (2016) have proposed that simulated practice is a type of mental simulation. They state that it is effective for tasks that require many cognitive activities. Professionals are assumed to invest mental effort in advance; thus, when they are faced with complex situations, their mental capacities are less charged. Third, simulating possible challenges and obstacles facilitates goal pursuit by reducing anxiety because professionals are better prepared to face contingencies (Gollwitzer & Sheeran, 2006; Kappes & Morewedge, 2016; Taylor et al., 1998). Fourth, as a consequence, professionals intuitively perform successfully in future situations (Klein, 1997). However, there is little empirical research about mental simulations and their contribution to intuitive decision-making. Crisis response work is one of the domains in which professionals must make intuitive decisions; thus, it is a promising field for linking mental simulation and intuition.

CRISIS RESPONSE WORKERS

Crisis response workers are trained volunteers who are called to particular emergencies, such as sudden deaths or accidents with severe injuries or deaths. They offer on-site spiritual support, counsel, and other mental assistance to the victims, relatives, and other affected individuals (Martens, 2004). Crisis response workers do not offer trauma therapy; rather, they provide short-time interventions. They aim to reactivate individuals' social networks after these individuals have overcome the first emotional reactions. They also try to prevent the development of future trauma (Müller-Lange & Autschbach, 2013). Their operations can last up to three hours.

Because intuitive decision-making is used in uncertain non-routine situations, crisis response work is a promising area of research. After all of the possible tasks have been considered, the least and most professionally demanding operations can be distinguished (Müller-Lange & Autschbach, 2013). The least demanding task is accompanying the police to inform relatives of the sudden death of a family member. A more demanding task is being on the scene of an incident and accompanying individuals who witnessed or were involved in a major traffic incident, e.g. a traffic accident.

Crisis response workers also have to work in unfamiliar terrain (Müller-Lange & Autschbach, 2013), for example, streets and railroad tracks. These operations are more complex because more individuals are involved. The scene is usually confusing; consequently, the specific task to be done might not be evident upon arrival. For example, who is in charge or who is to be taken care of is often unclear in the first moments. Crisis response workers are called for supporting a specific individual and must take their orders from the director of operations (Müller-Lange & Autschbach, 2013). In major incidents, they may supervise and coordinate colleagues.

Regarding the development of professional expertise, two characteristics of the crisis response worker's tasks must be noted. First, crisis response workers rely on professional peer supervision groups for information and feedback (Ziemer, 2008). Second, they usually work individually during operations. Even when multiple workers are on the scene, they have different tasks and aims, thus do not collaborate as a team.

RESEARCH QUESTIONS AND AIMS

Some of the crisis response workers' decision-making is intuition-demanding because they work in uncertain and non-routine situations on the basis of incomplete or contradictory information. Nevertheless, little research focused on this issue. In explaining how and why crisis response professionals use mental simulation, this chapter improves our understanding of the role of mental simulations in the development of intuition that could be applicable to other professions. The presented study focused on three research questions:

1. How does intuitive pattern recognition help crisis response workers to perform successfully in novel and complex situations?
2. How do crisis response workers use mental simulation to prepare for challenging tasks?

3. How does mental simulation help crisis response workers to develop solutions in novel and complex situations?

DATA COLLECTION

To answer these research questions, 11 interviews were conducted by the first author of the chapter. They followed a modified critical incident interview approach (Klein et al., 2010) using a semi-structured interview guideline (König et al., 2005). Five participants were directly contacted to take part in the interviews. These participants then helped contact the remaining interviewees. The participants (five females and six males) had experienced between three and more than 500 operations over two to more than 20 years of experience. The experience levels were almost equally distributed: four participants with 0–3 years (novices), three with 8–10 years of experience (intermediates), and three with more than 20 years of experience (experts). One participant did not provide information about experience. All of them were members of voluntary German church organizations. The interviews were based on participants' recollection and did not occur immediately after an incident.

The first part of the interview was about previous operations in which these crisis response workers had made intuitive decisions. They were asked to think about situations that were complicated, new to them, had an unexpected event, and/or required decisions to be made under uncertain circumstances. They described their course of action, their sensations, and how that effected their decisions (e.g., "How did you know what to do in that situation?"). The questions in the second part of the interview focused on mental simulations (e.g., "How do you think through possible challenging operations?"). The interviews lasted 49–118 minutes. With the subjects' consent, the interviews were digitally recorded and transcribed verbatim. The transcripts were analyzed using qualitative content analysis in accordance with Braun and Clarke (2006), Mayring (2008), and Schreier (2013). The software application MAXQDA v18 was used to support all of the analyses.

QUALITATIVE CONTENT ANALYSIS

Nine main categories were theoretically derived. The category system was revised and finalized after 25 percent of the interviews were coded. All of the interviews were then analyzed using the revised system. Summarizing and structuring techniques were used. The deductively derived main categories include professional biography, other activities supporting professional development, and the main categories presented in Table 18.2. The subcategories were derived deductively and inductively; they are noted in the table in italics.

Table 18.2 Content analysis

Main Categories/*Subcategories*	**Definition**
Intuition-demanding situations	
Professionally challenging operations	Reactions confronting crisis response workers: situations involving children, complicated relationship constellations of the individuals on the site, involvement of many individuals, incomprehensible and chaotic situations, missing resources on the part of the individuals in need, rejection from individuals, and support for individuals with different religious backgrounds that are different from the worker's
Unexpected occurrences	Counseling needed by someone other than the expected individual, the individuals on site having different needs than expected, extreme mourning reactions, differing relationship constellation of the individuals on the site, more individuals involved than expected, sudden dangers (e.g., dogs), and foreign languages
Decisions based on intuitive knowledge base	Necessary proposals for individuals in need (e.g., accompanying them to a hospital outside the administrative district), advising relatives to visit the scene of an accident, others whom the mourners have not considered that may need to be informed, others who may need on-site assistance, the timing for ending the operation and leaving the individuals, the resources that the mourning individuals may not be aware of, the timing for offering physical contact (e.g., a hug, an arm on someone's shoulder), the use of self-defense, and the need for reinforcements
Pattern recognition	
Orientation strategies	Obtaining initial information from the police or emergency personnel on site and getting a general overview on their own
Patterns that offered intuitive insight	Needs of the affected individuals, relationship constellations on site, individuals' behaviors, living conditions of affected individuals, overall situation of the operation, indications for ending the operation, communication from the police or emergency personnel, and indications for requesting reinforcements
Examples of mental simulations	(1) Questions concerning contextual information, (2) hypothetical answers, (3) hypothetical answers, and how they guide their decision-making (4) hypothetical answers several steps ahead
Triggers of mental simulation	News, peer supervision, and the journey to the operation
Assumed outcomes	Having action rules, making a larger number of correct hypotheses, feeling prepared for operations not previously experienced but mentally simulated, and investing less mental effort in finding explanations or developing plans in situations

FINDINGS

First, the chapter will report the findings on intuitive pattern recognition, including the decision points and decision characteristics. Second, the findings on mental simulation will be presented, including examples, triggers, and outcomes.

Intuitive Pattern Recognition

The interviewees offered insights into two types of intuition-demanding situations: professional challenges and unexpected occurrences. One crisis response worker described an example of the latter. He was driving someone home after that person had witnessed the deadly car accident of a friend:

> Then his phone rings on the way. Yes, in times of WhatsApp … it can be difficult. I briefly ask him, "Who is it?" It was the girlfriend of the dead person. Then I whispered to him, "Say nothing. Do not tell her like this on the phone. We will drive there. Do you know where she lives?" "Yes." "Can you accompany me there?," I asked him. (IV3)

This is an example of an intuition-demanding decision because there is no routine solution for this situation: The crisis response worker had to manage a situation (i.e., make a decision) in which a new person is involved (i.e., unexpected occurrence), during a telephone conversation (i.e., limited time span), when he did not know what the other individual already knows (i.e., incomplete information).

All the crisis response workers recognized patterns that offered intuitive insight, that is, spontaneous access to their tacit knowledge. The themes that arose included crisis response workers having to individually decide when to end an operation. A worker tried to describe how he knew when to leave bereaved individuals:

> That concrete grasp.… On this meta level, that you feel there is a human being who is steady.… People … clearly talk about their feelings … I don't mean saying, "Everything is alright, and I get along. No problem." Well, then I would say … hiding behind a mask doesn't work. Saying something like, "I just felt bad, and now … I feel it's sinking somehow.…" When people think and share their thoughts with me. (IV4)

The crisis response worker struggled to explain the cues for knowing when to leave individuals on their own; however, he could provide some of the indications for ending an operation.

Four crisis response workers were able to name the changes in their pattern recognition processes and to describe their own images of situations based on their experiences. One worker used a mistake he had made because of missing situational awareness. A couple was at a dialysis appointment when the man died. The worker was called to support the wife who was still at the hospital:

> Because the task was the wife of the deceased is already at dialysis, you have to go there and take care of the wife.… They had isolated her nicely. Everything was fine. It went perfect. But those five nurses that were standing in the lobby. I would address them next time, too. Those are the things that change. You take it more calmly. You get more of this: Firstly, stand still. Firstly, get yourself an overview. (IV6)

The crisis response worker stated that he would not make such a mistake again because he had developed a more deliberate situational awareness and now consciously takes the time to get a holistic impression of a situation and to analyze the scene confronting him.

Mental Simulation

The major portion of the interviews was about mental simulations. Based on the interviews four different types of mental simulation could be identified according to the detail and complexity in which they were applied.

First category: The crisis response workers' questions concerned only initial contextual information, that is, they had an idea of the possible important decisions without presuming the specific information. This supports them in guiding their situational awareness and prioritizing information:

> So the first operation was this motorcycle accident. There I had been super nervous because I did not know what I can expect. And then I always thought, "What should you do now? Do you go to the other motorcyclist? Or do you go to the one who slipped underneath the car?" (IV1)

Second category: The crisis response workers had questions concerning initial contextual information, and they developed hypothetical answers based on their mental models:

> Well, one thing is to medically check, for example, when you have someone who stays home after a death. Is that person medically stable? So my question is always: "Is that person I am seeing healthy? Or is there a precondition of depression, suicide risks? Or do they have to take any medicine at any time?" (IV9)

Third category: The crisis response workers had hypotheses for the situations they could face and the effects of these hypotheses on their decision-making:

> When the neighbor suddenly comes, could she be helpful? Yes. Include her. When the neighbor comes and she is not helpful, send her to the street to look out for the ambulance, grandchildren, whoever comes. Always have something prepared: "What do you do when this or that happens?" (IV6)

Fourth category: The crisis response workers had hypotheses for situations they could face several steps ahead: the decision-making based on their hypotheses, the effects of these decisions on the situation, and the additional decisions emanating from the initial ones. One crisis response worker described the simulation of a suicide by train, a challenging operation that he had not yet experienced. He could identify several decisive pieces of information (e.g., Who else is on the site? Are these individuals witnesses, or are they not affected? Are children involved?). The possible answers would guide his actions (e.g., different needs for someone who only noticed the train stopping versus someone who witnessed the incident, different kinds of support for children). He also simulated the possible obstacles (e.g., the train's power might go out, and there will be no heat or light). The worker went into even more detail about the many options he would have to consider and their influence on the possible courses of action.

Another activity linked to expertise development is seeking and obtaining professional feedback. A recurring theme in the interviews was the lack of feedback. The crisis response workers would leave an operation without receiving any information on the extent to which the affected individuals considered their actions supportive and empathic:

> And then I've had the feeling after every operation: Well, was that right that way? Did you do the right thing? Because no one says at the end, "Here is an evaluation form, and you helped me really well." That is not the case. (IV4)

The only feedback they receive occurs during the supervision sessions in which they discuss operations. But this feedback is only indirect because the peers usually had not been at the scene.

The participants described triggers of mental simulations. Although some stressed that they tried to avoid thinking through operations in advance in order to maintain healthy mental hygiene, four crisis response workers stated that they start the simulation on the way to an operation on the basis of the information from the control center. Such information must be considered carefully because it could be faulty. Nevertheless, they start thinking about the possible type of operation and related important information and decisions because this helps them prepare even if they have to modify their image of the situation later.

Five crisis response workers described the learning outcomes from mental simulations. One of them used a playing card metaphor to explain how he applies the courses of action that he had simulated:

> So you don't need a house of cards, but it is good to have a hand prepared. Having a deck with you is a nice thing, but just having it with you and only having to think, "So we'll try this one." And I put the card on the table, and my opposite says, "No, it doesn't work." That is no issue; then the card can be put away. I still have a whole hand. And I think this is very important in crisis response work because you have many situations you can't get under control with routine methods. (IV 6)

This crisis response worker stressed that he has developed different courses of action that he simply tries to apply; consequently, he does not have to start the planning during a situation. He is prepared with multiple methods. Another worker stated that fewer cognitive resources are needed during an operation:

> And then you can check again: "This is also something that could work." Due to that, [crisis response workers] automatically learn to build hypotheses and to see there are just many different possibilities that could cause this indication. And when I have thought about everything in advance, I do not have to do that for every operation because I have already done that. (IV11)

DISCUSSION

How Does Intuitive Pattern Recognition Help Crisis Response Workers Perform Successfully in Novel and Complex Situations?

As has been indicated in previous studies (Chase & Simon, 1973; Dreyfus & Dreyfus, 1986), intuitive pattern recognition seems to help crisis response workers perform successfully. They recognize patterns in uncertain and novel situations. For example, they are aware of individuals' needs in complex situations when those individuals are unable to express them. The workers know that individuals need stability; however, specific solutions for each individual are required in extraordinary situations. In other words, they use their tacit knowledge to perceive small differences (e.g., behaviors and living conditions) that distinguish situations (Chase & Simon, 1973; Glöckner & Witteman, 2010). Situational awareness helps them organize information and prioritize needs, and this becomes the basis for pattern recognition. They use operations closer to those of *System 1* because they do not invest cognitive resources during decision-making. One crisis response worker used physical contact as an example: "And I also know whether I am allowed to touch them, or I am not allowed to touch them, or I squat down or hug them. I just know this" (IV2). In summary, intuitive pattern recognition helps the workers discern situations and access their tacit knowledge (Klein et al., 2010).

How Do Crisis Response Workers Use Mental Simulation to Prepare for Challenging Tasks?

The interviewed crisis response workers used mental simulation very heterogeneously. Some pointed out that they did not actively think about future operations, not even on the journey to the operation. They argued that they are guided by a humanistic image and aim to avoid presuppositions. Others emphasized that thinking through possible operations or building hypotheses about the operation on their way to the scene helped them be more prepared. In other words, they have an idea about the important information to be checked before taking the first steps and the possible course of action that could ensue (Klein, 2008). In addition, they are open to the possibility that their initial idea might have to be modified or completely changed. But having different courses of action available and checking only the applicable one is easier than entering a situation without any possible course of action prepared (Kappes & Morewedge, 2016). This confirms the assertion of Taylor et al. (1998) that mental simulation improves goal implementation and self-regulation. Performance was not measured; consequently, no definitive statements can be made regarding possible positive effects of mental simulation on performance. It must also be noted that all the crisis response workers might have prepared initial steps, but they were unwilling or unable to express them during the interviews.

Four categories of mental simulations were identified. They vary in detail and complexity with which crisis response workers use them. First category: The crisis response workers had questions that guided their situation awareness. Second category: They had questions and could formulate hypothetical answers. Third category: They had hypotheses about a potential situation and its influence on their decision-making. Fourth category: They had hypothesized possible decisions and the influence of those decisions on a situation several steps ahead. Only the last two categories appear to contain enough elaboration to build an intuitive knowledge base. Six participants were able to make statements about mental simulations of the fourth kind. They had specific hypotheses and ideas about the effects of their actions on situations. These six participants, in addition to two others, were the workers who used mental models as a basis for making decisions. This outcome leads to the assumption that rich mental models can be developed through mental simulations, as has been previously proposed (Taylor et al., 1998). There seems to be an added value: Richer mental models could help professionals engage in even more detailed mental simulations. Consequently, the usage of the fourth category of mental simulation may support professionals in the development of their intuition.

The recurring theme of inadequate feedback was based on some of the crisis response workers' perceptions that it is detrimental to their professional development. Feedback is a factor in the development of expertise (see Goller, 2017); thus, in its absence, the workers had to rely more heavily on other factors, such as mental simulation, for the development of intuition and expertise.

How Does Mental Simulation Help Crisis Response Workers Develop Solutions in Novel and Complex Situations?

The exploratory nature of this study is most evident in the above question because no previous studies have explained the relationship between mental simulation and intuitive decision-making. The following five insights on the ways in which mental simulation supports the development of knowledge needed for intuitive decision-making can be proposed. (1) The crisis response workers who used more elaborated kinds of mental simulation also tended to use mental models to explain their decision-making. It can therefore be assumed that mental simulation supports the development of richer mental models that facilitate mental simulation of more complex situations, which may lead to more intuitive decision-making. (2) The crisis response workers who worked with mental simulations felt better prepared for some of the non-routine and complex operations and tasks even without prior experience. They had mentally evaluated various courses of action. As Klein et al. (2010) suggested, this is an outcome of mental simulation. The workers do not have to engage in spontaneous planning; rather, they merely detect important cues that were simulated in advance and choose the course of action that applies or could be applied with modifications – in other words: they decided intuitively. (3) The workers have concrete goals on which they focus and aim to achieve. Goal implementation helps with the intuitive development of solutions in novel situations because the workers are aware of specific goals and actions that need to be taken to achieve them (Taylor et al., 1998). (4) Mental simulations help the workers learn to focus on the important cues in a situation. On the basis of simulations, they enter operations with greater situational awareness; thus, their focus is related to previously simulated cues. They have more tacit knowledge which allows them to intuitively recognize patterns. (5) The experienced workers described taking the time to gain an overview and to become aware of situational patterns instead of being as nervous as they had been during their first operations. This decrease in anxiety has also been reported in the literature (Gollwitzer & Sheeran, 2006).

CONCLUSION

The study aimed to identify intuitive pattern recognition in crisis response work. As the findings revealed, professionals indeed identify patterns based on their situational awareness. In accordance with the literature, recognized patterns allow crisis response workers to make appropriate decisions spontaneously, that is, to act intuitively, in complex non-routine situations. Some findings reveal the exploratory character of our study; they offer initial insights into the contributions of mental simulation to the development of intuitive decision-making. One of these is that mental simulation appears to be important in domains in which other factors for nurturing the development of expertise are missing, feedback being a prime example. However, mental simulations have different qualities that need to be further explored.

A limitation of the study is the small sample size. In addition, there is a need for replication using objective measures of intuitive decision-making, such as skin conductance analysis. Interviews alone cannot provide an objective description of situational awareness or a measurement of performance quality. Eye-tracking is another method that could be used for linking situational awareness more closely to pattern recognition. Future research should also investigate how the four identified qualities of mental simulation develop on different experience/expertise levels, what is their influence on learning outcomes, and their contribution to the improvement of intuition.

REFERENCES

Baylor, A.L. 2001. A U-shaped model for the development of intuition by level of expertise. *New Ideas in Psychology*, 19(3): 237–244.

Billett, S., Harteis, C., & Gruber, H. 2018. Developing occupational expertise through work activities and interactions. In K.A. Ericsson, R. Hoffman, A. Kozbelt, & A. Williams (Eds.), *The Cambridge handbook on expertise*: 105–126. Cambridge: Cambridge University Press.

Braun, V., & Clarke, V. 2006. Using thematic analysis in psychology. *Qualitative Research in Psychology*, 3(2): 77–101.

Bruner, J. 1962. *On knowing*: *Essays for the left hand* (8th ed.). Cambridge, MA: Belknap Press of Harvard University Press.

Busby, S., & Witucki-Brown, J. 2011. Theory development for situational awareness in multi-casualty incidents. *Journal of Emergency Nursing*, 37(5): 444–452.

Chase, W., & Simon, H. 1973. The mind's eye in chess. In W.G. Chase (Ed.), *Visual information processing*: 215–281. Oxford: Elsevier.
Dreyfus, H.L., & Dreyfus, S.E. 1986. *Mind over machine: The power of human intuition and expertise in the era of the computer*. New York: Free Press.
Dreyfus, S. 2004. The five-stage model of adult skill acquisition. *Bulletin of Science, Technology & Society*, 24(3): 177–181.
Epstein, S. 2010. Demystifying intuition: What it is, what it does, and how it does it. *Psychological Inquiry*, 21(4): 295–312.
Ericsson, K.A. 2006. The influence of experience and deliberate practice on the development of superior expert performance. In K.A. Ericsson (Ed.), *The Cambridge handbook of expertise and expert performance*: 683–703. Cambridge: Cambridge University Press.
Ericsson, K.A. 2018. The differential influence of experience, practice, and deliberate practice on the development of superior individual performance of experts. In K.A. Ericsson, R.R. Hoffman, A. Kozbelt, & M.A. Williams (Eds.), *The Cambridge handbook of expertise and expert performance*: 745–769. Cambridge: Cambridge University Press.
Evans, J.S.B.T. 2011. Dual-process theories of reasoning: Contemporary issues and developmental applications. *Developmental Review*, 31(2–3): 86–102.
Glöckner, A., & Witteman, C. 2010. Beyond dual-process models: A categorisation of processes underlying intuitive judgement and decision making. *Thinking & Reasoning*, 16(1): 1–25.
Goller, M. 2017. *Human agency at work: An active approach towards expertise development*. Wiesbaden: Springer VS.
Gollwitzer, P., & Sheeran, P. 2006. Implementation intentions and goal achievement: A meta-analysis of effects and processes. *Advances in Experimental Social Psychology*, (38): 69–119.
Gruber, H. 1999. *Erfahrung als Grundlage kompetenten Handelns* [*Experience as foundation of competent action*]. Bern: Huber.
Hammond, K.-R. 1993. Natural decision making from a Brunswikian viewpoint. In G. Klein (Ed.), *Decision making in action. Models and methods*: 205–227. Norwood, NJ: Ablex Publishing Corporation.
Harteis, C. 2017. Intuition as crucial component of professional competence: Its relevance for competence-based vocational and professional education and training. In M. Mulder (Ed.), *Competence-based vocational and professional education*: 971–984. Cham, Switzerland : Springer International Publishing.
Kahneman, D., & Klein, G. 2009. Conditions for intuitive expertise: A failure to disagree. *The American Psychologist*, 64(6): 515–526.
Kappes, H., & Morewedge, C. 2016. Mental simulation as substitute for experience. *Social and Personality Psychology Compass*, 10(7): 405–420.
Klein, G. 1997. Developing expertise in decision making. *Thinking & Reasoning*, 3(4): 337–352.
Klein, G. 2003. *Intuition at work: Why developing your gut instincts will make you better at what you do*. New York: Currency/Doubleday.
Klein, G. 2008. Naturalistic decision making. *Human Factors*, 50(3): 456–460.
Klein, G., Calderwood, R., & Clinton-Cirocco, A. 2010. Rapid decision making on the fire ground: The original study plus a postscript. *Journal of Cognitive Engineering and Decision Making*, 4(3): 186–209.
König, E., Volmer, G., & Bentler, A. 2005. *Systemisch denken und handeln: Personale Systemtheorie in Erwachsenenbildung und Organisationsberatung* [*Systemic thinking and acting. Personal system theory in adult education and organisational consulting*]. Weinheim: Beltz.
Martens, E. 2004. Notfallseelsorge [Crisis response work]. *Notfall & Rettungsmedizin*, 7(8): 539–546.

Mayring, P. 2008. *Einführung in die qualititative Sozialforschung: Eine Anleitung zu qualitativem Denken* [*Introduction into qualitative research in social science: An introduction for qualitative thinking*] (5th ed.). Weinheim, Basel: Beltz.
Müller-Lange, J., & Autschbach, M. (Eds.) 2013. *Handbuch Notfallseelsorge* [*Handbook of crisis response work*]. (3rd ed.). Edewecht: Stumpf + Kossendey.
Norman, D.A. 1983. Some observations on mental models. In D. Gentner, & A. Stevens (Eds.), *Mental models*: 7–14. Hoboken: Taylor & Francis.
Schreier, M. 2013. *Qualitative content analysis in practice* (2nd ed.). Los Angeles: Sage.
Sinclair, M. 2011. An integrated framework of intuition. In M. Sinclair (Ed.), *Handbook of intuition research*: 3–16. Cheltenham, UK and Northampton, MA, USA: Edward Elgar Publishing.
Sloman, S.A. 2002. Two systems of reasoning. In T. Gilovich (Ed.), *Heuristics and biases. The psychology of intuitive judgment*: 379–396 (14th ed.). Cambridge: Cambridge University Press.
Sonnentag, S., & Kleine, B.M. 2000. Deliberate practice at work: A study with insurance agents. *Journal of Occupational and Organizational Psychology*, 73(1): 87–102.
Taylor, S.E., Pham, L.B., Rivkin, I.D., & Armor, D.A. 1998. Harnessing the imagination: Mental stimulation, self-regulation, and coping. *American Psychologist*, 53(4): 429–439.
Ziemer, J. 2008. *Seelsorgelehre* [*Pastoral care teaching*] (1st ed.). Stuttgart: UTB GmbH.

19. Enhancing intuition in problem solving through problem finding

Paola Iannello, Barbara Colombo, Serena Germagnoli and Alessandro Antonietti

In everyday life people encounter issues, which – most times – are not familiar. The increasing complexity of society continues to confront individuals with ill-defined and new problems – concerning economic, social, or political domain – that cannot be solved by automatically relying on strategies and methods used with past problems or by applying default algorithms and standard operating procedures. Defining, delimiting, clarifying, or reframing a problem, though, may facilitate the achievement of its solution. These operations are associated with problem finding, which refers to the first stages of creative problem solving and may affect the quality and the effectiveness of the problem-solving process (Okuda et al., 1991; Reiter-Palmon, 2017), to the point that some authors regarded the ability to "find a problem" as more relevant and at the same time more important than its solution (Getzels & Smilansky, 1983; Smilansky, 1984; Wertheimer, 1945).

Problem finding has been defined as "the ability to think, initiate, and formulate questions or problems in an ill- or moderately-structured problem situation" (Lee & Cho, 2007: 114) and, more in general, "the posing and formulating" (Getzels & Csikszentmihalyi, 1975: 90), besides "conceiving, and identifying a problem to be solved" (Barber, 1981: 7). Problem-finding skills come into play when people, faced with an unusual situation, try to answer some questions derived from the situation itself by questioning implicit assumptions and by trying to adopt the proper approach (for example: "What is the actual problem to solve?," "Which are the factors involved and connected to the problem?"). Problem finding, which leads to problem definition in a more original way, is vital to problem solving. It has been suggested as a significant predictor of quality of problem-solving outcomes (Basadur et al., 1982; Fontenot, 1993; Mumford et al., 1994; Okuda et al., 1991; Runco & Nemiro, 1994).

Problem finding implies different essential steps: considering the interrelations among a problem's elements, exploring alternative problems, and identifying the most effective questions (Ramirez, 2002). Thus, the problem-finding process requires the ability to generate and deal with alternative views of a problem, manage a network of interrelated elements, go beyond established links among these elements to discover and eventually create new non-existent-yet bonds (Tan & Caleon, 2015). It also requires tolerance to a certain level of ambiguity (Mumford et al., 1994) and openness and receptivity to change (Maloney & Konza, 2011). Given its features, the problem-finding process shows some overlaps with intuition and, specifically, with insight.

INTUITION AND INSIGHT

Intuition and insight are not the same (Hogarth, 2010). Even though they have been sometimes used synonymously (Fischbein, 1987; Schooler & Dougal, 1999), they are two distinct phenomena (Brock, 2015; Hogarth, 2010). Intuition can be described as a set of tacit hunches and non-conscious feelings that come to mind quickly with scarce effort and little conscious awareness of processing (Dane & Pratt, 2007). Insight, on the other hand, has been defined as a process of restructuring the situation in question (Wertheimer, 1945) by forming novel connections between concepts (Bowden et al., 2005). Although its explicit and conscious awareness arrives suddenly, an extended period of incubation usually precedes the insight itself (Brock, 2015).

As a result, both intuition and insight may be defined as non-analytical thought processes yielding an outcome that is not (only) based on a deliberate and stepwise search for a solution (Zander et al., 2016). Both processes are characterized by the interaction between tacit and explicit thought. Specifically, intuition is intrinsically tacit and non-conscious, even if it strongly influences the conscious level of thought. On the contrary, insight is an explicit awareness that mostly results from a tacit process. This difference and partial overlap have led intuition researchers to mainly refer to a continuity model, in which intuition and insight build upon each other in a gradual and cumulative fashion (Bowers et al., 1990; Zander et al., 2016), whereas insight researchers tended to choose a discontinuity model where an initial representation of the problem would negatively affect possible solution attempts and has hence to be overcome. Within this framework, no intuitive precursors of insight in terms of a subjectively felt nearness toward a solution are assumed (Zander et al., 2016). The existence of these two theoretical frameworks has implicitly caused some theoretical and experimental confusion regarding the relationship between intuition and insight.

To clarify this ambiguity, it has been suggested that more research is needed, especially using tasks that might help highlight similarities between intuition and insight. Possible tasks could be related to divergent thinking (Zander et al., 2016). Such recommendation makes sense because the close relationship between intuition and insight is particularly evident in the creativity domain. Creative intuition results in an explicit insight during the "Eureka moment" and implies the subjective experience of "gut feelings" or "hunches" that may lead to an impending insight, a "fringe consciousness of an association-train is in the state of raising consciousness which indicates that the fully conscious flash of success is coming" (Wallas, 1926: 97). There is a body of experimental evidence supporting the idea that creative turns are preceded by an incubation stage, which provides people with a "feeling-of-knowing" (Hélie & Sun, 2010), a sense that a "right" and "fruitful" idea is to be generated (Davidson, 1995; Sundgren & Styhre, 2004).

Problem-solving literature distinguishes between two different paths to solve problems. Besides solving problems in an analytical and logical way, individuals can use insight, that is, rely on finding the solution in an unpredictable way. Experiencing insight implies a sudden realization of a new and original approach to the problem, which is typically a result of the restructuring (finding a new interpretation) of the problem. Features of the problem-finding process suggest a link between problem finding and creativity. To raise new questions or to look at established problems from a different point of view necessarily requires imagination and creativity. Problem finding itself has been defined as a creative process (Paletz & Peng, 2009); some authors consider it the most important component of creativity (Getzels & Smilansky, 1983). Specifically, given its characterization in terms of exploration, openness to new and original alternatives, holistic and simultaneous synthesis of little contradictions, willingness to change one's point of view, problem finding partially overlaps with intuition and, specifically, with insight.

Aims of the Presented Research

This chapter explores the potential of a problem-finding training aimed to enhance the use of intuition in problem solving by primary school students. In this perspective, the potential role of intuition in problem solving is threefold. First, if we conceive intuition as a process which enables individuals to achieve an overall comprehension of the situation so that its deep structure becomes evident, we can design training that guides them to discover those questions implicitly embedded in situations that should increase their ability to solve problems. Such outcome is assumed because effective problem solving, as mentioned before, relies on one's understanding of the actual meaning of a situation to be faced, an operation that is implied in problem finding.

Second, if we understand intuition as a way to solve problems that is far from the mechanical application of previously learned algorithms or of automatic or automatized procedures, then as a strategy it requires to reach behind the surface or the formal aspects of situations. Under these conditions, it is likely that a problem-finding training will improve the ability to inhibit the tendency to rely on such mechanisms and help people become aware of the mistakes they produce. This is to be expected since problem finding guides trainees toward thinking about what the situation means before applying any rule or computation.

Finally, if we associate intuition with insight (an association which concerns also children's problem solving, see Antonietti & Nava, 1995), we may assume that training in problem finding would enhance the number of solutions to insight problems. This is likely to happen because trained individuals might become aware of a possible hidden meaning of the elements of a problem, which is the core of insight problem solving.

An additional consideration is that a problem-finding training should change also the understanding of what problem solving entails since it leads to realization that a successful solution does not rely on the amount of acquired notions nor on reasoning speed or memory. Rather, it relies on the capacity to adopt the relevant point of view and discover an aspect of the situation that was previously neglected.

METHODS

Sample

Three hundred and eighty-five primary school children attending 3rd, 4th, and 5th grade in different primary schools located in Northern and Southern Italy were involved in the study. Participants were randomly assigned to the intervention (N = 202; mean age = 116.5 months, SD = 15.6) or control (N = 141; mean age = 116.7 months, SD = 18.3) group. Because of missing data in the protocols, the number of participants varies across the analyses.

Materials

Assessment

All participants filled out the instruments described below at pre-test and post-test time. According to the three main hypotheses mentioned before, three different kinds of problem-solving tests were employed.

To assess the general problem-solving skill, a standardized test employed in Italian schools – named *AC-MT* (Cornoldi & Cazzola, 2004) – was applied. Since in the school setting problem-solving skills are trained mainly in the domain of mathematics, the test is based on mathematical tasks. A specific version of the test is available for each school grade. Five problems, chosen according to the level of competence of students in the corresponding grade, are included in each version. The total score is equal to the number of problems correctly solved. In this study we used three versions corresponding to three grades our participants attended. To make scores comparable across the three versions, rough scores were converted into z-scores.

To measure the ability to inhibit automatic behaviors in problem solving, that is, to resist the temptation to apply rules and computation immediately without becoming aware of the actual meaning of the problem, the *IRP* (Impulsive/Reflective Problem solving) test was used. The test – inspired by the Cognitive Reflection Test (CRT: Frederick, 2005) and developed by a research group of the Catholic University of Milan (Oldrati et al., 2016) – consists of six questions that children are required to read carefully and then answer as quickly as possible. An example of the items of the test is: "A farmer has 4 piles of hay in a corner of the field and 5 piles of hay in another corner. If you put them all together, how many haystacks will he have?" The impulsive, wrong response is 9 since the problem elicits immediately the sum of the numbers of piles mentioned, whereas the correct answer is 1 since, once the piles have been collapsed, the final result is one (bigger) pile. The total score corresponds to the number of correct responses given. The test is available in two versions (A and B). To make the two versions comparable, rough scores were transformed into z-scores.

The *IPS* (Insight Problem Solution) test was employed to evaluate the ability to solve problems relying on insight. The test – developed by a research group of the Catholic University of Milan – consists of three multiple-choice questions. For each question participants are asked to find the correct answer. An example of items is: "Two fathers and two sons killed three deer. Each brought home one deer. How was it possible?" The given responses are:

A. They bought the missing deer from another hunter
B. They were grandfather, father, and son
C. The fourth deer had only been wounded by the hunters (therefore they killed only three deer), but then it died and it was picked up by the fourth hunter
D. They were a father, his natural son, and the son of the new partner.

The correct answer (B) requires restructuring the usual interpretation (believing that the persons in question are four) and realizing that a person can play the role of both father and son (being the son of the first person and the father of the third one). The total score corresponds to the number of problems solved correctly. This test is available in two versions (A and B). Following the procedure mentioned above, in our study the rough scores were converted into z-scores.

To assess what participants believed about mathematical problem solving, the *MeMa* test (Caponi et al., 2012) was administered. It consists of nine statements that focus on the problem solving process, the specific skills that it involves, and the individuals' attributions concerning failure and success. Respondents are asked to endorse the statements they share. Each statement has been devised to highlight possible misconceptions about mathematical problem solving, which are grounded in a narrow view that it is a matter of memory, speed, luck, and so on, but not a case where understanding is required. The responses are converted into a score according to the standardized scoring system of the test.

Training

The intervention group was involved in a problem-finding training (Rahmani et al., 2016), which consists of 30 situations designed to improve the ability to identify possible underlying problems (see Appendix to this chapter for an example). For each situation participants are required to identify the final question, which is missing. The main focus of the training is to teach students how to identify questions that could be derived from the problem. This should lead participants to reflect more on the text of the problem, and hence develop a model of solution without incurring automatisms and biases. To further support this process, students are encouraged to focus on specific words used to phrase the problem and try to understand the actual meaning of each sentence. This process happened through all three phases of the training.

During the first phase (section A = analysis) students were asked to identify and highlight data that were relevant to understand the key elements. During the second phase (section Q = question), participants tried to identify the most pertinent question to ask. This was the key phase of the intervention. Students were induced to start by asking all the questions that came to their mind, relevant or irrelevant. Then they proceeded to classify questions as useful or not, starting from the available data. The phase ended with the choice of the best question to ask. The last phase (S = solution) focused on the solving process itself: Students were asked to provide the solution. More complicated problems also included an intermediate phase (L = links), which focused on the missing data that were necessary to discover in order to connect the question and the solution.

Procedure

An A (pre-test) – B (training) – A (retest) design was used. After being randomly assigned either to the intervention or the control group (because of the composition of the school classes, the number of children assigned to the two conditions was not the same), half of the sample received version A of the *IRP* and *IPS* tests in the pre-test phase and version B in the post-test phase. The other half of the sample received first version B at the pre-test and then version A during the post-test. When parallel versions of the same test were not available (i.e., *AC-MT* and *MeMa*), the same version was administered twice (at pre-test and at post-test).

After the pre-test, students in the intervention group completed the problem-finding training, whereas the control group was involved in a mathematical skill training based on traditional teaching methods. Both the problem-finding training and the mathematical skills training were delivered during five 20-minute sessions over three consecutive weeks.

RESULTS

A mixed ANOVA 2 (group: intervention vs. control) X 2 (phase: pre vs. post training) was run for each of the dependent variables with children's age (expressed in months) as a covariate. Results showed a significant interaction effect between group and phase in all the tests. Mean scores and standard deviations for each test in the two groups in the two phases of the study are reported in Tables 19.1–19.4.

In the *AC-MT* test the intervention group obtained in general (i.e., by collapsing the performance in the two phases) scores higher than the control group ($F(1,379) = 23.67$; $p < .001$; partial $\eta^2 = .059$) and no difference between the phases emerged ($F(1,379) = 1.33$; $p = .025$; partial $\eta^2 = .003$), whereas the interaction between the two variables was significant ($F(1,379) = 16.64$; $p = .004$; partial $\eta^2 = .042$): The ability to solve school mathematical problems increased in the post-test phase more in the experimental than in the control group.

The same was true for the *IRP* test, where differences between the two groups emerged ($F(1,293) = 29.30$; $p < .001$; partial $\eta^2 = .091$), but the overall performance was not significantly different in the two phases ($F(1,293) = 0.12$; $p = .734$; partial $\eta^2 < .001$). The interaction effect was significant ($F(1,293) = 25.86$; $p < .001$; partial $\eta^2 = .081$): Students in the intervention group showed an increased ability to inhibit mechanical responses after the intervention whereas such an improvement failed to occur in the control group.

Table 19.1 *Mean scores (Standard Deviations in parentheses) for the AC-MT scores in the two groups in the two phases*

Phase	Group	
	Control	*Experimental*
Pre	–1.08 (1.34)	–0.80 (1.48)
Post	–0.26 (1.53)	0.63 (1.27)

Table 19.2 *Mean scores (Standard Deviations in parentheses) for the IRP scores in the two groups in the two phases*

Phase	Group	
	Control	*Experimental*
Pre	0.04 (1.06)	0.18 (1.02)
Post	0.10 (1.09)	1.01 (0.97)

Table 19.3 *Mean scores (Standard Deviations in parentheses) for the IPS scores in the two groups in the two phases*

Phase	Group	
	Control	*Experimental*
Pre	0.08 (1.04)	–0.04 (0.94)
Post	–0.13 (1.18)	0.17 (1.25)

Table 19.4 *Mean scores (Standard Deviations in parentheses) for the MeMa scores in the two groups in the two phases*

Phase	Group	
	Control	*Experimental*
Pre	39.35 (16.83)	41.98 (17.12)
Post	41.09 (16.04)	49.23 (11.60)

In the *IPS* test neither the group ($F(1,299) = 0.91$; $p = .342$; partial $\eta^2 = .003$) nor the phase ($F(1,299) = 0.52$; $p = .471$; partial $\eta^2 = .002$) effects were significant, but the interaction effect was ($F(1,299) = 5.86$; $p = .016$; partial $\eta^2 = .020$). Children in the intervention group were worse than controls in the pre-test but outperformed them in the post-test by solving a greater number of insight problems.

Focusing on *MeMa* scores, a significant effect due to the group emerged ($F(1,382) = 16.50$; $p < .001$; partial $\eta^2 = .041$), whereas no significant differences between the phases were found ($F(1,382) = 1.15$; $p = .283$; partial $\eta^2 = .003$). The interaction effect was significant in this case as well ($F(1,382) = 9.81$; $p = .002$; partial $\eta^2 = .025$). Students in the intervention group changed their view of mathematical problem solving, by sharing beliefs about the role of understanding, more than the controls did.

DISCUSSION AND CONCLUSIONS

The study described in this chapter constitutes the first attempt at exploring the potential of a problem-finding training in enhancing the use of intuition in problem solving among primary school students. Specifically, the study aimed to investigate the relationship between problem-finding and problem-solving abilities, by testing whether the strengthening of problem-finding ability could enhance problem solving through intuition.

Results supported our hypothesis, since the intervention group – after a training focused on the search for the most relevant question that should be asked to solve a specific problem – achieved significant improvements in: (a) the number of correct solutions to mathematical problems; (b) the suppression of the tendency to activate impulsive mechanical responses; (c) the number of correct solutions to insight problems; and (d) the awareness that mathematical problem solving requires deep understanding of thc problem itself.

First, the problem-finding training induced participants to practice how to think of questions implicitly contained in the situation, which, in turn, increased their ability to solve problems. As discussed earlier, both problem finding and problem solving require an overall understanding of the situation that makes its deep structure clear and explicit. Reaching a better comprehension of the problem – through problem-finding training – resulted in better problem-solving abilities. The training presented in this chapter included several work sessions organized in three phases, which makes the training highly structured, and thus would suggest that it does not involve intuition. However, it is worth noting that the core of the training lies in the second phase, which focused on the question-finding task. The process that led to identifying the question would not happen by applying step-by-step or systematic procedures. Rather, students were encouraged to rely on their own spontaneous thoughts. The importance of considering all aspects of the described situation, including some not-declared assumptions (for instance, concerning the agents' goals and intentions) was constantly stressed. Moreover, students were encouraged to identify the relevant perspective (which could have been different from the usual one) not by analytical reasoning but by focusing on a global approach. This approach fostered intuition.

Second, the problem-finding training promoted in the intervention group the tendency to think about the meaning of the situation before applying any automatic rule or procedure. This may have improved participants' ability to inhibit any impulsive responses and, on the contrary, to facilitate comprehension of what the situation actually means. As stated earlier, we intended intuition as a path to problem solving, which requires individuals to avoid the application of mechanical algorithms and automatized procedures, in favor of the tendency to go beyond the formal – and somehow superficial – aspects of the problem. A specific form of intuition leading to insight is involved in the training. Insight, according to its classical description (Wertheimer, 1945), requires, in order to emerge, that mechanization in thinking is avoided. In our specific case, mechanization biases were avoided by continuously encouraging children to try to deeply understand the situation before implementing computational algorithms.

Third, by enhancing participants' awareness of the existence of possible hidden questions within the situation, the problem-finding training might have also facilitated the process that culminates in an explicit awareness of a novel and restructured way to look at the problem. If intuition is aimed at restructuring situations cognitively, we can assume that it was fostered by the training since students were taught to try to assume different viewpoints.

Last, the practice of problem finding led participants to become aware that an effective problem-solving process does not rely on personal knowledge, reasoning speed or luck, but rather on the ability to deeply understand the situation, adopt alternative points of view, and identify a novel element (or novel relationships among elements) within the situation itself (see Antonietti et al., 2000). Intuition is linked to this outcome of the intervention because of the three previous claims: If the training was focused on holistic processing, deep understanding, and restructuring, these aspects of intuition should be enhanced as well.

As argued at the onset of the chapter, the relationships between intuition and insight are not unanimously understood. What is clear is that both intuition and insight share a set of common features: They fail to follow a well-structured way of dealing with information, do not proceed step-by-step, arise in a quick and rather unpredictable manner, and operate beyond consciousness, without deliberation, and effortlessly. However, intuition as a broad mental approach may generate only a feeling or impression concerning the situation in question. Insight, on the other hand, produces a cognitive restructuring of the situation, which may be the base of its creative re-interpretation. If the situation at hand is a problem, insight leads the individual to overcome the tendency to apply automatic reasoning mechanisms, to go beyond the common way of reading the problem, and to discover the hidden solution. Sometimes a situation does not appear to be structured as a problem. In that case, insight – thanks to the re-interpretation that it implies – can help the individual become aware of the underlying problem(s) (problem finding), which is the stage preceding and fostering problem solving.

The results reported in this chapter are particularly relevant given the fact that when we face everyday situations, we may come to the realization that something is missing, wrong, or unsatisfactory, but we often fail to understand what is lacking. This prevents people from being able to address those situations successfully and transform them to better fit specific needs or goals. The perception of the mentioned gaps, inconsistencies, or deficits can be supported by intuition, which, thanks to the fast and overall understanding of the situation, might lead the individual to become aware that changing the approach or finding a new interpretation is necessary.

Solving such ill-structured problems that we meet in our everyday life requires the ability to restructure the elements and focus on the most relevant aspects of the given data in order to successfully change a problematic situation. This is where using a problem-finding approach to train people to be more intuitive in an effective way becomes potentially relevant. This occurs, as suggested by recent data collected by Hill and Kemp (2018), because everyday experience of insight reaches beyond cognitive problem solving. Following this line of reasoning, a new approach that can indirectly improve problem-solving strategies in everyday life, by enhancing the way we use intuition in problem solving, seems particularly relevant. This is the case especially since it is not easy to train intuitive skills and most training tends to provide explicit sets of fixed procedures that should be applied to solve a problem (Branchini et al., 2016). Obviously, traditional training would not be effective to address everyday problems and would not successfully increase intuition as a strategy to solve ill-defined problems. Yet, intuitive approaches can be relevant since they allow people to identify the main aspects to be addressed and suggest productive ways of managing the situation. On the other hand, the problem-finding-based training we tested in the present study resulted in an effective way to improve intuitive thinking and increased the successful rate in problem solving of primary school children. This has implications for teaching, suggesting a possible approach to enhance intuitive processes in learners (Iannello et al., 2011). The training in question represents also an alternative to direct stimulation of brain regions to foster the occurrence of intuition in thinking (Iannello et al., 2014a).

Besides the obvious implications for educational settings (by suggesting a teaching method to improve problem-solving skills), these findings might be relevant for organizations as well. In management literature, intuition is a widely studied topic, even though it has been mostly conceptualized as judgment (Dörfler & Ackermann, 2012). Intuition is mainly intended as a judgment or a choice made through implicit synthesis of information previously acquired or through the application of past learned rules (Miller & Ireland, 2005). Management literature suggests that intuition plays an important role in managerial decision-making processes, highlighting the tendency for senior expert decision makers to rely more on their intuition, especially when confronted with messy decisional settings and short time (Colombo et al., 2010; Iannello et al., 2014b, 2015; Raffaldi et al., 2012). On the contrary, the role of intuition in creativity has been poorly investigated in management research, apart from a few exceptions (see Sinclair, 2010). However, beside intuition as expert knowledge, management research might benefit from considering intuition also as a process that can actually produce a *novum* (Dörfler & Ackermann, 2012). Organizations could gain value from promoting and favoring managers' ability to employ creative intuition, especially when the decision to be taken requires reaching beyond the existing knowledge. We believe that our contribution provides useful hints for the enhancement of managers' creative intuition through the employment of the problem-finding training.

Lastly, our results may be read not only as a confirmation of the efficacy of a problem-finding approach that increases effective intuition in problem solving, but also as an indirect support for the very close link among intuition, problem finding, and problem solving. Future studies should further explore this link by studying different populations, looking, for example, for specific possible gender differences.

REFERENCES

Antonietti, A., Ignazi, S., & Perego, P. 2000. Metacognitive knowledge about problem-solving methods. *British Journal of Educational Psychology*, 70: 1–16.

Antonietti, A., & Nava, B. 1995. Solution of an insight problem at different age levels. *Perceptual and Motor Skills*, 80: 1215–1218.

Barber, L.J. 1981. *Children's problem finding and creative responses in and between reading and art* (unpublished master's thesis). Vancouver, Canada: University of British Columbia.

Basadur, M., Graen, G.B., & Green, S.G. 1982. Training in creative problem solving: Effects on ideation and problem finding and solving in an industrial research organization. *Organizational Behavior and Human Performance*, 30: 41–70.

Bowden, E.M., Jungbeeman, M., Fleck, J., & Kounios, J. 2005. New approaches to demystifying insight. *Trends in Cognitive Sciences*, 9: 322–328.

Bowers, K.S., Regehr, G., Balthazard, C., & Parker, K. 1990. Intuition in the context of discovery. *Cognitive Psychology*, 22: 72–110.

Branchini, E., Bianchi, I., Burro, R., Capitani, E., & Savardi, U. 2016. Can contraries prompt intuition in insight problem solving? *Frontiers in Psychology*, 7: 1962.

Brock, R. 2015. Intuition and insight: Two concepts that illuminate the tacit in science education. *Studies in Science Education*, 51: 127–167.

Caponi, B., Cornoldi, C., Falco, G., Focchiatti, R., & Lucangeli, D. 2012. *Test MeMa – Valutare la metacognizione, gli atteggiamenti negativi e l'ansia in matematica [MeMa Test – Assessing metacognition, negative attitudes and anxiety in mathematics]*. Trento: Erickson.

Colombo, B., Iannello, P., & Antonietti, A. 2010. Metacognitive knowledge of decision-making: An explorative study. In A. Efklides & P. Misailidi (Eds.), *Trends and prospects in metacognitive research*: 445–472. New York: Springer.

Cornoldi, C., & Cazzola, C. 2004. *Test AC-MT 6-11. Test di valutazione delle abilità di calcolo e problem solving [Test AC-MT 6-11. Numeracy and problem-solving skills test]*. Trento: Erickson.

Dane, E., & Pratt, M.G. 2007. Exploring intuition and its role in managerial decision making. *Academy of Management Review*, 32: 33–54.

Davidson, J.E. 1995. The suddenness of insight. In R.J. Sternberg & J.E. Davidson (Eds.), *The nature of insight*: 125–155. Cambridge, MA: MIT Press.

Dörfler, V., & Ackermann, F. 2012. Understanding intuition: The case for two forms of intuition. *Management Learning*, 43: 545–564.

Fischbein, E. 1987. *Intuition in science and mathematics*. Dordrecht: Reidel.

Fontenot, N. 1993. Effects of training in creativity and creative problem finding upon business people. *Journal of Social Psychology*, 133: 11–22.

Frederick, S. 2005. Cognitive reflection and decision making. *Journal of Economic Perspective*, 19: 25–42.

Getzels, J.W., & Csikszentmihalyi, M. 1975. From problem solving to problem finding. In I.A. Taylor & J.W. Getzels (Eds.), *Perspectives in creativity*: 90–116. Chicago, IL: Aldine.

Getzels, J.W., & Smilansky, J. 1983. Individual differences in pupil perceptions of school problems. *British Journal of Educational Psychology*, 53: 307–316.

Hélie, S., & Sun, R. 2010. Incubation, insight, and creative problem solving: A unified theory and a connectionist model. *Psychological Review*, 117: 994–1024.

Hill, G., & Kemp, S.M. 2018. Uh-oh! What have we missed? A qualitative investigation into everyday insight experience. *Journal of Creative Behavior*, 52: 201–211.

Hogarth, R. 2010. *Educating intuition*. Chicago, IL: University of Chicago Press.

Iannello, P., Balconi, M., & Antonietti, A. 2014b. Analytical versus intuitive decision making modulates trust in e-commerce. *Neuropsychological Trends*, 16: 31–49.

Iannello, P., Betsch, C., & Antonietti, A. 2011. Intuition in teaching. In M. Sinclair (Ed.), *Handbook of intuition research*: 168–179. Cheltenham, UK and Northampton, MA, USA: Edward Elgar Publishing.

Iannello, P., Colombo, B., & Antonietti, A. 2014a. Non-invasive brain stimulation techniques in the study of intuition. In M. Sinclair (Ed.), *Handbook of research methods on intuition*: 130–143. Cheltenham, UK and Northampton, MA, USA: Edward Elgar Publishing.

Iannello, P., Perucca, V., Riva, S., Antonietti, A., & Pravettoni, G. 2015. What do physicians believe about the way decisions are made? A pilot study on metacognitive knowledge in the medical context. *Europe's Journal of Psychology*, 11: 691–706.

Lee, H., & Cho, Y. 2007. Factors affecting problem finding depending on degree of structure of problem situation. *Journal of Educational Research*, 101: 113–125.

Maloney, C., & Konza, D. 2011. A case study of teachers' professional learning: Becoming a community of professional learning or not? *Issues in Educational Research*, 21: 75–87.

Miller, C.C. & Ireland, R.D. 2005. Intuition in strategic decision making: Friend or foe in the fast-paced 21st century? *Academy of Management Executive*, 19: 19–30.

Mumford, M.D., Reiter-Palmon, R., & Redmond, M.R. 1994. Problem construction and cognition: Applying problem representations in ill-defined domains. In M.A. Runco (Ed.), *Problem finding, problem solving, and creativity*: 3–39. Westport, CT: Ablex.

Okuda, S.M., Runco, M.A., & Berger, D.E. 1991. Creativity and the finding and solving of real-world problems. *Journal of Psychoeducational Assessment*, 9: 45–53.

Oldrati, V., Patricelli, J., Colombo, B., & Antonietti, A. 2016. The role of dorsolateral prefrontal cortex in inhibition mechanism: A study on Cognitive Reflection Test and similar tasks through neuromodulation. *Neuropsychologia*, 91: 499–508.

Paletz, S.B.F., & Peng, K. 2009. Problem finding and contradiction: Examining the relationship between naive dialectical thinking, ethnicity, and creativity. *Creativity Research Journal*, 21: 139–151.

Raffaldi, S., Iannello, P., Vittani, L., & Antonietti, A. 2012. Decision-making styles in the workplace: Relationships between self-report questionnaires and a contextualised measure of the analytical-systematic versus global-intuitive approach. *Sage Online* (DOI: 10.1177/2158244012448082).

Rahmani, L., Gagliardi, C., Girani, E., Antonietti, C., & Antonietti, A. 2016. *Pensare la matematica. Dai numeri ai significati: un training al problem finding [Thinking about mathematics. From numbers to meanings: a problem-finding training]*. New York: PsyPrint (CreateSpace Independent Publishing).

Ramirez, V.E. 2002. Finding the right problem. *Asia Pacific Education Review*, 3: 18–23.
Reiter-Palmon, R. 2017. The role of problem construction in creative production. *The Journal of Creative Behavior*, 51: 323–326.
Runco, M.A., & Nemiro, J. 1994. Problem finding, creativity, and giftedness. *Roeper Review*, 16: 235–241.
Schooler, J.W., & Dougal, S. 1999. The symbiosis of subjective and experimental approaches to intuition. *Journal of Consciousness Studies*, 6: 280–287.
Sinclair, M. 2010. Misconceptions about intuition. *Psychological Inquiry*, 21: 378–386.
Smilansky, J. 1984. Problem solving and the quality of invention: An empirical investigation. *Journal of Educational Psychology*, 76: 377–386.
Sundgren, M., & Styhre, A. 2004. Intuition and pharmaceutical research: The case of AstraZeneca. *European Journal of Innovation Management*, 7: 267–279.
Tan, Y.S.M., & Caleon, I.S. 2015. Exploring the process of problem finding in professional learning communities through a learning study approach. In Y.H. Cho, I.S. Caleon, & M. Kapur (Eds.), *Authentic problem solving and learning in the 21st century: Perspectives from Singapore and beyond*: 307–326. Singapore: Springer.
Wallas, G. 1926. *The art of thought*. New York: Franklin Watts.
Wertheimer, M. 1945. *Productive thinking*. New York: Harper & Row.
Zander, T., Öllinger, M., & Volz, K.G. 2016. Intuition and insight: Two processes that build on each other or fundamentally differ? *Frontiers in Psychology*, 7: 1395.

APPENDIX

Consider the following text:

"*A mother gave her children money to buy school supplies. Luke spent 28 € for books and 2 € for a pencil-case. John instead spent only 10 € for his books.*"

After having identified the data – 28 € spent for Luke's books, 2 € spent for Luke's stationery, 10 € spent for John's books – students are asked to think about the possible questions raised by reading the text.

Examples of possible questions asked by children:

- *How much were Luke's books more expensive than John's books?*
- *How much money did the two brothers receive?*
- *How much did the two brothers spend to buy only the books?*
- *How many books did Luke and John buy?*
- *How much did the two brothers spend in total?*

In this phase of brainstorming students are free to propose all the questions they consider suitable to address the presented situation.

Subsequently, the questions are divided into questions to which it is possible or impossible to respond based on the available data. For each question, students must focus their attention on the request contained within them; in particular, for impossible questions, students must reflect on what information is further needed to answer the question.

Taking up the previous example:
Possible questions:

- *How much were Luke's books more expensive than John's book?*
- *How much did the two brothers spend to buy only the books?*
- *How much did the two brothers spend in total?*

Impossible questions:

- *How much money did the two brothers receive?*
- *How many books did Luke and John buy?*

Finally, among all the possible questions, students are asked to select the best question.

Among the questions identified earlier in the example, the best is: "*How much did the two brothers spend in total?*" In this case, a person can answer the question just by using all the data reported in the problem. The introductory phrase explains that the mother gave money, without specifying the amount, to her sons Luke and John to buy the school supplies. Knowing how much the two boys spent overall can be interesting in order to know if the money they have available is enough to buy books and stationery.

PART V

RESEARCHING INTUITION FROM NEW PERSPECTIVES

20. Talking intuitions into existence: the role of ventriloquism figures

Nora Meziani

In many organizational settings, intuition is hardly legitimate, and often disqualified. One of the things that prevents intuition from existing and mattering in organizations is its ineffability – that is, it cannot be expressed in words. This ineffability has many important practical and concrete consequences in organizations where we are often asked to justify our reasoning and provide "hard facts" – not feelings – to make our case. How can we rely on something that we cannot put into words? How can we share our intuitions with our colleagues, in teamwork, if we cannot verbalize them? If an intuition cannot be expressed verbally, then it cannot be debated easily during a meeting, nor discussed in a team. When one does express one's intuition, it is not supported by any argument. After having said "I have a bad feeling," one can expect his/her colleagues to reply "How's that?" or "Can you elaborate?" or even "So, you have a 'feeling'… is that all you have to say?" But nobody responds "I do not agree with what you said!" Intuition is removed from deliberation, excluded from debate.

This chapter explores the non-verbal aspect of intuition in relation with teamwork: intuition's ineffability and the importance, nevertheless, of being able to put one's intuitions into words. It also focuses on how people can find a way to circumvent, mostly inadvertently, the organizational necessity and injunction to produce arguments to gain the support of their colleagues or their boss. In so doing, the presented findings complement research on intuition which has started to show how practitioners experience their intuitions but has not yet investigated the rhetorical and discursive aspects of intuitive experiences' narratives.

This chapter is organized as follows: it begins by introducing how intuition challenges our heritage from the Enlightenment, especially around the topic of deliberation. Then, it reviews the literature on the difficult but essential skill in teamwork: how to put intuitions into words. Next, it describes the used data, consisting mostly of secondary data, extracted from press interviews with artists (film directors, composers, writers, illustrators, etc.). Finally, it presents and discusses the findings by showing how the figures of the "song," the "film," or the "character," enable artists to put their intuitions into words in an audible and legitimate way, thus allowing to share them. In doing so, these individuals make their intuitions matter in decision-making and become able to make them exist in collective settings.

INTUITION, DELIBERATION AND DECISION-MAKING

In Western countries, we inherited values of transparency and deliberation from the Enlightenment period. This period is known for having promoted the use of reason – over passions. One of the most famous philosophers of the time, Diderot, who edited with d'Alembert the *Encyclopédie* [*The Encyclopedia*], has widely used deliberative discourse in philosophical reflection. In the iconic *Supplément au voyage de Bougainville* [*Supplement to Bougainville's voyage*] – a philosophical tale – Diderot uses a novel way to write about philosophical issues: a fictitious dialogue between two characters (called A and B). The entire dialogue is based on argumentation. Recent work in philosophy, political sciences and sociology note that these values of deliberation have played a key role in the public debate and argumentation in democracy (Urfalino, 2005).

Intuition challenges these values, as well as the modalities of collective decision and deliberation. The French sociologist Philippe Urfalino (2000, 2005) has developed an original approach to collective decision-making and deliberation. While his work does not explicitly analyze the involvement of intuition in collective decision-making, it nonetheless offers a relevant lens to look at how intuition challenges our heritage from the Enlightenment. Urfalino (2005: 1) explains that when we deliberate, for instance during a meeting, we faithfully reproduce the Ancient Greek definition of "deliberation": "deliberation is a discussion with the aim of making a collective decision." Typically, a meeting would start with a round table, where every member of the team would present his or her idea and recommendation before a final collective decision is made, for instance through a vote. Organizational situations try to follow the "conversational deliberative model" (Urfalino, 2005: 3). This model suggests that in collective settings, we respect the strength of the best argument, as well as the exclusive use of arguments without the use of any emotion. In this model, intuition challenges the notion of collective deliberation because intuition cannot be discussed, debated and argued. Intuition seems incommunicable and therefore does not fit the normative and argumentative structures of organizational and collective decision-making processes.

PUTTING INTUITIONS INTO WORDS: AN ESSENTIAL (BUT DIFFICULT) SKILL

The ability to share intuitions within a team has long been underexplored while being depicted as essential in many situations. For instance, entrepreneurs, who often use their intuition when making decisions (e.g., Ravasi & Turati, 2005; Vaghely & Julien, 2010), have to articulate a less equivocal message through metaphor development to convince their own partners, or potential investors and stakeholders, of the value of their projects (Cornelissen & Clarke, 2010; Hill & Levenhagen, 1995). Managers and other organizational actors also rely on their intuitions, especially when they have to solve problems (Kahneman & Klein, 2009; Salas et al., 2010), be creative

(Dörfler & Ackermann, 2012; Kirton, 2003) or are engaged in teamwork (Dayan & Di Benedetto, 2011; Dayan & Elbanna, 2011). In all these situations, the ability to put intuitions into words in collective contexts is part of practitioners' knowledgeability (Giddens, 1984). While the ability to express one's intuitions seems key in many professions, this ability is challenged by the ineffable nature of intuition.

Any practitioner finds it difficult to verbalize their intuitions (Nisbett & Wilson, 1977) and to express them in some written or spoken form (Baskerville & Dulipovici, 2006). Gertler (2003: 77) asserts that people can encounter "inadequacies of language in expressing certain forms of knowledge" such as tacit knowledge. The subjectivity of the intuitive experience reinforces the inability to put one's intuitions into words. Thus, when individuals have an intuition, they know more than they can tell, as Polanyi (1966) said about tacit knowledge. The challenge of any attempt to communicate intuitions is reinforced by the fact that intuition may be unusual, confusing (Sadler-Smith & Shefy, 2007) and embodied (e.g., Bastick, 1982; Bechara et al., 1997; Dane & Pratt, 2007; Sadler-Smith, 2016). Hence, intuition "cannot be literally spoken" (Blackman & Sadler-Smith, 2009). The unconscious nature of intuition (e.g., Epstein, 1994; Hogarth, 2001; Jung, 1976) can also explain the difficulty of putting intuition into words. Dual process theories of the mind associate intuitive processing with "System 1" (Kahneman, 2003) (also known as "experiential system," Epstein, 1994). Within this system, processes are automatic, unconscious, associative, implicit and fast. They occur outside the realm of words, which explains why intuition remains inaccessible to individuals, or "difficult-to-articulate and difficult-to-capture" (Sadler-Smith, 2008: 494). The unconscious nature of the intuitive process, and the feelings associated with its outcome (Dane & Pratt, 2007; Sadler-Smith, 2008), make the intuitive experience puzzling (Sadler-Smith & Shefy, 2007; Sinclair, 2011, 2014).

Yet, some researchers have asked practitioners to talk or write about their intuitive experiences. Lipshitz and Shulimovitz (2007) for instance, asked bank loan officers to report their personal experience of a credit decision involving their intuitions, while Huang and Pearce (2015) observed monthly meetings involving experienced entrepreneurial investors and interviewed them about why and how they make their investment decisions. More recently, Sadler-Smith (2016) examined the subjective experience of intuition by asking human resources practitioners to write about "what happens when [they] intuit." While these studies, among others (Akinci & Sadler-Smith, 2018; Fenton-O'Creevy et al., 2011; Hensman & Sadler-Smith, 2011; Huang and Pearce, 2015; Lipshitz & Shulimovitz, 2007; Miles & Sadler-Smith, 2014; Sadler-Smith, 2011, 2016; Woiceshyn, 2009), have opened perspectives to learn more about the subjective experience of intuition and about "intuition-in-use in the contexts of their (informants) job roles and their organization" (Hensman & Sadler-Smith, 2011: 54), they did not analyze in minute detail discourse on intuition.

To explore that aspect, I use secondary data, mostly from artists' press interviews. I explain in the next section why press interviews with artists (e.g., film directors, composers, etc.) constitute privileged data to study how people put their intuitions into words.

ARTISTS AS RESEARCH CONTEXT

The idea of exploring how people talk about their intuition emerged from a research project on intuition in filmmaking. During this time on the field, I conducted interviews and observations, and spent a great amount of time in the filmmaking circles for a period of three years. I found that among all the ways film workers talked about their intuitions, one stood out. When some film workers were talking to me or to their colleagues about an intuition they had about a casting, a project or a film they were editing, they connected their intuition to the "film" – by saying "the film needs it," "the film orders me to do that" or "the film does not like that sequence, I can feel it, I think we have to cut it." They talked about the "film" as if it were a human being: the "film" can act, can command. It has a life of its own.

Inspired by that observation, I started to collect secondary data from press interviews (written and spoken) in which, typically, the journalist interviews an artist (a director, a singer, a writer, a composer, an illustrator …). Artistic professions tend to value intuition (Coget et al., 2009), hence we can infer that they do not feel uncomfortable revealing intuitive-based decisions. The questions asked were related to the artists' past decisions, their artistic choices and their creative process. For instance, journalists asked about their background and past experiences, how they decided to write on a specific topic, and so on.

From that basis, I started to read or to listen to all the press interviews collected, in order to find sequences in which the artists talk about the involvement of their intuitions in their work. Then, I analyzed the discourse they developed around and about their intuitions, with a special focus on the figures similar to the "film" they could use when talking about their intuitions.

"I DO NOT DECIDE, THE SONG DOES"

As I was reading an interview with director Abdellatif Kechiche who won *La Palme d'Or* at Cannes Festival for his internationally acclaimed film *Blue is the Warmest Color*, I was struck by the way he talked about his intuitions:

> Journalist – How did you chose your two main actresses?
>
> Abdellatif Kechiche – I had the intuition that it would be possible to bring the two actresses together and that something would burst from their unlikely encounter. (…) I love when I lose control, when the character says "no", *when the film tells me: "no, this is not the direction you should take"*. (…) By experience, I know that explanations and analyses are useless. (…) Sometimes, it is just immediately magical. I can work on a scene for 5 days or a week, but in the end, I cut the scene because *I feel like the film did not want it*." (Interview with Abdellatif Kechiche by Olivier Séguret and Didier Péron, in *Libération*, 2013)

When replying to the journalist's question, Abdellatif Kechiche immediately refers to his intuitions. Intuitions, he says, are central to many of the most important decisions he has to make as part of his role of film director, such as selecting the actors of his latest film, cutting scenes during editing. Importantly, he uses the figure of the "film" to talk about his intuition by saying "the film tells me: 'no, this is not the direction you should take'" or also, "I cut the scene because I feel like the film did not want it." What is the "film," what does it mean, what role does it play regarding the ability to put one's intuition into words in teamwork? Is Abdellatif Kechiche the only film worker to connect his intuition to the "film"?

Far from being anecdotal, I noted that some film workers I have met used the figure of the "film" to talk about their intuitions. More broadly, additionally to film workers, artists such as sculptors, drawers, writers, or singers, use figures directly related to their work in their press interviews and communication activities. For instance, during an informal email exchange, Albert, a film editor I had met during my field research, told me that he often uses his intuition in editing. To illustrate his point, he shared a conversation he had with a director during the editing of his film. We can note that Albert talks about the film as if it were a human being, someone to "trust" or not to trust:

> I often follow my intuition when I edit films, and if I start looking for words to explain what I am going to do, I lose very quickly that little thing that arose inside of me, and I am left only with words and no intuition. (…) A producer asked me to come and edit a film that is already in postproduction. The director made rough cuts of his own film, and my focus was on cutting: the film lasts 2 hours 30 minutes, and we are asked to have 1 hour 40 minutes. The director, who edits very well, says: "I don't see why your perception would be more legitimate than mine." I answered what I thought, totally guided by my intuition and my instinct: "*You do not trust your film*," I said. This sentence had a strong influence on the rest of the editing! (Albert, editor, October 2016)

In the same vein, in a press interview, Mina Tindle, a composer and a singer, used the "song" to talk about how she used her intuition when she composed and wrote her latest album, *Parades*:

> For *Parades*, (…) it [was] always the *song that decide[d]*. (…) *The song orients itself* towards a direction or another. It is very intuitive. (Interview with Mina Tindle by Maxime de Abreu, in *Les Inrockuptibles*, 2014)

We can note that artists talk about their intuitions through a specific figure (the "song," the "film," and so on). The "film" and the "song" want, order, decide, talk, ask and need. What are these figures? What role do they play in the discourse on intuition? I suggest looking at these figures and at what they do to, and with, intuition, using a Communication as Constitution of Organizations (hereafter CCO) lens (e.g., Cooren, 2000).

VENTRILOQUISM FIGURES

The main idea underlying the "communicative constitution of organizations" perspective (Cooren, 2000) is that discourse, and more largely communication activities, have organizing properties and therefore create, maintain and transform organizations. In other words, communication activities are not just (cheap) "talk," they have effects. Hence, connecting the narration of an intuitive experience or an intuitive decision to the "film" or to the "song" is not neutral. These figures are not ornamental in the discourse on intuition.

The CCO perspective is rooted in a specific, post-structural ontology, which considers that agency is not just a property of human being, but instead is distributed among human and non-human actors. Accordingly, artifacts "such as tools, documents, settings, bodies, numbers, and even more 'abstract' elements such as emotions and values, what [Cooren] calls 'figures'" (Sergi & Bonneau, 2016: 382) matter, in the sense that they make a difference. Communication activities are done through multiple figures connected to one another and made present, or "presentified," in conversations (Benoit-Barné & Cooren, 2009). For instance, in our case, artists use figures such as the "film" or the "song" to talk about their intuitions. For Fairhurst and Cooren (2009), making things present through discourse can make a significant difference in a given situation, such as an argumentation or a discussion during a meeting, for example. They argue that presence is something that cannot be taken for granted, that it has to be created to produce an effect in the situation. For instance, when artists use the figure of the "song" or of the "film" to talk about their intuitions, they find a way to circumvent the ineffable. These figures enable artists to create a bridge between the world of words and the world of the ineffable. In doing so, they make their intuitions present, they talk them into existence.

Making things present can happen through a variety of modalities, such as mentioning them, showing a picture of them or imitating them. For instance, Cooren (2000) shows how, through ventriloquism, one can make someone or something present in a conversation. The notion of ventriloquism shows people's abilities to "make other beings say or do things while [they] speak" (Cooren, 2012: 1), such as a ventriloquist would do with his/her dummy. One can make a procedure speak ("I am sorry, I can't accept your application, the procedure wants that candidates sign in online first"), one can make a feeling speak ("A little bird told me that we should not go that way"). In doing so, people make these things present in the conversation and make them say things. In our case, the "film" (in inverted commas) is not the film (i.e., the movie); it is a ventriloquism figure. So is the "song." Considering the "film" or the "song" as ventriloquism figures that make one's intuition present in conversations renders visible the idea of polyphony (Cooren & Sandler, 2014), that is, the idea that multiple voices are made heard in a conversation and influence the unfolding of the situation. In our case, when a film worker says "the film decides," and when a composer says "the song wants it," we can hear them talking, we can hear the film/the song talking, and we can also hear their intuition talking to us.

THE ROLE OF DOMAIN-BASED FIGURES

Making these figures speak, order or ask to express intuitions has a significantly different effect than saying "a little bird tells me," "my guts tell me," or also "my intuition tells me," even though these three popular expressions are also ventriloquism figures. A little bird, as well as guts, intuitions or songs, do not literally speak. What is the specificity and the strength of these figures (e.g., the "song"), compared to the little bird or the guts? We offer to explore that in this section.

The "little bird tells me," "my guts tell me" or the "song tells me," give one's intuition a shape (of a personified œuvre that can act and decide), a frame (instead of the diffuse and uncapturable intuition) and a name (the "song," the "novel," etc.). The specific strength of ventriloquism figures such as the "film," the "song," or the "novel," compared to a "little bird" or the "guts," is that for artists, the "œuvre" is part of the professional jargon highlighting the importance of their work, their œuvre, above all. These ventriloquism figures are domain-based figures, audible and legitimate professional jargon that makes sense to all artists. By invoking these domain-based figures to talk about their intuitions, they evoke another order of reality that is undisputable as long as it is the symbol of their work. In doing so, these ventriloquism figures transform the mysterious phenomenon of intuition into a meaningful and sharable account.

These domain-based figures are frequently used by artists, not only to talk about intuitions. Here lies another strength of these figures: they are interpretatively flexible, in addition to being legitimate. Luz, a famous illustrator at Charlie Hebdo – a French satirical newspaper, narrates in a press interview how he came to use color in the drawings of his latest book, which was unusual for him:

> Then the drawing told me: "Use colours, buddy!" I do not consider myself as a good colourist. But suddenly, it felt like the colour was a character per se. (Interview with Luz by Frédéric Potet, in *Le Monde*, 2015)

Interpretative flexibility is a key feature of these ventriloquism domain-based figures. During an informal conversation with a film producer on my field research, he told me that when a film director invokes the "film" and says that this is the film that needs this or that, he would consider seriously the request because he has the feeling that the request is not (only) driven by the director's ego and wishes but by "what is best for the film," which is built by a whole team, and not only by one's wishes. As Dominique Villain, a former French film editor, explained during a meeting of an association of film editors in which I participated in 2016: Saying that "the film wants it" can bear a strong meaning and ultimately can make a difference. It can mean, for instance for editors, that the comments are not just the outcome of the scenario and what the team intended to do. At some point, there is a matter that has its own existence, and when editors work, they have to deal with this matter that exists and cannot be modified.

CONCLUDING THOUGHTS

In this chapter, a communication-based approach called CCO was used to reflect on intuition's ineffability and the importance to verbalize it nevertheless in collective contexts. Drawing upon secondary data extracted from press interviews of artists (film directors, composers, writers, illustrators, etc.), it illustrates how people can find a way to share their intuition among their team by using domain-based figures such as the "song," the "film," or the "character," to talk about it. By making these figures speak (i.e., by acting as a ventriloquist with them), they circumvent intuition's ineffability and discursively share their intuition in an audible and legitimate way. Hence, they can make their intuitions matter in decision-making and thus become able to make them exist in collective settings.

The ventriloquism and domain-based figures give a substance to intuition, they make it more concrete as they give it a shape, a frame and a name. Above all, these figures make intuitions exist, they give intuition a legitimacy and an authority. These figures invite researchers to pay attention to the use of professional artifacts and objects (e.g., a 3D model for architects, a scalpel for surgeons, etc.) in discourse in order to better understand their specific role in the process of sharing intuitions in collective contexts. Future research could build on the CCO perspective – and generally a discursive perspective – to further develop our understanding of intuition in collective contexts. For instance, management scholars could explore the role of domain-based figures in non-artistic organizational settings: how does the use of such figures to share intuitions affect collective action? What can we say about the role of these figures in the process of sharing intuitions in contexts such as finance (the "market"), marketing (the "brand"), firefighting (the "fire") or policing (the "investigation")? Exploring the effects of these discursive aspects has practical implications for teamwork, as intuition pervades organizations and informal day-to-day conversations while remaining an unthought-of in organization studies.

Generally, this chapter contributes to intuition research and practice in management by adopting a communication perspective. Recently, management scholars have started to explore how practitioners experience their intuitions, but they have remained focused on the subjective experience of each individual, and have not studied how these individuals make their intuition exist for others. In particular, they have not yet looked in minute detail into the rhetorical, discursive, and more broadly communicational, aspects of intuitive experiences' narratives. Future research could explore this aspect further, as it is of utmost importance for practitioners. For instance, entrepreneurs constitute a privileged field research on intuition (e.g., Baldacchino et al., 2014, 2015; Blume & Covin, 2011), mostly with the aim of understanding the role of intuition in decision-making during venture founding processes. However, pitching projects and convincing of their value are at the core of the entrepreneurial activity, hence there is a need to explore in minute detail the role of communication in entrepreneurs' ability to convey and share their intuitions in an appealing or convincing way.

REFERENCES

Akinci, C., & Sadler-Smith, E. 2018. Collective intuition: Implications for improved decision making and organizational learning. *British Journal of Management*: 1–20.

Baldacchino, L., Ucbasaran, D., Cabantous, L., & Lockett, A. 2015. Entrepreneurship research on intuition: A critical analysis and research agenda. *International Journal of Management Reviews*, 17: 212–231.

Baldacchino, L., Ucbasaran, D., Lockett, A., & Cabantous, L. 2014. Capturing intuition through concurrent protocol analysis. In M. Sinclair (Ed.), *Handbook of research methods on intuition*: 160–175. Cheltenham, UK and Northampton, MA, USA: Edward Elgar Publishing.

Baskerville, R., & Dulipovici, A. 2006. The theoretical foundations of knowledge management. *Knowledge Management Research & Practice*, 4(2): 83–105.

Bastick, T. 1982. *Intuition: How we think and act*. Hoboken, NJ: John Wiley and Sons.

Bechara, A., Damasio, H., Tranel, D., & Damasio, A.R. 1997. Deciding advantageously before knowing the advantageous strategy. *Science*, 275(5304): 1293–1295.

Benoit-Barné, C., & Cooren, F. 2009. The accomplishment of authority through presentification: How authority is distributed among and negotiated by organizational members. *Management Communication Quarterly*, 23(1): 5–31.

Blackman, D., & Sadler-Smith, E. 2009. The silent and the silenced in organizational knowing and learning. *Management Learning*, 40(5): 569–585.

Blume, B.D., & Covin, J.G. 2011. Attributions to intuition in the venture founding process: Do entrepreneurs actually use intuition or just say that they do? *Journal of Business Venturing*, 26: 137–151.

Coget, J.-F., Haag, C., & Bonnefous, A.-M. 2009. The role of emotion in making intuitive decisions: Focus on the director-decision-maker during filming. *M@n@gement*, 12(2): 118–141.

Cooren, F. 2000. *The organizing property of communication*. Amsterdam, the Netherlands: John Benjamins Publishing.

Cooren, F. 2012. Communication theory at the center: Ventriloquism and the communicative constitution of reality. *Journal of Communication*, 62(1): 1–20.

Cooren, F., & Sandler, S. 2014. Polyphony, ventriloquism, and constitution: In dialogue with Bakhtin. *Communication Theory*, 24(3): 225–244.

Cornelissen, J.P., & Clarke, J.S. 2010. Imagining and rationalizing opportunities: Inductive reasoning and the creation and justification of new ventures. *Academy of Management Review*, 35(4): 539–557.

Dane, E., & Pratt, M.G. 2007. Exploring intuition and its role in managerial decision making. *Academy of Management Review*, 32(1): 33–54.

Dayan, M., & Di Benedetto, C.A. 2011. Team intuition as a continuum construct and new product creativity: The role of environmental turbulence, team experience, and stress. *Research Policy*, 40(2): 276–286.

Dayan, M., & Elbanna, S. 2011. Antecedents of team intuition and its impact on the success of new product development projects. *Journal of Product Innovation Management*, 28(s1): 159–174.

de Abreu, M. 2014. Minda Tindle, l'interview: 'J'ai abordé le deuxième album avec beaucoup de sérénité.' *Les Inrockuptibles*. https://www.lesinrocks.com/2014/10/07/musique/mina-tindle-linterview-11528265/ (accessed February 24, 2020).

Dörfler, V., & Ackermann, F. 2012. Understanding intuition: The case for two forms of intuition. *Management Learning*, 43(5): 545–564.

Epstein, S. 1994. Integration of the cognitive and the psychodynamic unconscious. *American Psychologist*, 49(8): 709–724.

Fairhurst, G.T., & Cooren, F. 2009. Leadership as the hybrid production of presence(s). *Leadership*, 5(4): 469–490.
Fenton-O'Creevy, M., Soane, E., Nicholson, N., & Willman, P. 2011. Thinking, feeling and deciding: The influence of emotions on the decision making and performance of traders. *Journal of Organizational Behavior*, 32(8): 1044–1061.
Gertler, M.S. 2003. Tacit knowledge and the economic geography of context, or the undefinable tacitness of being (there). *Journal of Economic Geography*, 3(1): 75–99.
Giddens, A. 1984. *The constitution of society: Outline of the theory of structuration.* Cambridge: Polity.
Hensman, A., & Sadler-Smith, E. 2011. Intuitive decision making in banking and finance. *European Management Journal*, 29(1): 51–66.
Hill, R.C., & Levenhagen, M. 1995. Metaphors and mental models: Sensemaking and sensegiving in innovative and entrepreneurial activities. *Journal of Management*, 21(6): 1057–1074.
Hogarth, R.M. 2001. *Educating intuition.* Chicago: University of Chicago Press.
Huang, L., & Pearce, J.L. 2015. Managing the unknowable: The effectiveness of early-stage investor gut feel in entrepreneurial investment decisions. *Administrative Science Quarterly*, 60(4): 634–670.
Jung, C.G. 1976. *Psychological types.* Princeton: Princeton University Press.
Kahneman, D. 2003. A perspective on judgment and choice: Mapping bounded rationality. *American Psychologist*, 58(9): 697–720.
Kahneman, D., & Klein, G. 2009. Conditions for intuitive expertise: A failure to disagree. *American Psychologist*, 64(6): 515–526.
Kirton, M.J. 2003. *Adaption-innovation: In the context of diversity and change.* Hove, UK: Routledge.
Lipshitz, R., & Shulimovitz, N. 2007. Intuition and emotion in bank loan officers' credit decisions. *Journal of Cognitive Engineering and Decision Making*, 1(2): 212–233.
Miles, A., & Sadler-Smith, E. 2014. 'With recruitment I always feel I need to listen to my gut': The role of intuition in employee selection. *Personnel Review*, 43(4): 606–627.
Nisbett, R.E., & Wilson, T.D. 1977. Telling more than we can know: Verbal reports on mental processes. *Psychological Review*, 84(3): 231–259.
Polanyi, M. 1966. *The tacit dimension.* New York: Doubleday.
Potet, F. 2015. Luz: Envie de passer à autre chose. *Le Monde.* http://bandedessinee.blog.lemonde.fr/2015/05/18/luz-envie-de-passer-a-autre-chose/ (accessed February 24, 2020).
Ravasi, D., & Turati, C. 2005. Exploring entrepreneurial learning: A comparative study of technology development projects. *Journal of Business Venturing*, 20(1): 137–164.
Sadler-Smith, E. 2008. The role of intuition in collective learning and the development of shared meaning. *Advances in Developing Human Resources*, 10(4): 494–508.
Sadler-Smith, E. 2011. The intuitive style: Relationships with local/global and verbal/visual styles, gender, and superstitious reasoning. *Learning and Individual Differences*, 21(3): 263–270.
Sadler-Smith, E. 2016. 'What happens when you intuit?': Understanding human resource practitioners' subjective experience of intuition through a novel linguistic method. *Human Relations*, 69(5): 1069–1093.
Sadler-Smith, E., & Shefy, E. 2007. Developing intuitive awareness in management education. *Academy of Management Learning & Education*, 6(2): 186–205.
Salas, E., Rosen, M.A., & DiazGranados, D. 2010. Expertise-based intuition and decision making in organizations. *Journal of Management*, 36(4): 941–973.
Séguret, O., & Péron, D. 2013. J'aime que cela m'échappe, que le personnage, le film, me disent non [I love when I lose control, when the character and the film say 'no']. *Libération.* https://next.liberation.fr/cinema/2013/10/04/j-aime-que-cela-m-echappe-que-le-personnage-le-film-me-disent-non_937161 (accessed February 24, 2020).

Sergi, V., & Bonneau, C. 2016. Making mundane work visible on social media: A CCO investigation of working out loud on Twitter AU. *Communication Research and Practice*, 2(3): 378–406.

Sinclair, M. 2011. *Handbook of intuition research*. Cheltenham, UK and Northampton, MA, USA: Edward Elgar Publishing.

Sinclair, M. 2014. *Handbook of research methods on intuition*. Cheltenham, UK and Northampton, MA, USA: Edward Elgar Publishing.

Urfalino, P. 2000. La délibération et la dimension normative de la décision collective. In J. Commaille, L. Dumoulin, & C. Robert (Eds.), *La juridicisation du politique*: 165–193. Paris: L.G.D.J.

Urfalino, P. 2005. La délibération n'est pas une conversation. Délibération, décision collective et négociation. [Deliberation is not conversation. Deliberation, collective decision and negotiation] *Négociations*. No. 2.

Vaghely, I.P., & Julien, P-A. 2010. Are opportunities recognized or constructed? An information perspective on entrepreneurial opportunity identification. *Journal of Business Venturing*, 25(1): 73–86.

Woiceshyn, J. 2009. Lessons from 'good minds': How CEOs use intuition, analysis and guiding principles to make strategic decisions. *Long Range Planning*, 42(3): 298–319.

21. Researching intuition through metaphor

Heather Cairns-Lee

Intuition research has advanced significantly with attention to understanding conceptual considerations and descriptions (Sadler-Smith & Shefy, 2004), the evocation process (Teerikangas & Välikangas, 2014) and the micro-dynamics of intuitive experience (Petitmengin, 2014). Yet the research remains challenging due to lack of agreement on what intuition is (Dane & Pratt, 2007; Sinclair & Ashkanasy, 2005), the need to differentiate between the process of intuiting and the outcome of intuition (Dane & Pratt, 2007; Sadler-Smith, 2016), and its association with non-conscious holistic processing (Epstein & Pacini, 2001; Jung, 1921; Rowan, 1986; Sinclair & Ashkanasy, 2005), which is difficult to observe and measure. Despite being a significant construct in both academic and practitioner circles, there is limited empirical work on intuition (Dane et al., 2012; Khatri & Ng, 2000; Sadler-Smith, 2016; Teerikangas & Välikangas, 2014) and further integration of research and practice is necessary (Sinclair, 2014). This is particularly important in management research as Dörfler and Eden (2014) report that the role of intuition tends to be mistrusted in management even though it is broadly accepted in the development of scientists' knowledge.

Despite differing definitions, there is broad "agreement about the fundamental features of intuition" (Dörfler & Eden, 2014: 265). These include descriptions of the process as rapid, spontaneous and alogical (i.e., not following the typical rules of logic) and reaching the outcomes of intuitive knowledge tacitly, holistically and with confidence. Many scholars also concur that metaphor plays a substantial role in intuition (Crossan et al., 1999; Li, 2014; Petitmengin, 2014; Sadler-Smith, 2016; Sinclair & Ashkanasy, 2005).

This chapter highlights an elicitation technique, Clean Language, that illuminates intuitive knowledge accessed through metaphor. Furthermore, it provides an in-depth example of how intuition was described through metaphor and illustrated in a drawing by a business leader. This builds on previous research about the role of intuition in managerial decision-making (Khatri & Ng, 2000; Sadler-Smith & Shefy, 2004) and the role of metaphors in intuition (Crossan et al., 1999; Li, 2014). Like several other studies about intuition (Dörfler & Eden, 2014; Teerikangas & Välikangas, 2014), this study did not set out to explicitly explore intuition, rather the findings emerged from a secondary reading of the data which shows correspondences between leaders' metaphors describing the elicitation process and descriptions of intuition.

EXECUTIVES AND INTUITION

The desire for leaders to show the way in uncertain situations is a timeless demand despite modern reference to the volatile, uncertain, complex and ambiguous (VUCA) nature of the world (Stiehm & Townsend, 2002). Yet how do they know which way to take, let alone how to show this way? Whilst much leadership development relies on developing "skills and behaviours required for success that can be observed" (Korn Ferry, 2014–2015), it is how leaders think and make sense of situations that makes that difference. Although leaders often rely on analytical thinking to make sense of business situations, they rely on their conceptual thinking and intuition to make meaning of ambiguous and complex environments (Sinclair & Ashkanasy, 2005). Indeed cognitive flexibility involving both analysis and intuition is important for much leadership, innovation and learning (Akinci & Sadler-Smith, 2013). The holistic, non-conscious nature of intuition is typically described as having a non-verbal quality that relies on the use of images and metaphor (Sadler-Smith & Shefy, 2007; Sinclair & Ashkanasy, 2005). Metaphor grasps the similarities between apparently unrelated situations and helps explain the unknown (Morgan, 2016). Thus metaphor can assist leaders to understand and show the way in uncertain and complex environments. Yet despite the promise of metaphor to facilitate access to intuition, there is little research on how leaders actually do this in practice.

METAPHORS AND INTUITION

Metaphors play an important role in intuition, as analogical thinking and preverbal imagery are associated with developing intuitive awareness (Sinclair & Ashkanasy, 2005). Through its indifference to verbal logic (Koestler, 1964) metaphor is claimed to be "the central mechanism to create tacit and novel knowledge" (Li, 2014: 34). Furthermore, language that describes intuition is "replete with metaphors" (Sadler-Smith, 2016: 1079), such as "two minds in one brain" (Evans, 2003), thus turning to metaphorical language is not as a useful way to understand intuition. Like intuition, metaphor is processed non-consciously, often appearing in vivid images that precede verbal understanding. Metaphor is, therefore, a natural companion to intuition as it tends to illuminate complex, vague and difficult-to-express subjects, psychological states or processes in compact holistic images (Ortony, 1993). This has two implications: first, it is important to adopt a multi-modal approach to metaphor that goes beyond the verbal and pays attention to the images in which metaphors are expressed. Second, it is important to pay attention to the link that metaphors make between intuition and interpretation in the four "I" model of learning (Intuiting, Interpreting, Integrating and Institutionalizing) (Crossan et al., 1999).

Metaphor has been used extensively in organizational studies (Cornelissen, 2005; Cornelissen & Kafouros, 2008; Morgan, 1986; Oswick & Grant, 1996) to understand a range of complex topics including leadership (Alvesson & Spicer, 2011), change (Barner, 2008; Marshak, 1993), sensemaking (Cassell & Bishop, 2014; Patriotta

& Brown, 2011; Weick et al., 2005) and strategy (Bürgi & Roos, 2003; Oliver & Roos, 2007). Yet much research with metaphors has been deductive, relying on researchers' metaphors to understand phenomena (Cornelissen et al., 2008). This has led to a restricted range of metaphors used to describe leadership that is surprising, given the complexity of leadership and the differing contexts in which it is practised. Furthermore, most metaphors reported in organizational research are verbal, with limited use of other ways of knowing, such as embodied cognition or visual metaphor. This has led to the lamentation that whilst metaphors provide "many ways of thinking," there seems to be "only one way of thinking about metaphors," namely verbal (Oswick et al., 2002: 301). Turning to leaders' own naturally occurring metaphors provides an inductive understanding of leadership from the "inside-out" and illuminates their intuitive ways of knowing. Furthermore, the elicitation of multi-modal metaphors in naturally occurring language addresses a significant gap in organizational research (Cornelissen et al., 2008) by going beyond the deductive and verbal to provide insight into the contextualized, embodied and visual ways that leaders "know" about their leadership.

THE RESEARCH SAMPLE

This chapter is based upon the elicitation of metaphors for leadership from a group of 40 practising female business leaders. This purposive sample comprised women from 22 nationalities from all major regions of the world including Europe, Africa, the Middle East, Asia, Australia, the United States and Latin America. The women were aged between 35 and 68 years and came from diverse sectors, including international businesses and non-governmental organizations. These leaders were attending a two-day retreat following a leadership development program for women at a major European business school. The women were asked to respond to the question: "When you are leading at your best, that's like what?" All women in the sample developed a metaphor for their leadership. Follow-up interviews were held with a smaller sample of the group to understand how they experienced the process of surfacing and exploring their metaphors and whether they experienced their intuition in this process. The approach to elicit these leaders metaphors was based on Clean Language, which is now described as a promising method for illuminating intuitive knowing.

ELICITING INTUITON THROUGH CLEAN LANGUAGE

Clean Language is an approach to questioning that validates an individual's experience through precise use of their verbal and non-verbal expressions. Furthermore, Clean Language limits the influence of the interviewer's assumptions through the use of specific "clean" questions. Clean Language Interviewing (Tosey, Lawley and Meese 2014) is particularly useful for developing authentic accounts, which are fundamental for phenomenological approaches to understanding lived experience (Husserl, 1982; Moustakas, 1994). Furthermore, like the elicitation interview that elucidates "the microdynamics of intuitive experience" (Petitmengin, 2014: 197), Clean Language Interviewing illuminates the inner world. To make clear the appeal of Clean Language to researchers studying intuition, its origins and two key principles are now introduced. These principles are the validation of inner experience with particular attention to metaphor, and clean questions that direct attention to the inner world and minimize the influence of the interviewer. A practical example, drawn from the above sample, is then provided to illustrate how Clean Language works in practice.

David Grove, the originator of Clean Language, recognized the importance of embodied metaphors in understanding experience and stated that Clean Language creates an environment conducive to exploration of the inner world, by utilizing "the client's intuitive knowledge" that is typically expressed in symbols and metaphor (Grove & Panzer, 1989: 35). He claimed that Clean Language encourages an individual's internal process by ensuring that their "meaning and resonance remain wholly intact, uncontaminated by the therapist words" (Grove & Panzer, 1989: 1). Whilst Clean Language originated in counselling, it is now used broadly in education (McCracken, 2016), coaching (Way, 2013), leadership development (Cairns-Lee, 2015, 2017) and management research (Tosey, Lawley and Meese, 2014). These applications have been encouraged largely by practitioners Lawley and Tompkins (2000) who worked closely with David Grove.

One of the key principles of Clean Language is to validate the inner world so that a person can find out more about intuitive information held in metaphor. As the purpose of Clean Language is self-discovery and exploration, there is no interpretation or paraphrasing from the interviewer but rather an exquisite attention to the exact verbal and non-verbal expressions of an individual, which validates their inner experience. Lawley and Tompkins suggest that "Clean Language both validates the client's experience and facilitates the 'bringing into form' or giving life to information normally out of everyday awareness" (2000: 1). This is important for facilitating intuitive awareness, which is typically claimed to reside outside of everyday awareness.

A second principle of Clean Language is the use of "clean" questions which minimize the introduction of content or presuppositions from the interviewer thereby "contaminating" an individual's process as little as possible, hence the term "clean." These questions aim to honour the individual's experience, to send them on a search for more information and to provide maximum room to answer from their own perspective and the modality they choose (words, metaphors, gestures etc.). As the questions do not introduce content but direct an individual's attention to explore their experience, "clean" questions have similarities to the "content-empty" and "directive" questioning suggested by Petitmengin (2014: 192) to explore the micro-dynamics of intuitive experience. As Grove developed Clean Language during years of clinical practice, he established a core set of classically clean questions. These questions are based on the assumptions that people represent their experience

Table 21.1 Classic Clean Language questions

ATTRIBUTES
- And what kind of X is that X?
- And is there anything else about X?
LOCATION
- And where/whereabouts is X?
REFLEXIVITY
- And how do you know X?
METAPHOR
- And that's X like what?
RELATIONSHIP
- And when X, what happens to Y?
- And is there a relationship between X and Y?
- And is X the same or different as Y?
AFTER
- And then what happens?
- And what happens next?
SOURCE
- And where does/could X come from?
BEFORE
- And what happens just before X?

Note: "X" and "Y" are the interviewee's exact words or gestures.
Source: Tosey, Lawley and Meese, 2014.

in metaphor and that these metaphors are located in perceptual space and that most human experience is part of a sequence of events (Nehyba & Lawley, 2019). The core classically clean questions are outlined in Table 21.1.

The questions appear deceptively simple and whilst this simplicity is part of the appeal of Clean Language, their use is greatly enhanced by training, which is publicly available (e.g., https://www.cleanlanguage.co.uk/). This means that Clean Language can be systematically learnt and applied to explore the inner world of intuitive knowledge. This offers an exciting development for those interested in researching intuition and builds on understanding the experience of intuiting (Dane & Pratt, 2007; Petitmengin, 2014; Sadler-Smith, 2016) by maximizing attention to the inner experience of intuiting and minimizing interference from the outside. This is important as previous research on intuition has highlighted the need to study how intuition is evoked (Teerikangas & Välikangas, 2014).

The manner in which Clean Language questions are asked contributes to their effectiveness. This follows from Grove's assertion that the paralinguistic delivery of questions is vital to their efficacy. Clean questions are asked slowly to give the individual time to think and they are delivered in a consistent and curious tone of voice that values all parts of the individual's experience equally. These paralinguistic qualities signal acceptance and interest conducive to establishing a sense of safety for the individual to discover more about their own intuitive inner knowledge. As metaphors

Table 21.2 Eliciting intuition with Clean Language

Validating Inner Experience	Minimizing External Interference
1. Precision in replicating the individual's experience through words, tone and non-verbal gestures.	3. Clean questions minimize the introduction of content or presuppositions that do not come from the individual.
2. Focus on the individual's inner world channels their attention to revealing and exploring it rather than explaining it.	4. Limited eye contact frees the individual to explore their inner world without having to attend to the interviewer.

do not conform to ordinary logic and may therefore appear quite bizarre, this acceptance is paramount for individuals to surface and explore their metaphorical world. Four suggestions useful for eliciting intuition using Clean Language are outlined in Table 21.2. The first two suggestions maintain the focus on the individual's inner world while suggestions three and four limit interference from the external world to provide individuals the space to explore their inner world of intuitive thinking. These suggestions correspond to Sadler-Smith and Shefy's recommendation that individuals need methods to take a step back and a "contemplative space" to develop their intuitive awareness (2007: 201).

ILLUMINATING INTUITION THROUGH METAPHOR

The following example shows how Clean Language was used to elicit an understanding of intuition from one of the leaders in the study described above.

> Interviewer: And intuition is like what?
>
> Leader: Intuition is like crystal.
>
> Interviewer: Ah, and like crystal. And where is that crystal?
>
> Leader: It exists at the centre of my mind or my brain. In my mind / brain, there are lots of thoughts and feelings growing, very dense and almost dark like jungle.
>
> Interviewer: And what happens with all these thoughts and feelings?
>
> Leader: Things get entangled. It's hard to figure out what they are. Some thoughts are beautiful, some thoughts are ugly or even poisoned.
>
> Interviewer: And when things get tangled, what happens to intuition?
>
> Leader: Sometimes, suddenly, an access to my intuition appears. Nothing but only crystal hovering in the air. No sound, no colour.
>
> Interviewer: And intuition appears like a crystal. And is there anything else about that intuition?
>
> Leader: Intuition is solid, firm, and transparent like a piece of crystal. No bias. Sparkling. I don't know how but when necessary, the path instantly appears just like it happens in the fairy tale … Intuition, for me, relates closely with an action of making "a" decision or choosing "a" thing without doing any analysis or evaluation. Intuition tells what is right.

> Interviewer: And how do you know what is right?
>
> Leader: The jungle vanishes at once if I can see inside myself and come back to my own internal cosmos, and in that world, the access to intuition is free. No obstacles.

Following the elicitation of intuition, the leader was asked to draw it. This is illustrated in Figure 21.1.

Figure 21.1 Intuition – like a crystal inside a jungle

This example illustrates how Clean Language functions by precisely replicating the words of the individual and then asking a "clean" question to direct the individual to find out more about their intuition. The metaphors elicited through this process are so vivid with the entangled jungle that the individual is able to draw her internal cosmos of intuition as a crystal surrounded by jungle. Drawing is a normal practice in Clean Language that helps make the invisible visible and encourages further reflection. It is also possible and effective to inverse the process and ask people to draw an image and then ask "clean" questions about the image.

The above example is particularly lovely, not only due to the vivid metaphors used and the exquisite drawing but also because of the relative ease with which the individual was able to describe her intuition. It is quite usual, even when using Clean Language, for many more questions to be necessary to elicit metaphorical knowledge. This example illustrates that directing attention to leaders' metaphors provides a way for them to access and make sense of their intuition. Furthermore, the example shows that intuitive knowing originates “beyond consciousness” (Sinclair & Ashkanasy, 2005: 356), often in metaphor, and that individuals make sense of their intuitive thinking in their own ways (Sadler-Smith & Shefy, 2007). The use of metaphor to describe intuition supports theories that the conceptual system is largely hidden, out of awareness and metaphorical in nature (Lakoff & Johnson, 1980).

It is important for leaders to surface their intuitive, internal felt experience of leadership as a precursor to developing their self-awareness, which is foundational for authenticity (Kernis & Goldman, 2006) and leader development (Day et al., 2014). This intuitive understanding of leadership is also a necessary pre-condition for leaders to shape and share their mental model of leadership with others. The study provides empirical evidence of how leaders make sense of their intuition through use of metaphors, “to help explain their intuition to themselves and share it with others” (Crossan et al., 1999: 527). Moreover, observations from this study empirically support Crossan et al.’s (1999) theory that metaphors are a critical link between intuiting and interpreting, which are the first two stages in their four “I” model of learning. The above example illustrates how leaders can make sense of their intuition through attention to and interpretation of their own naturally occurring metaphors, and how verbal and visual metaphors express intuitive knowing which creates “new knowledge from intuitions” (Sadler-Smith, 2008: 503).

Clean Language complements work on the elicitation of intuition (Petitmengin, 2014) that directs attention to the intuitive experience, rather than the content of the intuition, through attention to both the experience of elicitation and the content of people’s intuitions. The practice of Clean Language supports the suggestion that the micro-behaviours of the researcher are vital to “the emergence and maturation of the intuition” (Petitmengin, 2014: 196) and identifies the following behaviours as particularly important: speaking slowly in a tone of curiosity that treats all information as equal value, precise replication of words and gestures, and limited eye contact. These behaviours combine to minimize researchers’ influence or interpretation, which helps create “kind” conditions for intuition to be expressed (Hogarth, 2001). Furthermore, as Clean Language elicits metaphors trans-modally (verbally, visually and in gesture), it is particularly suited for further research about intuition because intuitions appear trans-modally (Petitmengin, 2014) through a mixture of feelings, thoughts and images.

In conclusion, this chapter highlights Clean Language as an elicitation technique that offers much promise for intuition researchers through its attention to an interviewee’s inner world of intuition and metaphors. With minimal introduction of content from the interviewer, Clean Language creates an environment conducive to intuitive insight (Hogarth, 2001). This empirical work responds to calls to develop intuition in executives (Sadler-Smith & Shefy, 2004), explicating how metaphors reveal tacit, visual and embodied intuitions. Importantly, the study illustrates how leaders come to know what they know, through attention to their naturally occurring metaphors, which give form to their intuitive knowing. When leaders can make sense of their intuition, they are better placed to show and lead the way in uncertain times.

REFERENCES

Akinci, C., & Sadler-Smith, E. 2013. Assessing individual differences in experiential (intuitive) and rational (analytical) cognitive styles. *International Journal of Selection and Assessment*, 21: 211–221.

Alvesson, M., & Spicer, A. (Eds.) 2011. *Metaphors we lead by. Understanding leadership in the real world.* London and New York: Routledge.

Barner, R. 2008. The dark tower: Using visual metaphors to facilitate emotional expression during organizational change. *Journal of Organizational Change Management*, 21: 120–137.

Bürgi, P., & Roos, J. 2003. Images of strategy. *European Management Journal*, 21: 69–78.

Cairns-Lee, H. 2015. Images of leadership development from the inside out. *Advances in Developing Human Resources*, 17: 321–336.

Cairns-Lee, H. 2017. *An exploration of leadership and its development through the inner worlds of leaders using metaphor.* PhD dissertation, University of Surrey.

Cassell, C., & Bishop, V. 2014. Metaphors and sensemaking: Understanding the taint associated with dirty work. *Qualitative Research in Organizations and Management: An International Journal*, 9: 254–269.

Cornelissen, J.P. 2005. Beyond compare: Metaphor in organization theory. *Academy of Management Review*, 30: 751–764.

Cornelissen, J.P., & Kafouros, M. 2008. Metaphors and theory building in organization theory: What determines the impact of a metaphor on theory? *British Journal of Management*, 19: 365–379.

Cornelissen, J.P., Oswick, C., Christensen, L.T., & Phillips, N. 2008. Metaphor in organizational research: Context, modalities and implications for research introduction. *Organization Studies*, 29: 7–22.

Crossan, M., Lane, H., & White, R. 1999. An organizational learning framework: From intuition to institution. *Academy of Management Review*, 24: 522–537.

Dane, E., & Pratt, M.G. 2007. Exploring intuition and its role in managerial decision making. *Academy of Management Review*, 32: 33–54.

Dane, E., Rockmann, K.W., & Pratt, M.G. 2012. When should I trust my gut? Linking domain expertise to intuitive decision-making effectiveness. *Organizational Behavior & Human Decision Processes*, 119: 187–194.

Day, D.V., Fleenor, J.W., Atwater, L.E., Sturm, R.E., & McKee, R.A. 2014. Advances in leader and leadership development: A review of 25 years of research and theory. *Leadership Quarterly*, 25: 63–82.

Dörfler, V., & Eden, C. (Eds.) 2014. Research on intuition using intuition. In M. Sinclair (Ed.), *Handbook of research methods on intuition*: 264–276. Cheltenham, UK and Northampton, MA, USA: Edward Elgar Publishing.

Epstein, S., & Pacini, R. 2001. The influence of visualization on intuitive and analytical information processing. *Imagination, Cognition and Personality*, 20: 195–216.

Evans, J.S.B.T. 2003. In two minds: Dual process accounts of reasoning. *Trends in Cognitive Sciences*, 7: 454–459.

Grove, D.J., & Panzer, B.I. 1989. *Resolving traumatic memories; metaphors and symbols in psychotherapy.* New York: Irvington Publishers.

Hogarth, R.M. 2001. *Educating intuition.* Chicago: Chicago University Press.

Husserl, E. 1982. *Ideas pertaining to a pure phenomenology and to a phenomenological philosophy – first book: General introduction to a pure phenomenology.* Dordrecht, Boston, London: Kluwer Academic Publishers.

Jung, C.G. 1921. *Psychological types.* London: Routledge.

Kernis, M.H., & Goldman, B.M. 2006. A multicomponent conceptualization of authenticity: Theory and research. *Advances in Experimental Social Psychology*, 38: 283–357.

Khatri, N., & Ng, H.A. 2000. The role of intuition in strategic decision making. *Human Relations*, 53: 57–86.
Koestler, A. 1964. *The act of creation*. New York: Penguin Books.
Korn Ferry 2014–2015. *FYI – For your improvement*. Korn Ferry. https://www.kornferry.com/fyi-resources (accessed February 25, 2020).
Lakoff, G., & Johnson, M. 1980. *Metaphors we live by*. Chicago: University of Chicago Press.
Lawley, J., & Tompkins, P. 2000. *Metaphors in mind: Transformation through symbolic modelling*. London: The Developing Company Press.
Li, P.P. 2014. Toward the geocentric framework of intuition: The Yin-Yang balancing between the Eastern and Western perspectives on intuition. In M. Sinclair (Ed.), *Handbook of research methods on intuition*: 28–41. Cheltenham, UK and Northampton, MA, USA: Edward Elgar Publishing.
Marshak, R.J. 1993. Managing the metaphors of change. *Organizational Dynamics*, 22: 44–56.
McCracken, J. 2016. *Clean Language in the classroom*. Carmarthen: Crown House Publishing Ltd.
Morgan, G. 1986. *Images of organization*. Thousand Oaks, CA: Sage.
Morgan, G. 2016. Commentary: Beyond Morgan's eight metaphors. *Human Relations*, 69: 1029–1042.
Moustakas, C. 1994. *Phenomenological research methods*. New Delhi: Sage.
Nehyba, J., & Lawley, J. 2019. Clean Language Interviewing as a second-person method in the science of consciousness. *Journal of Consciousness Studies*, 27(1–2): 94–119.
Oliver, D., & Roos, J. 2007. Beyond text: Constructing organizational identity multimodally. *British Journal of Management*, 18: 342–358.
Ortony, A. 1993. *Metaphor, language and thought*. Cambridge: Cambridge University Press.
Oswick, C., & Grant, D. 1996. The organization of metaphors and the metaphors of organization: Where are we and where do we go from here? In D. Grant, & C. Oswick (Eds.), *Metaphors and Organizations*: 188–198. London: Sage.
Oswick, C., Keenoy, T., & Grant, D. 2002. Metaphor and analogical reasoning in organization theory: Beyond orthodoxy. *Academy of Management Review*, 27: 294–303.
Patriotta, G., & Brown, A.D. 2011. Sensemaking, metaphors and performance evaluation. *Scandinavian Journal of Management*, 27: 34–43.
Petitmengin, C. 2014. Researching the microdynamics of intuitive experience. In M. Sinclair (Ed.), *Handbook of research methods on intuition*: 188–198. Cheltenham, UK and Northampton, MA, USA: Edward Elgar Publishing.
Rowan, R. 1986. *The intuitive manager*. Boston and Toronto: Little Brown and Company.
Sadler-Smith, E. 2008. The role of intuition in collective learning and the development of shared meaning. *Advances in Developing Human Resources*, 10: 494–508.
Sadler-Smith, E. 2016. 'What happens when you intuit?': Understanding human resource practitioners' subjective experience of intuition through a novel linguistic method. *Human Relations*, 69: 1069–1093.
Sadler-Smith, E., & Shefy, E. 2004. The intuitive executive: Understanding and applying 'gut feel' in decision-making. *Academy of Management Executive*, 18: 76–91.
Sadler-Smith, E., & Shefy, E. 2007. Developing intuitive awareness in management education. *Academy of Management Learning & Education*, 6: 186–205.
Sinclair, M. (Ed.) 2014. *Handbook of research methods on intuition*. Cheltenham, UK and Northampton, MA, USA: Edward Elgar Publishing.
Sinclair, M., & Ashkanasy, N.M. 2005. Intuition: Myth or a decision-making tool? *Management Learning*, 36: 353–370.
Stiehm, J. Hicks, & Townsend, N.W. 2002. *The U.S. army war college: Military education in a democracy*. Philadelphia, PA: Temple University Press.
Teerikangas, S., & Välikangas, L. 2014. Exploring the dynamic of evoking intuition. In M. Sinclair (Ed.), *Handbook of research methods on intuition*: 72–87. Cheltenham, UK and Northampton, MA, USA: Edward Elgar Publishing.

Tosey, P., Lawley, J., & Meese, R. 2014. Eliciting metaphor through Clean Language: An innovation in qualitative research. *British Journal of Management*, 25: 629–646.
Way, M. 2013. *Clean approaches for coaches: Create the conditions for change using Clean Language and symbolic modelling*. Fareham: Clean Publishing.
Weick, K.E., Sutcliffe, K.M., & Obstfeld, D. 2005. Organizing and the process of sensemaking. *Organization Science*, 16: 409–421.

22. Intuition: scientific, non-scientific or unscientific?

Viktor Dörfler and Alina Bas

There has been a recent rejuvenation of interest in the phenomenon of intuition in scholarly research, especially in the area of psychology, as well as in management and organization scholarship. This research interest has increasingly intensified over the past 15 years, resulting in a large number of academic papers on intuition. As part of this development, the scope of what is included in the academic research became a contested topic of conversation. Besides minor disagreement among researchers, we have found bigger gaps in understanding between some practitioners and academics who study intuition. In order to identify and explore these gaps, we introduce the concept of *intuition practitioners* as those who intentionally use intuition in their practice, even when the scientific underpinnings of it are missing or not fully understood, and *intuition scholars* as those who conduct academic research on the topic of intuition using some form of a scientific method. We believe it is important for intuition scholars to not leave out something significant by labeling the 'not yet understood' as 'unscientific.' Therefore, in this book chapter we propose an extension of the scope of intuition research by shedding light on the process of *intuiting* (the outcome of which is intuition), utilized by intuition practitioners and not yet understood by intuition scholars.

We craft our argument without being dismissive of the scientific approach, and also without dismissing ideas that currently do not fit into what is scientifically accepted. We illustrate the fruitfulness of this extension by proposing a new two-stage model of intuiting. It is important to note that the idea for this model originated as a result of a discrepancy between the way intuition scholars and intuition practitioners describe intuiting. Intuition practitioners' claims are frequently dismissed by academics, but it does not mean that intuition practitioners' views are unfounded. Our model provides foundation for claims by intuition practitioners, while at the same time, accounting for the observations made by intuition scholars.

We first describe some of the least contested dimensions of intuition. Then, in order to understand the disagreement between intuition scholars and intuition practitioners, we outline the dynamics between the scientific, non-scientific, and unscientific knowledge, taking a historical perspective on the interplay between the three. To this end, we introduce the notion of 'three knowledge buckets.' Using the three buckets, we show the way for bringing under scientific scrutiny, without compromising the scientific rigor, aspects of intuiting that were previously dismissed. Subsequently we outline the current understanding of intuiting by intuition scholars and then by intuition practitioners, pointing out the gap between the two perspectives.

We attempt to explain the gap by proposing a two-stage model of intuiting: *sensing + sensemaking*. Finally, in our commentary, we demonstrate that the proposed two-stage model of intuiting is compatible with the current academic understanding of intuition, and enriches it by providing additional depth. Our aim for this chapter is to reconcile intuition scholars' and intuition practitioners' views of intuiting, and offer a *sensing + sensemaking* model for consideration, conceptual criticism and empirical testing by other scholars.

WHAT IS INTUITION?

Until about 30 years ago, intuition as a whole was poorly understood as a concept, poorly defined, and as a result, under-studied (Akinci & Sadler-Smith, 2012). Gradually, as the scholarly understanding of intuition started to emerge, several aspects of intuition were brought into the scientific realm. This includes explaining intuiting in terms of dual processes (e.g., Epstein et al., 1996; Hodgkinson et al., 2008; Kahneman & Frederick, 2002; Neisser, 1963; Stanovich & West, 1998; Tversky & Kahneman, 1983), expertise (e.g., Dörfler & Stierand, 2017; Hogarth, 2001; Kahneman & Klein, 2009; Prietula & Simon, 1989; Salas et al., 2010), as well as heuristics and biases (e.g., Kahneman, 2003; Kahneman et al., 1982; Tversky & Kahneman, 1974). There are still ongoing debates about whether it is meaningful or useful to classify intuition by types, that is, expert intuition (Kahneman & Klein, 2009), strategic intuition (Duggan, 2013), entrepreneurial intuition (Kickul & Gundry, 2011), and so on.

Intuiting can be conceptualized as a way of 'direct knowing,' that is, knowing "without any use of conscious reasoning" (Sinclair & Ashkanasy, 2005: 357). Although this is certainly not a precise definition, it is generally accepted in the intuition scholarship. Direct knowing means that knowledge is not achieved by the step-by-step reasoning, which typically characterizes the academic view of knowing, but through a process that somehow seems to bypass these steps.

The beginning of the renewed interest in intuition in management and organization studies was marked by Chester Barnard's (1938) seminal book *The functions of the executive*. Although Chester Barnard was a practitioner, his book has been widely accepted in the academia. The first academic inquiry to account for intuiting was Herbert Simon's work on *Administrative behavior* (first edition published 1947). It led to one of the most cited maxims on intuition: "Intuition and judgment – at least good judgment – are simply analyses frozen into habit" (Simon, 1987: 63). This was followed by the first empirical study by Weston Agor (1986), in which he explored both successes and failures of intuition. This book is halfway between academic and practitioner publications. Currently, some major characteristics of intuiting have been generally accepted by both scholars and practitioners; these characteristics will be discussed below in detail. As we review these characteristics, we point out one significant disagreement between intuition scholars and intuition practitioners: whether intuition can be intentional as well as spontaneous. The concept of the three knowledge buckets, and the movements of knowledge between them, will help expand our understanding of intuition and intuiting.

THE THREE KNOWLEDGE BUCKETS

We suggest that any knowledge, whether obtained through practice, academic research, or by any other means, fits into one of the three metaphorical buckets: scientific, non-scientific, and unscientific. *Scientific* knowledge is accepted as true in science based on scientific evidence obtained through a scientific method. *Unscientific* is rejected as false by science based on scientific evidence obtained through scientific method. *Non-scientific* is currently not covered by science; it is neither accepted nor rejected based on scientific evidence.

Before any scientific inquiry has been made about a particular phenomenon, the pre-existing explanation is always in the non-scientific bucket. When a scientific study is undertaken, one of the four things can happen:

1. If the scientific inquiry supports the pre-existing explanation, thus legitimizing it as a scientific explanation, this explanation is placed in the scientific bucket.
2. If the pre-existing explanation is dismissed (conclusively proven false) by the scientific inquiry, it is transferred into the unscientific bucket. Dismissing the pre-existing explanation as unscientific may go together with obtaining a new scientific explanation that is incompatible with the pre-existing explanation, this new explanation will then be put into the scientific bucket.
3. If the scientific inquiry neither proves nor falsifies the pre-existing explanation of the phenomenon, it will remain in the non-scientific bucket.
4. Finally, there may be cases, where a new scientific explanation is obtained, and placed in the scientific bucket, while the pre-existing explanation will remain in the non-scientific bucket, as the scientific explanation neither contradicts nor supports it. Thus, the two explanations can continue to coexist.

Everything science has proven wrong eventually moves from the non-scientific to the unscientific bucket, and everything, for which science has sufficient supporting evidence, moves from the non-scientific to the scientific bucket. However, there will always be knowledge remaining in the non-scientific bucket, containing whatever science did not prove (yet) to be right or wrong. Unfortunately, those who worship science, have a tendency to treat the non-scientific bucket in the same manner as the unscientific one, dismissing its content as wrong, without well-founded evidence. Even though it may not always be possible to differentiate immediately in which knowledge bucket a particular explanation (or part of an explanation) belongs, this should not lead to a premature assumption that the explanation is unscientific. Intuition is one such phenomenon: it has parts of explanations in the scientific and some in the non-scientific knowledge buckets.

We believe we have found something on intuiting in the non-scientific bucket deserving a closer look through a scientific prism. It is an explanation of intuiting provided by intuition practitioners, which focuses on the sensory aspects of intuition. This non-scientific explanation can potentially be transferred from non-scientific into scientific, as it passes scientific scrutiny. While it may be easy to dismiss intuition practitioners' explanation as unscientific, we insist it is essential to prevent moving ideas into the unscientific from the non-scientific bucket without examination.

The academic explanation of intuiting is an amalgamated body of knowledge grounded in and supported by systematically gathered and tested evidence. In contrast, the practice-based explanation focuses on the individual experiences, and relies on a fragmented body of knowledge, un-systematized terminology, and anecdotal rather than systematic evidence. Until about 25 years ago, nearly all knowledge about intuiting belonged in the non-scientific bucket (and was often dismissed as unscientific by the academic community at large). Gradually, the scientific understanding of intuiting began to emerge. As a result, some aspects of intuiting are currently in the scientific bucket, as they already have scientific explanations, while other aspects of intuiting are in the non-scientific bucket, with practice-based explanations.

Our comprehensive model conceptualizes the intuitive process as sensing + sensemaking, and creates a pathway for moving more aspects of intuiting from the non-scientific to the scientific bucket through scientific exploration, and without giving up the understanding obtained through the practice-based explanations. Intuition practitioners understand intuiting through their senses rather than explanations, while intuition scholars understand intuiting through explanations rather than sensing; the two types of understanding do not contradict each other.

WHAT INTUITION SCHOLARS KNOW

The literature on intuiting within the management and organization scholarship identified six necessary and sufficient characteristics that define intuiting (cf. Dane & Pratt, 2007; Dörfler & Ackermann, 2012; Dörfler & Stierand, 2017; Kahneman, 2003: 698; Sadler-Smith, 2008: 13; Sinclair, 2010):

- Intuiting is *rapid*, meaning that it occurs almost instantaneously, and in this respect, it is similar to guessing. However, it is guessing which is "frequently correct" (in line with Simon, 1983: 25).
- Intuiting is *alogical*, meaning that it operates independently of the general principles of reasoning that we call logic, therefore it is neither *logical* nor *illogical*, as it neither follows nor contradicts the rules of logic.
- Intuiting is *holistic* or *gestalt*, as it is about the 'big picture' of the situation, including the broad context, and far-reaching implications. It even takes into account what we could call 'invisible parts' inaccessible to deliberate step-by-step reasoning, sometimes referred to as the 'unknown unknowns.' Furthermore, intuiting also involves the totality of the intuitor.

- Intuiting is *tacit* in the sense that intuitors can describe the outcome, but not the way they arrived at it. Although intuitors are often good at defending their intuitive judgments or insights, there is no evidence that the justification has anything to do with the way the intuiting was used.
- Intuition, as the outcome of intuiting, has an *intrinsic certainty*: intuitors are confident they have the right answer. This does not make intuiting infallible, and intuitors do not usually claim infallibility. We will revisit what is known about the reliability of intuiting below.
- Finally, intuiting is considered to be *spontaneous*. This means that intuiting does not require conscious effort, at least at the moment when it happens. This is the one feature where intuition scholars and intuition practitioners are in disagreement.

These features are grounded in empirical research – predominantly interviews with practitioners, including decision takers and creative problem solvers.

Besides the above-mentioned six features of intuiting, it is also often mentioned that intuiting is frequently accompanied by somatic (visceral) effects and affective charges. While the role of affect in intuiting and intuition has been addressed (e.g., Coget, 2011; Dane & Pratt, 2007; Sinclair, 2010), the somatic aspects are much less understood (e.g., Tantia, 2011, 2014). Although presence of affect in the intuitive process and outcome does not contradict any of the findings in intuition research, it still lacks solid foundation, and empirical support. Affective and somatic aspects of intuiting are mentioned cautiously by intuition scholars, since these two aspects are not yet solidly in the scientific bucket, but they can be pertinent in terms of relating to the intuition practitioners' view of intuition.

It is important to note that the scholarly discourse on intuiting is tightly linked with the notion of *expertise*. Domain expertise is not limited to disciplinary expertise; it can be expertise in a particular problem area which is transdisciplinary. With this broad view of expertise, it can be argued that nearly all scholarly knowledge on intuiting either refers to experts' intuiting or is based on it. A closer look at studies claiming to have provided experimental evidence on the failure of intuiting (including Bowers et al., 1990: 97; Schoemaker & Russo, 1993: 27; Trailer & Morgan, 2004) reveals that these experiments targeted novice intuition. In contrast, those (including Burke & Miller, 1999 in management; Hayashi, 2001 in leadership; Keren, 1987 in the game of bridge) who have found empirical (predominantly non-experimental) evidence of intuiting working well typically focused on people at a high level of domain expertise (Dane et al., 2012; Mielonen et al., 2009). Dane et al. (2012) conducted two comparative experiments, which confirmed the importance of expertise in reliability of intuiting. Kahneman and Klein (2009) concluded the same in their conceptual discourse grounded in years of research on intuition. Expert intuition is the best understood phenomenon within intuition research, although this does not imply that it is fully understood. Interestingly, once people become experts in their respective domains, intuiting becomes their predominant way of thinking in their domains (Dörfler & Ackermann, 2012; Kahneman & Klein, 2009). Expertise aids "fast thinking" (Kahneman, 2011) by enabling rapid pattern recognition (Chase & Simon, 1973), and recognition-primed decision-making (Klein, 2015).

There is still a great deal of knowledge about intuiting in the non-scientific bucket. Unfortunately, academic hubris can push to dismiss everything about a particular phenomenon in the non-scientific bucket as unscientific, once there is substantial knowledge accumulated in the scientific bucket. The claim is that if there was any evidence supporting the scientific foundation of something in the non-scientific bucket, it would have already come into the light, which lacks basis. It is therefore useful to look from time to time at what practitioners do in the same area as scholars: if something seems to work in practice but did not make its way into the scientific bucket yet, it is worth exploring. This is why we now focus on the way intuition practitioners see intuiting.

WHAT INTUITION PRACTITIONERS KNOW

Practice-based explanation of intuiting is founded on accounts of intuition practitioners, who consistently use intuiting, intentionally, on cue. Intuition practitioners do not describe intuiting as scientific, non-scientific or unscientific. Instead, they explain intuiting as *practical*: they claim to have tacit or explicit understanding of the way intuiting works, use it intentionally, and even help others become more attuned to their intuiting (Day, 1997). Their understanding of intuiting is typically rejected within the realm of science because it is not based on evidence acquired through a scientific method. Still, it does not prevent practitioners from using their intuiting.

Furthermore, intuition practitioners see intuiting as a sensory-based, *direct way of obtaining awareness* of phenomena, which is in line with what is usually viewed as lacking scientific foundation. There are numerous reasons why this makes some scientists uncomfortable: some scoff at the subjectivist approach to knowing, others object to lack of scientific method for exploring the sensory-based phenomena, while others are simply oblivious to the sensing aspect of intuiting. Interestingly, *affect and visceral sensations* in intuiting, which are somewhat marginalized by intuition scholars, are essential to intuition practitioners: affective and visceral cues typically serve as starting points that make intuition practitioners pay attention to intuiting (Bas, 2013). Intuition practitioners employ a sensory-based way of obtaining awareness of phenomena, achieving first-hand experience. By 'sensory' we imply perception based on the five primary senses, as well as visceral (e.g., hunger), affective (e.g., love), and mental sensations (e.g., pride) (Burton, 2009: 37). It is a way of coming to know something, without necessarily knowing how this knowledge was obtained.

While intuition practitioners may or may not describe intuiting as rapid, tacit, holistic, alogical, and having intrinsic certainty, as scholars do, they often talk about intuition as *both spontaneous and intentional* (Day, 1997). In contrast to the academic literature, which provides ample examples of intuition occurring to people spontaneously (Dane & Pratt, 2007; Sadler-Smith, 2008), there has been recent additional evidence from practitioners, suggesting that intuiting can also be produced on cue (Beck, 2011: 137; Day, 1997: 23, 2009: 41; Mielonen et al., 2009). For example, intuitive flashes could be conjured up by asking oneself a question about a situation, or defining a desired outcome, and staying attuned with soft focus to sensory and environmental cues emerging in response to the initial inquiry (Day, 1997, 2009). After posing a question, intuition practitioners may listen and look for shifts in the mental, physical and affective states (see also 'passionate intention' in Bradley, 2011: 210; and 'indwelling' in Dörfler & Stierand, 2018). These shifts seem to occur without apparent causes either from the external environment or from internal processes, and hence become labeled as intuitive.

Intentionality of intuiting is currently often dismissed by scholars as unscientific, without examination, as it is so poorly understood. An intuition practitioner may explain intentionality in intuiting much like developing musicality while learning to play a musical instrument (Bas, 2013: 9). At first, a music student must learn all the notes by name, as well as the practical mechanics of the instrument. The first equivalent step in intuiting would be an attempt to notice and differentiate between sensory experiences. After learning the names and graphic representations of the notes, a student would learn to *hear* the difference between the notes, and *feel* the difference between the notes in the fingers, much like intuition practitioners would learn to sense individual 'notes' in their range of physical, emotional, and mental perception. After plentiful practice of corresponding the written notes to the touched keys, and the heard sounds, gifted and well-trained students would be able to play what is seen on a page, and to play what is heard by the ear, as well as to hear in their mind's ear the music written on the paper. Similarly, a trained intuition practitioner can decipher sensory-based cues, and translate them into meaningful and useful information beyond the actual sensation.

An analytical thinker, not experienced in paying attention to sensing, may wonder how it is possible to get intuitive information seemingly out of nowhere, unless one is able to justify it as expertise. For intuition practitioners, however, expertise is much less tied to intuiting than the scholarly literature implies. Intuition practitioners suggest that over time, a student of intuiting could learn to understand various sensations underpinning their intuiting, such as the colors, words, images, tastes, textures, and intentionally making sense of these sensations can create a useful, actionable narrative. To the musically challenged, observing someone differentiate between F# and G in the third octave just by hearing the sounds may sound like a lucky guess or a sort of a magic trick. Similarly, when it comes to intuiting, it may seem just as mysterious to observe someone differentiate among the meanings of other sensory signals (Bas, 2013). A person who is not particularly musical or musically trained will not be able to tell with certainty whether F# and G are different sounds or the same sound, unless the sounds are played back to back without interference or delay between them. To highly trained musicians, even the notion of confusing F# and G may seem strange, because they perceive the two notes as two distinct sounds. A trained intuition practitioner is similarly able to distinguish between, for example, an intuitive signal and hope.

Intuition practitioners rarely argue with scholars' explanations of intuiting. In our view, this increases the credibility of the explanations of intuiting in the scientific bucket. However, a discrepancy between something that works in practice but cannot be accounted for by the knowledge in the scientific bucket is alerting. It implies that either intuition scholars made a mistake (e.g., lack of rigor in applying the chosen scientific method or unjustified claim of validity) or simply did not cover all the bases yet. We will now try to unpack one such discrepancy.

WHY INTUITION SCHOLARS AND INTUITION PRACTITIONERS SEE DIFFERENTLY

Intuition scholars accept only the aspects of intuiting that can be scientifically explained. If they dismiss everything else, they will only see what is in the scientific bucket. Intuition practitioners accept all aspects of intuition that work. This means that intuition practitioners see both the scientific and the non-scientific buckets. Practitioners may or may not be aware of the intuiting features described by intuition scholars. They may have a feeling or may know from reading that intuiting is rapid, alogical, holistic, tacit, has intrinsic validity, and is often spontaneous, but they do not necessarily think about it or are able to articulate it. They would not argue with the scientific view, and would add that intuiting can be intentional as well as spontaneous.

The main difference between the views of intuition practitioners and intuition scholars is in the way they think about sensory inputs. Intuition practitioners aim at attaining insight into hidden truths through immersing themselves in a phenomenon, thus the focus is on the personal (individual) experience. This means taking the subjectivity to the extreme in order to reach understanding. In contrast, intuition scholars, at least traditionally, aim at attaining insight into hidden truths by getting rid of everything personal and subjective, and penetrating the phenomenon in an impersonal objective way. As Schrödinger (1958) argues in his discourse on the so-called 'scientific method,' science is also ultimately sensory-based: even if we design a machine that designs another machine that does the measurement and the processing in itself, there is still a starting point somewhere, where the initial machine was designed by a human using a sensory-based approach. Similarly, there is also always a human interpretation of the outcome at the end of whatever data the machines collected and processed, which is why Gummesson (2003) claims that all research is interpretive.

Intuition practitioners' and intuition scholars' views of intuiting bring to mind a famous Indian parable about blind men and an elephant. As each of the blind men was touching a different part of an elephant, they described their experiences very differently, making it seem as if they were interacting with entirely different entities. Intuition practitioners and intuition scholars have different purposes for, and different roles in, understanding intuiting, which may make it seem like they are looking at different phenomena. As we will demonstrate below, this may not be the case.

Perhaps intuition practitioners' views can inform and enable the scientific inquiry, and we can reconcile the difference between the two modes of knowing.

COMPREHENSIVE VIEW OF INTUITING: SENSING + SENSEMAKING

In this section we bring together the intuition scholars' and the intuition practitioners' views of intuiting, covering both the scientific and the non-scientific buckets. If we were only practitioners, we would not need to do this because, as we stated above, intuition practitioners can see both scientific and non-scientific. However, we make an attempt to synthesize the views as scholars, thereby extending the scope of the scientific bucket by providing a scientifically acceptable explanation of aspects of intuiting currently in the non-scientific bucket.

Both intuition scholars and intuition practitioners acknowledge that some interpretation takes place as a part of the intuiting process. We call this the *sensemaking* aspect of intuiting. This sensemaking can be described by five of the six characteristics identified by intuition scholars: it is rapid, holistic, alogical, based on tacit processing, and carries intrinsic certainty. We have identified one characteristic on which intuition scholars and intuition practitioners disagree when describing the way intuiting works: intentionality. Intuition practitioners' explanation allows for a possibility that the intuiting process can be initiated on cue, while the scholarly explanation claims that intuition is spontaneous, not allowing for intentionality.

This discrepancy may be explained by the fact that the scholarly view disregards the sensory aspect of intuiting, while for intuition practitioners, intuiting is *rooted* in the sensory, and it is in the sensory realm where intentionality of the intuiting process can be achieved. Although *intuition as an outcome* is naturally spontaneous, *the process of intuiting* may or may not be spontaneous; it is plausible that practice-based and scholarly explanations address different phases of the intuiting process.

Looking at the process of *intuiting*, the product of which is *intuition*, we divide the process of intuiting into *sensing* and *sensemaking*. It can then potentially be understood what each phase entails, and how one's ability to capitalize on each phase can be improved. The model allows for both practitioner and scholarly claims about spontaneity versus intentionality of intuiting to be possible at the same time. On the input side of sensing, there are sensory signals, which in the process of sensing are transformed into *sensations*. These sensations, tacit or explicit, are the inputs of the sensemaking process, the output of which is *meaning*. Thus the process of intuiting, described as 'sensing + sensemaking,' produces 'sensations with meaning,' that is, intuition. While not all 'sensation with meaning' is intuition, all intuition is 'sensation with meaning.'

The sensing aspect of intuiting entails perceived signals. One example is a visual image either in a mind's eye or in a tangible world, which suddenly catches a person's attention. Other examples include auditory sensations (again, either in a mind's ear, or also potentially observable to others), tactile sensations, or changes in one's physical and emotional state (Mielonen et al., 2009). Intuiting presents to each person in a sensory language, which is unique to him or her due to physiological and psychological differences, and therefore it cannot be standardized. For instance, the same visual image can represent different ideas to different people, or even to the same person in different contexts. Hence, sensing must be followed by sensemaking in order for sensing to acquire additional meaning, and thus become usable.

Sensemaking (Weick, 1979, 1995) is the aspect of intuiting concerned with *revealing the meaning* of signals perceived through *sensing*, and appears to be tied to one's domain expertise, relevant to the particular situation. One may not be aware of the sensing part at all, as one only perceives the signals of which one has already made sense. It may seem unclear, vague, and unexplainable to scholars what happens (or *whether* anything happens) during the sensing stage. This dismissal, or lack of understanding, keeps the *sensing* part of intuiting in the category of non-scientific. In this light, it is understandable why scholars may not distinguish between 'the outcome of intuiting,' which is intuition, and 'the output of sensemaking,' which is meaning. This also explains why intuiting is tightly linked with domain expertise in the scholarly view: domain experts are competent at interpreting all sorts of inputs within their area of expertise. Ignoring the sensing aspect of intuiting makes the concept of intuiting incomplete.

COMMENTARY

By offering the *sensing + sensemaking* model of intuiting, we open up new avenues of research on intuiting, for which this model can serve as a conceptual framework. Furthermore, the model, which can be useful for people who are interested in making better use of their intuition, bridges the practical and the scholarly view. It enables training the sensing aspect of intuiting without leaving the realm of the scientific mindset.

Sensing in the process of intuiting is equivalent to perceiving and differentiating among sounds in the process of becoming a musician. It requires practice in learning to sense the difference, and getting accurate feedback during practice (Ericsson & Pool, 2016: 17). Sensemaking in the process of intuiting is equivalent to knowing what each note represents on an instrument, and making decisions as a result of having this knowledge.

Based on this model, it is possible to get more specific about educating intuiting. The sensing phase of intuiting can be improved through developing physical, emotional, and intellectual self-awareness, while the sensemaking phase can be educated through increasing domain expertise or context expertise (Dörfler & Stierand, 2017; Sinclair, 2010; Sinclair et al., 2002). The Western educational system is fully focused on the latter, while the sensing is systematically repressed (Bergson, 1911; Hogarth, 2001). Top professionals in any area of expertise – be it musicians, chefs, athletes, designers, or scientists – are esteemed precisely for their 'sense of the game' in their domains, even when formally they are recognized for expertise (Bruner, 1977:

67), so sensing is worth developing along with sensemaking in order to achieve the highest levels of performance.

There is nothing in the intuition practitioners' view of intuiting that contradicts scientific evidence. The disagreement we have identified is between *opinions* of intuition practitioners, and scholars. The scholarly opinion is informed by the scientifically obtained evidence that intuition *can* manifest spontaneously. However, this does not mean that 'spontaneous' is *the only way* in which intuiting can manifest. There is no scientific evidence that contradicts the claim of the intuition practitioners' view that intuiting *can be* originated intentionally as well as spontaneously. This means that intuition practitioners' claim of possible intentionality of intuiting belongs in the non-scientific bucket, rather than in the unscientific one. With further research, it has potential to move to the scientific bucket, provided that the *sensing + sensemaking* model of intuiting sustains scientific scrutiny.

REFERENCES

Agor, W.H. 1986. The logic of intuition: How top executives make important decisions. *Organizational Dynamics*, 14(3): 5–18.

Akinci, C., & Sadler-Smith, E. 2012. Intuition in management research: A historical review. *International Journal of Management Reviews*, 14(1): 104–122.

Barnard, C.I. 1938. *The functions of the executive*. Cambridge, MA: Harvard University Press.

Bas, A. 2013. *Skeptic's guide to intuition: How developing intuition can improve the way you live and work* (Kindle edition): The Difference Press.

Beck, M. 2011. *Finding your way in a wild new world: Reclaim your true nature to create the life you want*. New York: Simon & Schuster.

Bergson, H. 1911. *Creative evolution*. New York: Henry Holt and Company.

Bowers, K.S., Regehr, G., Balthazard, C., & Parker, K. 1990. Intuition in the context of discovery. *Cognitive Psychology*, 22(1): 72–110.

Bradley, R. 2011. Resolving the enigma of nonlocal intuition: A quantum-holographic approach. In M. Sinclair (Ed.), *Handbook of intuition research*: 197–213. Cheltenham, UK and Northampton, MA, USA: Edward Elgar Publishing.

Bruner, J.S. 1977. *The process of education* (2nd ed.). Cambridge, MA: Harvard University Press.

Burke, L.A., & Miller, M.K. 1999. Taking the mystery out of intuitive decision making. *Academy of Management Executive*, 13(4): 91–99.

Burton, R.A. 2009. *On being certain: Believing you are right even when you're not*. New York: St. Martin's Press.

Chase, W.G., & Simon, H.A. 1973. Perception in chess. *Cognitive Psychology*, 4(1): 55–81.

Coget, J. 2011. The critical decisions vortex–interplay of intuition, reason and emotion: Comparison of three dynamic industries. In M. Sinclair (Ed.), *Handbook of intuition research*: 133–144. Cheltenham, UK and Northampton, MA, USA: Edward Elgar Publishing.

Dane, E., & Pratt, M.G. 2007. Exploring intuition and its role in managerial decision making. *Academy of Management Review*, 32(1): 33–54.

Dane, E., Rockmann, K.W., & Pratt, M.G. 2012. When should I trust my gut? Linking domain expertise to intuitive decision-making effectiveness. *Organizational Behavior and Human Decision Processes*, 119(2): 187–194.

Day, L. 1997. *Practical intuition: How to harness the power of your instinct and make it work for you*. New York: Broadway Books.
Day, L. 2009. *How to rule the world from your couch*. New York: Simon & Schuster.
Dörfler, V., & Ackermann, F. 2012. Understanding intuition: The case for two forms of intuition. *Management Learning*, 43(5): 545–564.
Dörfler, V., & Stierand, M. 2017. The underpinnings of intuition. In J. Liebowitz, J. Paliszkiewicz, & J. Gołuchowski (Eds.), *Intuition, trust, and analytics*: 3–20. Boca Raton, FL: Taylor & Francis.
Dörfler, V., & Stierand, M. 2018. *Understanding indwelling through studying intuitions of nobel laureates and top chefs*, AoM 2018: 78th Annual Meeting of the Academy of Management, Chicago, IL.
Duggan, W. 2013. *Strategic intuition: The creative spark in human achievement*. New York: Columbia University Press.
Epstein, S., Pacini, R., Denes-Raj, V., & Heier, H. 1996. Individual differences in intuitive-experiential and analytical-rational thinking styles. *Journal of Personality and Social Psychology*, 71(2): 390–405.
Ericsson, A., & Pool, R. 2016. *Peak: Secrets from the new science of expertise*. New York: Houghton Mifflin Harcourt.
Gummesson, E. 2003. All research is interpretive! *Journal of Business & Industrial Marketing*, 18(6/7): 482–492.
Hayashi, A.M. 2001. When to trust your gut. *Harvard Business Review*, 79(2): 59–65.
Hodgkinson, G.P., Langan-Fox, J., & Sadler-Smith, E. 2008. Intuition: A fundamental bridging construct in the behavioural sciences. *British Journal of Psychology*, 99(1): 1–27.
Hogarth, R.M. 2001. *Educating intuition*. Chicago, IL: University of Chicago Press.
Kahneman, D. 2003. A perspective on judgment and choice: Mapping bounded rationality. *American Psychologist*, 58(9): 697–720.
Kahneman, D. 2011. *Thinking, fast and slow*. London, UK: Penguin Books.
Kahneman, D., & Frederick, S. 2002. Representativeness revisited: Attribute substitution in intuitive judgment. In T. Gilovich, D. Griffin, & D. Kahneman (Eds.), *Heuristics and biases: The psychology of intuitive judgment*: 49–81. Cambridge, UK: Cambridge University Press.
Kahneman, D., & Klein, G. 2009. Conditions for intuitive expertise: A failure to disagree. *American Psychologist*, 64(6): 515–526.
Kahneman, D., Slovic, P., & Tversky, A. 1982. *Judgment under uncertainty: Heuristics and biases*. New York: Cambridge University Press.
Keren, G. 1987. Facing uncertainty in the game of bridge: A calibration study. *Organizational Behavior and Human Decision Processes*, 39(1): 98–114.
Kickul, J.R., & Gundry, L.K. 2011. Entrepreneurial intuition. In M. Sinclair (Ed.), *Handbook of intuition research*: 88–96. Cheltenham, UK and Northampton, MA, USA: Edward Elgar Publishing.
Klein, G. 2015. A naturalistic decision making perspective on studying intuitive decision making. *Journal of Applied Research in Memory and Cognition*, 4(3): 164–168.
Mielonen, S., Keinänen, M., Raami, A., & Rouhiainen, L. 2009. Intuitive knowledge processes among design students, professional designers and expert intuitive practitioners, *Communicating (by) Design 2009*, Brussels, Belgium.
Neisser, U. 1963. The multiplicity of thought. *British Journal of Psychology*, 54(1): 1–14.
Prietula, M.J., & Simon, H.A. 1989. The experts in your midst. *Harvard Business Review*, 67(1): 120–124.
Sadler-Smith, E. 2008. *Inside intuition*. London, UK: Routledge.
Salas, E., Rosen, M.A., & DiazGranados, D. 2010. Expertise-based intuition and decision making in organizations. *Journal of Management*, 36(4): 941–973.
Schoemaker, P.J.H., & Russo, J.E. 1993. Pyramid of decision approaches. *California Management Review*, 36(1): 9–31.

Schrödinger, E. 1958. Mind and matter. In E. Schrödinger (Ed.), *What is life? With mind and matter and autobiographical sketches*: 91–164. Cambridge, UK: Cambridge University Press.

Simon, H.A. 1947. *Administrative behavior: A study of decision-making processes in administrative organization* (1st ed.). New York: Macmillan.

Simon, H.A. 1983. *Reason in human affairs*. Stanford, CA: Stanford University Press.

Simon, H.A. 1987. Making management decisions: The role of intuition and emotion. *Academy of Management Executive*, 1(1): 57–64.

Sinclair, M. 2010. Misconceptions about intuition. *Psychological Inquiry: An International Journal for the Advancement of Psychological Theory*, 21(4): 378–386.

Sinclair, M., & Ashkanasy, N.M. 2005. Intuition: Myth or a decision-making tool? *Management Learning*, 36(3): 353–370.

Sinclair, M., Ashkanasy, N.M., Chattopadhyay, P., & Boyle, M.V. 2002. Determinants of intuitive decision making in management: The moderating role of affect. In N.M. Ashkanasy, W.J. Zerbe, & C.E.J. Härtel (Eds.), *Managing emotions in the workplace*: 143–163. New York: M.E. Sharpe.

Stanovich, K.E., & West, R.F. 1998. Individual differences in rational thought. *Journal of Experimental Psychology: General*, 127(2): 161–188.

Tantia, J.F. 2011. Viva las vagus! The innervation of embodied clinical intuition. *The USA Body Psychotherapy Journal Editorial*, 10(1): 29–37.

Tantia, J.F. 2014. Is intuition embodied? A phenomenological study of clinical intuition in somatic psychotherapy practice. *Body, Movement and Dance in Psychotherapy*, 9(4): 211–223.

Trailer, J.W., & Morgan, J.F. 2004. Making 'good' decisions: What intuitive physics reveals about the failure of intuition. *Journal of American Academy of Business, Cambridge*, 4(1–2): 42–48.

Tversky, A., & Kahneman, D. 1974. Judgment under uncertainty: Heuristics and biases. *Science*, 185: 1124–1131.

Tversky, A., & Kahneman, D. 1983. Extensional versus intuitive reasoning: The conjunction fallacy in probability judgment. *Psychological Review*, 90(4): 293–315.

Weick, K.E. 1979. *The social psychology of organizing* (2nd ed.). New York: McGraw-Hill.

Weick, K.E. 1995. *Sensemaking in organizations*. Thousand Oaks, CA: Sage Publications.

Index